Reading, Writing, and Riches

Education and the Socio-Economic Order in North America

Edited by

Randle W. Nelsen and David A. Nock

between the lines

© 1978 Between the Lines

Typeset by members of the Workers Union of Dumont Press Graphix, Kitchener, Ontario

Printed and bound in Canada

 COVER DESIGN

ISBN 0-919946-07-0 bd.   ISBN 0-919946-08-9 pa.

Canadian Cataloguing in Publication Data

Reading, writing and riches

ISBN 0-919946-07-0 bd. ISBN 0-919946-08-9 pa.

1. Educational sociology — North America —
Addresses, essays, lectures. 2. Education and
state — North America — Addresses, essays,
lectures. 3. Education — North America —
Economic aspects — Addresses, essays, lectures.
I. Nelsen, Randle W., 1943-   II. Nock, David A., 1949-

LC189.R43   370.19'3'097   C78-001454-5

Table of Contents

Introduction

Education and the economy have been more widely discussed and written about than any other of our modern institutions. As topics of conversation which can be counted upon to elicit heated discussion and conflicting opinions, education in schools and the economy have come to replace the older standbys of religion and politics. From cocktail parties and union meetings to campus seminars and scientific studies, Commons debates and governmental briefs, education has been hailed as the deliverance and accused as the death of our present-day capitalist economy; similarly, today's corporate socio-economic arrangements have been viewed as being responsible for emphasizing a technological education which is mind expanding and sustains life, and alternately, a C.O.D. type of learning which is mind deadening and threatens our survival.

Reading, Writing, and Riches is an attempt to provide a coherent collection of articles on the educational system in North America as it is related to the economy. Our conscious purpose has been to bring together primarily original articles unified by a coherent logic. Even a cursory glance at the Table of Contents should make clear the major unifying themes. All articles are (1) *critical* rather than accepting *of the status quo*; (2) *anti-pluralist and anti-liberal* (as explained by Nelsen and Bleasdale); (3) *concerned with making evident the close linkage of education and the economy*, as opposed to the view that education is somehow autonomous from the economic system; (4) *focused* in large measure *upon the specific economic system of capitalism* as it influences and affects education; (5) *focused upon critique in relation to proposal*.

This last point suggests why these themes are so crucially important to all contributors. They are derived from a desire to move from a critical understanding of education in a corporate and monopoly capitalist system to changing this system, and consequently, changing "education" in North America. It is this desire for fundamental change, then, that is responsible for the shared themes which give this collection its wholeness.

If we have a single overall criticism of prior books in the field, it is that they most often have been excessively eclectic. However, this criticism should not be interpreted to mean that readers will find no differences in the various articles comprising this collection. For while we are critical of analyses grounded in pluralistic theory, we believe that pluralism in style and method is desirable for social science as a whole. Therefore, differences having to do with writing style, tone of address, method used, and data collected are readily observable in this volume. We expect that many readers will feel a closer affinity to certain articles than to others on the basis of style

5

and method alone. Some will like more quantitative data which they feel constitute ''hard'' evidence, while others will respond more favourably to more qualitative data which for them help convey a feeling of closeness and immediacy to the subjects discussed. In the final analysis, we hope readers will share our view that this diversity in research style and method constitutes an attractive feature of this book.

Further perusal of the contents should reveal an almost even amount of Canadian and American material. This occurrence is not merely happenstance; nor can it be explained by the fact that one of the editors was born and grew up in the United States, the other in Canada. Rather, our work as social analysts provides strong support for our belief that capitalism as a social structure creates broad similarities in institutions and ideologies. Just as other authors have shown how capitalism produces institutional similarities in different capitalist countries (see, for example, Ralph Miliband's comparison of political systems in *The State in Capitalist Society*), we believe *Reading, Writing, and Riches* shows the similarity in development and maintenance of the educational institution in our two adjacent capitalist societies.

We are aware of recent work by Canadian scholars which attempts to show that the unequal development of capitalism results in domination and imperialism; that is, some countries and regions become marginal ''hinterlands'' relative to the more developed centres of capitalism. While this book does tend to emphasize capitalism as a homogeneous force, the papers from Friedenberg and Davis, in particular, do warn us to consider Canada and the U.S. as differentially developed segments of the overall, worldwide, capitalist system.

We believe that a book with so much comparative material may be unique in the field of Canadian-American studies. Too many books are focused only on one country or the other, or merely provide token recognition by including an article or two on the neighbouring nation. One of our primary interests is to begin drawing out a Canada-U.S. comparison grounded in economic analysis. To facilitate this, readers already may have noticed that we have begun each section with a ''Canadian'' paper, followed by an article in which the focus is upon ''American'' data.

Given the sharp debate currently underway concerning Canadian unity, some readers may question the lack of Quebec material. While we could point out selected references to Quebec in the Davis paper, as well as implications found in other papers with regard to self-governance of Quebec by Quebecois, we believe that Quebec deserves a much fuller analysis.

This analysis should treat Quebec as a national society — with national features of distinctiveness including language, history, culture, geographical territory — regardless of whether it continues as part of the Canadian State or whether a new Quebecois State is formed as a consequence of the 1976 election. Yet, for all of its distinctiveness, those who study Quebec should not forget that it remains a capitalist society and thus, capitalism shapes the Quebecois as it does the rest of us. Bearing this in mind, we strongly support the view that Quebec institutions, including education, are best studied at length by Quebecois scholars themselves.

In this volume's coverage of the various levels of formal schooling, some readers may question what might appear to be an overemphasis upon higher education. As university professors our day-to-day activities to an extent make mandatory a strong interest in post-secondary education. Accordingly, we feel that the papers by Barkans and Pupo, Luckhardt, Nelsen (multiversity), Pupo, Davis, and parts of the Bleasdale and Nelsen section adequately, but not excessively, cover the university system. Relatedly, the American community college is covered by Pincus, and while we await, and are currently involved in a project which may help provide, a more complete analysis of Canadian community colleges, references to the Colleges of Applied Arts and Technology (C.A.A.T.s) in Canada can be found in both the papers by Pupo and by Barkans and Pupo.

However, those readers most interested in finding material drawn from primary and secondary school experiences will not be disappointed. The articles by Friedenberg, Nock, Ahern, Hanson, Garber, and parts of Bleasdale and Nelsen speak to education at this level. Furthermore, while the Steinhause and Harding papers focus upon the more all-encompassing matter of adult learning within the context of community education, Harding's work can also be viewed as providing a beginning to further analysis of learning at the pre-school level. In this regard, he asks questions and makes some suggestions concerning development of structured learning situations outside the family setting for pre-school children.

In sum, then, although there are not equal quantities of material covering each level of schooling, the most important priority for us and all our contributors has been to draw out certain themes, and to show how they apply to any and every level of the North American educational system. For the point we wish to emphasize is that the close linkage of education to the prevailing capitalist economy makes schooling at every level, in a very important sense, all part of a single system.

Finally, while most of the more explicit proposals concerning educational change are to be found in the last five articles, the authors of every paper in the book at the very least imply certain proposals which extend beyond the limits of critique. We have not attempted to provide a cut-and-dried blueprint for change; in fact, some papers even have somewhat contradictory emphases (as an example, see Hanson and Garber). For we believe that significant, fundamental change will not be created from a dependency upon unilinear programmes but rather, from the clash of evaluative debate and confrontation over on-going practice.

Our aim, then, is not simply to familiarize readers with theoretical criticism which negates status quo ideology, but to move them, and us, towards using these critiques as a basis for proposing and practising constructive alternatives to our present system of education. Since it is a system in which schools have been created and maintained by a socio-economic elite in order to serve its class interests, the fundamental goal accompanying this new practice must be to free people and their imaginations so that we might begin changing, rather than reproducing, the oppressive socio-economic arrangements of today's corporate capitalism. As a beginning, we invite and urge readers to engage in a dialogue with us by relating your personal learning and school experiences, and ideas concerning educational change to the various critiques and proposals found in this collection.

SECTION I

Liberal Values in Education and the Capitalist System

The capitalist system, like any other economic structure, is something more than simply a particular way in which goods and services are produced, distributed, and consumed. Equal in importance to the explicit structural relation between capitalist socio-economic arrangements and their products are the prevailing value and normative definitions which grow out of and guide this production-consumption process. Due to the very pervasive and powerful effects these definitions have upon the collective consciousness of North Americans, it can be argued that the most significant product of our system is the creation of a "capitalist style of life".

The two papers which follow discuss and are critical of this style of life as it is transmitted through the school, an agency socializing students to fit in and adjust to the prevailing socio-economic structure. It is school values and the way they are used in attempts to legitimize capitalist socio-economic arrangements which constitute the subject matter of Graham Bleasdale's paper.

Drawing mainly upon Canadian data, he traces growth of capitalist educational values from the beginnings of secular, state education in the mid-nineteenth century to their present form under corporate capitalism. Bleasdale argues that a variety of institutionalized techniques (tracking, testing, grading, certifying) have been used to mystify and/or distort the ideals of liberal education — to achieve progress, promote academic freedom, create educational equality, teach tolerance, and protect social order. His work emphasizes the important role schools play in helping to replace these liberal ideals with market values such as consumerism, pragmatism, elitism, sexism, individualism, and competition.

Nelsen's article continues to emphasize this central theme concerning the interrelation between the educational institution and the larger socio-economic system. His criticism of different varieties of the education-as-autonomous argument presented by Clark, Riesman, and Jencks, shows that these "leading" theorists share one thing in common — a pluralistic view of the structure of power. Nelsen argues that they, like all who subscribe to pluralist ideology, focus upon the supposed dispersion and variety of power and thereby, fail to adequately understand institutional interconnections. The result is that these theorists try to represent higher education as autonomous

9

— colleges and universities are separated from the socio-economic context within which they are created and maintained — making it easier for an upper class elite to continue to dominate and recreate without fundamental change the current capitalist order.

Towards a Political Economy of Capitalist Educational Values

GRAHAM BLEASDALE

BEYOND VALUE CONSENSUS

Much post-war sociology of education has been confined to functionalist or neo-functionalist treatments of educational structures and their value systems.[1] Briefly, functionalism has sought to explain social phenomena in terms of how they "function" to maintain an equilibrium throughout the social structure. Probably the most influential social theorist in this tradition has been Emile Durkheim, whose belief in the necessity of social solidarity led him to call for a new "moral order" in modern society that would reconstitute a social consensus.[2] Hence the "value consensus" tenet of orthodox sociology, which has itself been perceived as a social function.

Even when the educational systems of the West have been challenged as in some way socially unequal, the smooth functioning of the social system has remained as the major reference point. So-called common values present in the education system, such as "support of evolutionary changes", have for the most part been uncritically accepted as if they were scientifically valid explanations. That is, what have been perceived as social values have simply been imputed to existing conditions.[3] Values have been defined in ahistorical, subjectivist terms, e.g. "man is perfectable", "achievement orientation".[4] The result has been an uncritical acceptance of a pregiven consensus and any "deviance" from it has been viewed as a failure on the part of the individual to adapt to the socialization process. Orthodox economics, in its analysis of education, has also reflected an "order" model of society by defining economic efficiency as the primary educational outcome. Issues such as social equality and the qualitative nature of educational outcomes have, for the most part, eluded the "human capital" economists.[5] Again, a value consensus within the capitalist system is assumed.

My own approach recognizes that social conflict is inherent in human societies and that value systems are social products whose characteristics are

11

defined by the social distribution of wealth and power. Social values are not simply free-floating end-states adrift in some nebulous "organic whole". Social values, as cultural predispositions or social choices, are symbols of a given society's economic and political goals. And they are not simply social phenomena; they are also ideological to the extent that they give credence to the existing social division of labour and the social relations which enforce it.

Ideologies contain a mixture of theoretical representations, beliefs, and values. In a class society, their content is directly related to social classes whose interests they represent in a more or less coherent form. An ideology may be seen as a dialectical unity reproducing in its own structure social conflict and structural contradictions within the economic and social milieu which gave it birth. In a word, ideologies are part fact, part fiction. They act in a "positive" way to imbue individuals with the cultural ability to be useful members of society, and in a "negative" way by distorting and obscuring the essence of that social reality.[6] With this perception of the nature of an ideology, I shall be examining the ideology of liberal education — the dominant educative ideology in contemporary capitalist society. It will be seen as a dialectical structure, encompassing both values.

To comprehend the nature and significance of liberal educational values, we must attempt to see beneath the veneer of established, "official" explanations of how the education system functions and what its goals are. Initially, we need to risk a statement of the obvious and in so doing define a framework for analysis.

Schools have always had a dual purpose: to select young people for adult roles and to prepare the young for satisfactory performance of those roles. Under capitalism, the reproduction of labour power may be seen to require both a reproduction of skills and a reproduction of submission to the dominant ideology.[7] The training function, as it is sometimes called, is the transmission of cognitive knowledge and skills so that the technical division of labour can be accomplished. The content of this process is the formal curriculum of separate subject areas. The so-called socialization function of education is perhaps more realistically to be referred to as the indoctrination function of schooling. The social institution of education has now displaced the Church and to a growing extent, the family, as the most powerful social control agency in industrialized societies. Since the genesis of universal "popular" education in the nineteenth century, state authorities and educators alike have recognized how essential to the established order it was to have young people inculcated with the correct social attitudes and norms of behaviour — and at a deeper level of social consciousness, the social values of bourgeois society. These evaluative forms of knowledge have made up the informal or hidden curriculum that has been taught both directly in the form of teacher attitudes, and indirectly as a consequence of the social organization of educational knowledge. The hidden curriculum of evaluative knowledge can perhaps best be viewed as underlying the formal curriculum itself.

At both functional levels of education there has occurred an unequal social division of knowledge originating with the unequal social division of labour in capitalist society. The social relationships of liberal education, the lines of authority, modes of behaviour, have reproduced in education capitalist social relations of production.

In the following, the aim will be to show how the ideology of liberal education has evolved since the introduction of universal schooling. Some of the major organizational techniques used by contemporary liberal education (bureaucratization, testing, streaming) in the reproduction and institutionalization of capitalist values will be analysed. Finally, an assessment is offered of contradictions within capitalist education and their relation to the coming crisis in educational values.

THE RISE OF UNIVERSAL SCHOOLING:
A PRODUCT OF THE TECHNICAL AND SOCIAL DIVISION OF LABOUR

Liberal education as we now know it — secular, "free" (state-supported) schooling — became a real possibility only when the development of productive forces within capitalism made it an economic and political necessity for the bourgeoisie.

Up until the mid-nineteenth century, Mandeville's infamous dictum that the poor had simple needs, none of which included an education,[8] summarized well the prevailing view held by aristocrat and bourgeois alike in class societies. The nobility feared the political implications of an enlightened populace, especially after what they regarded as the excesses of the French Revolution, while the motives of the middle class were more characteristically philistine though equally self-interested. Since the beginning of the Industrial Revolution, the mines and factories of the bourgeoisie had been profitably exploiting child labour. What education for the workers and poor there was, taught essentially religious knowledge via biblical and Church catechisms in village Sunday schools or in the Church-sponsored voluntary schools.

Universal schooling was eventually to come about for two major reasons — both related to the dictates of capital. Industrial technology requires more knowledgeable workers. Secondly, there was considerable fear of social revolution from 1789 to 1848.[9] Poor and working class children had to be protected from "pernicious opinions" about the prevailing social order and their rightful place in it. Specialized occupational and social training for adult roles have thus evolved as the twin functions of liberal education. These functions of education will be seen to interact and conflict as two aspects of the social division of knowledge.

As human knowledge — notably technology — progressed and the technical division of labour increased, schooling would gradually replace apprenticeship as the basic mode of learning work skills.[10] The introduction of capitalist production and its social organization, the factory, had destroyed cottage industry and along with it the production and socialization functions of the family. As machine technology advanced, the need for literacy and numeracy on the part of operatives became critical. In short, schools would have to ensure that the workers' children had sufficient knowledge of the "three R's" so that they would be useful (i.e. profitable) in the production process.

Very early in the rise of universal schooling in both England and North America, the social organization of education was structured by the superimposition of an already existing social division of labour. A division of labour into manual work for the "labouring classes" and intellectual work or else no work at all for the "superior classes" had existed prior to the Industrial Revolution. Through the nineteenth century, a class-stratified system of education grew up on both sides of the Atlantic. When universal schooling was introduced through state intervention in England (1870) and somewhat earlier in both the U.S. and Canada (1840s and 1850s), a hierarchical education system reproduced all too accurately the unequal social division of labour characteristic of capitalism. The working class was to be almost totally limited to primary schooling until the turn of the century in North America and until 1944 in England, while in general only middle class students[11] were permitted into the secondary schools.[12] During the early years of the twentieth century, school knowledge was itself socially divided along class lines — vocational knowledge for the working class and academic knowledge for the middle and upper classes.

The social organization of mass education was, in its early form, an almost exact replica of factory organization. The monitorial system made famous by Lancaster and Bell in the early nineteenth century proved, prior to the introduction of universal education, that the efficiencies of large-scale production could be successfully applied to schooling. This would be, in all crucial respects, the prototype of the modern school. By the use of classroom assistants or monitors, a division of labour made possible the "teaching" of hundreds of children simultaneously. Methods were, as one might expect, unabashedly didactic — dictation and repetitive drills were techniques used to achieve memorization of facts. Teacher-student relations were authoritarian in nature. Utilitarian motivations were used to attain the maximum "good", including competition for prizes, corporal punishment, and solitary confinement. The model utilitarian school of Bentham's at Hazelwood used only material rewards for learning. In short, the Bell and Lancaster system incorporated all the educational versions of the social relations of capitalist production. Bell referred candidly to his school as being " . . . like the steam engine or spinning machine, it diminishes labour and multiplies work."[13] This model of bourgeois reasoning, albeit in technocratic form, is still with us.

Monitorial schools were continuing, on a larger scale, the indoctrination tasks earlier affected by the voluntary school movement of the late eighteenth century. The result was a curious but potent ideological blend of moralizing and utilitarian authoritarianism. Although their future forms would change, the fundamental liberal educational values were present in their social organization and techniques of pedagogy. These included competition, elitism, authoritarianism, pragmatism, and materialism. The first of Bell's National Schools in Canada was established in Halifax in 1814. Where it was not actually adopted, the monitorial system's methods were nevertheless popular. Interestingly, in the U.S., this system was later practised by the philanthropic New York Free School Society.[14] A similar development would occur in turn-of-the-century Canada, guided by the Child Saving Movement and the Temperance Movement, which would see children of the poor and "under-privileged" the objects of moral "rescue" by upper class women.

Once the issue of child labour was solved by the onslaught of industrial technology, general bourgeois opinion concerning universal elementary education began to change. In America, the middle class reformers were not at all reluctant to point out how education for all would materially benefit society. Horace Mann, the famous Secretary of the Massachusetts' Board of Education who led the fight for the first "free" school system in North America would thus write: "It is . . . by accomplishing greater results with less means, by creating products at once cheaper, better, and by more expeditious methods that the cultivation of the mind may be truly said to yield the highest pecuniary requital. Intelligence is the great money maker".[15] The link between learning and capital could not be made any clearer. Unimpeded by a landed aristocracy, the champions of universal schooling won early victories in industrialized New England, and after the Civil War state-supported compulsory schooling spread all over the United States. Yet, the major benefactors of universal schooling were the children of sea captains, professionals, and businessmen — that is, of the affluent.[16]

In its embryonic stage, Canadian education was modelled on British lines in content and pedagogy, with organizational forms more susceptible to American influences.[17] Before these began to be felt in the years following Confederation, education in Upper Canada was classically colonial with British themes and texts.

With the ushering in of industrialization during the 1840s and 1850s, the aspiring bourgeoisie, like their British and American counterparts, saw a need for compulsory elementary schooling — something that had been stiffly resisted by the landed Family Compact. The reformers' most energetic and persevering protagonist was Egerton Ryerson, Chief Superintendent of Education in Ontario during the formative years 1844-1876. Like his contemporary, Horace Mann, Ryerson saw universal education as a way of combatting "social diseases" such as poverty, delinquency, and alcoholism, brought on by rapid industrialization. There was left little doubt that schooling was to be valued for its social training function as much as for its technical advantages. Furthermore, this political aspect of compulsory schooling was openly portrayed as a class phenomenon. Ryerson stated his preference for a system of education that was " . . . in harmony with the views and feelings of the better educated classes". An educated people, he professed, would be " . . . the best security for a good government and constitutional liberty."[18] Indeed! As the views and feelings of the dominant classes were that the "common people" should have only sufficient education for a lifetime of work, it is clear that Canadian public education (Ontario as the most wealthy and populous of the provinces set the pattern for English Canada) would be just as elitist as education in the imperialist countries. From the very beginning of their development in the nineteenth century, the public schools were perceived by their middle class promoters as a means of guaranteeing the political security of the social order and the economic requirements of capitalist industry. That political and economic guarantee made by the bourgeoisie to itself, remains unbroken.

The way in which education was socially organized as an avowedly universal system reflected the class biases of its promoters and benefactors. By 1871, the traditional grammar schools had evolved into American-style high schools. And like American high schools, Canadian secondary schools were primarily for the children of the "superior classes" of the day. The Ontario high schools, for example, were very selective — using the British-type competitive examinations to filter intake. In 1891, Ontario secondary schools admitted approximately one-half of the qualified candidates.[19]

As in Europe, competition by examination became the major internal technique by which aristocratic patronage was replaced by bourgeois merit. Competition in the schools was seen as an altogether logical complement to what was found in the real world of laissez-faire capitalism. The Social Darwinism of H. Spencer chose the competitive elements in Darwin's evolutionary theory, while largely ignoring cooperation and Darwin's notion of dependence in the struggle for survival. Spencer's views gave to competition the false aura of natural necessity and provided a quasi-scientific justification for social competition. As in their drive for professionalization (i.e. the monopolization of knowledge in the occupational structure), the bourgeoisie could claim that competition was fair because it produced mobility by merit. For obvious reasons, they preferred to overlook the glaring evidence that social competition, like economic competition, was a rigged race: the contestants were competing for educational chances in a game whose rules were written by the winners. Prior inequalities handicapped working class students, which is why so relatively few ever won. However, in the name of merit, competition became a key educational value.

The high schools also charged fees, thereby limiting enrolment in a more direct way to those who could afford it — a class barrier that remained in the Canadian education system well into this century in some provinces; in Manitoba, high school fees were still charged up until the 1950s. In the early 1900s the elementary schools provided the only formal education for 95 per cent of all Ontario children: an education for the "poorer classes" that would prepare them for their future lot in life.[20] Early techniques such as competitive examinations and tuition fees characterized an educational structure embodying elitism as a central value, even as "equality of educational opportunity" gained in popularity as a liberal slogan.[21]

The appearance of the large industrial corporation, an organizational form that evolved during a period of rapid industrialization between Confederation and World War I, signalled a demand by employers and reformers alike for more technical secondary education. In the early 1900s, the Canadian Manufacturing Association led a well-organized lobby for state-provided vocational education, explicitly linking the goal of manufacturers' prosperity with a technically trained "class of labour".[22] In Canada, as in England, the grammar school humanists were vocal in their opposition but they were on a losing side. Spencer's book on education and T. Huxley's essays, both advocating a more pragmatic education relevant to an industrial society, apparently had been widely read by English Canadian educators.[23] By the turn-of-the-century, the Huxley-Arnold debate was over in Canada. Manual training was included in both the elementary and secondary curricula in Ontario as of 1904.[24] Vocational education in schools and a more "useful" academic knowledge was now an official creed. The foundation had been laid for the modern class system of education as we know it. A vocational-based curriculum would be provided for immigrant and working class children while a traditional academic curriculum was reserved mainly for affluent children from bourgeois or petty bourgeois families. Pragmatism had become an indispensable value in an educative ideology that, in part, functioned to create a social consciousness in the young compatible with the capitalist work ethic. In short, vocationalism was introduced into the schools under the guise of a universalism that promised advantages from a more practical education both to the individual and to society. Truth to tell, vocationalism would primarily benefit business and would at the same time provide a convenient route for working class children who might otherwise challenge the middle class monopoly on prestige positions in the occupational hierarchy.

The organizational preconditions for the efficient reproduction of social stratification and capitalist values were provided in the form of bureaucracy. Under the slogans of merit and equality of opportunity, the bureaucratization of the schools proceeded to rationalize the class control of education.[25] From the mid-century onward, educational reform under Ryerson's tutelage had centralized administrative and social control. Provincial examinations guaranteed that there was little deviation in the classroom from the official course of study. Grading by age group, first introduced in the hope of eliminating the rabid competitiveness found in the monitorial system, merely reintroduced competition at the level of the graded class. Its latent function, though, had been the fragmentation of knowledge into centrally controlled "courses" of study with centrally approved high-circulation textbooks. Textbooks, apart from arbitrarily limiting the definition and scope of knowledge by standardizing it, were often explicitly political. Canadian school texts were in fact frequently British, complete with British imperial propaganda. Canadian themes were largely ignored — just as they were in the American texts which replaced the British ones in the post World War II era. Centralization was to permit, then, the mass inculcation of both liberal educational ideals and liberal social values at a level never before possible.

Unhampered by the localism of American jurisdictions,[26] the bureaucratizing process has progressed this century in Ontario and subsequently in the rest of Canada, in the form of a highly centralized, classical Weberian model.[27] Social relations in the school system have reconstituted the hierarchical lines of authority typical of capitalist society: administrator-principal-teacher-student. The institutionalization of authoritarianism in the educational value system has been the major result. And as we shall see, the large, rationalized public school system has not produced equality of educational opportunity. Bureaucracy in education has, however, served to make the class biases more methodical and more efficient. Bureaucratization of the social relationships of education has, as in other social institutions, served to legitimize established norms and values. By preparing the young for alienating and bureaucratized work roles, bureaucracy in education provides the organizational bridge between education and society.

CLASS BIASES IN LIBERAL EDUCATION:
THE MYTH OF MERITOCRACY AND EQUAL EDUCATIONAL OPPORTUNITY

The class barriers to education have been well documented. Inequality of income is perhaps the most obvious social barrier to individuals seeking an equal chance to be educated. In Canada, as in other capitalist countries, class bias is present in both secondary and university attendance.[28] Regional and religious differences have historically compounded income inequities, benefiting white, Anglo-Saxon Protestants in urban areas. The central fact, however, is that if you are from an affluent family you are much more likely to succeed in school, both in terms of educational performance[29] and actual number of years of schooling attained.[30] And these inequalities are self-perpetuating. Education, like physical capital, is transferred to the children of the privileged — only it is intangible and untaxed. The children of university-educated parents in Ontario, for instance, were found to be six times more likely to attend university than children who have elementary-educated parents.[31] Both American and Canadian data show that economic pressures,[32] and hence educational aspirations,[33] are themselves subject to class bias. Elitism has become "built-in" to the structure of liberal education and it remains as an omnipresent object lesson for survival in a capitalist society. What is astounding is that the official interpretation of this reality is that the education system provides equality of educational opportunity.

By reproducing the unequal sexual division of labour, liberal education reinforces another related dimension of elitism — sexism. Composing some 40 per cent of the labour force, women occupy the lower rungs of the occupational ladder — traditionally employed in the service sector of the economy as waitresses, domestics, nurses, bank tellers, and teachers. They are paid significantly less than men, for equal work.[34] Schools prepare women for the social and sexual inequalities they will have to face as mothers and workers. Girls are more often streamed into commercial and other terminal programmes, while boys are more likely to be placed in academic programmes. Twice as many boys as girls obtain a university education in Canada. Controlling for scholastic and financial variables, it becomes apparent that inequality results in part from attitudinal differences.[35] This sexist attitudinal structure is taught as part of both the formal and informal curriculum.

In the school media, women are usually portrayed in traditional social roles — as wives, mothers or possibly in male-supportive roles such as nurses or secretaries. Many schools in Canada still have segregated classes, for example in cooking, industrial arts, physical education, and music. The curriculum structure guides girls into traditionally female subject-areas and away from traditionally male subject-areas. In this way, the educational aspirations of girls are channeled into learning areas, the products of which the occupational structure can handle.

More insidious is the way in which the hidden curriculum teaches both boys and girls sexism. Boys have male counsellors, and girls have women counsellors. Most elementary teachers are women, most secondary teachers are men. And most of the 30 per cent of secondary teachers who are female still teach in the traditionally female subjects: home economics, physical education, languages, and secretarial skills. None of the high school principals or school superintendents in British Columbia are women.[36] Children learn from examples such as these, lessons which have become part of the social relations of education.

Women are not the only social group to be discriminated against by the education system. Native Indians and immigrants have historically been the subjects of racial bias in society and in the schools.

Europeans stole not only Indian land, but with it their culture and very identity. Natives were left to work for whites (e.g. in the B.C. fish canneries), when work was available, and were forced to send their children to missionary residential schools. Here, separated from their bands and parents, they were indoctrinated with the white man's religion and values. Native languages, religious practices, and values were ignored, or still worse, denigrated. When the state took over native education in the 1950s, assimilation of natives into white society was the explicit goal of government education policy.[37] The indoctrination function would remain in the public schools for natives; only the form by which it was expressed would change. Religious values would be replaced by capitalist ones.

Over 50 per cent of the British Columbia prison population are native Indians. In some Indian bands in Canada, the unemployment rate is higher than the employment rate. Not surprisingly, the drop-out rate among native children is higher than for any other ethnic group. The schools have little of value or relevance to native Canadians. By treating native children as if they were white children, the informal curriculum teaches native children inferiority and white children discrimination. There are fewer than one hundred native teachers in B.C schools, but if an equivalent ratio of native teachers to native students existed, there would need to be another 1000 teachers. A stereotyped role model is reinforced in the formal curriculum, where native cultures are largely ignored or discussed only as a side-issue in the history of the white man's progress.[38]

Historically, immigrants have been used by Canadian capitalists as cheap labour. A classic example of this was the importation by the Canadian Pacific Railway of thousands of Chinese workers to construct the transcontinental railway. The survivors formed the nucleus of B.C.'s Chinese communities. The net effect of immigration upon the class structure has been the compounding of economic competition within the working class. Immigrant workers have generally competed unsuccessfully due to their cultural handicaps — East Indians in B.C., for instance, often occupy the low status jobs in the forest industry. In the schools, this phenomenon has taken the form of discrimination by teachers and students alike.

Race remains, for thousands of Canadian children, a barrier to equal educational opportunity. That barrier will not be lifted, however, until economic inequalities have been resolved. Racism will remain as a dominant educational value until such time as the economic and cultural needs of ethnic groups are met prior to the dictates of capitalist growth. A Marxist as opposed to a liberal approach presupposes that economic exploitation must be abolished as a precondition for the ending of racial exploitation, upon which discrimination is based.

Clearly, the reality of liberal education contradicts its ideological rhetoric about equality of opportunity and reward by merit. Yet so long as isolated examples of "disadvantaged" students who "worked their way through college" can be enshrined as proof of the system's viability, then the liberal ideal of meritocracy sustains itself. Indeed, what has been called the "technocratic-meritocratic ideology"[39] is surely the most subtle and appealing of all liberal educational notions. This quality of meritocracy lies in its half-truth: individuals do progress through the system according to merit. But what the education system defines as merit has very little to do with intellectual ability. Recent research indicates that the system's definition of merit includes the ability to conform to established norms and attitudes. With ability measured by scholastic achievement (test scores and grades), it has been found that intellectual achievement on its own does not determine school or economic success. In fact, character traits such as perseverance, discipline, and punctuality were found to be almost as good predictors of grades as standardized test scores.[40] It would appear that school performance has much more to do with social class membership than arbitrary criteria such as test scores.

What the meritocracy in education does seem to succeed at accomplishing is the legitimation of a role allocation mechanism that assigns individuals to unequal social roles in the occupational structure. Defenders of the status quo have suggested that a hierarchical, unequal division of labour in society is both technically and socially necessary. Yet these apologists for social inequality have treated the social division of labour as if it were a natural phenomenon when it has been a social product, created by human beings.[41] Under capitalism, the private ownership of social productive forces, including labour itself, means that individuals must compete for a share of society's rewards. The merit system in liberal education provides an essential object-lesson to the young who will have to survive under such a system: competition. For without this social value, which builds upon the worst in human behaviour, capitalism would not work.

The transition from an aristocratic inculcation of one's proper station in life to a bourgeois "democratic citizenship" did not change the class nature of education, only its social form.[42] There have, of course, been differences in the structuring of role allocation between capitalist societies — differences which have reflected the societal relations of dominant classes to their respective class structures. For our purposes, the relevant comparison most often made has been the English-American one. Its relevance lies in the fact that the Canadian educational structure has been influenced by the application and theoretical perceptions of both mobility models, previously labelled "sponsored mobility" and "contest mobility" respectively.[43]

British education has historically been tied, even in modern times, to an aristocratic model of social mobility, albeit modified by the bourgeoisie's insistence upon competition as a means of access for their children. The English education system has been, like most European ones, one in which nominated individuals proceeded up educational ladders to a prescribed destination. Selection of nominees has been at a relatively early age (the old "eleven-plus") and switching from one educational ladder to another has been difficult if not impossible — an efficient and convenient social control mechanism.

The American bourgeoisie has been unencumbered by a politically powerful nobility.[44] There has been greater access to educational ladders, though schools have subsequently developed sophisticated screening devices by which the social organization of the school itself has become a "mechanism of social differentiation". Organizational sponsorship and social class membership have been shown to be key criteria in an "informal" selection process.[45]

Canada's educational mobility structure has, like the economy itself, been shaped by both British and American capital. But, as intimated earlier, the American model has become increasingly dominant, especially since World War II. The importation of organizational forms, such as the high school, was followed, perhaps inevitably, by the Americanization of what is taught in Canadian schools and universities. Generations of Canadian children have grown up in an ideological climate nurtured by the propagation of American ideals (free enterprise, progress, anti-communism) and the American social values of consumerism and pragmatism. The liberal educative ideology combined with the liberal continentalist ideology (even in its present modified, pseudo-nationalist garb) may well have succeeded in destroying any fabric of national identity or "will" left in the Canadian people.[46]

Yet, if the comparative differences between national mobility structures have been significant, the similarities in the capitalist nature of educational mobility have produced profound and trans-national distortions in the educational chances of individuals and of whole social classes. Canadian academics have sought, in typical fashion, a compromise — indicative of a colonial mentality — between sponsorship and contest mobility, between the educational goals of academic standards and equality of access.[47] However, standards have been arbitrarily defined and bureaucratically set, while equality of opportunity has been prelimited by class bias. There is no correct choice, because there is no real choice. The techniques may differ, but the end result is the same: inequality and privilege. Indeed, the "academic standards versus equal opportunity" debate is locked into the same liberal dichotomy of theory and practice, academic and vocational knowledge, politics and economics, the division of the state (political being) and civil society (social being) in capitalist society.[48] Under the ideological umbrella of slogans like equality of educational opportunity and universality, liberal educators have continued to view education in either elitist or instrumentalist terms. The so-called pendulum effect in education swings in both directions, in so far as the booms and recessions of the capitalist economy permit it to, but the whole mechanism continues to churn out a majority of individuals who are imbued with a capitalist social consciousness.

THE SOCIAL DIVISION OF KNOWLEDGE: TESTING AND STREAMING

By whatever name, streaming or tracking, ability grouping of children is the major technique used in the role allocation system that sorts and selects individuals for different work roles: factory work, white collar work, management, and so on.

It is in the organizational technique of streaming that the twin functions of liberal education, training and indoctrination, merge. Put technically, streaming is the social division of both cognitive knowledge (skills) and evaluative knowledge (norms, attitudes, and values).

Efficiencies of scale and the rational bureaucratization of organizations have characterized the development of both the work place and the school during this century. Specifically, the organizational structures of the modern corporation and of the modern school share characteristics that are fundamental to the social relations of capitalist production. In Canada, what has been called the industrial model of schooling has been, and continues to be, a dominant one.[49] In many ways, the history of testing and streaming may be seen as the imposition of hierarchic social relations onto the social organization of knowledge.

In England, for instance, when there was a post World War I demand for universal secondary schooling by the political representatives of the working class, sheer numbers became a social and political problem for the capitalist state. The actual numbers of those qualified for secondary school entrance in 1919, for example, far outweighed the available spaces by at least 18,000 children.[50] Consequently, the emphasis through the 1920s and 1930s was less and less upon actual school performance and increasingly upon capacity or promise measured by arbitrary standards of ability — as material expansion of secondary education was ruled out on political grounds.[51] The English ruling class, frightened by the economic crisis that marked the Depression, was understandably opposed to altering a school system in which the middle class child was four times as likely to receive a secondary education as a working class child.[52]

The technology of streaming was to be developed in the U.S., where objective testing had first been experimented with on a large scale by the U.S. Army in 1917. Large-scale industry, Henry Ford's assembly line production, and a new form of social organization, the large, vertically-integrated business corporation, had already appeared by the turn of the century. This was the age of the Rockefellers, the Carnegies, and the Vanderbilts, who had reaped huge profits commencing in the 1880s and 1890s through the creation of cartels of suppliers and producers. The publication of F.W. Taylor's *The Principles of Scientific Management* in 1911 was to provide the requisite organization theory, a theory that stressed the importance of material rewards in pursuit of maximization of efficiency (time and motion studies) and hence of profits. But if standardization and maximum output were now on the corporate agenda, they would very soon be a priority of the mass educators in the burgeoning public school systems. Taylorism in the classroom meant production-line style regimentation — the "lock-step" approach to learning, and the wholesale importation of "business values" into the schools.[53] The educationist version of time and motion studies would be standardized testing.

The progressive philosophy that education must meet the "needs of the individual child" was used to give objective testing a certain pedagogical rationale. Yet, objective testing in practice made schooling more efficient, with larger classes ranked by tested ability.[54] But the real fixation and allure of objective testing lay in its pseudo-scientific cloak. Established psychology maintained that moral character, social worth, and intelligence were all genetically linked and inherited. The authors of the intelligence tests, Thorndike and Terman, claimed a direct correspondence between Intelligence Quotient (test-measured intelligence in relation to an average intelligence score) and occupational status. As a totally inborn trait, intelligence was held to be constant and hence measurable. Individual needs, it was argued, could better be met in homogeneous groups ranked by both age and I.Q. This is the rationalization behind what has been called the "I.Q. Ideology".[55] Even though the scientific arguments for its use in education have long ago been discarded, the use of standardized I.Q. tests in streaming children has become, since World War II, a fixture of contemporary liberal education.[56]

The use of I.Q. test scores as a major criterion for evaluating ability has been described by a recent, comprehensive American study of educational inequalities, as purely a "bureaucratic convenience".[57] There appears to be a positive correlation between income level and I.Q.[58] Working class children are handicapped from the outset, as the content of the tests is biased in favour of more verbally expressive, problem-oriented, and literate middle class children. I.Q. tests actually measure achievement as well as "aptitude", that is, they purport to measure innate intelligence when in fact they measure the sum total of what a child has learned.[59] Standardized tests measure socio-economic background as much as they claim to measure native intelligence. In this obvious sense, testing reproduces class biases and specifically, elitism as an educational value.

Perhaps most damaging of all arguments about the validity of standardized testing is that I.Q. becomes a self-fulfilling prophecy. Low I.Q. scores are used as a rationalization for low expectations of learning — expectations which students proceed to meet. Teachers who judge their students' capacities on their respective I.Q. scores get caught in the same Catch 22. Research has shown how children placed in streams other than those they would normally be in, performed according to the stream norm.[60] Once labelled slow or non-university material, the student is counselled or placed in the appropriate "terminal" (vocational or general curriculum) stream. In this way, arbitrary test measurements of ability result in an enormous waste of human talent.[61] Just as the capitalist economy is plagued by the under-consumption/over-production of goods as a result of the unequal distribution of wealth, so too capitalist society is necessarily inhibited by the under-utilization of talent and knowledge produced by the unequal social division of knowledge.

The net effect of standardized testing upon the social relations of education is the creation of a utilitarian attitudinal structure which perceives education as an instrumental, as opposed to creative, process. Teachers and students alike develop a test-knowledge approach to learning — the "teach to the test" syndrome. The underlying value being transmitted is pragmatism — a belief in what is deemed practical or expedient as opposed to what may or may not be intrinsically good.

The Social Division of Cognitive Knowledge

Streaming is the practical means used to socially divide forms of knowledge and skills. The most common form it takes in Canada is groupings of secondary academic and vocational programmes, with supplementary terminal programmes sometimes added in the larger secondary schools. It also occurs at the elementary level, more informally, as division into slow and fast reading groups (the Rabbits and Turtles). Even here in the elementary grades the role allocation mechanism is at work informally, with selection a function of the teacher's discretion.

That streaming effectively provides different kinds of knowledges and skills to children from different socio-economic backgrounds, is no longer disputed. A disproportionate number of working class children are tracked into vocational and commercial programmes in preparation for blue-collar and low-level white-collar service jobs, while a disproportionate number of middle and upper class children are placed in academic programmes in preparation for university and professional or management positions.[62]

This central feature of capitalist education is perhaps its most fundamental one. Theory and practice, thinking and doing, are estranged from each other and, at the same time, divided along class lines. Working class children face a gauntlet of tests, counsellors, peer group, and teacher attitudes, before reaching the competitive plateau of more affluent children. Elitism emerges as a structural phenomenon intrinsic to the capitalist education system. The smug, condescending attitude of upper stream (academic programme) students to their "vocational" or "occupational" peers is a manifestation of the degree to which elitism has become a part of the social consciousness of students.

It is the social rivalry generated by the meritocratic system of testing and streaming that exhibits an express ideological dimension. Apart from legitimating an unequal allocation of social roles, the social division of cognitive knowledge engenders competition as a social value in educational social relationships. Students, consciously and unconsciously, compete for scarce academic programme places, while teachers compete for the status and better working conditions of teaching the "bright" kids. School is a race, and only the hardest workers and smartest students win. So runs the mythology in our society, but this myth runs counter to significant sociological research.

The Social Division of Evaluative Knowledge

Non-intellectual skills, though more difficult to evaluate, are undoubtedly — even our common sense tells us — a prominent factor in determining educational performance. This view is made more credible by the recent finding that academic test scores, when controlled for other factors, do not explain differences in educational performance.[63] The positive relationship existing between length of education and income would indicate, however, that schooling transmits something useful to employers.[64] That there is little apparent relationship between educational attainment and actual job performance leads us to further question the effect of cognitive development alone on success in both school and society.[65]

School, as part of its indoctrinating function, teaches students evaluative forms of knowledge by rewarding the development of certain capabilities while penalizing others. The social structure of liberal education — of the social organization of knowledge and the accompanying social relations of education — accomplishes this indoctrination function by reproducing and reinforcing the growth of a social consciousness containing the social norms, attitudes, and values which will enable the individual to adjust to the capitalist production process.

The education system no longer uses blatantly material rewards as a kind of substitute wage for educational production. Today, in keeping with post-

Taylor human relations theory, the social organization of knowledge is meant to create motivation through social rewards which nevertheless remain external to the individual. These include grades, honour roles, promotion/failure, teacher approval, rules, and certification. This externalization of social control, because it is legitimated by the social organization of knowledge, is internalized by the individual. It is by means of this institutionalized normative order that the essential components of the "bureaucratic mentality" required by capitalist production are created.[66] The personality characteristics demanded by bureaucratized production for adequate job performance have been identified by recent research done by Bowles and Gintis.[67] They report that whereas traits such as creativity and independence went unrewarded, dependability, perseverance, discipline, consistency, and reasonableness were rewarded in the form of subject grades. One can induce that the values underlying these behaviour norms — elitism, pragmatism, and competition — were being reinforced.

Further evidence points to the social division of evaluative knowledge. Authoritarian norms such as consistency, punctuality, conformity, discipline, and external motivation were found to be stressed in high schools, while universities permitted individual autonomy and a more open social atmosphere.[68] The rapidly growing community college system in the U.S. and Canada, designed to train future service and middle-level workers, was also found to reproduce a normative structure similar to that of the high school.[69] What is indicated here is that the education system is capable of accommodating different forms of evaluative knowledge for different levels of role allocation. This phenomenon in fact reappears both between schools in differing socio-economic areas and between curriculum streams within schools.

A recent study of two Toronto schools, one an inner-city working class neighbourhood school and the other in an affluent area, found a negative, imposed discipline in the former and a positive, self-discipline in the latter.[70] The same class division of the informal curriculum takes place between streams in composite secondary schools, streams which we have already seen to be class divided in cognitive terms. Vocational programmes were found by American researchers to emphasize rule-following, while academic programmes permitted more intellectual and social freedom.[71] Significantly, the identical phenomenon is indicated by class differences in child-rearing techniques.[72]

What has now become readily apparent is that the value system of the educative ideology itself accommodates class distinctions made by the social division of evaluative knowledge. For working class children, the dominant norms are proscriptive: punctuality, conformity, and discipline. The educational value reinforcing these is authoritarianism. Conversely, for middle and upper class children, the dominant norms are essentially prescriptive: including self-discipline, delayed gratification, and individuality. The value mediating this normative order might be called a kind of individualism, but it is no longer the rugged individualism of a century ago. Rather, it is a new social value more in keeping with the organization of monopoly capitalism: corporatism.

The trade-off here would appear to be the internalization of self-perpetuating behavioural norms and school values on the part of individuals who will fill the upper slots in the occupational structure. Once the appropriate social norms have become second nature to the individual, close supervision is unnecessary. The future corporate leader defines the system's needs as his/her own: class values now become personal values.

The End of the Track?

The contemporary state of streaming in Canada is in flux, the issue being complicated by provincial jurisdiction over education. In British Columbia, formal streaming had been terminated along with Grade 12 written university entrance examinations during the reforms of the early seventies. That the reform is permanent, however, is not yet clear. The B.C. government, following Ontario's lead, is demanding a "core curriculum" in the public schools, implying the concomitant need to measure achievement vis-à-vis Departmental standards. Once testing is reestablished, the necessary preconditions for traditional streaming will exist. The popularity of "competency tests" in the U.S. and Canada, such as the B.C. post-secondary English placement examination, may very well lead to the reintroduction of traditional streaming.

What appears to have happened in the interim is that formal streaming has been largely discontinued. However, a more subtle but equally effective informal streaming process has replaced it.

I would argue that any kind of homogeneous ability-grouping tends to channel working class children into the lower end of the occupational hierarchy and more affluent children into the upper levels. What is happening in the "detracked" secondary schools today is similar to what is happening in elementary schools where children have been placed in homogeneous reading groups. Our knowledge of how children respond to learning expectations leads us to believe that non-tested, non-compulsory ability grouping will produce essentially the same results as the formal kind.[73] The role allocation mechanism must in some way redirect the occupational aspirations of a growing number of students. The old "meeting individual needs" rationale, used earlier this century to justify streaming, is reappearing under the guise of an "adaptation of programmes to pupils" approach.[74] The "cooling-out" function[75] of schools becomes more significant under conditions of nonobjective selection. Guidance counselling, always a major factor in streaming decisions, appears (when combined with teacher evaluation and grades) to be the key criterion for informal streaming.[76] As both counsellor/teacher evaluations and grades are subject to class bias, we can expect these decisions to be just as class biased as the traditional, formal ones.[77]

THE COMING CRISIS IN CAPITALIST EDUCATIONAL VALUES

The liberal dilemma, unchanged in its essentials from the one it has faced since universal education was first introduced over a century ago, is that modern capitalism requires both trained and politically quiescent workers. The limits to economic growth and the social effects of the growth in human knowledge (e.g. technology) now threaten to transform the dilemma into a crisis within liberal education and its ideology.

The Limits to Capitalist Educational Growth

The huge growth in the sixties of enrolments, particularly in higher education, has challenged the existing role allocation mechanism of both European and North American education systems. A so-called revolution of rising expectations, created by the rapid post-war economic growth rate, has conflicted with the unequal division of labour and prestige in capitalist societies. To put the issue bluntly: the old equation of education and jobs has broken down. How has this come about?

As production capacity expanded into the post-war "affluent society", the occupational structures of the industrialized countries began a period of radical change. The resulting transformation of corporate manpower requirements was reflected in the dramatic growth of technical, clerical, and service sectors in the Canadian occupational structure which have gone from 24.4 per cent of the labour force in 1931 to 38.6 per cent in 1961, and now probably represents close to 50 per cent of the total work force.[78] The unionization of more white collar workers and some professional groups (e.g. teachers, nurses) attests to the accompanying decrease in status differences between blue collar and white collar workers, in a work environment subject to the methodical rationalization of production. In short, the working class has been expanding as automated and large-scale production processes have taken away the traditional independence from the white collar and even petty bourgeois elements of the class structure.[79] This proletarianization process has resulted in the fact that 83 per cent of all Canadians work as employees earning their living in the form of wages or salaries.[80]

Automation, by making industry less labour-intensive and by demanding fewer skills for those jobs remaining, has created new forms of technological unemployment and underemployment — Ph.D. mail carriers. There are now over a million Canadians unemployed. Forty-six per cent are youth, many of them high school or, increasingly, university graduates.[81] In the economic crisis confronting us, there are simply not enough jobs to go around in an economy still based upon natural resource exportation. Further- more, with the bureaucratization and alienation of corporate-style white collar work spreading into middle-management positions, there are fewer prestige jobs left.

School once provided an avenue of access to good jobs for the children of the middle and upper classes, but this mobility corridor is narrowing. A whole generation of university graduates, conditioned by the "human capital" incantations of counsellors, teachers, and government television adver- tisements, were told that x number of years at university equals y amount of life-time earnings. This generation discovered for itself the myth of the meritocracy. Once the demand for marketable skills diminishes, the liberal ideal of mobility via merit becomes absurd. And still present in the educative ideology is a materialism reproduced most blatantly by credentialism. Raising the educational ante has induced an artificial scarcity of talent, but it has also latently served to exacerbate a commodity fetishism of certificates and degrees perceived as symbols of knowledge, consumed as a means in acquiring other commodities. The liberal ideal of educational progress masks a bourgeois definition of progress as material progress and its underlying value of materialism.

The French Fouchet plan to restrict enrollment in university arts faculties and the construction of a separate community college system in the U.S. and Canada (and polytechnics in England), have been two different attempts by capitalist states to adjust the role allocation mechanism while preserving the unequal distribution of economic rewards and prestige. In Canada, direct state manipulation in order to match graduates with jobs has so far been avoided as it would conflict too obviously with the contest system's ideal of equality of educational opportunity. Income incentives and the cooling-out of students' expectations have been cited as "voluntary" alternatives.[82] Yet, the raising of university tuition fees will no doubt have the desired effect. In addition, within the educational structure's content, a core curriculum trend may also be viewed as an attempt to tailor cognitive knowledge, and indi- rectly evaluative knowledge as well, to the realities of adult work roles — notably by deemphasizing critical inquiry and creativity.

So long as there has been a scarcity of qualified personnel in the occupation hierarchy, the social division of knowledge has remained for most people a non-issue, just as economic growth until now has prevented for the most part any critical political examination of the social division of wealth. The continuity of growth economies in the "affluent society" made it possible for all social classes to receive proportionally larger pieces of the economic pie. Attention has been focused on equalizing the allocation process as opposed to the distribution of unequal rewards, which is its end.[83] In other words, equality of educational opportunity has been used as a red herring to obscure the prior inequalities inherent in capitalist society. But its usefulness as an ideological foil for elitism may not last much longer. In the deepening economic crisis, capital is caught in a predicament of its own making — it can either promote inflation or unemployment in its attempt to produce economic growth. Similarly, capitalist states must reduce their educational output in order to bring it in line with economic requirements. If output is arbitrarily reduced (as in France), the long-term problem for capital is alleviated, but educational expectations will remain unmet by the educational system. If output is not reduced, the long-term problem of manpower requirements will be unresolved and expectations will be unmet in the job market itself. In both circumstances, the ideal of equal opportunity will be subject to social forces which it may not be able to withstand.

Human Knowledge as as Productive Force and the Demise of Liberal Educational Values

The fundamental contradiction inherent in liberal education will remain between the growth requirements of productive forces, including knowledge and labour, and the reproduction of alienating social relations of education and their accompanying values. The growth of human knowledge and its qualitative development, including the demands of future workers for more relevant knowledge, are pushing capitalist educational values to their breaking point.

In the late twentieth century, the capitalist ideology of education is being transcended by new forms of human knowledge. That it is no longer possible to know all there is to be known (human knowledge is now doubling every few years) means that the industrial model of education, upon which the liberal educative ideology is based, is out-moded. This model, first refined by Bell and Lancaster in England during the early nineteenth century, is the social organization of education in which individuals are taught distinct bodies of knowledge or subjects as if their minds were, as Locke would have put it, a "tabula rasa". The implicit assumption that youth are raw material to be treated and processed into a prescribed educational product is no longer appropriate for contemporary, increasingly automated, production. And the values attached to the industrial or factory model of education — including pragmatism, competition, and authoritarianism — will no longer be logical or meaningful once this model is discarded.

The irony of the crisis in liberal educational values is that capital's need to reproduce labour power — to train workers to become more productive — has created at the same time expectations on the part of workers for literacy, social mobility, and social justice. In other words, liberal education has, in spite of itself, given the ''lower classes'' the knowledge with which to critically comprehend social reality and their own situation within it. Social scientific knowledge, commencing with the *Philosophes* but only achieving any scientific cogency and significance for industrial humanity with the social theory of Marx, has since illuminated the myriad, often subtle, relationships between environment and consciousness so vital to human destinies. To the extent that the existing education system fails to meet the majority's need for relevant, developmental knowledge, the dominant values underlying the training function itself — elitism, racism, sexism, and materialism — will become less and less defendable.

The training and indoctrination functions of liberal education, once integral to the economic and social needs of an early industrial capitalism, now conflict with contemporary needs. This contradiction reconstitutes itself within the education system's need to train and to placate. The growth of new forms of human knowledge, including technology, means that the working class must acquire new kinds of training; while the unequal social division of labour has required the continuation of an unequal social division of both cognitive and evaluative forms of educational knowledge. In short, human knowledge as a productive force,[84] is being stifled by a dilapidated educational structure.

Within the ideology of liberal education, this underlying contradiction has created the preconditions for a heightening of tension between the reality of capitalist values and the illusory ideals of liberal education. The dominant values of the ideology of liberal education — elitism, competition, pragmatism, authoritarianism, corporatism, and materialism — are the foundation of a social consciousness appropriate to the economic and social requirements of a capitalist mode of production. At the same time, the liberal education ideals of equality of educational opportunity, merit, universality, intellectual freedom, and educational progress respectively, pose as so-called educative values while serving to mask the underlying capitalist values so essential to the existing educational order. The dominant value system mediates and directs the search for, and social uses of, human knowledge. As class values, liberal educational values mystify, particularize, and fragment human knowledge and in the process, human beings. Just as human beings in capitalist society have become alienated from their full potentialities, so human beings have become alienated from knowledge and their own consciousness.

The ultimate resolution of the crisis in capitalist educational values will become a possibility only with the communal ownership of knowledge: the abolition of the unequal social division of knowledge is its fundamental precondition. Only then will the structural preconditions exist for the nurturing of a new social consciousness in which will grow a different, humanist set of educational values. Not yet definable in their precise content or form, the new values will both reflect and help shape an education for the future and the present — an education that is at once theoretical and practical, cognitive and affective, scientific and joyful.

NOTES

1. For a useful review of functionalist and conflict theories of education see R. Collins, "Functional and Conflict Theories of Educational Stratification", *Education: Structure and Society*, ed. B. R. Cosin, London, 1972, pp. 175-199.

2. E. Durkheim, *The Division of Labour in Society*, New York: Free Press, 1964. Also, his *Moral Education*, New York: Free Press, 1961. On the ideological overtones of Durkheim's "social order" bias, see I. Zeitlin, *Ideology and the Development of Sociological Theory*, Englewood Cliffs: Prentice-Hall, 1968, especially p. 234.

3. M. F. D. Young, "On the Politics of Education Knowledge", *Economy and Society*, May 1972, Vol. 1, No. 2, p. 198.

4. See, for example, F. Kluckhohn and F. Strodbeck, *Variations in Value Orientations*, Evanston, Ill.: Row, Peterson, 1961; also, D. McClelland, *The Achieving Society*, Princeton, N. J.: Van Nostrand, 1961.

5. A summary of orthodox economics of education is provided by S. Bowles, *Planning Educational Systems for Economic Growth*, Cambridge: Harvard University Press, 1969, pp. 1-10. On the human capital approach to education, see T. W. Schultz, *The Economic Value of Education*, New York: Columbia University Press, 1963.

6. The identification and analysis of bourgeois ideology, and indeed of ideology per se as we now perceive it, was first explored by Marx. See K. Marx and F. Engels, *The German Ideology*, New York: International, 1947. For a selection of Marx's writings regarding ideology, see *Karl Marx: Selected Writings in Sociology and Social Philosophy*, eds. T. Bottomore and M. Rubel, London: Watts, 1956. For a critical discussion of modern capitalist ideology, see H. Lefebvre, *The Sociology of Marx*, New York: Random House (Pantheon), 1968, Chapter 3; also, N. Poulantzas, *Political Power and Social Classes*, London: NLB, 1973.

7. L. Althusser, *Lenin and Philosophy and Other Essays*, New York: Monthly Review Press, 1971, pp. 123-173.

8. B. Mandeville, "The Fable of the Bees", *The Educating of Americans*, ed. D. Calhoun, Boston: Houghton Mifflin Co., 1969, p. 6.

9. R. Williams, *The Long Revolution*, New York: Columbia University Press, 1961, pp. 146-147.

10. P. Aries, *Centuries of Childhood*, New York: Knopf, 1962, pp. 194, 369-370.

11. In the context of the nineteenth century, the term "middle class" is a synonym for the bourgeoisie. Once the bourgeoisie had in effect become the ruling class, only the petite bourgeoisie (small businessmen, professionals, etc.) remained as a middle class. The issue becomes ambiguous in the contemporary context when "white collar" sector workers are often misleadingly labelled middle class.

12. In England, education was explicitly viewed as a class structure by the ruling class and their agents. This is made quite clear in the Taunton and Bryce Commissions on education. See B. Simon, *Studies in the History of Education: 1780 - 1870*, London: Beekman, 1960; also, D. Wardle, *The Rise of the Schooled Society*, London: Routledge and Kegan Paul, 1974. The same class attitudes were apparent in Canada. See, for example, "Urban Industrial Change and Curriculum Reform in Early Twentieth Century Ontario", *Studies in Educational Change*, eds. R. Heyman et al., Toronto: Holt, Rinehart and Winston, 1972.

13. E. Midwinter, *Nineteenth Century Education*, U.K., 1970, p. 29.

14. This was the epitome of what Michael Katz has called "Paternalistic Voluntarism". Katz writes: "This was a class system of education. It provided a vehicle for the efforts of one class to civilize another and thereby ensure that society would remain tolerable, orderly and safe." M. Katz, *Class, Bureaucracy, and Schools*, New York: Praeger, 1971, pp. 7-15.

15. From H. Mann, "The Use of Educated Labour", rep. in M. Katz, *School Reform: Past and Present*, Boston: Beacon, 1971.

16. See Katz's excellent *The Irony of Early School Reform*, Cambridge: Harvard University Press, 1968.

17. The impact of American educational structures (e.g. high schools) would be followed by American pedagogical techniques (e.g. testing) and the importation of a "branch-plant" type of culture. American influences became more pervasive paralleling the growth of American industrial capital vis-à-vis Canadian finance capital. American capital was in a predominant position vis-à-vis British capital by the end of World War I.

18. J. D. Wilson, "The Ryerson Years in Canada West", *Canadian Education: A History*, eds. J. D. Wilson et al., Toronto: Prentice-Hall, 1970, p. 218.

19. "Urban Industrial Change and Curriculum Reform in Early Twentieth Century Ontario", *Studies in Educational Change*, p. 15.

20. *Ibid.*, p. 25.

21. The system has changed very little in its essentials, including its value system. Competitive examinations and tuition fees have simply been applied to post-secondary education with the general rise in qualifications required by employers. Elitism and competition remain as dominant education values.

22. *Ibid.*, *Studies in Educational Change*, p. 60.

23. R. M. Stamp, "Education and the Economic and Social Milieu: The English Canadian Scene from the 1870's to 1914", *Canadian Education: A History*, p. 294.

24. *Ibid.*, pp. 63-68.

25. See M. Katz, *Class, Bureaucracy, and Schools*, esp. p. XVIII.

26. *Ibid.*, p. 18.

27. For a useful review of bureaucratization in the schools, see L. Lind, "The Rise of Bureaucracy in Ontario Schools", *This Magazine*, Summer 1972.

28. One of the first and still one of the best studies is J. Porter's *The Vertical Mosaic*, Toronto: University of Toronto Press, 1965, esp. Ch. 6. The new community college system does not appear to have escaped class bias either. In 1968-69, whereas 39.2 per cent of university students came from families with incomes over $10,000, only 23 per cent of community college students came from this income level. See *Reviews of National Policies for Education: Canada*, O.E.C.D., Paris, 1976, p. 49 (Table 6).

29. J. Porter, *Vertical Mosaic*, pp. 180-184.

30. See the classic study by Pat Sexton, *Education and Income*, New York: Viking Press, 1961, p. 28; also, J. Porter, p. 184.

31. J. Buttrick, "Who Goes to University in Ontario", *This Magazine*, Summer 1972.

32. See J. Porter, *The Vertical Mosaic*; W.G. Fleming, *Educational Opportunity*, Toronto: Prentice-Hall, 1974. For U.S. data, see C. Jencks et al., *Inequality: A Reassessment of the Effect of Family and Schooling in America*, New York: Basic, 1972, pp. 19-20.

33. P. George and H. Kim, "Social Factors and Educational Aspirations of Canadian High School Students", *Social Process and Institution*, eds. J. Gallagher and R. Lambert, Toronto: Holt, Rinehart, and Winston, 1971, pp. 351-363.

34. Women receive some 47 per cent less pay than men in management positions, while in clerical work, for which most women are prepared in school, women receive on the average 38.5 per cent less pay. Data from Stats. Canada.

35. E. Harvey and J. Lennards, *Key Issues in Higher Education*, Toronto: Ontario Institute for Studies in Education, 1973, pp. 74-77.

36. Data from B.C.T.F.'s *Equality of Educational Opportunity Kit*, Vancouver, 1976.

37. See H. Cardinal, *The Unjust Society*, Edmonton: M.G. Hurtig, 1969.

38. For a detailed examination of racist curriculum content, see *Our Tomorrows*, pub. by Manitoba Indian Brotherhood, 1974.

39. S. Bowles and H. Gintis, *Schooling in Capitalist America*, New York: Basic, 1976.

40. For a topical and comprehensive review of several related studies, see *Ibid.*, pp. 111 and 131.

41. In social theory, social inequality has been in effect defended by the Davis and Moore thesis. It suggests that differential material rewards are a "functional necessity". Social solidarity or cohesion, à la Durkheim, is presumed. The argument hinges, of course, on a functional equilibrium in society being taken as

pregiven — the claim of functional necessity then becomes, like the organic analogy upon which it is based, circular in reasoning. Scarcity of talent or training for instance, is a *social* phenomenon (like its opposite — unemployment) and it is created by a specific set of social relations of production shaped by human beings in response to the natural and social environment. Another attempt to naturalize what are social phenomena, is the functionalist definition of human nature. Based on the Hobbesian assumption that human beings are innately selfish and competitive, individuals are seen to be motivated solely by external rewards (be they material or social). By suggesting that a hierarchical social division of labour is naturally and therefore, socially necessary, the defenders of social inequality implicitly defend established values such as elitism and competition. See. K. Davis and W.E. Moore, "Some Principles of Stratification", *American Sociological Review*, April 1945.

42. R. Miliband, *The State in Capitalist Society*, London: Quartet Bks., 1973, p. 215.

43. See R. Turner, "Modes of Social Ascent through Education: Sponsored and Contest Mobility", *Education, Economy, and Society*, eds. A.H. Halsey et al., New York: Free Press, 1961. Sponsored mobility refers to selection by upper class patrons and the institutions they control; contest mobility, while influenced by factors related to socio-economic class background, refers to a selection process based upon "merit", supposedly made formal by open and competitive examinations.

44. C.W. Mills, *The Power Elite*, New York: Oxford, 1956, Ch. 1.

45. See the important study by A. Cicourel and J. Kitsuse, *The Educational Decision-Makers*, Indianapolis: Bobbs-Merrill, 1963, esp. pp. 70-74.

46. On the social and political consequences of Americanism for Canada, see G. Horowitz, "Mosaics and Identity" and also G. Grant, "Liberalism and Nationalism" in *Making It: The Canadian Dream*, eds. B. Finnigan and Cy Gonick, Toronto: McClelland and Stewart, 1972.

47. E. Harvey and J. Lennards, *Key Issues*, p. 3.

48. By exclaiming "Equality" as one of the inalienable Rights of Man, the bourgeois revolutionaries of the eighteenth century meant a sectarian, political equality (and even then, a highly qualified one until this century) as distinct from economic or social equality. In liberal social and educational theory (Locke, Mill, Spencer, Dewey, et al.) the schism between private and public, between the economic or material and the political, has reflected the failure of capitalist society to bridge the gap between human beings and social forces out of their control. The universalization of education, like the universalization of suffrage was no human emancipation — a semi-religious source of authority was merely displaced by a new, secular class one. On the distinction between political and human emancipation, see K. Marx, "On the Jewish Question", *Karl Marx: Early Writings*, ed. T. Bottomore, New York: McGraw-Hill, 1964.

49. A recent survey by the Organization for Economic Cooperation and Development stated in part: "It is interesting to note how far many Canadian schools have moved towards a traditional, industrial concept of the organization of educational services. More importantly, nearly everywhere the Examiners found a further

development in this direction stated as the ideal model to aim for." See *Reviews of National Policies for Education: Canada*, O.E.C.D., Paris, 1976, p. 106.

50. B. Simon, "Classification and Streaming in English schools: 1860-1960", *History and Education*, ed. P. Nash, Philadelphia: Philadelphia Book Company, 1970, pp. 99-100.

51. *Ibid*.

52. D. Glass, "Education and Social Change in Modern England", *Education, Economy, and Society*, eds. Halsey et al., p. 398.

53. On the educational impact of the Taylor system, see R.E. Callahan, *Education and the Cult of Efficiency*, Chicago: University of Chicago Press, 1962.

54. B. Simon in *History and Education*, ed. P. Nash.

55. S. Bowles and H. Gintis, "The I.Q. Ideology", *This Magazine*, Winter 1972/73.

56. In the mid-sixties for instance, it has been determined that every American school child took on average three standardized ability tests each year. See D.A. Goslin and D.C. Glass, "The Social Effects of Standardized Testing in American Elementary and Secondary Schools", *Sociology of Education*, Spring 1967, Vol. 40. We would assume that the Canadian usage of standardized tests has not been substantially different from the American experience.

57. C. Jencks et al., p. 36.

58. See P. Sexton, p. 39. Jencks et al. find that the relationship though there, has been exaggerated in the past, see *Inequality*, p. 81. This would appear to point to the importance of non-cognitive factors in school performance, including social norms and values.

59. Jencks et al., p. 56.

60. See F. Howe and P. Lauter, "How the School System is Rigged for Failure", *The Capitalist System*, eds. R. Edwards et al., Englewood Cliffs: Prentice-Hall, 1972, pp. 230-235.

61. J. Porter, *The Vertical Mosaic*, p. 197.

62. See "Class Bias in Toronto Schools", *This Magazine*, Fall/Winter 1971. Also, George and Kim, in *Social Process and Institution*, eds. Gallagher and Lambert; R. Breton, "Academic Stratification in Secondary Schools and the Educational Plans of Students", *Social Stratification: Canada*, eds. J. Curtis and Wm. Scott, Toronto: Prentice-Hall, 1973.

63. Jencks et al., p. 77.

64. J. Porter, *Canadian Social Structure: A Statistical Profile*, Toronto: McClelland and Stewart, 1967, p. 119 (Table G7).

65. See I. Berg, *Education and Jobs: The Great Training Robbery*, Boston: Beacon Press, 1971, p. 85.

66. H. Gintis, "Activism and Counter-Culture: The Dialectics of Consciousness in the Corporate State", *Telos*, Summer 1972.

67. H. Gintis, "Education, Technology and the Characteristics of Worker Productivity", *American Economic Review*, May 1971, Vol. 61. Bowles and Gintis review the relevant data in *Schooling in Capitalist America*, p. 40.

68. Bowles and Gintis, especially Part III.

69. *Ibid.*, p. 208. The class bias present in Canadian community college enrollments indicates a similar pattern, see note no. 28.

70. L. Lind, "Two Schools", *This Magazine*, March 1974.

71. Bowles and Gintis, p. 132.

72. M. Kohn, *Class and Conformity: A Study of Values*, Homewood, Ill.: Dorsey Press, 1969.

73. Recent research shows how both teachers' and students' learning expectations are highly context-bound. Hence, social categorization of knowledge and abilities is likely to persist in unstreamed classrooms. See Nell Keddie, "Classroom Knowledge", *Knowledge and Control*, ed. M.F.D. Young, London, 1971.

74. The recent O.E.C.D. report on education in Canada warns that the "adaptation of programmes to pupils" approach " . . . may easily build in a form of selection into even the primary school." *Reviews of National Policies for Education: Canada*, p. 45.

75. This refers to the role allocation mechanism's redirection of student hopes within educational organizations (e.g. high schools and community colleges) in order to align them with limited opportunities. See B. Clark, "The Cooling-Out Function in Higher Education", *The American Journal of Sociology*, May 1960, Vol. 65.

76. See A. Cicourel and J. Kitsuse, p. 16. R. Breton found grades and counsellor/teacher evaluation ahead of test scores as streaming criteria in Canadian (Ontario) secondary schools. See R. Breton, p. 138.

77. Cicourel and Kitsuse report that middle and upper income adolescents were seen more frequently by counsellors as "natural" college prospects than low-income students with comparable school performances. "Unrealistic" aspirations were perceived as needing to be redirected, or in other words cooled out. See Cicourel and Kitsuse, pp. 70-74.

78. J. Porter, *The Canadian Social Structure*, p. 93. With agricultural and menial labour sectors removed from the labour force, the white collar sector represented 45.7 per cent of the total labour force as of 1961. Data reported by Leo Johnson, "The development of class in Canada in the twentieth century", *Capitalism and the National Question in Canada*, ed. G. Teeple, Toronto: University of Toronto Press, 1972.

79. On the decline of the petite bourgeoisie in Canada (i.e. of the middle class), see *Ibid.*, p. 151.

80. *Ibid.*, p. 153.

81. Data released by Statistics Canada, March 15, 1977.

82. E. Harvey and J. Lennards, *Key Issues*, p. 29.

83. *Ibid.*, p. 93.

84. Marx foresaw how ''general social knowledge'' had become a ''direct force of production'' in the application of science and technology to industrial production. In the transformation of living labour to objectified labour (e.g. machinery), production based on exchange value would necessarily break down. See K. Marx, *Grundrisse*, London: Penguin, 1973, pp. 704-706.

The Education-as-Autonomous Argument and Pluralism: the Sociologies of Burton R. Clark, David Riesman, and Christopher Jencks

RANDLE W. NELSEN

The education-as-autonomous argument is based upon the assumption that the school has become the central institution of the American social system. This argument treats schools as being closer to independent, rather than dependent, variables. Thus, the education-as-autonomous argument assumes that changes in the educational, rather than the economic, institution are fundamental in changing that complex of institutions which comprise the socio-economic structure of the larger social system.

This view of social change is shared by, among others, three of the most prominent sociologists currently observing the growth of higher education in the United States — Burton R. Clark, David Riesman, and Christopher Jencks.[1] For Yale's Professor Clark, America's colleges and universities are more than just autonomous in relation to the larger socio-economic system; rather, he argues that higher education has become an "active force" shaping this system.[2] Harvard's Professor Riesman, supports this "active" view of higher education. Paradoxically, he contends that the modern university maintains a relatively independent existence apart from other institutions of American society. Moreover, like Clark, Riesman argues that the growth and development of the scientific disciplines, the "racecourses of the mind", has produced *The Academic Revolution* that is in large part responsible for shaping the current socio-economic order.

Riesman's Harvard colleague and collaborator in developing this academic revolution thesis, Professor Jencks, has since added an interesting variation to their education-as-autonomous argument. According to Jencks serendipitous accidents rather than schools are central to the maintenance of the current social system. Jencks continues to conceive of the school as autonomous, independent of existent socio-economic arrangements, likening the school to the nuclear family while presenting evidence that questions the effect of schooling with regard to income and occupational inequalities among individuals.[3]

It is the argument of this paper that these inequalities are reinforced by the work of the three sociologists reviewed herein; Clark, Riesman, and Jencks, by holding higher education to be largely independent of the surrounding socio-economic system, seem to have obligated themselves to play a supportive role in legitimating and sustaining that system. Further, it is argued that this obligation is, in large part, a result and a reflection of their commitment to a pluralistic view of the structure of power in the United States; summarily stated, a view that assumes a rather wide dispersion of power among a rather large number of people representing a variety of groups and issues.[4] Focusing upon the dispersion and variety of power, their analyses share a characteristic common to most pluralists — failure to see the "big picture".[5] Thus, each author makes higher education autonomous, separating colleges and universities from the socio-economic context within which they are created and maintained; the result is the legitimation, and thereby reproduction, of the current socio-economic system.

THE PLURALISM OF BURTON R. CLARK: COLLEGES AND UNIVERSITIES AS "ACTIVE AGENTS" AND CULTURAL INNOVATION

Burton Clark begins his discussion of education in the "expert society" by noting the increased public concern over education's role in an age marked by a supposed second scientific revolution; civic clubs, professional associations, academic disciplines, and a variety of other interest groups all seem to be out to "save education" — to make it relevant to a world transformed by atomic energy and computers.[6] Clark argues that this concern is not misplaced for "technology with a vengeance" will continue to alter the role of education in today's society. "The effect of technological advance is to increase the pre-eminence and power of the expert, and with this, to increase the commitment of education to technical and professional preparation."[7]

This task of preparing future experts is, according to Clark, consistent with the traditional function of the educational institution as it continues to become "society's main vehicle of cultural indoctrination". For Clark, it is clear that "society expects education to do its bidding, transmitting a heritage and preparing the next generation in approved ways."[8] However, he notes that fulfillment of these expectations is complicated by the pluralism of American society: "the volume of knowledge is large, groups differ over what should be taught, and the general values of society contain many contradictions."[9] Thus, responsibility for determining educational policy rests with an ever-increasing variety of groups having different interests and ideas about questions regarding "what to teach, who shall be educated, the direction of change".[10] In brief, Clark argues that both professors and students are becoming increasingly important educational interest groups formulating and answering these and similar questions as "education in a technological society becomes itself an active force, one of the important institutions in innovation and in changing what men think."[11]

What men and women (to include that half of the population forgotten in the Clark analysis) think is not, however, a matter that is completely relative to and dependent upon changing opinions of the various interest groups. For although Clark argues that the quality of excellence of the cultural material transmitted by formal schooling cannot be judged by absolute standards, he also contends that "there are major pockets of social agreement." Thus, Clark believes "an observer can roughly assess quality in education on the basis of its appropriateness for the requirements of adulthood."[12] Accordingly, on the next page Clark informs his readers: "In this book I attempt to edge toward a 'clinical' judgment of quality, on the basis of how adequately education prepares the young for adult life."

By assuming this relation between quality in education and preparation for adult life, Clark also assumes the legitimacy of, and helps to reproduce, the current socio-economic system within which adult life in the United States is lived. These assumptions are a logical extension of Clark's view that there is a second scientific revolution — different in kind from the first, the industrial revolution — responsible for producing a society of *trained* experts.[14] As the title of his book indicates (*Educating the Expert Society*), Clark assumes the expert society and a quality education that is independent of, but trains potential experts to fill vacancies within, the larger socio-economic system. In short, students *receive* an education that encourages them to emulate Clark, who neglects questions concerning the developing character of American society in favor of inquiries that focus analysis on problems of training experts to serve the society as given.

This emphasis upon training experts in numerous specialities is in keeping with Clark's pluralistic view of American society — a view that is strengthened by his conception of professors and students as interest groups important in restructuring society. Thus, according to Clark, education should no longer be seen as merely a "passive instrument" doing society's bidding, but rather, as an "active force" shaping the social system.[15] He claims that three facts characterizing the operation and effects of present-day schooling support this argument that the educational institution is now a "prime contributor to change in society": Education (1) produces new culture, (2) liberalizes attitudes, and (3) differentiates culture.

Clark argues his first point, education produces new culture, by stressing "the increasingly large role of the university as an inventor of knowledge and technique".[16] He supports this statement by citing statistics that emphasize the development of the university as a research center; these statistics are in turn used to assert that colleges and universities serve as "centers of innovation and change, of investigation of the application of knowledge to current needs, and of re-examination and criticism of society.''[17]

Clark might have had cause to re-examine this assertion concerning the role of university research in bringing together and fostering a connection between innovation and criticism, had he attempted to specify whose "current needs" are served by "the application of knowledge". Such an examination might have tempered his active view of professors: "Oriented to critical thought and set apart from many pressures of the market place, academic men can and do become free intellectuals, critical and innovating.''[18] In brief, Clark's failure to examine professorial practice — "the topic of teaching as a profession is barely broached, being touched upon only here and there in an offhand fashion''[19] — conveniently permits him to posit a new interest group, the "free intellectuals"; convenient, because in this way, Clark is able to add increased variety to his pluralistic model of American society.

The tolerance required to sustain this pluralism seems to be developed in large part, according to Clark, in the classroom. In presenting evidence to support this second point in his active argument, schooling liberalizes attitudes, Clark emphasizes the fact that "a growing body of evidence indicates that education leads toward tolerant and humanitarian attitudes.''[20] For Clark, then, the proof that validates his "education as an active agent" argument is found not only in the research orientation of universities staffed by free intellectuals, but also in the development of tolerant attitudes among students. However, in his determination to emphasize a positive relation between education and tolerant attitudes, Clark seems either to be ignorant of, or to simply ignore, other explanations which might question his "tolerance" conclusion.

For example, in citing studies that find a positive relation between amount of formal schooling and more liberal student attitudes toward ethnic and racial groups,[21] Clark fails to inform his readers of a most significant fact: namely, that much of the social science literature on stereotyping shows stereotypic images are reassessed, and often break down, with increased contact between the typer and the typed.[22] Consequently, the liberal, and supposedly more tolerant, attitudes found among certain college graduates — attitudes that Clark attributes to their time spent in the classroom — may simply reflect the separation and isolation of their lives from those of most Blacks, Indians, and other minorities.

Similarly, Clark's emphasis upon scientific studies that show a positive relation between education and liberal attitudes toward a democratic political system,[23] may reflect a tolerance that need never be practiced by the "tolerant". Thus, it might be easier to be "democratic" when a college education has certified one to be part of the management group of administrative technocrats, than if one is part of the managed group of laborers.[24] Further, it might not be terribly difficult to sustain a favorable belief in a multiparty political system (regarded by many observers as the most important measure of democratic attitudes) when reality continues to become increasingly uni-dimensional[25] — when the choice is between "tweedle-dee" and "tweedle-dum", both owing allegiance to that small number of powerful individuals who, in governing America, have pre-selected the group from which the candidates themselves are chosen. In such an environment, most college-graduate liberals can be fairly confident that the defeat of a personal preference at the polls will not lead to changes in the prevailing socio-economic order which might threaten their privileged positions; for the most successful and very powerful capitalists are not likely to radically alter current corporate arrangements that recreate and confirm the value configuration of a culture profitable to them.

This culture, according to Clark, becomes increasingly differentiated — the third point in his active argument — as tolerant (more liberal) students continue to be trained by free (critical and innovating) intellectuals. For Clark, the major reason why education differentiates culture is the fact that after a certain number of years, common schooling gives way to individual preparation for an occupation. Fast becoming characteristic of modern technological society — that is, the United States — is the replacement of higher education's "integrative function" which emphasized a core curriculum with training in diverse disciplines for specialized occupations. What results is, according to Clark, "the widening cultural split between men of science and men of the humanities".[26]

Such a split is to be expected because: "The specialization trend, which is irreversible, means that individuals are allocated to a widening spectrum of adult subcultures that are hooked to occupational subworlds."[27] This specialization, and the pluralism that it implies, is in Clark's view accentuated by the academy itself, through "the process of fields giving rise to subfields" and "variation in the character" of the more than 2,000 colleges in the United States.[28] For Clark, the many types of colleges — the Protestant, the Catholic, the liberal-arts, the state, and so on — "represent a cultural diversity in themselves; they educate and train differently, and their 'products' are not of a piece."[29]

Once again, Clark's emphasis on pluralism — supposedly evident in higher education's diversity — seems to infer causal connections that are, at best, highly questionable. For example, the fact that colleges and universities are increasingly involved in attempting to train students for work in a wide variety of fields, should not necessarily lead to the conclusion that these students are less and less like one another. On the contrary, it could be that students — largely because of the way (how) they are taught, not what they are taught — and their schools are growing more and more alike.[30]

This interpretation, however, no matter how closely it corresponds with current experience among those involved in higher education, is not likely to be subscribed to by Clark. For to accept this view is to question the pluralism of American society, severely diminishing the supposed power of various student and faculty interest groups by emphasizing their inability to implement the educational changes they desire. Similarly, if it could not be argued that education was in large part responsible for producing liberal student attitudes, the validity of a pluralistic model of the power structure in the United States would again be a matter for scepticism. Likewise, the research orientation of colleges and universities must produce free, rather than 'bought and sold', intellectuals if the pluralistic doctrine is to remain unquestioned.

Moreover, the pluralism that makes education active can also, according to Clark, solve the problems of the educational institution. For example, if students are becoming more and more alike and this is perceived as a problem, pluralism will provide a solution. Thus, what Clark refers to as "mass processing" in higher education — the lengthy registration line, the large lecture hall, and the anonymous graduation — can be countered if colleges and universities can create: "Excitement, identification, a sense of belonging to a *different* organization — these are means by which some high schools and colleges reach and shape their students."[31] These are the means by which Clark sees membership for the mass transformed into "an exciting rather than a routine matter".[32]

For Clark, then, pluralism as a problem producer is also its own problem-solving antidote. The pluralism that will make higher education "more dispersed and disparate" in the future — "a crazy quilt patched with materials of varied hue and size"[33] — will also provide educational leaders trained to "counter drift with design by building organizations and fashioning programs that *steer change in desired directions*."[34] (my emphasis) Clark argues that it is the special interest in education — as opposed to economics, politics, religion — which empowers this leadership group to give direction, to make higher education exciting rather than routine.

The pluralism that separates education from economics, from politics, from religion and so on, is compatible with Clark's view that higher education is an "active agent". This view in turn reaffirms the basic assumption of pluralism, that there is a rather wide dispersion of power within current socio-economic arrangements, by interpreting higher education as autonomous. Pluralism associates individuals involved in higher learning with various educational interest groups, each group possessing — dependent upon the agreement between interests and the issue in question — a relative measure of influence and autonomy. In Clark's words, "Autonomous agencies can be critical and innovative; dependent ones usually cannot."[35] Thus, the pluralism that supports and is supported by his active argument — colleges and universities are "centers of innovation and change" — permits Clark to make higher education autonomous by definition.

In sum, not only does Clark's pluralism make institutions of higher learning autonomous, innovative; it is also a blueprint for managing the innovations. Change is directed, the future anticipated, by a pluralistic view of the power structure that has become a mechanism of self-service. It is a mechanism that is scientifically applied by trained experts to predict and correct those problems which might prevent the supposed pluralistic base of the present social system from being brought into the future. Free intellectuals and their tolerant students not only connect today and tomorrow by solving the problems of transition from one to the other, but in so doing they shape the future in the image of the present. In this way, the routine can be made more exciting — that is, more pluralistic — and if leaders feel it is necessary, the exciting more routine. Thus, change becomes the current order as pluralism, like Clark's sociology that reaffirms it, supports the existent socio-economic arrangements of corporate capitalism.

THE PLURALISM OF DAVID RIESMAN: ACADEMIC DISCIPLINES AS "RACECOURSES OF THE MIND" AND ACADEMIC REVOLUTION

David Riesman, like Clark, has long been concerned with higher education's role in directing cultural change; as early as 1956, he made known his concern that the leading American universities were "directionless . . . as far as major innovations are concerned."[36] Rjesman, like Clark, charts a direction for universities by using his pluralistic view of the American social system to make higher education active and autonomous. In brief, Riesman argues that the universities themselves, by virtue of the fact that they house what he calls "the intellectual veto groups", will be increasingly responsible for determining the direction of higher learning in the United States.

Implicit in all I have said is the notion that what my collaborators and I speak of in *The Lonely Crowd* as the 'veto groups,' the political and social blocs and groupings that frustrate political action in the United States, operate also in the intellectual realm, in terms of departments and fields. Each prevents the others from growing too big, from encompassing too much. While it takes tremendous energy and courage and vision to inaugurate a new field . . . the nationalistic investments of less courageous and less dogmatic men can serve to maintain an old field and even to give its development a certain autonomy.[37]

Thus, "the push and pull" of disciplines as veto groups (pluralism) helps provide autonomous, yet balanced, direction to the directionless universities. Allowing for both the development of old fields and the inauguration of new ones, the academic disciplines serve as both mediators and "evocators";[38] they both constrain and add variety, balancing and blending academic parochialism with creativity. The Riesman emphasis is, however, on constraint and not creativity; the disciplines become, in his words, "the racecourses of the mind''.[39] Rather than encouraging professors and students to create new courses, Riesman views the disciplines as keeping them on course by ''stabilizing the market for ideas, policing it to some extent and thus controlling the worst charlatanry, and making large-scale reorganizations of large-scale universities about as difficult as comparable re-organizations in the political realm.''[40]

Over the past two decades, Riesman with the help of, among others, Christopher Jencks, has reiterated this thesis that the veto power possessed by professors trained on one of a variety of racecourses permits them to direct and shape higher education. The power of professors, then, as in the Clark analysis, is due to the fact that they are specialized experts, while the very existence and proliferation of these numerous specialities seems to be the fact upon which Riesman reaffirms his commitment to pluralism. Thus, fifteen years after his initial discussion of the racecourses, Riesman restates his view that: ''Looked at in comparative and historical perspective, American higher education is astonishingly pluralistic.''[41]

According to Jencks and Riesman, this academic pluralism is fast becoming transformed by the professors into power. The power of academic pluralism prohibits the wishes of such interest groups as clinical psychologists and psychiatrists, corporate administrators, engineers, state legislators, students, and even educators themselves,[42] from falling outside the boundaries demarcated by the professors' racecourses. Consequently, Jencks and Riesman argue that this variety of groups — each group holding quite different ideas about education — has ''ended up pursuing increasingly convergent goals by ever more similar means''.[43] The major reason for this convergence is ''the colleges' universal preference for undergraduate faculty trained in the standard disciplines at the leading national graduate schools''.[44] In brief, it is the growth and development of academic power in shaping higher education — ''the academic profession increasingly determines the character of undergraduate education in America''[45] — that Jencks and Riesman refer to as *The Academic Revolution*.

This ''revolution'', while controlling the power of several interest groups outside the university, seems to be largely confined to the campus; in brief, it seems to have brought about few, if any, changes in the prevailing socio-economic arrangements of corporate capitalism. The conclusion that there is or ever could be revolution arising from and confined almost solely to the universities, may be yet another artifact of a commitment to pluralism that encourages the authors to disregard the interrelations between education and other societal institutions. Thus, while Jencks and Riesman introduce their analysis by claiming that the problem to which they have addressed themselves is ''the relationship between higher education and American society'',[46] this relation is quickly submerged by their concern with the supposed growing influence of the academic disciplines on the development of higher education. In backing Riesman's racecourse thesis, the authors seem to have forgotten who owns the tracks; more than likely, they never knew. For the pluralism of academic veto groups, like Clark's education-as-active argument, makes it unlikely that Jencks and Riesman would look beyond the academy and its racecourses to the power structure of the larger socio-economic system; instead, as with Clark, they see higher education as autonomous.

In fact, according to Jencks and Riesman, the university is more than autonomous, it is fast becoming the most fundamental institution of the American social system:

The American graduate school has become the envy of the world, a mecca for foreign students and a model for foreign institutions. It has also become one of the central institutions of American culture . . . . The university has, indeed, become the new Maecenas, and its decisions to give or withhold patronage shape much of American life. What the graduate schools define as "research" will get done; what they exclude is likely to languish . . . .[47]

This view of an autonomous higher education rapidly emerging as the central institution of today's America is maintained by an analysis that invests the university with enough power both to separate from — the campus is seen as a world apart — and also to control changes in, the other institutions comprising the larger socio-economic system. Thus, on the one hand the authors are able to argue that the "character of American life" is in large part determined "within such diverse and sporadically conflicting enterprises as the Chase Manhattan Bank and the Treasury Department, the Pentagon and Boeing Aircraft, the Federal Courts and the National Council of Churches, CBS and *The New York Times*, the State Department and the Chamber of Commerce, the Chrysler Corporation and the Ford Foundation, Standard Oil and Sun Oil."[48] At the same time, they use the next 530 pages to argue that the university, made powerful by the growth and development of academic disciplines, has in large part replaced this "mixed bag" of established institutions in determining the character of life in America. In brief, Jencks and Riesman redirect the supposed diversity and conflict from these several institutions to a very powerful single institution, education: "The graduate departments and the ideology for which they stand have thus far managed to win over or override all the major interest groups which might have forced them to deviate from their chosen path."[49]

This path, like the authors' analysis that separates education from the larger socio-economic system, leads to other analytical divisions that are both confusing and questionable. Most often these divisions break up reality in a way that further isolates education from other institutions of the social system. For example, pure is contrasted with applied work, and research made separate from teaching as Jencks and Riesman differentiate the intellectual from the academic, and the academic from the practical.[50] This intellectual-academic-practical distinction corresponds with the plurality of student groups — each group holding different value configurations — that Clark labels the non-conformist, the academic, and the vocational subcultures. The attachment of students to this variety of subcultures (interest groups) not only helps prepare them to join Clark's "occupational subworlds", but it also helps to widen the "generation gap" that separates the young from the old.[51]

Professors too play an important role in dividing the generations by becoming more professional — to use the Jencks-Riesman terminology, they become more "colleague-oriented" as opposed to "client-oriented".[52] As the following passage makes clear, this collegial orientation of professors fosters, and fits nicely within, the author's view of higher education as autonomous:

Unlike a doctor or lawyer, an able scholar does not have to persuade non-professional customers to respect his expertise; his "customers" are other scholars. Of course he needs non-professional financial support, but he gets this in ways that give the non-professionals only minimal power to direct or even evaluate his work.... Research grants come mostly from large bureaucratic organizations. While such a bureaucracy may adopt the overall priorities of laymen rather than professionals, it usually hires academicians to work out the details of its relationships with the academic profession. This means that decisions about how research will be done, who will get to do it, and even (on a de facto basis) what the research will really be about, are made by members of the guild.[53]

Jencks and Riesman elaborate this argument as they continue developing their fantasy of education as an autonomous institution in a discussion of graduate school reform entitled, "'Pure' versus 'Applied' Work":

We begin with departmentalism and specialization. The basic problem here is how to determine the research agenda of individuals and groups. At present there are two conflicting tendencies. The academic profession is eager to ensure that everyone will draw up his agenda to please his colleagues.... In this context the test of good research becomes how much influence it has on other scholars. The government and the major foundations, on the other hand, have a different set of priorities. They are primarily interested in non-academic problems, and they finance research in the hope that it will illuminate these problems.... This divergence about the proper subjects of research does not, however, usually extend to methodology. On the contrary, government agencies and foundations subsidize academic research primarily because they are impressed by the methodological competence of university professors. They may want to redirect this competence into new areas, but they make relatively little effort to influence the technique. That, indeed, is why the marriage between government research agencies and the academic profession has proved fairly satisfactory; many academicians are not particular about the areas in which they work so long as they are free to choose the methods, and the government frequently has no preconceptions about the method so long as it controls the areas....[54]

In all this and more,[55] there is no discussion of alternative explanations of this "marriage". For example, it is possible that the Jencks-Riesman wedding may be of the "shotgun" variety, initiated by the Department of Defense; or it may by that the "two conflicting tendencies" is yet another one of the authors' creative abstractions that bifurcate reality. For as the role of government in the historical development of science within American colleges and universities suggests, there has been, from the beginning, little conflict.[56] Further, whatever conflict did exist has been resolved not by an autonomous and powerful education institution, but instead by a higher education that has maintained the favor — that is, the financial support — of the government and the major foundations. Thus, the point is, the Jencks-Riesman analysis notwithstanding, that in the great majority of cases if the researcher can please the government and/or foundation sponsor, then his/her colleagues will also be pleased.[57]

Just as Jencks and Reisman attempt to disconnect the common interests of the academy and government, they also use their intellectual-academic-practical distinctions to attempt to keep education separate from industry, the university from business.

The only interest groups that have shown a continuing capacity to compete with the academic profession in the training of high school graduates are enormous bureaucratic and corporate enterprises: the Armed Services and the major corporations . . . . (The Department of Defense is said to spend more on education beyond high school than all the state legislatures in the country combined, and General Electric spends more than any but the largest universities).

Nonetheless, we see little prospect that these in-house training programs will emerge as genuine alternatives to those conducted by academicians . . . .[58] (my emphasis)

Once again, the pluralism of Jencks and Riesman that encourages the division and subdivision of reality causes them to overlook possible interpretations that counter their analysis. In this instance, their separation of education and industry ignores the possibility that relations between higher education and the larger socio-economic system may make American colleges and universities "in-house training programs" for "enormous bureaucratic and corporate enterprises" like the Armed Services and General Electric.

Such an oversight is to be expected on the part of sociologists so deeply committed to pluralism as are Jencks and Riesman. For them, the argument that education is autonomous is more than the idea that the academic profession shapes the educational institution with the acquiescence, if not always the approval, of a variety of groups representing a kaleidoscope of interests; it is also the embodiment of America's humanistic heritage. Thus, Jencks and Riesman logically extend their autonomous argument to suggest that improving the racecourses of the mind is perhaps synonymous with advancing the human condition:

... Other professional schools justify themselves (and their budgets) in terms of external problems and needs. The graduate academic departments are for the most part autotelic [roughly translated, autonomous]. They resent even being asked if they produce significant benefits to society beyond the edification of their own members, and mark down the questioner as an anti-intellectual. To suggest that the advancement of a particular academic discipline is not synonymous with the advancement of the human condition is regarded as myopic. Perhaps, considering the affluence of American tax-payers and the relatively ample supply of talented, well-educated college graduates, it really is.[59]

This implied relation between affluence and higher education is, however, bothersome to Jencks and Riesman. They argue — in a chapter entitled, "Social Stratification and Mass Higher Education" — that there has been "a good deal of social mobility in America" because the United States falls closer to an "equality" rather than a "hereditary" model.[60] The role played by education in this model remains somewhat unclear to the authors as they puzzle over the relation between educational attainment in school and occupational status.

In brief, Jencks and Riesman argue that type of work and amount of formal schooling, for most Americans, do not seem to match — to be positively correlated — as might be expected if the United States is an "equality" society. Yet, as the authors quite elaborately explain, this fact does not invalidate the mobility-through-educational attainment argument. For while it is the children of the upper-middle class who continue to find employment that enables them to maintain their class position, it is also they who, when compared to children of other socio-economic classes, remain in school the longest.[61]

For those readers who remain unconvinced that this apparently close relation between amount of schooling and type of employment for many in the upper-middle class could be transferred to the children of lower classes, making them more equal, Jencks and Riesman point to what they see as a kind of fairness in the way most colleges selectively admit and continually reevaluate students. Thus, while the authors acknowledge the fact that colleges tend to "pre-select the upper-middle class", they are quick to remind their readers that when reevaluation (grading) is added to this admission process it is not only the youngsters from lower-strata families who are eliminated, but also a substantial fraction of upper-middle children. Of course, the reasons for elimination are different for both groups; most lower-class individuals "have 'the wrong attitudes' for academic success", while many in the upper classes "drop out" because "they lack academic competence and dislike feeling like failures year after year."[62]

Since Jencks and Riesman do not carry further their discussion of these upper-middle class youth who withdraw from school, one is left to speculate.

Keeping to the logic of their argument concerning the maintenance of upper-middle class status over generations, one might reasonably presume that some who drop out are able to use their class background in helping them to, when convenient, drop back in. In these cases, a phone call from father to a friend who is dean of a law school, a membership in the right country club, and/or similar "achievements" may replace school evaluations in separating future lawyers from laborers. In this way, the "equal" society is perpetuated — members of the various socio-economic classes are kept in their respective places generation after generation.[63] In fact, this matter of keeping and knowing one's place is an important concern for Jencks and Riesman. This concern is nowhere better illustrated than in the content and interpretation of the following creative anecdote:

Suppose, for example, that Yale must choose between two applicants. One is an obviously gifted boy from the wrong side of the tracks in Bridgeport. The other is a competent but unremarkable youngster whose father went to Yale and now practices medicine in New York. All right-thinking people assume that Yale should choose the first boy over the second. We agree. Nonetheless, this decision almost certainly causes more individual misery than the alternative. If a Bridgeport boy is refused a place at Yale and goes to the University of Connecticut (where he still has a fair chance of discovering a new world) or even to the University of Bridgeport (where this is conceivable if less likely), he will be disappointed but seldom shattered. The University of Connecticut is a smaller step up than Yale, but it may in fact more nearly fit his temperament if not his talents. The New Yorker who fails to make Yale and winds up at the University of Connecticut, on the other hand, will very likely feel himself branded a failure. Connecticut may suit his talent, but probably not his temperament. The verdict will seem doubly harsh for being just. The rejected Bridgeport boy can blame his fate on snobbery and feel it is not his fault but "the system". The New Yorker has no such defense.

. . . .

    Nonetheless, there is a point of diminishing returns beyond which the advantages of meritocracy and mobility to society as a whole may no longer offset their disadvantages to individuals who fail to meet the test . . . . If, to revert to our earlier example, there are talented boys who do not want to go to Yale and mediocre ones who do, is any useful purpose really served by recruiting the former and excluding the latter? . . .

    What all this suggests is that further efforts to increase mobility may be not only fruitless but undesirable. What America most needs is not more mobility but more equality . . . .[64]

In sum, the sociology of Riesman and colleague Jencks, like that of Clark, amounts to ideological maintenance of an "equality" that preserves and perpetuates existing socio-economic arrangements. Riesman's pluralism creates "intellectual veto groups" who, by running the "racecourses of the mind", have directed a revolution that has made higher education autonomous. While Jenks and Riesman attempt to argue that this academic revolution is largely confined to the campus, they do allow that the autonomy of colleges and universities gives to higher education the power to in large part replace "established institutions" in determining the character of American life. They argue that the pluralism which altered the university is currently modifying a socio-economic system that continues to make Americans both more affluent and talented. Thus, equality is considered within the interest-group context of a pluralism that, like Riesman's sociology, continues to keep "the system as a whole expanding",[65] and individuals in place — knowing their interests and groups — within the corporate context of today's capitalism.

THE PLURALISM OF CHRISTOPHER JENCKS: THE SCHOOLS AS NUCLEAR FAMILIES AND ACCIDENTAL INEQUALITY

More recently, Christopher Jencks, with the assistance of several collaborators, has attempted a rigorous and scientific re-examination of this notion of equality. Jencks draws two distinctions that are crucial for him to any discussion of the way in which schooling might affect policies of social reform, and that consequently, have been the center of much criticism concerning *Inequality*. The first is between equality of opportunity and equality of condition; the second is between equality as related to groups and equality as related to individuals. These distinctions underlie the following statement written by Jencks in response to critical comments concerning his book, and summarizing the direction, major findings, and conclusions of his work:

In any event, the purpose of *Inequality* was not to argue the case for socialism, which is complex and problematic. Neither, as the book makes clear, was its purpose to argue against school reform. Rather, the aim of the book was to show that one specific, widely-held theory about the relationship between school reform and social reform was wrong. According to that theory, the degree of inequality in income is determined by the degree of inequality in skills. These, in turn, depend on family background, genes and schooling. The evidence presented in *Inequality* seems to me to show that variations in family background, IQ genotype, exposure to schooling, and quality of schooling cannot account for most of the variation in individual or family incomes. This means we must reject the conservative notion that income inequality is largely due to the fact that men are born with unequal abilities and raised in unequal home environments. We must also reject the liberal notion that equalizing educational opportunity will equalize people's incomes. The evidence in *Inequality* cannot carry us much further, even though its rhetoric sometimes tries.[66]

The reason that neither the evidence, nor the rhetoric of *Inequality* is able to carry us much further than a rejection of "the liberal notion that equalizing educational opportunity will equalize people's incomes" can be found in the seeming inability of Jencks to clarify what his evidence means in relation to whom. Critic Lester C. Thurow puts the matter this way: "*Inequality* might be summarized as 'nothing affects anything.' Or, more accurately, as fifty to seventy per cent of what goes on does not seem to be explained by anything else that goes on."[67] His summary is echoed by Stephen Michelson, one of the book's collaborators, who states the problem with these words: " . . . what most bothers me about the concept of equality in *Inequality* is that I cannot pin it down. I don't know whose inequality is being cared about, and what relationship this has to the way society operates."[68]

Perhaps this is so because the Jencks explanation of adult inequality in occupational status and income replaces such commonly-accepted predictive factors as I.Q. scores, school examination scores, and years of formal schooling with the "noncognitive" traits of personality and luck; the obvious difficulty in scientifically predicting and controlling the effects of such capricious factors as personality and luck might in large measure explain the difficulty Jencks has in relating his evidence on inequality to people. Or, perhaps the Jencks inability to make clear the relation between inequality and "the way society operates" should be seen as an outcome of his commitment to pluralism. For to be unable to specify which people are being talked about, to clarify "whose inequality is being cared about", is characteristic of analyses based upon a pluralistic view of the structure of power. In the words of Jencks' colleague, Riesman, "there is no longer a 'we' who run things and a 'they' who don't, or a 'we' who don't run things and a 'they' who do, but rather that all 'we's' are 'they's' and all 'they's' are 'we's'."[69]

Evidently Jencks agrees with this most arguable assumption concerning the undirectedness of life in today's America, for he forecloses the possibility of finding both direction and directors with an analysis that has "ignored extreme cases".[70] The result is, in Michelson's words, "the deliberate choice of methodology which is weighted by the number of individuals within a category."[71] Thus, even though there is factual evidence that most of the wealthiest Americans inherit their wealth, if Jencks included non-labor income in his correlations they would be, according to Michelson, "scarcely affected". He would still find almost no relation between family origin and current income. In brief, the Jencks statistical approach is conveniently unable to analyze actual differences in family income for identifiably different individuals; conveniently, because just a few families control the great majority of wealth in the United States and they, as it happens, are among the extreme cases Jencks has chosen to ignore. Michelson writes:

Jencks thus chooses hypotheses and methods which neither ask *whom* tests of "merit" serve, nor how they do so. It is clear that testing *does* "maintain the privileges of the economic elite" operating through meritocratic selection for schools. But testing serves a different purpose for the ruling class, the few owners of the means of production. They inherit their status directly. They, however, want to preserve the characteristics of a society which allows this direct inheritance for a very few under a rhetoric of merit equality. . . . Jencks has estimated the net result of these contradictions. The "optimal" amount of status transmission in a competitive market society with a small property-owning ruling class would be described by a father-son status correlation greater than zero (because high-status parents must see a better than random chance of passing on status) and less than one (because low-status parents must see some chance of their children surpassing them). Although estimating the actual correlation is not a trivial task, neither is it a politically telling one. [72]

While this criticism is basically both well-reasoned and accurate, to suggest that the Jencks analysis is not politically telling is most inaccurate. For what it tells about, and in the end legitimates, are the institutional interconnections of the existent socio-economic system. This legitimation is accomplished, as in the Clark and Riesman analyses, by separating one institution from another. Jencks, like other pluralists, has difficulty seeing the "big picture".

Thus, just as Jencks must separate the extreme from the middle levels of the socio-economic structure in order to find a nonrelationship between people and their own inequality, he must also separate school from factory in order to disconnect the personal from the political. Jencks argues that schools "serve primarily as selection and certification agencies, whose job is to measure and label people, and only secondarily as socialization agencies, whose job is to change people. This implies that schools serve primarily to legitimize inequality, not to create it." [73] In other words, since personality and luck, rather than education, explain most of the variance in adult occupations and incomes, the expectation that changing the schools will reduce inequality (equalize economic differences) is "fantasy"; a more realistic strategy is, according to Jencks, "to make the system less competitive by reducing the benefits that derive from success and the costs paid for failure." [74] Jencks thinks that this could be accomplished if the school was to become more like what he says it is, a family rather than a factory. [75]

Such a vision of future schools supports the privileged position of the few wealthy families the Jencks analysis ignores. It is a plan for educational reform that attempts to make the school more equivalent to the American family, the nuclear family, thereby attempting to make the school more autonomous; conceptualizing the school as family, Jencks argues that the school, unlike the factory, is relatively separate and independent of its socio-economic surroundings. What Jencks fails to see is that to maintain even the idea of independence, the school, like the nuclear family, has become a "service station" molded to the contours of capitalism in its corporate form. [76] Thus, children taught in schools modelled upon today's nuclear family are no less "products" ready for service in the corporate order than is the case when schools are patterned after today's factory. In brief, the Jencks proposal for educational reform succeeds in moving schools away from functioning as he says they do, legitimating inequality by measuring and labelling, towards recreating inequality by passing on ideology that serves to help reproduce the current socio-economic system.

Let us return for a moment to the example of father's phone call that compensates for unsatisfactory academic performance and permits his son to attend law school. In the Jencks analysis, the effect of this call can be subsumed, written off, under either personality and/or luck. Likewise, a son may not have to develop his ability "to persuade a customer" or "to look a man in the eye without seeming to stare",[77] if his father can do it for him. Similarly, "chance acquaintances who steer you to one line of work rather than another, the range of jobs that happen to be available in a particular community when you are job hunting, the amount of overtime work in your particular plant",[78] may not matter much if your father owns the plant. In short, the mobility that leads to economic success, like the change that brings about educational reform, can be interpreted in the Jencks view as an individual, or family, enterprise — enterprise that does not disturb the institutional relations of corporate capitalism.

Such enterprise conforms to Jencks' argument that differences among individuals are more relevant than group differences (attention to which, Jencks contends, was responsible for the failure of the 1960s' "War on Poverty") as the focal point for social reform.[79] If he is correct, the problem for public policy makers, as Thurow has pointed out, is to some extent analogous to the basic problem of quantum mechanics. "While it is impossible to predict the path of individual particles or atoms it is possible to predict the effect of groups of particles. If true . . . public policies can be designed to help groups of individuals but they cannot be designed to help particular individuals."[80]

Thus, for Jencks the fact that a father's phone call — like the recommended choice of the one Yale applicant over the other — permits the upper class to pass on privileged position to a new generation can simply be translated as the unofficial (not public) policy of an enlightened social order; for the emphasis of the Jencks argument is that it is more important to eliminate inequality *within* groups rather than differences *between* groups in order to eliminate dissatisfactions.[81] For those individuals of middle and lower class origins, who usually find official public policy even less amenable to personal needs than do the upper class, and who are without the unofficial phone call or a well-positioned influential father, they too can use the schools to keep abreast of the other members of *their* group. In these cases education can be seen, using the Jencks perspective, as a risky, but possibly profitable, investment — *profitable* not to the middle and lower classes as groups, but *to particular individuals only*.

The Jencks pluralism, then, emphasizes the individualistic competition of all 'we's' and 'they's' for a greater share of scarce resources (larger individual incomes), without analyzing the social system within which this competition takes place. His pluralism assumes disconnectedness between the personal and the political; it also posits the answer to this problem — namely, maintenance of the existing social system. For Jencks, the educational institution, as well as all others, is justifiable within the corporate socio-economic arrangements that currently prevail. He writes:

... The general implication of our work may [therefore] be that reformers should concentrate more attention on the internal workings of institutions and less on the relationship between institutions. Perhaps what America needs is more radical innovation in what might be called micro-politics and less concern with what might be called macro-politics.[82]

This reform strategy that discourages attempts to work out the relations between institutions nicely complements Jencks' inability, in large part an attribute of his pluralistic bias, to analyze the socio-economic system as a whole. This inability, in turn, leaves him unable to suggest viable alternatives by implementing his own reform strategy of applying his scientific evidence to the workings of any single institution. Thus, the school, like the nuclear family, in becoming more autonomous via the Jencks argument — that is, separated from its socio-economic surroundings — permits students to make the personal political only within the confines of the existent social system. Accordingly, Jencks tells us that despite finding such commonly-used measures as school examination scores and academic credentials are poor predictors of occupational performance,[83] "staying in school has a modest effect on many of the noncognitive traits [for instance, ambition and persistence] that employers value."[84]

This message to stay in school begins to look like an advertisement for the current socio-economic order when it is remembered Jencks argues that these noncognitive traits of the personality, along with luck, are largely responsible for the wide variation in individual incomes. If income is randomly distributed because it is pulled out of a personality/luck magic hat unresponsive to the machinations of science, then one logical outcome of the Jencks argument might be to help shift social policy from saying that we do not know how to control incomes to the position that incomes are uncontrollable.[85] In this way, the powerful and privileged position of one extreme group that Jencks ignores, the very wealthy (the group that Michelson calls "the ruling class"), could be solidified within the current socio-economic system; the positions of the less-privileged middle and lower classes could also be solidified, and their members encouraged to try harder. This extra effort could then be translated to mean more schooling. Indeed, Jencks, in his reassessment of *Inequality*, seems to argue that the way in which school attendance affects adult occupation and income is not quite so unimportant as his evidence may have first suggested:

If those who earn low incomes are almost all being punished for failings they cannot prevent, like having poor parents, black skins, or low IQ scores, it seems clear to me that their incomes ought to be supplemented by those who have been more fortunate. *But* if those with low incomes are mostly being punished for failings they can remedy, such as not wanting to work, the case for redistribution is more problematic. This is also true if most of the poor are being punished for making the "wrong" choice at some time in the past, such as dropping out of school. *Society has a stake in discouraging certain kinds of anti-social behaviour, and if dropping out of school reduces an individual's capacity to contribute to the general welfare, it may make sense to punish this decision by paying drop-outs less.*[86] (my emphasis)

Thurow might have been wrong; rather than "nothing affects anything", often Jencks seems to be saying that "some things affect everything". Translated, this means that while the learning of ambition and persistence taught in school may not help one to a more comfortable job at a higher income, this training will help each individual to *adjust to* and *accept* their position within prevailing socio-economic arrangements. In the words of Jencks:

... There is no evidence that building a school playground will affect the students' chances of leaning to read, getting into college, or earning $50,000 a year when they are 50. Building a playground may, however, have a considerable effect on the students' chances of having a good time during recess when they are 8. . . .[87]

This strategy of school reform that attempts to guarantee a "good time" for all, should also continue to help guarantee a supply of happy workers "educated" to undertake the variety of jobs this society demands be done. It is a strategy that should once again give comfort to that group most often responsible for creating these demands, but ignored by Jencks, the very rich. After all, the members of this group have long believed that school should be little more than a "good time" extension of the family — that the most important things were usually learned not in classrooms, but by interacting with the members of one's own class in the drawing rooms and board rooms of family corporations.[88]

In sum, for Jencks inequality is something more than just the individual accidents his analysis suggests; all is *not* undirected drift.[89] Rather, school in the United States offers an education that is an important factor in shaping the adult "successes" who maintain, but do not create, present socio-economic arrangements. The Jencks infatuation with the family model of the school turns such an education into a reflection of his pluralism. Education becomes training in ambition and persistence *liberally* mixed with instruction in tolerance;[90] the result is subservient employees who, in accepting (tolerating) their own position in relation to others, are happy to do their part to help maintain and recreate the demands of a socio-economic system that has brought great wealth to their employers. The Jencks analysis is, then, a pluralistic view strongly reminiscent of colleague Riesman's notion of the "other-directed man"; the increasingly common North American character type who would, assuming instruction in family-like schools, continue to place his ability to be "at home everywhere and nowhere" in the service of societal demands.[91] In American society, the others to whom the other-directed man, as well as Jencks and his sociological pluralism, are directed, and serve, is a small group of very powerful and wealthy corporate capitalists.

CONCLUSION

The pluralism that holds higher education autonomous — permitting Clark, Riesman, and Jencks in turn, to view academe as being a creative agent, an institution in revolution, and like a family — is again very much in evidence in one of Riesman's more recent works, *Academic Values and Mass Education*. In summarizing this study of the early years of two new schools, Oakland University and Monteith College, Riesman reiterates his thesis that "American higher education is astonishingly pluralistic."[92] Pluralistic means, as it did before, that the educational institution is separated from its socio-economic surroundings. This separation once again results in a reaffirmation of both the education-as-autonomous argument and the current socio-economic system.

Accordingly, for Riesman, colleges and universities are characterized by fluidity and change;[93] they become Clark's creative agents. They hire professors who, being relatively uncontrolled by clients in setting work pace and standards (the academic revolution),[94] agree with Riesman in viewing teaching as a search for the "right strategy".[95] These schools and their professors are part of what Riesman calls a "non-system";[96] the same non-system, perhaps, that inspires Jencks to suggest a non-relationship between the American people, their social system, and their own inequality.

In brief, the pluralism that encourages Riesman to conceptualize teaching as a search for the right strategy also encourages Jencks to interpret his findings of inequality as individual accidents and Clark to argue for a creative education without any innovations that might threaten the existent socio-economic order. That the arguments of these three social scientists — the major figures involved in developing a sociology of higher education over the past twenty years — compliment and complement one another so well should not be surprising. For what they share is pluralism — a pluralism that permits each author to attempt to make higher education autonomous by isolating the educational institution from the larger social system.

It is this same pluralism which leads to thinking that professional refinement of academic disciplines will increase the professors' power to fundamentally reorganize the American political economy. This thinking is backwards. Why? Simply because it is not an accurate representation of today's socio-economic reality. The result of this backwards thinking is that it reinforces and perpetuates the socio-economic arrangements which permit a small group of corporate capitalists to continue dominating education and other institutions, and thereby, to continue exercising significant control over the daily interactions of the vast majority of the population. If progress towards ending this domination is to be made, then the Clark-Riesman-Jencks thesis and similar analyses must be discarded and this matter of institutional interrelations put the right way around. Fundamental social change does not take place as a result of what is initiated by educators in the schools; rather, it is changes in the larger political economy outside the school which alter our school learning by changing the conditions of individual relationships to the means of economic production, distribution, and consumption.

NOTES

1. Evidence as to the prominence of these three sociologists of education can be easily accumulated by constructing a summary review of their scholarly and professional activities. During Professor Clark's lengthy tenure in the Sociology Department of Yale University he has authored four major books on higher education, written several papers on education, served several times as chair for education sessions at the annual meetings of the American Sociological Association and other professional groups, and was chosen to write the education chapter in what has become a standard source book for sociologists, *The Handbook of Modern Sociology* (1964). More recently, he has reviewed the sociological literature on higher education in the Association's official educational journal; see "Development of the Sociology of Higher Education", *Sociology of Education*, Winter 1973, pp. 2-14.

   Professor Riesman has taught in the Department of Social Sciences at the University of Chicago, 1946-58; and at Harvard since 1958. His association with Harvard goes back to his entering undergraduate year of 1927. Over the past thirty years he has been a most prolific writer — having written numerous journal articles and authored or co-authored books on a variety of topics, at least four of which deal specifically with American higher education. He has served as an editor for several education journals and as a consultant to and member of various educational foundations, councils, and committees (for example, The Carnegie Commission on the Future of Higher Education and the American Council on Education), while also being involved in research activity as a Fellow of Stanford's Centre for Advanced Study in the Behavioral Sciences.

   Professor Jencks, in addition to his teaching duties at Harvard, has done recent research as a Fellow at the Cambridge Policy Studies Institute. He first became well-known in 1968 as co-author, with Riesman, of *The Academic Revolution*. More recently, he has written a number of articles in major journals in response to the controversy (see, for example, *Harvard Educational Review*, February 1973) occasioned by the publication of his other major work, *Inequality*. While Clark might be considered the foremost expert on higher education among professional sociologists and Riesman, the most widely-read and well-known analyst of American higher education, Jencks may well be the most widely-discussed North

American authority on schools over the past six years.

Perhaps it is well to mention here one other prominent social analyst, Ivan Illich. Although he neither claims to be a sociologist nor is accepted by other sociologists as a member of the discipline, in *Deschooling Society* (New York: Harper and Row, 1970) Illich makes an education-as-autonomous argument which can be linked to those of Clark, Riesman, and Jencks. For an excellent criticism of Illich's work, see Herb Gintis, "Towards a Political Economy of Education: A Radical Critique of Ivan Illich's Deschooling Society", *This Magazine Is About Schools*, Spring 1972, pp. 117-145.

2. This argument is found in Clark's *Educating The Expert Society*. The general theoretical orientation presented in this book has, as might be expected, influenced the presentation of his research findings: *Adult Education in Transition* (Berkeley: University of California Press, 1956), *The Open Door College* (New York: McGraw-Hill, 1960), *The Distinctive College* (Chicago: Aldine, 1970). However, since in these three studies he examines specific aspects of American higher education in a way that adds little to the more encompassing perspective presented in *Expert Society*, they have not been reviewed here.

3. This evidence and the accompanying thesis summarized here can be found in *Inequality*. Jencks has made attempts to clarify reader "problems" and "misunderstandings" of this 1972 publication and Riesman has joined him in attempts to clarify and elaborate upon their earlier collaboration on *The Academic Revolution*. Since the present analysis of their work does not go beyond the early 1970s, ending with Riesman's 1971 publication of *Academic Values and Mass Education* and Jencks' 1972 and 1973 publications of *Inequality* and "Inequality in Retrospect", the author has taken care to survey more recent work for indications of new thinking which might significantly alter the critique presented here. In the material surveyed, including a relatively recent article by Jencks and Marsha Brown ("Effects of Desegregation on Student Achievement: Some New Evidence from the Equality of Educational Opportunity Survey", *Sociology of Education*, Winter 1975, pp. 126-140) and book by Riesman and Seymour Martin Lipset (*Education and Politics at Harvard*, New York: McGraw-Hill, 1975), I find nothing that would significantly alter the present analysis.

4. There are many, an almost infinite variety of, pluralistic views. Among the many pluralists listed by Richard Gillam (*Power in Postwar America*, Boston: Little, Brown and Company, 1971, pp. 191-198), the "veto group" theory of David Riesman (*The Lonely Crowd*, New Haven: Yale University Press, 1950), the "dispersed inequalities" thesis of Robert A. Dahl (*Who Governs?*, New Haven: Yale University Press, 1961), and "the multi-influence hypothesis" of Arnold Rose (*The Power Sturcture*, New York: Oxford University Press, 1968) continue to be three of the most well-known and accepted arguments in this pluralistic tradition. In contrast, and more in accordance with the tradition of a "ruling class" view of the power structure, is the "power elite" thesis of C. Wright Mills (*The Power Elite*, New York: Oxford, 1956) and the "governing class" argument of G. William Domhoff (*Who Rules America?*, Englewood Cliffs: Prentice-Hall, 1967; *The Higher Circles*, New York: Random House, 1970).

5. For an excellent discussion of this phrase, the big picture, in relation to social theory, see C. Wright Mills, *The Sociological Imagination*, New York: Oxford University Press, 1959, especially Chapter One and most particularly, pp. 17-24.

6. Burton R. Clark, *Educating the Expert Society*, San Francisco: Chandler, 1962, p. 2.

7. *Ibid.*, p. 3.

8. *Ibid.*, p. 4.

9. *Ibid.*, p. 4.

10. *Ibid.*, p. 5.

11. *Ibid.*, p. 4.

12. *Ibid.*, p. 7.

13. *Ibid.*, p. 8.

14. *Ibid.*, Introduction, "Education in the Technological Age", especially pp. 1-3. The changing relationship between humans and the machines they have produced is, and should continue to be, of concern to all North Americans. However, to posit a second scientific revolution requiring an education that ensures the training of experts, whole-heartedly embraces the technological age — encouraging control of human begins by a machine-like logic that tends to perpetuate itself. In short, humans are encouraged to continue eliminating themselves from the process of living by becoming more efficient — that is, "being" in Clark's world, automated by the second scientific revolution, becomes increasingly automatic. Being becomes a job for the machine and/or the machine-like human. For similar thoughts on this matter, see Jacques Ellul, *The Technological Society*, New York: Random House, 1964.

15. Clark, pp. 25 and 26. For the "classic" discussion of education as a "passive instrument" that Clark has in mind here, see Emile Durkheim, *Education and Sociology*, translated by Sherwood D. Fox, Glencoe, Illinois: The Free Press, 1956, pp. 65 and 66.

16. *Ibid.*, p. 27.

17. *Ibid.*, p. 27. This quotation is taken from *The Price of Excellence*, Problems and Policies Committee, American Council on Education, Washington: October, 1960, p. 1. The statistics mentioned can be found on p. 28 of the *Expert Society*.

18. Clark, p. 29. For a view that sees most of today's academicians as much less free, critical, and innovating than they used to be and Clark claims they are, see C. Wright Mills, *White Collar*, New York: Oxford University Press, 1951, pp. 129-136. For data that supports the Mills interpretation, see Theodore Caplow and Reece J. McGee, *The Academic Marketplace*, New York: Basic Books, 1962; and James Ridgeway, *The Closed Corporation*, New York: Ballantine Books, 1968.

19. Clark, p. 9.

20. *Ibid.*, p. 30.

21. *Ibid.*, pp. 35 and 107-112. In citing these studies to support his view that education leads to more liberal (tolerant) attitudes regarding both racial and political matters, Clark fails to cite what was, at the time, probably the most well-known review and interpretation of research on this relation between education and attitudes — a review that strongly disputes Clark's view. See Philip E. Jacob,

Changing Values in College: An Exploratory Study of the Impact of College Teaching, New York: Harper and Row, 1957.

22. One of the earliest and probably most widely-known studies that suggests this conclusion is the "streetcar scene" demonstration of rumor reported in G. W. Allport and Leo Postman, *The Psychology of Rumor*, New York: Henry Holt and Company, 1947, p. 71.

23. Clark, pp. 30-35.

24. This is not to suggest that the managers are not themselves managed. See C. Wright Mills with Hans H. Gerth, "A Marx For The Managers", in *Power, Politics & People*, ed. Irving Louis Horowitz, New York: Oxford University Press, 1963, especially pp. 62, 64 and 67. Also, it should be noted that a small percentage of today's college graduates are opposed to becoming managers, actively choosing to become laborers instead.

25. On this point the reader is referred to Herbert Marcuse, *One-Dimensional Man*, Boston: Beacon Press, 1964.

26. Clark, p.38. He takes this distinction from C. P. Snow, *The Two Cultures and the Scientific Revolution*, Cambridge, England: Cambridge University Press, 1959.

27. Clark, p. 39.

28. *Ibid.*, p. 39.

29. *Ibid.*, p. 39.

30. Particularly good on this point is Jerry Farber, *The Student As Nigger*, Richmond Hill, Ontario: Simon & Schuster of Canada, 1970, especially his discussion of the "method", pp. 19-26. Also, see the excellent discussion of the "dominant style" in North America by Paul Goodman, *Like a Conquered Province*, New York: Random House, 1968, especially pp. 265-267; and in the same book his essay entitled, *People or Personnel*.

31. Clark, p. 283.

32. *Ibid.*, p. 283.

33. *Ibid.*, p. 287.

34. *Ibid.*, p. 288.

35. *Ibid.*, p. 40.

36. David Riesman, *Constraint and Variety in American Education*, Garden City, New York: Doubleday, 1956, p. 64.

37. *Ibid.*, p. 107.

38. Clark Kerr in his book, *The Uses of the University*, New York: Harper & Row, 1963, cites Riesman as having originally suggested this term "evocator". While the term is used here to refer to the academic disciplines, Kerr uses it in evaluating the role of today's university president; see pp. 29-41. A very brief discussion of this role by Riesman can be found in *Constraint and Variety*, pp. 30-32.

39. For the phrase and a brief discussion of what he has in mind, see Riesman,

Constraint and Variety, pp. 109, 110. For a more complete elaboration of the racecourse idea, see all of Chapter Two, "The Intellectual Veto Groups", pp. 66-119.

40. *Ibid.,* pp. 109, 110.

41. David Riesman, Joseph Gusfield and Zelda Gamson, *Academic Values and Mass Education: The Early Years of Oakland and Monteith,* Garden City, New York: Doubleday, 1971, p. 246.

42. Christopher Jencks and David Riesman, *The Academic Revolution,* Garden City: Doubleday, 1968, pp. 505, 508, 539.

43. *Ibid.,* p. 480.

44. *Ibid.,* p. 480.

45. *Ibid.,* p. 510. For a more lengthy statement of this "revolution", see pp. 25, 26.

46. *Ibid.,* p. XV.

47. *Ibid.,* pp. 513, 514.

48. *Ibid.,* p. 10.

49. *Ibid.,* p. 540. This quotation could be interpreted as very accurate; however, this could be so not because graduate department ideology is, as the authors suggest, *different from* the surrounding socio-economic system, but rather, because it is a *duplication of* that system. American higher education is not autonomous, but dependent.

50. *Ibid.,* pp. 243, 252. These distinctions help Jencks and Riesman, like Clark, make their argument more pluralistic by reaffirming a supposed cultural split between science and the humanities.

51. For Clark's discussion of these subcultures among college students, see Chapter 6, *Expert Society.*

52. Jencks and Riesman, p. 201.

53. *Ibid.,* p. 238.

54. *Ibid.,* p. 516.

55. *Ibid.,* see pp. 517-523.

56. For more detail, see Randle W. Nelsen, *Growth of the Modern University and the Development of a Sociology of Higher Education in the United States,* Ph. D. Dissertation, Hamilton, Ontario: McMaster University, 1975, pp. 23-90; Samuel Bowles and Herbert Gintis, "Capitalism and Education in the United States", *Socialist Revolution,* July-September 1975, Vol. 5, No, 3, pp. 101-138.

57. In considering the academic division of labor (the proliferation of subject matter specialties and specialists) in relation to this statement, one might want to question its relative validity when applied to diverse segments of the university faculty. To do so might make clear important qualifications bearing on the general point being made here. What would also likely be made clear is the poverty and irrelevance of much criticism of universities among "liberal" social scientists who claim that they and their colleagues in the humanities are less "bought" by

research sponsors than those working in the natural (physical) sciences, schools of business, etc.

58. Jencks and Riesman, p. 506.

59. *Ibid.,* p. 250.

60. *Ibid.,* p. 73.

61. *Ibid.,* p. 95.

62. *Ibid.,* p. 100.

63. These examples should help illustrate the unacceptability of the achievement-ascription distinction that many sociologists continue to make. For excellent discussions of how the educational institution continues to keep members of the various socio-economic classes in place generation after generation, see Samuel Bowles, "Unequal Education and the Reproduction of the Hierarchical Division of Labor"; Florence Howe and Paul Lauter, "How the School System is Rigged for Failure", *The Capitalist System*, eds. Richard C. Edwards, Michael Reich, Thomas E. Weisskopf, Englewood Cliffs, New Jersey: Prentice-Hall, 1972, pp. 218-235.

64. Jencks and Riesman, pp. 149, 150.

65. *Ibid.,* p. 150.

66. Christopher Jencks, "Inequality in Retrospect", *Harvard Educational Review*, February 1973, p. 164.

67. Lester C. Thurow, "Proving the Absence of Positive Associations", *Harvard Educational Review*, February 1973, p. 107.

68. Stephan Michelson, "The Further Responsibility of Intellectuals", *Harvard Educational Review*, February 1973, p. 104.

69. David Riesman, *The Lonely Crowd*, New Haven: Yale University Press, 1950, p. 260.

70. Christopher Jencks et al., *Inequality: A Reassessment of the Effect of Family and Schooling in America*, New York: Basic Books, 1972, p. 13.

71. Michelson, p. 102. The discussion in the remainder of my paragraph corresponds very closely with Michelson's comments, see pp. 102, 103.

72. *Ibid.,* p. 103.

73. Jencks et al., *Inequality*, p. 135.

74. *Ibid.,* p. 7.

75. *Ibid.,* pp. 255-257. For an excellent discussion of various models of higher education, see Robert Paul Wolff, *The Ideal of the University*, Boston: Beacon Press, 1969, Parts One, Three, and Conclusion.

76. For a superb analysis of the extent to which nuclear family units have become, if not factory-like, the major maintenance institution of corporate capitalism, and of the traditional role of women in providing this service, see Dorothy E. Smith, "Women, the Family and Corporate Capitalism", *Women in Canada*, ed.

Marylee Stephenson Toronto: New Press, 1973, pp. 5-35. Also, see Saul D. Feldman, "Impediment or Stimulant? Marital Status and Graduate Education", *American Journal of Sociology,* January 1973, pp. 982-994.

77. Jencks et al., *Inequality*, p. 227.

78. *Ibid.*, p. 227.

79. *Ibid.*, p. 14.

80. Thurow, p. 107.

81. Jencks et al., *Inequality*, p. 250.

82. *Ibid.*, p. 250.

83. *Ibid.*, see pp. 52, 53, and the remainder of Chapter Three. Also, p. 134.

84. *Ibid.*, p. 134. For his comments on the noncognitive traits of ambition and persistence in relation to schooling, see p. 132.

85. Thurow, p. 110.

86. Jencks, "Inequality in Retrospect", p. 156.

87. Jencks et al., *Inequality*, p. 29.

88. Particularly good on this point is G. William Domhoff, *Who Rules America?*, Englewood Cliffs, New Jersey: Prentice-Hall, 1967, especially Chapter One.

89. See C. Wright Mills, *The Power Elite* (New York: Oxford University Press, 1956), pp. 243-244, *infra*.

90. For an idea of the way in which the liberalism taught in the schools affects students, see Edgar Z. Friedenberg, *Coming of Age in America: Growth and Acquiescence*, New York: Random House, 1963, especially Chapter Three. Also, the work of John Kenneth Galbraith is exemplary of the way in which many liberals conceive of the relation between higher education and the current socio-economic order. See his *The New Industrial State*, New York: The New American Library, 1968, particularly pp. 271-385.

91. For this description of the other-directed character type as being "at home everywhere and nowhere", see Riesman, *The Lonely Crowd*, p. 26.

92. Riesman, Gusfield and Gamson, *Academic Values*, p. 246. For a complete citation see note 41. (For a relatively recent restatement by Clark of the education-as-autonomous argument, see "Development of the Sociology of Higher Education" — a complete citation is in note 1 — p. 11.)

93. Riesman, Gusfield, and Gamson, p. 75.

94. *Ibid.*, p. 69.

95. *Ibid.*, p. 267.

96. *Ibid.*, p. 246.

SECTION II

The Multiversity and the Capitalist System

The most important feature of today's capitalism in North America has to do with the tendency for wealth to become centralized and concentrated in a few large corporations which develop monopoly power over the goods and services they produce, distribute, and consume. Within the knowledge industry, the multiversity stands apart from other educational settings in the clarity with which it exemplifies this centralization and concentration of wealth that moves toward monopoly power. However, as all three papers below point out, in order to become a leading multiversity, the road travelled becomes a winding series of crossing intersections between private industry, schools and educational foundations, and the State. The toll taken during the course of this travel is extracted in education's service to the dictates and demands of corporate and increasingly, monopoly capital.

The paper by John Barkans and Norene Pupo is particularly informative as to how the increasingly important role played by the Canadian State fits in with the educational activities of Canada's most prominent capitalists. Their study of the Boards of Governors of eight Ontario universities underscores the fact that the power which shapes higher education is not widely dispersed throughout the socio-economic order. Rather, it is part of an increasingly close-knit State-private industry-education triangle, part of an increasing centralization and bureaucratization of political and economic spheres, in which power becomes further consolidated in the hands of an upper class elite. The result is that "the university is not autonomous in the most crucial sense, financially."

Ken Luckhardt shifts our attention from the Barkans and Pupo analysis of Canadian universities such as McMaster, Queen's, Western, and York, back across the border to American multiversities. He sees Harvard, Columbia, Chicago, the University of California, and other similar institutions as illustrative of the way in which American universities support the structural status quo by serving interests of the corporate ruling class. Luckhardt's overview of the postwar military-university complex describes and analyzes the workings of State monopoly capitalism by showing how today's universities have learned to "Goose Step" to the dictates of foundation grants and military contracts of the defense sector.

The paper by Nelsen continues to focus on this goose step. He returns to

67

the work of Riesman, Jencks, and Clark, this time to show how their widely-accepted celebration of the multiversity's growth and its service orientation is part of becoming socialized to a professionalism which teaches students to join faculty in recreating the capitalism of an increasingly profitable educational-industrial-governmental partnership. Thus, while this article echoes the first two papers of this section in its general outline of this partnership, in addition it provides a specific focus for understanding how learning within the multiversity is structured by professorial adherence to a predominant role model stressing a particular kind of professionalism. As Nelsen argues, it is a professionalism which encourages most multiversity professors and students to continue serving the interests of wealth and power.

Canadian Universities and the Economic Order

JOHN BARKANS & NORENE PUPO

A central problem explored in the literature on the role and functions of contemporary universities concerns the potential antipathy between two primary goals of these institutions. On the one hand, it is argued that universities should serve and be responsive to "national interests", while on the other hand, it is claimed that these bodies of higher learning must possess enough autonomy to guarantee academic freedom. While it is usually conceded that the resolution of the tension between these two ideals is always problematic, writers on the modern university have, in the main, claimed that the proper balance between the two has been achieved. Underlying this belief is an explicit or implicit assumption about the nature of our society, namely, that it can be best understood as a plurality of countervailing interest groups. Acceptance of this assumption allows one to argue that universities respond to a plurality of interests (that is, the "public") which make up the national interest and at the same time are not subservient to any one particular interest. Hence, they are relatively autonomous from all of these groups.

In this paper we attempt to reveal the inadequacies of the pluralistic conception of the university by examining the relation between Canadian institutions of higher learning and the capitalist class. It is argued that universities are, in fact, dominated by this class. However, we must emphasize that we are not arguing that universities are mere instruments of the capitalist class acting on its behest, nor that universities possess no autonomy. Rather, we claim that the degree of autonomy of these institutions can only be understood within the context of the concrete relation between universities and the capitalist class.

The relation between universities and the capitalist class can be understood as comprising both personnel and structural relationships. The first section of this paper analyzes the personnel who sit on boards of governors, the uppermost decision-making bodies of universities. The second section examines structural constraints on the university which make it susceptible to capitalist domination. In this second section, it is argued that the current economic crisis within Canada and the financial crisis in universities have helped to solidify capitalist domination of universities.

THE PERSONNEL RELATIONSHIP:
GOVERNING BODIES AND THE ECONOMIC ELITE

In any hierarchically organized institution one can delineate a set of upper-most positions and a group of people who fill these positions whom we may call an elite. In the case of the university, the top decision-making body corresponds to what is usually termed the board of governors or governing council, and the people who sit on these councils can be designated as the university elite. Here we are concerned with exploring the nature of this university elite. Data are given below which demonstrate that contemporary Canadian universities are dominated by what Wallace Clement terms the "corporate elite"[1] as well as by other businessmen. Before presenting this information, however, it is necessary to understand that the economic elite's involvement in universities is not a recent phenomenon but is part of a long standing historical relationship.

Canada's universities were not established primarily in response to popular demands but owed their existence to activities of certain key members of the dominant class. For example, the founder of King's College (later the University of Toronto) was John Strachan. Besides his involvement in the Welland Canal Company and the Bank of Upper Canada, Strachan was part of the inner circle of the "Family Compact", a group of merchants, landowners, and government officials who comprised the local ruling class of Upper Canada. Strachan designed the charter for King's College and was sent to England to negotiate its royal assent in 1826. In view of the way Strachan assumed control in organizing Ontario's first university, it is neither surprising nor is it mere coincidence that the college's charter provided that the Archdeacon of York, a position then held by Strachan himself, was to become the *ex officio* president of the institution. Along with Strachan, the first governing council of King's College was dominated by members of the Family Compact.[2] Its membership included H.J. Boulton, John Beverley Robinson, Honourable Thomas Ridout, Sir William Campbell, and Grant Powell.

As the nature of Canada's dominant class changed with the development of industrial capitalism, the new men of wealth and power — financial and industrial capitalists — assumed leadership positions within universities. Thus, in 1873 the fifteen member governing body of the University of Toronto included the following persons in the economic elite: Honourable Edward Blake, first president, Toronto General Trusts Company; John Morison Gibson, president, Dominion Power and Transmission Company and director, Canadian Westinghouse Company; James Thornburn, president, Imperial Loan and Investment Company of Canada; and Honourable Thomas Moss whose family was involved in the brewing industry in Toronto. Similarly, in 1904-5 the University of Toronto was governed by such people as Sir

B.E. Walker, president of the Canadian Bank of Commerce; J.H. Mason, president, Canada Permanent Loan and Savings Company; Honourable G.A. Cox, president, Canadian Life Assurance Company and director, Canadian General Electric Company and Dominion Iron and Steel Company; Sir C.S. Gzowski, president, London and Canada Loan and Agency Company and vice president, Ontario Bank; and John Hoskin, president, Toronto General Trusts Company and Consumers' Gas Company. A more detailed examination of the historical relationship between the economic elite and governing councils of universities would confirm the findings of the selected examples cited here.

While the economic elite's dominance within top decision-making bodies of institutions of higher learning dated back to their founding, it was not until 1906 with the passage of the University Act that this relationship was formally legitimized. The problem of university government had plagued Canadian universities from the outset. In an attempt to alleviate this problem, a committee was established at the University of Toronto in 1905 to make recommendations for reorganization of the university's system of government. The work of this committee resulted in several proposals which were implemented through the Act of 1906. Most significantly, the Act placed control and management of the university in a provincially appointed body, the Board of Governors.

Once appointed by the provincial authorities, the governors were to be virtually autonomous from political control. Members of the board of governors were, in effect, to become the voice of the provincial government in the university, with final vetoing power over all major university policies and decisions and absolute authority in financial matters.[3] In selecting governors a chief concern was to avoid political partisanship. The board was to be a lay body, representative of the mass of people, rather than of any one particular sector of society such as the political order. In practice, however, the upper levels of the university came to be dominated by members of the economic elite. Most significantly, this relationship was fully sanctioned by the University Act.

The first Board of Governors chosen under the new Act was heavily over represented by key corporate officials. These included: Sir B.E. Walker, John Hoskin and others who were also on the 1904-5 board; Joseph W. Flavelle, chairman of National Trust Company; E.B. Osler, member of the executive committee of the Canadian Pacific Railway; Chester D. Massey, president, Massey-Harris Company; J.L. Englehart, president, Imperial Oil Company; Sir Mackenzie Bowell, president, Farren Manufacturing Company; G.R.R. Cockburn, president, Ontario Bank; and E.C. Whitney, president, St. Anthony Lumber Company.

The fundamental features of Toronto's University Act which placed the economic elite in command posts of the university became the basis for other Canadian universities' systems of government and has, in fact, served as a model for contemporary universities. In an attempt to determine whether or not the economic elite also rules the contemporary Canadian universities, a study was undertaken in 1974 to examine boards of governors of eight Ontario institutions — Toronto, McMaster, Western, Waterloo, Carleton, York, Queen's, and Guelph.[4] These universities are of various sizes and are all public institutions subsidized by government funds. Theoretically and ideally, then, the boards should be representative of the "public". In fact, members of the economic elite dominate the uppermost power positions within these universities.

The number of governors for these eight universities totalled 258 and of these, 106 or slightly more than 41 per cent, were members of the economic elite[5] (see Table I). This figure, however, underestimates the extent of corporate dominance in general and business dominance in particular. Not included in this calculation are businessmen who operate medium and small-sized local concerns, members with kinship ties to the economic elite, and individuals who have had close and direct ties to corporations although they themselves have never held directorships (such as various researchers and consultants for corporations). While the inclusion of people with these types of backgrounds would raise representation of the economic elite on governing councils, they have been excluded and instead we focus on the 106 members with direct ties to the dominant Canadian corporations.

TABLE I

University	No. of Governors	No. in Economic Elite
Carleton	30	8
Guelph	23	6
McMaster	39	17
Queen's	37	21
Toronto	50	16
Waterloo	30	11
Western	23	11
York	26	16
Total	258	106

Overall, nearly 500 different corporations and financial institutions are represented in the directorships held by members of boards of governors. While these range from fairly local or regional concerns to the largest financial firms and multinational corporations, one *can* note a pattern of corporate connections which bring together various board members both within and across universities.

An analysis of directorships held by governors reveals a pattern of intricate connections within each set of university governors. For example, at McMaster several of the common directorships held include: J.P. Gordon, R.B. Taylor, and W.H. Young on the Steel Company of Canada; G.H. Blumenauer and F.H. Sherman on Dominion Foundries and Steel; and W.J. Cheeseman and W.P. Pigott on Westinghouse Canada. Space does not permit further elucidation of common directorships at McMaster and the rest of the universities studied; however, such connections abound within each university board and bring together a significant number of governors into a pattern of close interaction.

More impressive than the common economic links of governors within universities are those among the different universities. The major Canadian banks, insurance, trust companies and other financial institutions are well represented on boards of governors and serve as major unifying forces for personnel making up the university elite. For example, the Canadian Bank of Commerce is represented by nine governors who sit on six different university boards and five governors from five universities are directors of the Toronto-Dominion Bank. Further, if ownership and subsidiary patterns among corporations are examined, more detailed interconnections among universities are evident. Figures I and II display some of these ties which result for the subsidiaries and other interests revolving around the Canada Trust Company and the Montreal Trust Company.

Both intra-university and inter-university corporate ties serve to unite members of the governing councils. Mirroring these common economic linkages among governors are similarities in social patterns. A useful indicator in this respect is membership in Canada's exclusive social clubs. Club membership is patterned in such a way that there are ''local'' and ''national'' clubs which function to provide intra and inter-university unity among governors. For example, at least eight governors of McMaster University belong to the Hamilton Club while at least six governors of Western belong to the London Hunt and Country Club. These clubs are important local meeting places. Moreover, at least twenty-six governors from six different universities belong to the Toronto Club, Canada's most difficult club in which to gain membership.[6] Thus it is an important mingling place for the university elite of the various institutions.

In short, the structural interrelatedness of the corporate order and common social ties of the economic elite who sit on governing councils provide a basis for unity among this group. Along with this, their over representation on boards of governors provides the key to understanding the economic elite's domination of the university governing bodies. These men hold a conserva-

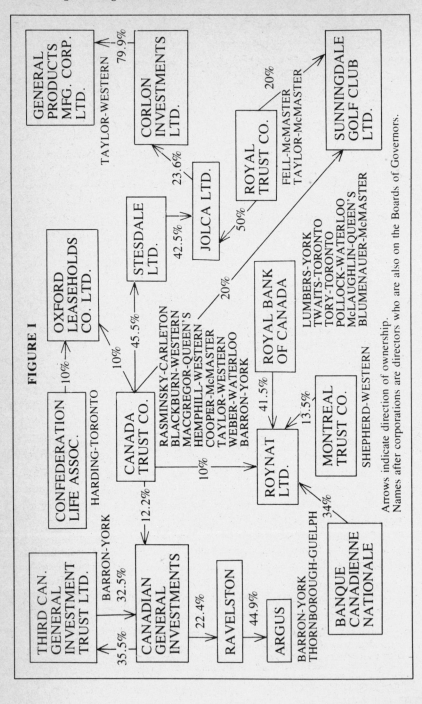

FIGURE I

Arrows indicate direction of ownership.
Names after corporations are directors who are also on the Boards of Governors.

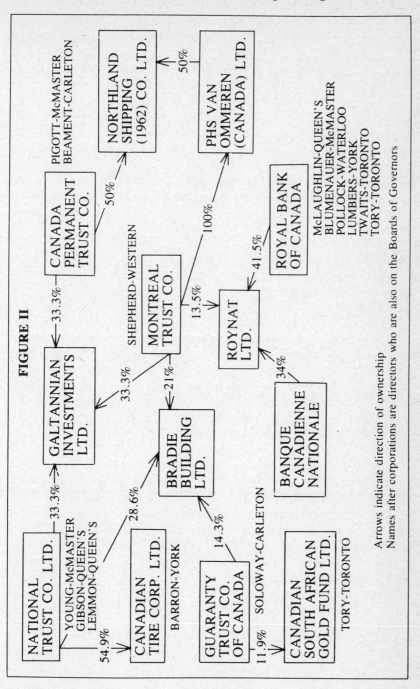

FIGURE II

Arrows indicate direction of ownership
Names after corporations are directors who are also on the Boards of Governors

tive ideology, one generally supportive of the status quo and existing economic system. Because of the authority conferred on them through their positions within universities' power structures, they can, in the main, shape policy to serve their interests. While these are complex problems and we cannot do justice to them here, a few words are in order on these matters.

First, although we do not have data on the attitudes and values of our sample of governors, other research has indicated that members of governing councils generally believe that running a university is like running a business and that a hierarchical system should exist in which decisions are made and passed from the top down to the rest of the university community.[7] Second, the question of power within the university is far more complex than merely delineating who participated in the making of various decisions. While it is no doubt true that universities' Senates, administrations, and various faculty bodies participate in making the majority of decisions, this begs the question of what interests were taken into account by participants. In addition, as Bachrach and Baratz have argued, there are "two faces of power" and part of the power of the powerful rests in their capability of preventing issues from arising which could challenge their interests.[8] Nevertheless, on occasion such issues arise when boards of governors do act and in these instances the power relationships are uncovered and underlined. Thus, at McGill in 1937 the Principal of the university, Arthur E. Morgan, was forced to resign because, as he put it, "the Board of Governors did not see eye to eye with me in regard to the relationship of the Principalship to the Governors."[9] While such examples do occur, we would argue that governors probably prefer to avoid such confrontations and, instead, exercise the "other face" of power. In this sense, they stand as the "gatekeepers" of the university, ruling with a velvet glove and attempting to mobilize bias in favour of their conception of the purposes and structure of the university.

In this section we have examined one aspect of the corporate elite's dominance of universities — their over representation on the uppermost decision-making bodies, the boards of governors. This is one aspect of the university's subservience to the economic order; however, concentration on this relationship leads to reformist implications for action to alter universities, namely, removal of these people and establishment of more representative governing councils. While such actions could potentially alter some aspects of the university, they alone would not fundamentally change the relation between the university and the corporate order. This is because this relation is primarily a structural one, a problem which will be analyzed next.

THE STRUCTURAL RELATION

The key to understanding the structural relation between the university and the capitalist class lies in recognizing that the university is not autonomous in the most crucial sense, financially. We will examine two sources of funds: (i) the state sector (ii) the corporations and individual capitalists. We argue that universities' dependence on such funding results in the domination of the post-secondary system by the capitalist class. This does not imply that the university possesses no autonomy and acts on the *behest* of the capitalist class. Rather, what is claimed is that the structural relation between the university and the capitalist class places severe limits on the university, ultimately resulting in the university functioning on *behalf* of the capitalist class.

The University and the State

The single most important source of funds for Canadian universities comes from the various levels and agencies of the state system. Thus, between 1920 and 1956 the proportion of universities' operating income accounted for by government grants fluctuated between 40 and 50 per cent.[10] Since then, however, universities' dependence on government sources has been rising and by the 1970s government funds accounted for 65 to 80 per cent of their operating income.[11] Our point of departure for understanding the implications of this is the recent works on the role of the state, such as those of Ralph Miliband,[12] Nicos Poulantzas,[13] and especially James O'Connor.[14]

O'Connor argues that the capitalist class dominates the state because of a basic objective structural fact — the state is dependent on a "healthy" economy for its own power and survival. "A state that ignores the necessity of assisting the process of capital accumulation risks drying up the source of its own power, the economy's surplus production capacity and the taxes drawn from this surplus (and other forms of capital)."[15] Applying this to the Canadian state,[16] the role of state funding of universities must not be seen solely as "political" intervention or state control of education; rather, it must be placed within the context of the general domination of the capitalist class as a whole over the state. At the simplest level, this reveals the way in which university dependence on government revenues can be related to the domination of the capitalist class over higher education. What is especially important is the way O'Connor develops this initial premise to analyze what he terms the "fiscal crisis" and, in turn, the way in which this can be applied to recent developments in state funding of Canadian universities.

O'Connor roots the fiscal crisis of the state, or the tendency for government expenses to exceed revenues, in the contradictions of monopoly capitalism. Monopoly capitalism, he argues, faces a crisis of profitability and accumulation,[17] and the state has had to intervene to ensure profitable accumulation. The result is that more and more of the costs of monopoly capitalism have become "socialized".[18] This, however, has created other contradictions since growth in the monopoly sector involves an increase in the physical capital-to-labour ratio and output per worker.[19] Hence, a greater percentage of the labour force must rely on employment in the competitive and state sectors while, at the same time, monopoly faces the problem of excess capacity/under consumption. These processes give rise to the two often contradictory functions of the state: on the one hand, it must aid accumulation while on the other hand this must be legitimized to maintain social harmony. The fiscal crisis results from the fact that monopoly capitalism requires the state to increase expenditures for both socialization of production and legitimation while the means of production are owned privately and, hence, profits are appropriated privately.[20]

The contradictions of monopoly capitalism and the fiscal crisis of the Canadian state have been analyzed elsewhere,[21] but what concerns us here are the implications of this on universities. Briefly, the fiscal crisis has resulted in the unleashing of two sets of forces upon universities — on the one hand, an attempt to restrain and cutback on university funding and on the other hand, a push toward a greater role for universities in training for the industrial labour market. The cutbacks in post-secondary education are directly related to the changing roles and responsibilities of the federal and provincial governments. The massive expansion of the universities since 1945 largely resulted from the initiatives and policies of the federal government. Between 1945 and 1965 federal government grants to universities were calculated on a *per capita* basis with the requirement that the grant be distributed to the individual institutions in proportion to the number of students. This method of directly funding universities was discontinued in 1965 when a new system was instituted whereby the federal government made a transfer payment directly to the provinces covering 50 per cent of the costs incurred by the provinces in the operation of post-secondary institutions. The new federal policy effectively gave the provincial governments full control over university funding.[22] The significance of this was that the share of federal spending on universities became dependent upon the amounts spent by provincial governments, subject only to a 15 per cent annual growth of the federal portion. Since the fiscal crisis is most prominent at the provincial (and municipal) levels of the state,[23] the new funding arrangements have placed the universities in vulnerable positions.

In Ontario, for example, the financial position of the government has had important implications for the province's universities. The provincial debt has been increasing during the 1970s, necessitating that a larger proportion of expenditures are allocated to the payment of this debt.[24] Consequently, there have been attempts to reduce expenditures and the university sector has been one of the major targets of financial restraint. Thus, in 1972-3, the province imposed a freeze, except under special circumstances, on new capital funding, suspended the funding of any new graduate programmes, and increased student tuition fees by $100 per year. These policies had an immediate impact on the universities. While direct government financial support increased, although at a rate below the cost of living between 1970 and 1972, during 1972-3 this support declined absolutely.[25] In 1974 further restraints were placed on university funding when the Ontario government moved from a financing formula based on enrolment to a "global budgeting approach". Prior to 1974 the Ontario government had established a basic amount to be granted for various designated categories of students. With the global budgeting approach, the total amount of funds to be allocated to universities is fixed. Hence, as enrolments increase, the average grant per student decreases. Overall, the effect of these government policies has been that between 1972-3 and 1975-6 the basic grant per student has increased substantially less than the cost of living.[26]

At the same time as the financial changes outlined above were being instituted in the universities, efforts by the state were also directed at creating a post-secondary system of education more directly responsive to the needs of the economic order. These latter efforts have involved two interrelated sets of policies. First, there has been an increased promotion of Colleges of Applied Arts and Technology (C.A.A.T.s) and secondly, within both the universities and the C.A.A.T.s, there has been a marked emphasis on programmes related directly to applied research and the acquisition of job related skills.

Generally, the growth of C.A.A.T.s was largely a phenomenon of the 1960s. In Ontario, for example, between 1961 and 1966 student enrolment at C.A.A.T.s grew by 188 per cent.[27] Moreover, the 1972 Commission on Post-Secondary Education in Ontario not only stressed the utility of C.A.A.T.s in providing pretraining, training, and retraining programmes for the labour market and advised that such programmes be expanded, but also recommended the formation of long-range funding policies for these institutions. The general promotion of the C.A.A.T.s in Canada is reflected by the faster growth rate of these institutions compared to the growth rate of universities as measured by enrolment statistics (see Table II). A more dramatic trend toward the community colleges is evident in Ontario (see Table III). The Ontario trends are especially significant given that this province's university system is the most developed in all of Canada and to some extent serves national interests.

Although the per student operating costs of the C.A.A.T.s are generally lower than those of universities, this fact has not been of primary importance in their promotion.[28] Rather, the utility of C.A.A.T.s in providing trained manpower for the economic order has been their chief selling point. As is evident from Table IV, a large majority of students in C.A.A.T.s are being directly trained for the industrial labour market. Further, new proposals in Ontario call for the strengthening of this function and the trimming of "frill" and general interest courses in these institutions. Thus, *The Report of the Special Program Review* recommended that the "Province's support for part-time general interest courses in Colleges of Applied Arts and Technology be phased out so as to put them on a full-cost recovery basis and the colleges be encouraged to direct their efforts towards providing vocational and technical training of the highest calibre."[29]

TABLE II
Full-Time Enrolments in Universities and Colleges of Applied Arts and Technology, Canada, 1972-73 to 1975-76

Year	Universities	C.A.A.T.s
1972-73	311,657	173,239
1973-74	325,161	194,234
1974-75	339,073	204,355
1975-76	363,188	215,322
1972-76:		
Increase	51,531	42,083
Percentage Increase	16.5	24.3

Sources: Calculated from Statistics Canada, *Enrolment in Community Colleges*, (Ottawa, various years), Catalogue No. 81-222; and Statistics Canada, *Fall Enrolment in Universities*, (Ottawa, various years), Catalogue No. 81-204.

TABLE III
Full-Time Enrolments in Universities and Colleges of Applied Arts and Technology, Ontario, 1969-70 to 1974-75

Year	Universities*	C.A.A.T.s
1969-70	105,235	24,742
1970-71	116,840	30,382
1971-72	126,642	34,354
1972-73	127,957	39,823
1973-74	133,132	51,878
1974-75	142,097	55,038
1969-75		
Increase	36,362	30,296
Percentage Increase	35.0	122.4

*excludes Ryerson Polytechnical Institute

Sources: The data for 1969-70 to 1970-71 is from *Report of the Ministry of Colleges and Universities*, 1971-72, (Toronto, 1972); 1971-72 to 1974-75 is calculated from *Ministry of Colleges and Universities Statistical Summary*, (Toronto, various years).

The push toward job related skills has not been confined to community colleges. A similar trend is apparent in universities. For example, the Ontario *Report of the Commission on Post-Secondary Education* advocated a closer interrelation of the university's teaching and research functions with the requirements of the economic order.[30] This view of the purpose of the university is also prevalent among top political officials at the federal level. According to Donald A. Chant, the vice-president and provost of the University of Toronto:

There are abundant signs in Canada that the dominant image of the university is that of training for jobs. . . . Recently, when meeting with a group of scientists in Ottawa, a senior cabinet minister strongly expressed the opinion that the *only* function of our universities is to produce trained manpower . . . more or less on order. When governments saw the need of additional trained people for the job market, university grants would be increased. When trained personnel were a glut on the market, the financial tap would be turned off. He actually denied the cultural and intellectual values of our universities . . . .[31]

Even prior to this renewed emphasis on pragmatic higher education, universities were scarcely divorced from meeting manpower requirements of industry. Based on a 1968-9 government survey of the university student population, Rick Deaton found that "nearly 44 per cent of all post-secondary school students are trained to meet the needs of industry (broadly defined)."[32] Although we are unaware of any follow-up survey which may update this statistic, there are indications that this process has continued. Significantly, the fastest growing university discipline has been business. Between the late sixties and 1976, the number of undergraduate business majors has more than doubled from 13,000 to 31,000 and the proportion of these students to the total undergraduate population has climbed from 5.8 per cent to 10 per cent. Similarly, during the same period, the full-time graduate enrolment in business master's programmes rose from 1,500 to 3,200 or from 10 per cent to 14 per cent of all master's students.[33]

TABLE IV

Field of Specialization of Community College Graduates, 1972, 1973

Year	Graduates in Field of Specialization as % of Total			
	Technologies & Vocational	Business & Commercial	Applied Arts	University Transfer Programs
1972	42.6	30.3	17.6	9.8
1973	52.0	26.6	15.8	5.6

*excludes P.E.I.

Source: Calculated from Statistics Canada, *Enrolment in Community Colleges*, Ottawa, 1974-75/1975-76), Catalogue No. 81-222.

In short, one aspect of the relation between universities and the capitalist class entails an understanding of the nature of the state and how its functions relate to the interests of the capitalist class. As argued above, the state performs both accumulation and legitimation functions. State expenditures on universities comprise both of these functions. However, Panitch argues that historically the Canadian state has largely promoted the accumulation role at the expense of the legitimation role.[34] This thesis is verified by recent developments within the universities. Acting under the aegis of the fiscal crisis, government policies have been directed at a general curtailment in university spending but not within those programmes designed to serve the labour market. In O'Connor's terms, state expenditures on education have increasingly assumed the functions of social investment; that is, the funds are earmarked toward socializing the costs of training labour power and increasing its productivity, thereby increasing the rate of profit for private capital.

The structural relation between the universities and the political order thus reveals the general domination of the university by the capitalist class. However, besides their dependency on the state for financing, universities are also directly dependent upon funds from corporations and private capitalists, a phenomenon to which we will now turn.

The Universities and Private Capital

Besides the state, another important source of funding for universities is the private sector. Through their corporate and private gifts a degree of control over the university is afforded to the capitalist class. Although it is often maintained that there is no relation between the source of money and domination of the university, the argument is, in fact, rejected by members of the dominant class. For example, the Industrial Foundation on Education, a corporate elite organization, has explicitly postulated a direct relation between university control and the source of funding. In arguing against free higher education and in urging further private support of universities, the Foundation's report stated:

Making education free implies the possibility of state control. It is a cherished tradition that free enterprise in higher education is a corollary of free enterprise in other areas of our society. Control normally follows the provision of the greatest proportion of finances.[35]

In view of our above argument, we would not separate state financing of education from capitalist class control. Nonetheless, this statement of the Industrial Foundation on Education is significant because it suggests that the corporate order perceives its funding of universities as a guarantee of control.

In this section we briefly examine the historical dependency of universities on private capitalists and the influence of these men in shaping the university. We then turn to an examination of the scope and significance of private capital in the contemporary university. It is argued here that because of the nature of the fiscal crisis in the seventies, the domination of the university by the capitalist class far exceeds what might otherwise be deduced from their proportional share in university funding.

Historically, the survival of universities depended on their ability to recruit funds from the private sector. Initially, the University of Toronto held a monopoly on state aid while other universities were forced to raise capital on their own. During this time George Munro Grant, Principal of Queen's, 1877-1902, set forth a policy for these latter schools:

A provincial system offers various advantages, including, in particular, the bringing together of young men of different denominations, and the cultivating of a breadth of view which we are glad to see is now appreciated. If any locality or any body of men considered it necessary to have other colleges, then . . . the necessity must be proved by the sacrifices their friends are willing to make, and the real extent of the necessity by the survival of the fittest.[36]

In this assertion laden with Darwinian assumptions, the "fittest" universities came to be defined as those most able to align themselves with the men of wealth and the corporations.

Thus, McMaster University largely owes its existence to the work and funds of William McMaster who was also founder and first president of the Canadian Bank of Commerce. Similarly, one of Canada's leading merchants and commercial capitalists, James McGill, left a large endowment and his Burnside Estate for the establishment of McGill University. In addition, even University of Toronto as well as the other institutions, when they became secularized and eligible for state funds, relied heavily on donations and grants from the private sector. For example, Toronto's board of governors were among its chief benefactors. Early donations included gifts from Colonel A.E. Gooderham and Sir John Eaton; the Massey family of the Massey-Harris Company left an estate of $1,300,000 to the university; J.W. Flavelle of the Robert Simpson Company donated annual post-graduate fellowships; E.B. Osler, long-time member of the executive committee of the Canadian Pacific Railway and J.L. Englehart, president of Imperial Oil, each gave $10,000 for research in medicine.

These donations and countless others conferred a certain amount of control of the university to members of the capitalist class. Their decisions on where and how much to invest influenced whether or not universities could be founded and whether they could survive, as well as how they were to expand and generally the variety of programmes they could provide. Other gifts more directly shaped the university curriculum to meet the donors' interests. For example, William C. Macdonald, the "tobacco king", supported various agricultural programmes at McGill; at the University of Toronto Colonel A. E. Gooderham, a prominent distiller, provided the equipment for the research department of zymology, the study of fermentation; and various bankers of Toronto along with the executive members of the Toronto Board of Trade organized a fund to support the developing business curriculum at the University of Toronto in the early 1900s.

This historical sketch provides a background for understanding the contemporary university's financial dependency on the corporate order. While undoubtedly the state's role in education has increased over the past century, this has not eliminated the importance of the university's ties to the private sector. In particular, during times of fiscal restraint, universities have been forced to embark upon a number of fund raising schemes. This solicitation of funds has centred on cultivating support from major corporations. As one York University official explained in the midst of a drive to acquire ten million dollars for this institution, only major corporations were to be approached. He said that York's fund drive "will be done by board room visitations. . . . We won't be standing on street corners with tin cans and tambourines."[38] Given the nature of the funding campaigns, it is crucial that universities are capable of summoning fund raisers who have access to board rooms. For example, the University of Toronto's fund drive benefited considerably from the active support of Ted Burton, president of Simpsons Ltd. Burton raised $500,000 and claimed that this was done "pretty easily. I just leaned on somebody and reminded them of what a great institution it is and of a corporation's public duty."[39]

Besides specific fund raising campaigns, another source of private capital input into universities is through various research grants. Table V shows sources of sponsored research income for Canadian universities. Most significantly, although governments contributed the largest share, the only source which has been rising in the last five years is from the private sector.

TABLE V
Percentage of University Sponsored Research Income by Source, Canada, 1971-72 to 1975-76

Source of Income	1971-2	1972-3	1973-4	1974-5	1975-6
Federal Govt.	71.1	68.2	66.4	62.9	62.0
Provincial Govt.	7.9	10.5	13.5	14.0	16.6
Municipal Govt.	0.1	0.2	2.2	0.1	0.1
Total Govt.	79.1	78.9	82.1	77.0	78.7
Gifts, non-govt.	15.7	15.5	15.9	19.9	17.5
Investment Income	1.3	1.3	1.3	1.2	1.1
Misc.	3.9	4.3	0.7	1.9	2.7

Source: Statistics Canada, *University — Financial Statistics*, (Ottawa, Oct. 1977), Catalogue No. 81-212.

While this indicates an element of control by the business community, more direct control is evident from the growing trend toward contract research. The growth of contract research stems from recent developments in government spending on research. Between 1973 and 1975 federal government support of pure research which is mainly carried out in universities has declined as a percentage of all research funding from 8.2 per cent to 7.4 per cent. Instead, federal funds have been diverted to applied research and these have been increasingly allocated to industry.[40] One way to compensate for the declining government grants is to promote contract research. As Allan Frosst, Director of Research Services, McMaster University explains: "We can foster more interaction with industry . . . and seek more industrial and government contract research." In order to accomplish this, however, Frosst points out, "the research must be of interest to [the contracting] industries. You've got to relate your interests to their needs."[41]This is precisely the course many universities have chosen to follow. For example, the University of Saskatchewan is launching the development of a $6 million research park for which the university will donate the land. As Balfour Currie, research adviser to the president, remarked: "We were willing to donate the land for the project because we think it will enhance the interplay between university and industry."[42] Similarly, McMaster University has been emphasizing contract research and in 1975 earned $1.1 million by engaging in mission-oriented research for corporations. Moreover, this money funded between 20 and 30 per cent of the total research in arts, science, and engineering during that year.[43]

In general, gifts and research grants from the private sector are crucial to the effective functioning of the universities. During the period of cutbacks in the seventies, these monies have provided the difference between the mere survival of any particular university and continued growth and claim to scholarly excellence. This has been aptly expressed by McMaster's president, A.N. Bourns, when he pointed out that government grants "are intended to provide only a basic level of support" but " 'to achieve and maintain the excellence of McMaster,' the University has always had to approach corporations, firms, and individuals for additional financial support."[44] Because the universities must at all times seek non-government support, an effort must be made to cultivate an image and to engage in activities which, if not in complete accord with, are at least not hostile to the interests of the private sector. This throws doubt on the question of the existence of an autonomous university and reveals another aspect of the domination of the university by the capitalist class.

CONCLUSION

Although a number of different forces act on the university, we have only been concerned here with analyzing the power of the capitalist class. The position of this class within the university structure consists of both personnel and structural relationships. It is this latter objective relation which is of primary importance for understanding the domination of the university by the capitalist class.

The universities' financial dependence, largely on the state but also on the private sector, underlines the structural relation of these institutions to the capitalist class. While state expenditures have increasingly been directed at socializing the costs of private enterprise, at the same time, the state has had to fulfill legitimation as well as accumulation functions. The Canadian state's historical neglect of the former in favour of the latter has been intensified in the 1970s with the economic and fiscal crises. The impact of this on universities has been that they are increasingly faced with budgetary cuts and financial constraints while at the same time pressure is being applied to strengthen their role in aiding private accumulation by developing curricula and policies more directly relevant to the task of training labour power.

The financial vulnerability of institutions of higher learning has, in turn, augmented the significance of private and corporate gifts and grants. While private sources of funding have historically been important, in the 1970s they have become crucial for capital hungry universities. One trend associated with this has been universities' increasing willingness to solicit the private sector for research grants and to emphasize mission-oriented research. Because such grants imply that university interests must more directly coincide with the needs of private capital, the result has been to more closely align the activities of institutions of higher learning with the interests of the capitalist class.

Universities' dependence on support by the capitalist class provides the key to understanding the significance of domination of boards of governors by members of the corporate elite. While universities require continued assistance of the business community, the capitalist class also requires the aid of universities for profitable accumulation, and their willingness to support universities is in some measure a reflection of the degree to which this function is fulfilled. This reciprocal relation which has developed between the university and the capitalist class is exemplified by Gilbert LaBine's remark. LaBine, a uranium tycoon, acknowledged that his appointment in 1940 to the University of Toronto Board of Governors was one of his most important "prizes".[45] For their financial contributions, LaBine and other members of the capitalist class have been placed in positions of esteem and power within the university structure and have thus been enabled to perform a "gatekeeper's" function over the development of curriculum and policy. In this process, the standards, rules, and ideals of the business community have become the guiding code of the university.

NOTES

1. Wallace Clement, *The Canadian Corporate Elite: An Analysis of Economic Power*, Toronto: McClelland & Stewart, 1975.

2. W. Stewart Wallace, *A History of the University of Toronto, 1827-1927*, Toronto: University of Toronto Press, 1927, pp. 20-1.

3. "The University Act of 1906" reproduced in W.J. Alexander, ed., *The University of Toronto and Its Colleges, 1827-1906*, Toronto: The University Library, 1906, Appendix J.

4. John Barkans and Norene Pupo, "The Boards of Governors and the Power Elite: A Case Study of Eight Canadian Universities", *Sociological Focus*, Summer 1974, Vol. 7, No. 3, pp. 81-98.

5. A member of a governing council was included in the economic elite if he/she, or their present spouse, was listed in either *The Canadian Who's Who, 1970-1972*, or the *Financial Post Directory of Directors*, 1973-1974 and held one or more corporate directorships.

6. Peter C. Newman, *The Canadian Establishment, Volume 1*, Toronto: McClelland & Stewart, 1975, p. 367.

7. See for example Rodney T. Hartnett, "College and University Trustees: Their Backgrounds, Roles and Educational Attitudes", in Elizabeth L. and Michael Useem, eds., *The Education Establishment*, Englewood Cliffs: Prentice-Hall, 1974, pp. 146-62.

8. Peter Bachrach and Morton S. Baratz, "Two Faces of Power", in Willis D. Hawley and Frederick M. Wirt, eds., *The Search for Community Power*, Englewood Cliffs: Prentice-Hall, 1974, pp. 167-77.

9. *Globe and Mail*, Apr. 28, 1937.

10. Industrial Foundation on Education, *The Case for Corporate Giving to Higher Education*, Report No. 1, Toronto: Dec. 15, 1957, Part II, p. 5.

11. *Hamilton Spectator*, Apr. 9, 1975, p. 39.

12. Ralph Miliband, *The State in Capitalist Society*, London: Quartet Books, 1973; and "Poulantzas and the Capitalist State", *New Left Review*, No. 82, Nov. - Dec., 1973.

13. Nicos Poulantzas, *Political Power and Social Classes*, London: New Left Books, 1976; and "The Capitalist State: A Reply to Miliband and Laclau", *New Left Review*, No. 95, Jan.-Feb., 1975.

14. James O'Connor, *The Fiscal Crisis of the State*, New York: St. Martin's Press, 1973.

15. *Ibid.*, p. 6.

16. For an application of O'Connor's and other Marxist theories of the state to Canada, see Leo Panitch, ed., *The Canadian State: Political Economy and Political Power*, Toronto: University of Toronto Press, 1977.

17. For a more detailed discussion of this crisis, also see Paul Baran and Paul

Sweezy, *Monopoly Capital*, New York: Monthly Review Press, 1966.

18. O'Connor, p. 24.

19. *Ibid.*, p. 15.

20. *Ibid.*, p. 40.

21. See Cy Gonick, *Inflation or Depression*, Toronto: James Lorimer & Company, 1975 and Rick Deaton, "The Fiscal Crisis of the State", in D. I. Roussopoulos, ed., *The Political Economy of the State*, Montreal: Black Rose Books, 1973.

22. *The Learning Society —Report of the Commission on Post-Secondary Education in Ontario*, Toronto: Ministry of Government Services, 1972, p. 14.

23. Deaton, p. 38.

24. *Report of the Special Program Review*, Ontario, Nov. 1975, pp. 3-5.

25. Howard Adelman, *The Holiversity: A Perspective on the Wright Report*, Toronto: New Press, 1973, p. 9.

26. Council of Ontario Universities, *New Structure, New Environment: Review, 1972-73 to 1974-75*, Toronto, p. 7.

27. This calculation is based on the figures in *The Learning Society*, p. 156.

28. For a comparison of the operating costs per student of the C.A.A.T.s and universities of Ontario, see *Ibid.*, p. 158. A rationale for the promotion of the C.A.A.T.s and a refutation of the argument that community colleges are promoted because they are less costly to run can be found in *The Learning Society*, p. 230.

29. *Report of the Special Program Review*, p. 129.

30. See *The Learning Society*, especially recommendations 13, 14, and 15, p. 173.

31. *Financial Post*, Jan. 10, 1976, p. 6.

32. Deaton, p. 25.

33. *Careers and the Job Market: A Special Report*, published by the *Financial Post*, Fall 1977, p. 35.

34. See Leo Panitch, "The Role and Nature of the Canadian State", in Panitch, ed., *The Canadian State*, pp. 18-22.

35. Industrial Foundation on Education, *The Case For Increasing Student Aid*, Report No. 2, Toronto: Jan. 1, 1958, p. 7.

36. Principal Grant, "Three Brief Addresses By Principal Grant on the Duty of the Legislature to the Colleges of the Province", Public Archives of Ontario, Pamphlet n.d.T., No. 5, p. 6.

37. Wallace, pp. 299-301.

38. *Financial Post*, Sept. 14, 1974, p. 11.

39. *Toronto Star*, Oct. 9, 1976, p. 7.

40. *Contact*, McMaster University, Vol. 7, No. 9, Oct. 30, 1975, p. 1.

41. *Ibid.*, p. 2.

42. *Financial Post*, Sept. 4, 1976, p. 4.

43. *Ibid.*, p. 4.

44. *Contact*, McMaster University, Vol. 7, No. 29, Apr. 1, 1976, p. 2.

45. Peter C. Newman, *Flame of Power*, Toronto: McClelland & Stewart, 1959, p. 152.

The Political Economy of the American Postwar Military-University Complex: The "Goose Step" Revisited

KEN LUCKHARDT

THE PROBLEM DEFINED

...the American college has not been organized on the principles of American government, but on those of American business; the college is not a state but a factory.[1]

Thus concluded Upton Sinclair in the final pages of his critical analysis of American colleges in the 1920s. Sinclair's book, *The Goose Step,* had resulted from a personal coast-to-coast tour of American colleges, a voyage which allowed him to witness first-hand the class nature of higher education in the country. Sinclair's chapter titles reflect upon the fact that the Robber Barons of the late nineteenth century, the ascendant industrial capitalist class, had fixed a heavy hand on the knowledge industry: the university of "the House of Morgan" (Columbia), "the Black Hand" (California), "the Lumber Trust" (Oregon), the "Anaconda" (Montana), "the Smelter Trust" (Colorado), "Wheat" (North Dakota), "the Ore Trust" (Minnesota), "Standard Oil" (Chicago), "Automobiles" (Michigan), and "the Steel Trust" (Pittsburgh and Pennsylvania).

The emergent pattern is one of American higher education controlled in its substance and directed in its orientation by a class of trustees and presidents who in their business careers have been the industrial and finance capitalists associated with the expansion of American capitalism across the continent. The internal structure of the institution, the political co-optation of faculty members to act in the interests of this same class, purges of those who care to challenge these class interests, and the socialization of the undergraduate masses to attach themselves practically and ideologically to this class structure — these are the basic elements and consequences of the class nature of American higher education.

For the working class children, Sinclair says,

In college after college we have seen the brains of the working class stolen away from them; we have seen young men and women who came from the working class, and who should fight for their class and save it, being seduced by the dress-suit bribe, the flummeries and snobberies of academic life, and becoming traitors to their class,

90

betrayers and even murderers of their class.[2]

In sum, Sinclair's journalistic description of the class structure of American universities in the early decades of the century should make us aware of the essential components of factory production in higher education. While Fordism (time and motion studies) was giving capital greater supervisory control over labour in the assembly line, the "Carnegie unit" — forerunner of the modern bourgeois grading system — assured the standardization and control of "quality" of the product of university — the graduate.

Sinclair's analysis raises the main questions that form the basis of this investigation into the post-war American Military-University Complex. What is the structural relation between the capitalist system of production and institutions of higher education? Can the socio-economic class relations in higher education — or education in general — be freer or more progressive than the capital-labour relation that defines the mode of production? If the form of university production resembles the form of factory/commodity production, can the content, and, more importantly, the product of higher education, be any more challenging to class domination than the content and product of factory production?

The central thesis of this article is that institutions of higher education are crucial to the reproduction of the capitalist social formation. The university in this system is that institution that (i) provides the skilled labour — technological, managerial, professional, and ideological — to the capitalist class which in turn (ii) employs that skilled labour in the process of *production and the creation of commodities that yield profit to the corporate sector*. As we shall see below, universities themselves divide up this general task by occupational and geographical specialization. It is in this sense that Upton Sinclair's depiction of universities as factories can already be appreciated. The rise of corporate industrial capitalism in the latter third of the nineteenth century in American society demonstrates very clearly the crucial relation between industrial capitalism and "meritocratic" universities; the latter were set in motion by the imperatives of capital accumulation and the skilled labour and products of that labour that universities were so organized to provide.

Yet universities are more than factories, or, more correctly, they are a special type of factory. The creation of skilled labour necessary to capitalist production requires, in contradictory fashion, an abstinence from production for a certain amount of time spent as students. Following Marx, the value of labour-power, as with the value of all commodities, is always determined by the amount of socially necessary labour to produce that labour-power. Hence, in capitalist society, the market exchange is obliged to recognize the amount of labour time lost to immediate production through the training of skilled labour for subsequent production. This is simply to say, in theory if not always in practice, the university graduate commands a greater exchange-value than the worker who lacks this credential, i.e., this abstinence from productive labour-time. Advanced degrees are then merely multiples of this original abstinence.

Commodities, however, command exchange-value only when they have a socially necessary use-value, utility. On this point the university production system distinguishes itself as a special type of factory in capitalist society. The vast majority of the commodities produced — graduates — enter the sphere of capitalist production distinguished not only by the skills they possess, but also in the way they subjectively view the capitalist world. From the standpoint of the capitalist class, this necessary abstinence from production is a minimal price to pay when compared with the ideological skilled labour that pours into corporate production four years later. University faculties vary in their open endorsement of capitalist relations of production: commerce/business administration faculties clearly accept those relations and agree to produce skilled labour to work within them; physical science faculties often pretend a sociological innocence and immunity from such mundane realities; and social science faculties occasionally criticize those relations albeit in a liberal reformist manner, and thus usually restrict their attention to "social problems" that emerge within capitalism.

The result on both the practical and ideological planes is predictable: few academics and hence few students ever talk, write, or learn about exploitation, class conflict, imperialism, or even alienation. The graduate, with diploma and skill in hand, marches hopefully to the corporate hiring hall, to the state's bureaucracy, or remains to eventually find a niche in the university factory itself. And, as Sinclair's quote testifies, the more recruits from the working class the better as class warfare becomes class attrition and the illusion of social mobility. The university factory, like all capitalist factories, prepares for the next production cycle, ever attuned to the "needs" of "society".[3]

STATE MONOPOLY CAPITALISM, IMPERIALIST WAR, AND THE UNIVERSITY

Sinclair, as we have seen, looked at the class nature of American universities within the context of American society of the early 1900s. Since that time, and upon that historical base, the U.S. economy has become fully monopoly capitalist, imperialist, and, in the post-1945 era, heavily committed to a permanent war economy. The exploitative relations of capitalist production have been greatly internationalized through the solidification of the American empire in the past three decades. Nevertheless, the capitalist world is gradually but decisively shrinking as national liberation movements allow colonized peoples to regain control of their own destiny (in Angola, Mozambique, Vietnam, etc.).

As the dominant imperialist power in the post-war era, the American corporate ruling class is required by the very nature of its class interests and class actions to be able to call upon a new type of expertise and assistance. The university, as one of the major institutions responsible for the production of this expertise and assistance, is now geared toward a closer harmony with the capitalist class in servicing the empire at home and especially abroad.

The basis of power in monopoly capitalism still derives from the ability of the capitalist class to appropriate profit and other surplus-value created by human labour-power. Yet, the *principal* profit maximizers and capital ac-cumulators today are the trans-national corporations.[4] Creation of surplus-value remains dependent on an assured access to strategic resources, raw materials,[5] and a mass of labour-power. However, the global distribution of these resources means that the capitalist class must now extract surplus-value in a geo-political context that can never be taken for granted. Consequently, monopoly capitalism is obliged to strike a new working relation with the state.

The state in any social system accepts and recognizes one set of relations above all other — the economic processes that establish the method of production, distribution and consumption. Despite the ideological claim of serving the vested interests of all segments of the society under its jurisdic-tion, the capitalist state recognizes the capital-labour relation as the *modus vivendi* through which all of society's important business must pass. To put it differently, the state need not be characterized as an institutional pawn of the ruling capitalist class; conspiracy theories are unnecessary to demonstrate that it is in the interests of the state to promote the interests of that ruling class. In practice, the primary role of the state in capitalism is to create conditions conducive to the accumulation of surplus-value. State policies range broadly from tax incentives and guaranteed access to natural resources on the domes-tic front, to loans, foreign aid, and military protection on the international scene. History shows quite clearly that the capitalist state defines the "free world" as that area of the globe "free" for the realization of capital invest-ment and accumulation.

An uncritical analysis of the state (often intentional in bourgeois social science) impedes investigation of the role of universities within monopoly capitalist society. Liberal thinking has created two inaccurate theories of the state in capitalist society. The state is regarded in one view as doing battle with the private sector dominated by the monopoly corporation; the alternate conception regards the state as a neutral or disinterested body representing the interests of no particular class, or, what amounts to the same thing, all classes within its jurisdiction. Uncritical theory, intentionally or not, fails to see that the state's unqualified acceptance of the dominant relations of production engenders the very conflicts which it must then adjudicate with an appearance of neutrality.

In American society, the service of the state in the enhancement of capital accumulation is scarcely concealed. While this service has not been restricted to the post-war era,[6] the last three decades have witnessed the extension of this process to new heights and broader parameters. Miliband is correct, when he argues,

... the state is by far the largest customer of the 'private sector'; and some major industries could not survive in the private sector without the state's custom and without the credits, subsidies and benefactions which it dispenses.[7]

The specific manifestation of this process in post-war American society is the permanent war economy.[8] Cold war ideology and rhetoric, stemming from the Truman Doctrine of 1947, reflected a carefully orchestrated program designed to create the illusion of imminent attack from "hostile" powers — first the Soviet Union, next China, and eventually any nation or people who dared to assert their self-determination and independence from imperialism. Alienated American people responded with characteristic fervour as concrete air-raid shelters soon dotted the American landscape, and the corporations performed their patriotic duty in protecting the "national interest" by stepping up military production and clearly establishing themselves as the "merchants of death".

Yet beneath this self-imposed and calculated hysteria, assisted by the machinations of careerist witch-hunters like Nixon and McCarthy, lies a basic economic reality: the U.S. economy could not maintain current levels of productivity — which is to say desired profit rates — without maintaining the war economy that had developed during the war years. Despite the public works programs of the 1930s, the only solution to unemployment and depression had been militarism and its attendant productive base. To ensure future domestic stability and to guarantee the process of capital accumulation, the corporate leaders responded in class chorus with harmonious appeals for expanded military production. The cold war was in reality an economic war and the contestants in battle were no longer primarily nation-states but rather capital and labour. Capitalists were successful in propagandizing the working class to identify their interests with national interests, and the effect was a permanent war economy at home and an unparalleled imperialist thrust abroad.

By the end of the 1950s, if not before, the collusion of state and monopoly capital in this new form became obvious. Corporation after corporation, from those associated in the consumer's mind with breakfast cereal to electric light bulbs, turned to military production. American society became an "armed society" not through the ascendancy or power of a military elite as C. Wright Mills would lead one to believe,[9] but instead through the civilian corporate sector that owned the means of production and needed the war economy more than the generals. The state and its functioning apparatus, also

largely composed of corporatists, responded with assistance to the imperatives clearly enunciated by the monopoly corporations. This exemplifies what
Miliband terms the " . . . vast range of social services for which the state in
these (monopoly capitalist) societies has come to assume direct or indirect
responsibility."[10]

Miliband's statement must, however, be qualified to avoid one possible
misunderstanding. These state-initiated "social services" are social only in
the sense that production itself is ultimately social; the vast array of benefits
accrue to the capitalist class in a decidedly unequal manner. A summary
listing of these services illustrates the specific class interests that are served:
(1) military agreements and arms sales to foreign nations of pro-capitalist
forces within these nations; (2) subsidization of military research and development, thus reducing the necessary costs of production of military industries; (3) foreign aid programs that assist private American capital in the
penetration of foreign economies; and, most relevant for the topic here, (4)
the subsidization of university research and development (R and D) and a
corresponding production of a skilled, technical labour force capable of
contributing to the future expansion of capitalist accumulation.

The commonality of class interests between the state and private sector is
far more than theoretical. Many scholars have demonstrated the movement of
individuals between the state system (government, administrative bureaucracy, military, judiciary) and the world of private wealth. In the six decades
from 1890 to 1950, over 60 per cent of the U.S. cabinet personnel were from
business corporations and this form of corporate penetration into key governmental decision-making positions seems to have increased in the past two
and one-half decades. This has led to greater state involvement in "solving"
capitalist crises. When business people move into public service, they not
only influence the nature of subsequent state intervention in the private sector
but they do so in a manner consistent with their business-and-profit-oriented
ideology. Again, to quote Miliband:

What the evidence conclusively suggests is that in terms of social origin, education
and class situation the men who have manned *all* command positions in the state
system have largely, and in many cases overwhelmingly, been drawn from the world
of business and property, or from the professional middle classes. . . . In an epoch
when so much is made of democracy, equality, social mobility, classlessness, and the
rest, it has remained a basic fact of life in advanced capitalist countries that the vast
majority of men and women in these countries has been governed, represented,
administered, judged, and commanded in war by people drawn from other, economi-
cally and socially superior and relatively distant classes.[11]

Our concern to this point has been the interrelation of superstructure and
base, of university and economy, to illustrate how production in the former
can advance the creation of surplus-value in the latter. We can now turn our
attention directly to university production in state monopoly capitalism.

UNIVERSITIES AND PRODUCTION

Capital's ability to extract surplus-value from productive labour over time is dependent upon continuous advances in the means of production. Through increases in the productiveness of labour — a greater amount of commodities produced in a given period of time — capital is simultaneously capable of reducing the value of labour power and increasing the proportion of labour-time in the working day that is extracted without compensation to the working class. In contemporary monopoly capitalism, these advances in the means of production are heavily dependent on developments in science and their application in technology. Torn from their social and political context, these advances are ideologically conceived as the measure of "progress". However, these advances should be seen as part of the mode of production itself because they become new methods of exploitation. That is, breakthroughs in science and technology, the form they take, and the use-value (utility) inherent in them can only be understood within the class relations of capitalist production.

Monopoly capital requires, in addition to transformations of the means of production, a highly skilled, technical labour force to develop, operate, and supervise the institutionalization of these transformations. Universities facilitate both requirements.

The "knowledge industry" becomes virtually synonymous with the "innovation industry" as universities effect the means of production (or means of destruction in the case of military research) through (i) research and development and (ii) the development of techniques of social control that are employed in the maintenance of the structural status quo at home and abroad. The university becomes in state monopoly capitalism a *de facto* business corporation, an essential component in the production and reproduction of the capitalist political economy. Knowledge and the manner in which it is employed are to be regarded as particular forms of skilled labour-power that reinforce the class structure and its inherent inequalities.

In postwar American society, a certain number of "elite" universities have essentially monopolized the dual functions outlined above. This is realized through an institutional collaboration of the state apparatus (especially the military, which accounts for the largest proportion of the state budget), the business sector (represented by the corporation and the private foundation), and the university. Collaboration refers in this context to the interrelations among these three institutional spheres and the interests shared in common by those who serve in a dominant decision-making capacity in their respective institutions. This model does not necessitate actual movement of individuals between these institutional spheres, but, on the other hand, this inter-institutional mobility is indeed an important feature in daily practice. In the final analysis, however, a general commitment to the maintenance of state monopoly capitalism is a sufficient condition for the functioning of this triple arrangement.

The state-corporation-university triumvirate expresses itself through three interrelated processes:

(1) Universities are financially-dependent production units that must generate their working capital from either the public sector (state) or the private sector (the propertied class). Insofar as power is derived from the accumulation of capital, and insofar as those who invest such capital do so in order to advance their own interests, we begin by analyzing the source and extent of *investment inputs* that go from the state and private foundations to universities. These investments are concentrated in a small proportion of American universities; this mirrors the concentration of capital that characterizes the economic sphere *per se*. Just as not all capitalist firms are monopolistic, so too we should not expect that all universities are essential components of the "Military-Industrial-University" complex.

(2) Secondly, capital investment carries with it demands upon the nature of production — the resultant use-values that all capitalist commodities share in common. Therefore, we want to examine the respective uses of the commodities, both material and ideological, that are associated with state and foundation investments in universities. The commodities produced by skilled academic labour will be referred to as *production outputs*.

(3) Finally, the collaboration of these three institutional spheres is evidenced by the interlocking directorates, e.g. the inter-institutional mobility of personnel. Academics and university administrators move from the university to the business, foundation, and state sectors; business directors dominate the key state bodies and are the largest force in university boards of trustees; similarly, former state decision-makers make their way to university and corporate boards. The major concern here is with the connections that tie the state and foundations to the university positions of power. These *interlocking directorates* are of crucial importance to a critical understanding of the structural relation between state, business and university.

These three processes identify the university's two-fold nature as a passive institution dependent upon outside investment and, simultaneously, a creative force (production outputs, interlocking directorates) in the service of monopoly capitalism. The question is not, as liberal theory would have it, whether or not universities are autonomous institutions, but rather how they (and the personnel who labour within them) employ what autonomy they have. Academic autonomy, commonly disguised as "academic freedom", is always practiced within a determinant political economy. To quote Miliband again,

... it is ... often the case that both university authorities and teachers endorse the (given) context, are part of it, and exercise their autonomy in ways which are congruent with that context, not because they are compelled to do so but because they themselves are moved by conformist modes of thought ... *the control over the "means of mental production" has been of great importance in legitimating capitalist rule.* (emphasis added)[12]

The minority of radical academics (students and professors) in American universities in no way denies the fact that the overwhelming majority of academics share a world view conducive to the maintenance of capitalist society. The latter may, and do, apply their skilled labour to the resolution of problems that emerge within the capitalist order, yet this problem-orientation is to be distinguished from a radical critique of the mode of production itself and the contradictions generated by it. Somewhat paradoxically, we find that the academic social stratum that constitutes the skilled labour required by monopoly capital expresses its passivity in its very creativity. It is these academics and their practice that must be examined in postwar American society.

THE STATE (MILITARY)-UNIVERSITY NETWORK[13]

In this day of scientific expertise, each administrator, admiral and general requires his own contingent of unleashed intellectuals who will perform on command like trained monkeys, writing persuasive analyses in highly sophisticated and quantitative language to support the whims, hunches, value judgements, and opportunism of agency officials, converting scientist and engineer into a new kind of lawyer of technology. ... In spite of bland claims that the new braintrusters demonstrate a high degree of pluralism, independence and objectivity, it is clear that they have to a considerable extent failed to protect public interests and public control, serving instead powerful coalitions of special interests on whose behalf they often invade the policy-making realms of the State.[14]

The historical origins of the contemporary state-university network can be traced to the large military research programs initiated on certain college campuses in the early 1940s. Conceived in a period of inter-capitalist conflict, the fact that these and subsequent projects had little or nothing to do with basic research seems to have been of minimal importance to a scientific community which had for a long time been desirous of Federal research subsidies. It goes without saying that not all Federal research projects are of a military or quasi-military nature; yet it would be mistaken to pretend that the genesis of the state-university network did not emerge with the permanent war economy of the 1940s. In the past three decades, this relation has been consistently characterized by "defense"-related concerns.

Four universities in particular — California, Chicago, Johns Hopkins, and MIT — were virtually transformed into wartime arsenals between 1939 and 1945. Through massive R and D subsidies, the government became a specialized customer for the production output of the scientists' labour, or, as Sidney Lens states: "As electronics and the atom bomb became instruments of war, the university was co-opted to supply brain power".[15] The remainder of this section will outline the post-war development of these state-university ties with regard to the three processes outlined in the prior section.

Investment Inputs

By 1967, Federal obligations to universities and colleges were rapidly increasing, more than doubling the amount allocated only four years earlier. Moreover, seven of every ten dollars expended went into Research and Development and R and D plant, the largest proportion of this coming from the military agencies of the state — e.g. the Department of Defence (D of D), the Atomic Energy Commission (AEC) and the National Aeronautics and Space Administration (NASA). In the same year, the military sector accounted for 15 per cent of total federal expenditures to universities and colleges ($505 million) and over 90 per cent of this amount was allocated for R and D.

Universities also receive state-military subsidization for what are known as Federally Funded R and D Centers (FFRDCs) which they have administered since World War II. Of the $800.8 million allocated to thirty-three FFRDCs in 1967, $768.8 million, or 96 per cent, came from military agencies. These centers are essentially mission-oriented research enclaves " . . . established at or near universities where they could draw upon the available scientific and technical manpower".[16]

State allocations to universities are highly concentrated geographically and by institutions. The following conclusions can be made regarding geographical distribution: four regions (New England, Middle Atlantic, East North Central, and Pacific) account for 68 per cent of total Federal R and D obligations; each of the largest state recipients (California, New York, Massachusetts, Illinois, and Pennsylvania) are located in these five regions; these five states account for 47.1 per cent of the total Federal R and D expenditures and 56 per cent of total military R and D expenditures; the proportion of military R and D varies from 28.8 per cent (Pennsylvania) to 64.5 per cent (Massachusetts). These five states house the "elite" university-factories in American society, accounting for over 34 per cent of all degrees awarded and over 41 per cent of Ph.D.s awarded in science and engineering; in these five states are located fourteen of the thirty-three FFRDCs.

By institution, approximately five per cent of the 2,056 universities and colleges receiving Federal support obtained 68.8 per cent of total funds. Furthermore, one hundred top recipients received 88 per cent of all monies earmarked for R and D, and ninety-six of these institutions awarded 90 per cent of all Ph.D.s in science and engineering (1965-66). To be even more specific, 51.3 per cent of Federal R and D obligations going to the ten largest recipients[17] came from the military. The military proportion of these funds by school varied from Wisconsin's 22 per cent to MIT's over 87.

It comes as no surprise to discover that the top twenty-five recipients are all involved in the administration of FFRDCs, either singly or as part of university consortia. In 1967 the six largest FFRDCs — the Jet Propulsion Laboratory (Cal Tech), Lawrence Radiation Laboratory (U of California), Los Alamos Scientific Laboratory (U of California), Argonne National Laboratory (U of Chicago and consortium of twenty-six schools), Lincoln Laboratory (MIT) and Brookhaven National Laboratory (consortium of nine schools) — received over 80 per cent of Federal R and D money and the military agencies accounted for this entire amount ($727 million).

Finally, in the 1960s, smaller universities and colleges began to express opposition to this concentration of R and D funding to the elite institutions. It was not a protest over the militarization of universities, but rather, a desire to be *a part* of that process. Consequently, the D of D created Project Themis in 1967 in an attempt to incorporate these smaller institutions in the agency's overall objectives.[18]

Having outlined the concentration of state and especially military investment inputs into universities and their FFRDCs, we must now consider the exact nature of the production being purchased. What services does the state purchase from the academic community?

Production Outputs

Research and Development is most closely associated with the physical sciences, yet it is no less important to consider the role that social scientists play in devising techniques of managing the American empire both militarily and politically. It may be helpful to think of the former as ''hardware'' research and the latter as ''software'' research. However, the distinction is often blurred in many of these mission-oriented projects. Again, only an overview can be presented here.

By far the most ominous, chemical and biological warfare (CBW) research, also became the most pervasive on college campuses in the 1960s as the U.S. ruling class carried out its genocidal war in Southeast Asia. Campus after campus was discovered to be directly complicit in CBW research and the deployment of CBW agents in Vietnam. Beginning with the University of Pennsylvania's Institute for Cooperative Research (ICR), where Air Force-sponsored projects Summit and Spicerack were directly involved in defoliation and counter-insurgency operations, the list of universities included Tulane, Oklahoma, Cornell, Berkeley, Illinois, Stanford Research Institute (SRI), Johns Hopkins, and Missouri. As early as 1964, over fifty campuses were receiving $36.3 million for CBW research; over half of these universities were among the top thirty Federal R and D recipients. Robin Clark concludes:

Today the United States has clearly found one way of circumventing the problem of not being able to attract research workers to chemical and biological warfare centres. It simply places contracts with scientists working at universities and colleges. This is the main reason why so many U.S. educational establishments are now engaged in chemical and biological warfare research.[19]

There were other types of "defense" laboratories that served the interests of the American ruling class. The thinktank style of research was perhaps best represented by the Institute for Defense Analysis (IDA), originally created as a non-profit organization by MIT, Stanford, Tulane, Case Institute, and Cal Tech in 1955-56. When student protests in 1968 led to a reorganization of IDA, it was revealed that seven additional universities had become involved. IDA paid academics healthy consulting fees to work on such projects as the weapons-coordinating program of the D of D's Advanced Research Projects Agency, and, with the emergence of non-conventional warfare priorities of the 60s, to work on projects such as "Chemical Control of Vegetation in Relation to Military Needs", "Night Vision for Counterinsurgents", "Behavioral Science Relevant to Military Operations: Government-Funded External Research Relevant to Persuasion and Motivation", and "Helicopter Aural Detection in Tactical Situations". Although Southeast Asia was the focal point of such research, Brazil, India, and Bolivia were also given special attention.

The IDA illustrates the synthesis of physical and social science in imperialist research. In 1958, while young American males were learning their military discipline in boy scout summer camps, forty academics — known as Jason Scholars — ventured to IDA's "summer camp" to study weapons systems, foreign policy, and problems of national defense. The Jason Scholars Program also made the transition to counter-insurgency work in the 1960s — e.g. Project Agile, which was designed to develop "techniques for detecting and combatting insurgents in remote-area conflicts". Similar projects yielded a total of $12.3 million in D of D contracts to the IDA by 1969.

The IDA transition from "hardware" to "software" research is indicative of the changing interests of state military agencies over the past two decades. Like colonial social science before,[20] imperialist social science now turns to gathering data on human populations abroad that can be of service to ruling classes at home. Social scientists often dependent upon these tainted funds, have been required to compromise further their independence and objectivity in the process. In American society, this "defense" compromise began with the Office of Strategic Services (OSS — forerunner of the CIA) during World War II, when the former looked to universities for area specialists to assist in intelligence operations. By 1967, the D of D Director of Defense, Research, and Engineering openly admitted sponsorship of seventy-six social science studies. One year earlier, a Department of State official commented on the strategic importance of academics to the Department's activities:

The colleges and universities provide us with a rich body of information about many subjects, countries, and people through special research studies prepared for many clients and purposes. For example, the U.S. government is spending $30 million this year on foreign affairs studies in American universities. Here in the Department (of State), in our office of External Research, we have on file information on more than 5,000 foreign affairs studies now underway in American universities. Our foreign affairs documentation center lends out to State Department officers and to offices of other agencies 400 unpublished academic papers each month. The Department receives each month over 200 new academic papers.[21]

Space limitations preclude an exhaustive inventory of the physical-social science research carried out under the control or guidance of American "cold warriors", but a few key organizations deserve at least passing mention. The Stanford Research Institute (SRI) stands out for its vested-interest research on counter-insurgency (COIN) and the development of appropriate weapons, surveillance, and reconnaissance systems. In turn, these projects were then handed over to corporations located in the nearby Stanford Industrial Park, a complex of spinoff firms established and/or supported by Stanford and SRI personnel. SRI has been involved in everything from technical questions of how to effectively disperse CBW agents to performing economic consultant work for the anti-communist government in Indonesia. SRI's most famous pundit was Eugene Staley who, in the minds of many, is largely responsible for the formulation of the "strategic hamlet" program utilized by American military forces in Vietnam. In over twenty years, the SRI received an estimated 50 per cent of its operating income from military agencies, and in 1969 alone the D of D contributed a total of $24.8 million. It should be kept in mind that Stanford University has also always been one of the top recipients of military funding to universities.

The importance of social science research to U.S. imperialist objectives led the Pentagon in 1968 to allocate $27 million to foreign policy-oriented research and approximately $40 million for research in foreign countries. George Washington University's Human Resources Research Office (HumRRO) and American University's Centre for Research in Social Science (CRESS) were key components in this research. HumRRO became a non-profit organization in 1969 following student protests against its Army contracts. Since that time HumRRO activities have been openly geared to the improvement of training soldiers via ROTC programs on college campuses, research on "man/weapons systems", and the training of U.S. military personnel to advise foreign military forces. In the words of James Ridgeway:

'HumRRO's mission is to discover, develop, and apply human factors and social science principles and techniques to improve Army training and operational performance' says a blurb for the (HumRRO) office. The research includes studies on the effects of music on Communists, a booklet on shooting entitled 'How Fast Can You Hit Him?' and a work on urinary responses to stress . . . . HumRRO has developed a short automated course in Vietnamese called MALT, works on counterinsurgency, provides hints for Army missions setting out from the Canal Zone to proselytize among the Latins. (And) it published a booklet called 'Optimum Kill Power of Man'.[22]

CRESS, originally known as Special Operations Research Office (SORO), is best remembered for its abortive Project Camelot, an estimated $6 million project which would employ social scientists to discover the causal factors leading to insurgency activities in Latin America. Under the polite bourgeois rubric of "social change", academics were clearly laying the basis of imperialist "social control" and the suppression of anti-imperialist movements. After Camelot in 1966, and the name change from SORO to CRESS, the latter was engaged in the collection, analysis, and distribution of social science studies related to counterinsurgency operations in the Third World. CRESS involvement in Vietnam focussed primarily on psychological and propaganda techniques associated with rural "pacification". On the domestic front, a 1966 research document suggested that police infiltrate "subversive" groups with intelligence agents, a practice that became quite common on American campuses in the late 1960s.

These are only a few of the examples from the physical and social sciences that demonstrate the type of services rendered by academics to American military and foreign policy programs. Having defined itself as the policeman of the "free world", that is, the part of the world where U.S. capital can "freely" and safely invest, American state monopoly capitalism demands up-to-date knowledge of peoples and cultures that fall within that orbit. The social scientist's complicity is a logical historical development out of the physical scientist's contribution to the era of conventional warfare. In the process, the state and especially the military agencies have found on university campuses a group of academic mercenaries whose production is well worth the original investments.

Interlocking Directorates

Overlapping memberships in powerful decision-making bodies of the state and the universities facilitate the process outlined above. W.F. Raborn, former CIA director, speaks of one strategic connection:

... in actual number we (the CIA) could easily staff the faculty of a university with our experts. In a way, we do. Many of those who leave us join the faculties of universities and colleges. Some of our personnel take leave of absence to teach and renew their contacts in the academic world. I suppose this is only fair; our energetic recruiting effort not only looks for the best young graduates we can find, but also picks up a few professors from time to time.[23]

This and other interlocking connections again have their roots in the 1940s and 1950s when four Scientific Advisory Panels (the Defense Science Board, the Army Scientific Advisory Board, the Naval Research Advisory Committee, and the Air Force Scientific Advisory Board) were established to create the infrastructure of the university-military network. Below these senior boards are an estimated one hundred advisory committees associated with various governmental agencies, all under the supervision of the President's Science

Advisor. According to a Stanford Research Institute report, university scientists make up the majority of members of these advisory boards.

A careful examination of the four senior boards in 1970 reveals that almost one-half of the total membership comes from the university community, or sixty individuals representing twenty-three universities (or their FFRDCs) and two university consortia. All but two of these twenty-three universities are among the top one hundred recipients of Federal R and D funds, and nine are among the top ten. These nine universities account for over 50 per cent of the university members of the four senior boards.

The President's Scientific Advisory Committee (PSAC) also reflects these trends. All but one of the seven Presidential advisors since 1950 worked either at the Los Alamos Scientific Laboratory (U of California) or the MIT Radiation Laboratory during World War II. In the mid-60s, twenty-nine of forty-one PSAC members had received graduate training at seven elite universities (California, Cal Tech, Chicago, Columbia, Harvard, MIT, and Princeton). In 1970, research indicates that 70 per cent of PSAC members are from eleven universities and one university consortium. All eleven schools are among the top fifty recipients of Federal R and D grants; four universities (Stanford, Columbia, California, and Harvard) are among the top ten. Similar degrees of concentration of universities and their representatives (mostly physicists) made up the IDA's Jason Scholars Program referred to above. Also, HumRRO, having been divorced officially from George Washington University following student protests, had a Board of Trustees that clearly reflected the full complement of the university-military research network: academics, a retired military officer, a business representative from one of the largest defense contractors, and a trio of lawyers.

Finally, the Department of State (D of S) cannot be overlooked for the role it plays in descending on academic conferences for the purpose of gathering and distributing foreign policy information. The D of S also operates the Foreign Area Research Coordination program through which academics are required to register prospective foreign research projects. In 1967, following briefing sessions by government spokesmen W.W. Rostow and M. Bundy to the American Political Science Association meetings two years earlier, it was revealed that two APSA officers were jointly serving with the CIA-funded research organization, Operations and Policy Research Inc. Subsequent investigation disclosed that the Asia Foundation, a CIA front, had been a second financial contributor to APSA.

In conclusion, all three processes — investment, production, and interlocking directorates — taken together point to the historical origins and subsequent expansion of this institutional collusion. Universities have provided the state with technical-intellectual resources in the form of skilled, mental labour and the products of this labour which in turn have been actively employed in the maintenance of the American corporate empire. One of the dominant institutions in this network, SRI, summarizes the role of the university, as follows:

The university is a *major performer of defense R and D*; *a supplier of advisors and consultants* to defense R and D agencies; *a producer of the technical professional workforce* that is the *prime production factor* in the many government, non-profit, industrial, and academic laboratories that produce R and D; and a *provider of continuing, updating education* to the defense R and D workforce.[24] (emphasis added)

THE FOUNDATION-UNIVERSITY NETWORK

They (the foundations) are no longer family trusts, but class institutions; they are conscious not merely of parochial economic interests but of the necessity of preserving a total social system, international in scope, on which their wealth, power, prestige — in a word, their whole way of life — depends.[25] . . .the 'seed money' they provide for important intellectual and cultural projects helps to shape the framework of American society to a great extent. . . . By encouraging some projects and discouraging others, the foundations create implicit values and set the limits within which cultural and intellectual quests are undertaken.[26]

This section focusses on the foundation, the most powerful institution in the private sector next to monopoly business itself. Under the ambiguous heading "international affairs", the corporate foundation's influence in directing university research is less direct and more subtle than the state's but in its "philanthropic" subtlety lies its power and efficiency. In many cases, the finances provided by the state for "hardware" research are complemented by foundation resources attached to mission-oriented foreign policy research.

First, it is necessary to debunk the popular myth that foundations are philanthropic or altruistic institutions created to return to society in general what the private sector has appropriated specifically — i.e. surplus-value. Foundations were, at the outset, responses to the anti-trust legislation that "threatened" to curb monopolistic control and regain a portion of the family fortunes of the 19th century Robber Barons of American industry. In reality, foundations should be recognized in their two-fold nature: they serve as tax-exempt depositories of accumulated wealth and, simultaneously, they further the process of capital accumulation through their granting priorities. The Carnegie, Duke, and Ford Foundations, while amassing fortunes from the exploitation of different segments of the working class, share the essential features of the Rockefeller Foundation:

(It) was built as a secure repository designed to insulate a great fortune from the legal and political assaults that plague overtly commercial institutions. It was a disguised tax-free holding company . . . . Forced to dispense huge resources to keep its status, it salvaged something from the situation by understanding that it had a unique opportunity for private interest to operate on the cultural, political, and social life of the society.[27]

Over the decades, these foundations have understandably concentrated their energies and resources in fashioning universities and educational institutions into institutions that reinforce the status quo. Foundation "venture capital" has altered the structure and priorities of American higher education in many ways: introduction of the Carnegie Unit standardized university enrollment and curricula; the Rockefeller money created the University of Chicago; and the latter strengthened academic social science through the creation of the Social Science Research Council (SSRC) in 1923. Foundation funds have had the tendency, once accepted by the recipient institutions, to create a "lead system" in higher education in that pressures toward conformity have a trickle-down effect among all universities and colleges. Harold Laski, writing in the 1930s, speaks to this point:

And, observe, there is not a single point here in which there is the slightest control from, or interference by, the foundation itself. It is merely the fact that a fund is within reach which permeates everything and alters everything. The college develops along the lines the foundation approves. The dependence is merely implicit, but it is in fact quite final. . . . where the real control lies no one who has watched the operation in process can possibly doubt.[28]

In retrospect, foundations in the pre-World War II era played a crucial role in integrating educational institutions with the industrial capitalist mode of production. This helped to create the hierarchical nature of the university system that replicates the more fundamental hierarchy of corporations in the economic sphere. As Horowitz puts it:

The carrot is always more efficacious and gentlemanly than the stick. As education became more and more bound up with the success of the industrial system, therefore, the nexus of control exercised over academics came increasingly to lie in the positive advantages which the established powers were able to bestow on a professionalism ready to serve the status quo and to withhold from 'partisan' scholarship ranged against it.[29]

In the post-World War II era, the emergence of the state as a major source of money for university research has had the effect of allowing foundations to concentrate on mission-oriented social science projects that bear upon American corporate and military activity abroad. This section will again only summarize data on foundation-supported research in "international affairs" studies carried out by university personnel.

Investment Inputs

Of the many categories of foundations in American society, General Purpose Foundations (Ford, Rockefeller, etc.) are those which have the most profound impact on the university community. *The Foundation Directory* (1967) accounts for 370 foundations (G. P.) having a combined total of $13.5 billion in assets and $721 million in grant expenditures. Within this category there are

237 "large foundations", those having assets of at least $10 million. Indeed, the degree of concentration is much greater than these figures suggest: the thirteen largest foundations have a combined total of $7.73 billion in assets, or 51 per cent of the assets of the "large foundations". The Ford and Rockefeller Foundations, whose activities are analyzed below, together hold $3.9 billion in assets, or nearly 20 per cent of the total assets of all 6,803 American foundations listed in the 1967 *Directory*.

Most important to the present discussion is the funding orientation of these large foundations. In 1966, Education and International Affairs received $442 million, or 59 per cent of all funds expended by these 237 foundations. Within International Affairs, the two largest sub-categories are International Studies and Education; the former accounts for eight foundations giving 47 grants worth $50.8 million, whereas the latter represents 58 foundations giving 139 grants worth $40.5 million. Of the $50.8 million expended for International Studies, $38 million (76 per cent) supported programs at American universities. The real significance of foundation support for International Studies programs is suggested however, by one all important fact: the Ford Foundation alone accounted for $50.3 million of this $50.8 million expenditure, or 99 per cent. The degree of Ford Foundation control, which has increased relative to Rockefeller and Carnegie support in the post-World War II era, obviously suggests that this foundation deserves special attention in the analysis.

Since its inception in 1951, Ford Foundation money has consistently dominated the arena of international research on U.S. campuses. Ford money is the principal source of financial support for 107 of the 191 foreign affairs research centers, 112 of which are geographically concentrated at twelve universities. Horowitz summarizes Ford's monopoly position:

In 11 of the 12 top universities with institutes of international studies, a single foundation, Ford, is the principal source of funds. Affiliated with the institutes at Columbia, Chicago, Berkeley, UCLA, Cornell, Harvard, Indiana, MIT, Michigan State, Stanford, and Wisconsin are 95 individual centers. Ford is a sole or major source of funds for 83 of these.[32]

Nine of these twelve universities are, not surprisingly, among the top ten recipients of Federal R and D funds; the remaining three are within the top forty. In sum, the same universities receive the largest proportion of state and foundation support in areas directly or marginally related to physical and social science research that bears upon the maintenance of the American empire. These are the elite universities *par excellence* in American society.

Finally, on the subject of foundation investments, the major interests of these "functionally oriented centers" (academic jargon for corporate think-tanks) and the number of institutes associated with these fields are as follows: socio-cultural change (17), political change and development (14), economic development (13), communism (13), international relations in general (11), international economics (10), national security (10), and population and demography (10). These fields in themselves reflect the harmony of interests that exists between academics in international studies programs and the corporate ruling class in the global imperialist empire. As in the last section, we now want to find out the qualitative nature of this vested-interest research.

Production Outputs

The influence of the rich in philanthropy focuses on the established institution, tends to maintain the status quo. It is rare, indeed, that major donations are made to encourage basic change or even minor dislocation of any aspect of established society.[33]

Having already isolated the "established institution(s)", we can now determine the way in which international studies programs strive to maintain the capitalist status quo.

Foreign studies institutes are largely a post-World War II phenomenon, the first such institute being the Rockefeller-funded Russian Institute at Columbia University in 1945. This was the "precursor of a host of foundation grants to what were to become known as university foreign language and area centers".[34] Soon, the Carnegie Institute began to fund non-Western Studies and in the 1950s the Ford Foundation grants emerged on a massive scale, "especially for maintaining the strength of the non-Communist nations and for assisting (sic) the social and economic development of the emerging nations."[35]

Rockefeller Foundation support for foreign language and area studies (Slavic, East Asian, Near Eastern, and Latin American) began as early as the 1930s, yet the grants doubled in the war years as these programs were used by the military for training and research purposes. The postwar Russian Institute was part of Columbia University's School for International Affairs (SIA), itself an outgrowth of Columbia's Naval School of Military Government and Administration.

Carnegie assistance between 1947 and 1951 reached an estimated $2.5 million and was directed toward training and research on Japan, India, the Near East, Southeast Asia, and Latin America. In addition, funds were disbursed to Harvard's Russian Research Institute and to the SSRC for graduate fellowships in foreign area studies.

The Ford Foundation, after 1951, assumed the burden of financing the largest proportion of such programs. In the first two decades, that is, through 1970, Ford spend over $70 million on foreign affairs research at American universities and colleges. In the space of four years, 1959 to 1963, grants totalling $42 million found their way to fifteen universities emphasizing East

Asian, East European, South or Southeast Asian, Near Eastern and African area and language communities.

One trend emerges from a consideration of the geographical and topical orientation of these institutes:[36] the support coincides directly with historical developments in the global political economy and the so-called trouble areas as defined by American brain-trusters and Cold Warriors. The ''Russia watchers'' were replaced by the ''Cuba watchers'' who in turn yielded to the ''China watchers''. In short, these foreign studies programs provided a vehicle for academics to move around the world yet remain attached to the comfort of their hallowed walls of ivy. They became no more nor less than consultants to the profit motive. Their names, two decades later, ring with the unpleasant sounds of B-52s over Vietnam and the noxious odors of napalmed bodies.

Columbia University's SIA was first headed by Schuyler Wallace, former director of the wartime Naval School; his associate status with the Ford Foundation and directorship of the Columbia University Press virtually assured that SIA researchers would get their studies funded and subsequently published. An SIA official report (1960) lists the CIA, the State Department, the Agency for International Development (AID), and the U.S. Information Agency (USIA) as post-graduate occupational priorities; by 1968, it was reported that 40 per cent of SIA graduates go directly into government service and another 20 to 30 per cent into international banking and business. Columbia's Russian Institute was composed of men like Wallace, all three Rockefellers, and G. T. Robinson (formerly with the OSS) all of whom sat concurrently on the Council on Foreign Relations (CFR), the key foreign policy association. Of the original five man coordinating staff, only one had a prior connection with Columbia University, although four had been with the OSS, three were in the CFR, and three were members of the upper-class Century Club.

Next came the East Asian and East European institutes at SIA in the late 1940s. The former was initially headed by ex-State Department and foreign service officers, while the latter was directed by Grayson Kirk, Columbia professor, Carnegie trustee, CFR member, and Mobil Oil director. When Kirk became president of Columbia in 1950, he was replaced by none other than Schuyler Wallace. As David Horowitz comments, ''Like the Hapsburg Royalty, they like to keep their family small and intimate.''[37] By the late 1960s, Ford money had replaced Rockefeller and Carnegie funding as the sole financial support for nine of fifteen SIA institutes and partial supporter of the remaining six.

Harvard's Russian Institute also combined Foundation directors and ex-OSS personnel (e.g. anthropologist Clyde Kluckhohn). The Institute was responsible for carrying out the Refugee Interview Project under the auspices of the U.S. Air Force; this entailed interviewing Russian refugees and, in turn, forwarding all information to the Department of Defense. Classified projects under D of D agencies, Rand Corporation, and Industrial War Colleges became the name of the game at Harvard.

In close geographical proximity emerged MIT's Center for International Studies in 1950. The objectives were stated as follows:

> ... MIT which has been engaged for some years in research on behalf of the U.S. Military establishment was asked by the civilian wing of the government to put together a team of the best research minds available to work intensely for three or four months to penetrate the iron curtain with ideas.[38]

This Center, more so than others, yields names that will forever be associated with genocide in Southeast Asia — W. W. Rostow, Max Millikan, Allen Dulles, all at one time with the CIA. Also, Harvard organized the Center for International Affairs "to provide training for civilians who might (sic) later be involved in the formulation of defense policy."[39] Funded by Ford and Carnegie money, we encounter Dean Rusk, later to become Secretary of State, and McGeorge Bundy, Kennedy's national security advisor and then head of the Ford Foundation. When Bundy left the White House, he was replaced by MIT's Rostow. The first associate director of the Harvard Center was the paragon of the Cold (and Hot) Warriors, Henry A. Kissinger.

Foreign area studies programs provided the link between the academics from elite universities and the interests of state monopoly capitalism. Without foundation support this would never have been possible on such a grandiose scale. It should always be kept in mind that foundation wealth itself presupposes exploitation of the labour-power of working people. These foundation programs have in the past three decades created a "lead system" which reinforced the hierarchical structure of American higher education and threatens to compromise the entire social science endeavour. Those academics who touch such questionable funds and allow them to determine or shape their research interests become, in no uncertain terms, social technicians involved in the manipulation of foreign populations. In addition, this "lead system" established by Foundation expenditures establishes the research trend for academics *not* associated with the elite schools. Just as all capitalists want to become bigger capitalists, status quo academics strive to become bigger, more powerful apologists, thereby gaining individual recognition in the process. In both cases, the inherent tendency of capital to expand dictates the logic and the behaviour of those who act in its interest. The smaller segment of the academic community which *explicitly refuses* to comply with the research priorities of capital, as opposed to those of labour, are generally excluded from Foundation research funding.

Before leaving the production carried out by Foundations, it is essential to make reference to their direct-action programs that intervene in the domestic affairs of underdeveloped countries. Both Ford and Rockefeller interests have demonstrated the desire to create a Third World governmental structure that pretends to guarantee the stability of the private enterprise system. Their funds also tend to go to areas where their corporate tenacles already have penetrated or will penetrate in the future . It is easy to understand the *raison d'être* behind 75 per cent of Rockefeller Foundation money allocated for "the creation of elites, modernization of infrastructures and purchases of goodwill overseas".[40] Whether under the guise of the "Green Revolution", family planning/birth control, or agricultural development, these so-called humanitarian interests dissolve into two complementary concerns: they serve either as means to expand the corporate capital of their respective conglomerates (e.g. petroleum products in the case of Rockefeller) or, what is even more sinister, they deprive Third World populations of future generations for the sake of short-run investment stability.[41] The basis of these projects also reflects a consciously false analysis by suggesting that the problems of underdeveloped nations are to be located in the spheres of distribution and population size. In fact, these "problems" are all symptomatic of the lack of indigenous control over production and reproduction — in a word, they are the symptoms of a barren imperialism.

In the 1960s, the eyes of the world were focussed on Asia. The following statements by critical researchers summarize the process.

In Burma:

Hoping to get capitalist expertise, if not dollars, U Nu invited American foundations to advise in the 'development' of Burma. As they had in Thailand, India, Indonesia, and elsewhere, the Ford Foundation, the Asia Foundation, and the Stanford Research Institute began altering the Burmese infrastructure in preparation for foreign (American) investment. The Ford Foundation, with the help of the University of Utah Business School, developed a crash program to create a managerial class, instituted rural pacification programs, and financially supported many of U Nu's Buddhist institutions.[42]

In the Philippines:

The orientation and basic materials of the present educational system and mass media are still dictated by the U.S. government and by U.S. monopoly firms. . . . U.S. governmental agencies like the AID and the Peace Corps and foundations like those of Asia, Ford, and Rockefeller still have a decisive say in the educational system from the elementary to the graduate level.[43]

In Indonesia:

Hoffman's Ford team laid the basis of a post-independence national bureaucracy trained to function under the new indirect rule of America — in Ford's words, to train a 'modernizing elite'.[44]

Finally, as we move through the direct action programs of the large foundations it becomes increasingly difficult to distinguish the "liberal" Rockefellers and Fords from the smaller openly reactionary foundations and their rightist friends. The Patman Congressional investigation revealed that, for instance, the J. P. Kaplan Fund (of New York) was a CIA front that had been receiving money from seven additional foundations. The money was then re-laundered to right-wing organizations such as Christianform which was involved in anti-Cuban propaganda and the American Friends of the Middle East.

The Lilly Endowment, seventh largest general purpose foundation in 1967, established the National Foundation for Education in American Citizenship which in turn gave the lion's share of its money for the publication of *Human Rights*, a reactionary magazine formerly edited by the founder of Christianform. This magazine was also tied to the late Texas oil billionaire, H.L. Hunt. In Texas alone, seven foundations were known to be affiliated with the CIA; Lyndon Johnson's financial ally Brown and Root Corporation, and the related Brown Foundation, were among this group.

Thus, foundation-sponsored production ranges from mission-oriented international studies programs on university campuses, to Third World action programs that enhance their parent corporations, to right wing causes in the U.S. proper. The significance of these projects in the maintenance of capitalism and imperialism is largely self-evident, and a quick study of interlocking directorates should forever put the lie to the foundations' altruistic rhetoric.

Interlocking Directorates

By documenting the class composition of foundation trusteeships one can get an indication of the close affinity of the power elite in business corporations, universities, state agencies, and foundations.

A classic study of foundation trustees was performed by Lindeman in 1936, in which he concluded,

In short, he [the foundation trustee] is a member of that successful and conservative class which came into prominence during the latter part of the nineteenth century, the class whose status is based primarily upon pecuniary success.[45]

G. William Domhoff's study, *Who Rules America?*, reaches similar conclusions 35 years later:

Twelve of the top 13 foundations are controlled by members of the power elite, with two-thirds of their trustees coming from the upper class (51 per cent) or major corporations (16 per cent) . . . The one-third of the trustees who are neither members of the upper class nor corporate executives are professional persons, most of them college presidents or college professors. Just over half of all trustees attended Harvard, Yale or Princeton; 22 earned Phi Beta Kappa keys; 20 are in the Links Club of New York; and eight are on the board of the RAND Corporation, the Air Force 'think factory' supported primarily by government contracts.[46]

All of Lindeman's criteria are present in Domhoff's trustee profile — class background, corporate affiliations, university connections, and club memberships.

Our earlier concentration on the Ford and Rockefeller Foundations leads us to examine their respective trusteeships in order to establish the coordinates of wealth and power represented. Representatives of the corporate ruling class dominate these positions, with university personnel (academics and administrators) accounting for a large proportion of the remaining trustees. Many of these individuals have moved back and forth between corporation and government service — especially during the Kennedy era.

Perhaps the most revealing interlock is that which exists between the dominant foundations and the Council on Foreign Relations (CFR), the latter being the key link between corporate capital and State policy. The CFR, established in 1921, began receiving Rockefeller and Carnegie foundation funding in the latter years of that decade.

In addition to its role of carving out American foreign policy, the CFR publishes the journal *Foreign Affairs* and organizes speakers to address CFR seminars organized in an estimated thirty American cities. Foundation financial support of the CFR continues to account for a large share of its activities, the *quid pro quo* being positions on the CFR for Foundation trustees. Domhoff has documented this interlock in the 1960s:

... 10 of the 14 trustees of the Carnegie Corporation were members of the CFR in 1961. The overlap of the CFR with other major foundations is as follows: 10 of the Ford Foundation's 15 trustees are also members of the CFR; 12 of the 20 from the Rockefeller Foundation; 18 of the 26 from the Carnegie Endowment for International Peace; 15 of the 26 from the Carnegie Endowment for the Advancement of Teaching; 12 of the 16 from the Sloan Foundation; 6 of the 10 from the Commonwealth Fund; 13 of the 20 from the Twentieth Century Fund; and 7 of the 18 from the Fund for the Republic.[47]

This CFR-Foundation network acts as an institutional context through which the academic contribution to the maintenance of the American corporate empire can be effectively channeled.

In conclusion, this discussion demonstrates the complementary role of foundation and state-university networks which serve the interest of the status quo. Neither network is more crucial to the realization of those interests, in that *both* emphasize the strategic importance of universities in producing a skilled labour force to meet the conflicts and contradictions inherent in the political economy of state monopoly capitalism.[48]

CONCLUSION: ACADEMICS IN THE SERVICE OF POWER

Thus far the military-university complex has been approached in structural and institutional terms. Yet one question remains: why do academics, who themselves for the most part are not members of the corporate ruling class, choose to participate in mission-oriented research? This is not a matter of individual psychology but rather an issue bearing upon the interrelationship between the individual and the larger social system. The ideology, motivation, and practice of academics, in this case, can only be properly understood by focussing on the social conditions in which academics operate.

Each mode of production is systematically reinforced by a naked power at the disposal of the ruling class-state apparatus and an ideology which legitimizes the dominant relations of production. To paraphrase Marx, the ruling ideas are the ideas of the ruling class. In capitalism, the ideology of the ruling class is that of privatized success. As Baran and Sweezy state:

Under capitalism the highest form of success is business success, and under monopoly capitalism the highest form of business is the big corporation. In this system the normal procedure for an ambitious young man must be to work himself up to as near the top as possible of as big a corporation as possible. Once he enters a given corporation, he devotes himself to two ends: ascending the managerial ladder and advancing the relative status of his company in the corporate world. In practice these two ends are indistinguishable: the young man's rise in the company depends on his contribution to improving the position of his company. This is the crux of the matter, and this is why we can say without qualification that the company man is dedicated to the advancement of his company precisely to the extent that he is dedicated to advancing himself . . . . *The character of the system determines the psychology of its members, not vice versa.* (emphasis added)[49]

In accepting the system of structured inequality, and in agreeing to work *within* that system, the individual's ideology is necessarily shaped by the objective determinants of class conflict.

This seems readily apparent for those who obviously stand in open confrontation with each other as personifications of capital and labour, but one may ask what relevance this has to the theory and practice of academics. Academics do not work for business corporations, at least not directly, and many might never be as loyal to their university as businessmen are to their companies. But such a narrow view of academics vis-à-vis corporate leaders fails to critically analyze the university as an "essential component" in the political economy of monopoly capitalist production. Once this conceptual impasse is broken, and once it is understood that universities are also involved in commodity production, then it follows that the objective relations and conditions of production will be accompanied by a corresponding ideology. In the case of academics, the "value-free" stance is itself the ideological commitment that on the one hand justifies all forms of research in the name of science and, on the other hand, consciously conceals the vested interests that most academics have in only interpreting the world and not transforming it.

Noam Chomsky has argued that intellectuals who have already achieved some degree of power and influence share a consensus that capitalist society and its values must be accepted. In American post-World War II society, for example, most academics attached themselves enthusiastically to the liberal doctrine of the Cold War and the necessity to protect the "free world" even when that "protection" entailed supporting a most genocidal war (the American involvement in Vietnam). Within this ideological perspective, each academic sets out to find a means of developing his/her science to contribute to that end.

There is no lack of evidence to support this position. We have already seen the extent of university involvement: universities sanction the training of military officers in ROTC programs; university R and D centers produce the technology and the technicians to maintain and expand the American empire; and university social scientists provide the research and the ideology to justify American foreign policy, a foreign policy which has clearly distinguished itself as opposed to the interests of the world's people. Whether academics always believe everything they say or write in advancing these objectives is often difficult to determine and largely irrelevant in any case. It is not what they say or think that is important — it is what they do!

The result is now obvious: university departments of the physical and social sciences have become willing agents of political control and domination. As McConnell states, "the values of the academic . . . have become the values of the marketplace or the governmental arena".[50] In the process, the academics come to identify themselves with the propertied class which they serve both at home and abroad. In the context of imperialism, Noam Chomsky puts it this way:

When we strip away the terminology of the behavioural sciences, we see revealed . . . the mentality of the colonial civil servant, persuaded of the benevolence of the mother country and the correctness of its visions of world order, and convinced that he understands the true interests of the backward peoples whose welfare he is to administer.[51]

It is important to point out that academics need not be born into the corporate ruling class to serve its interests. Indeed most are not. The issue of individual mobility within the capitalist class structure was best understood by Marx: "the more a ruling class is able to assimilate the most prominent men of the dominated classes, the more stable and dangerous its rule."[52]

In conclusion, this essay has outlined the functional role that universities play in maintaining and reproducing the capitalist mode of production in post-World War II American society. The structural collusion of state, corporate-foundation and university has not only assured the corporate ruling class of a mass of skilled labour power; it has also transformed the entire form and substance of American higher education. From the perspective of individual academics who accept and agree to work within these structural parameters, the objective necessities of this production system largely determine their subjective consciousness. This synthesis of objective and subjective conditions leads one to conclude that Upton Sinclair in *The Goose Step* only anticipated what Horowitz makes explicit:

... the prostitution of intellect has become so pervasive and profound that all but a small minority mistake it for academic virtue. . . . Most academics no more perceive the ideological basis of their work. . . . What may have seemed like an isolated scandal in 1966 (the MSUG Vietnam Project) can now be recognized as a universal condition of organized intellect in America. The saddest part is that academics have become such eager victims. They have internalized the limits placed upon them. They fiercely uphold a strict academic professionalism. But it is no more than expert servitude to oppressive power, to a system whose wages are poverty and blood. They do not see that what they have really embraced is the perverted professionalism of the mercenary and the hired gun.[53]

NOTES

1. U. Sinclair, *The Goose Step: Study of American Education*, Published by the author, 1923, p. 460.

2. U. Sinclair, p. 442.

3. The contemporary glut of university graduates in the marketplace in no way invalidates this analysis. Crises of over-production/under-consumption are nothing novel in capitalist history. Further, the crisis is not located in the sphere of exchange but in the production process itself. In this case, an excessive amount of labour time has been expended in the production of university commodities — i.e., skilled labour. The university factory does not require unique laws of economics to explain its internal dynamics and contradictions.

4. See P. Baran and P. Sweezy, *Monopoly Capital*, New York: Monthly Review, 1966. J. K. Galbraith, *The New Industrial State*, Boston: Houghton Mifflin, 1967.

5. Following Marx, raw materials are here distinguished from virgin, untouched resources in that they have been "filtered through previous labour". K. Marx, *Capital*, Volume I, Progress: Moscow, n.d., p. 174.

6. See G. Kolko, *The Triumph of Conservatism: A Reinterpretation of American History, 1900-1916*, Chicago: Quadrangle, 1967. Kolko's term "political capitalism" is synonymous with "state capitalism" used here. His analysis shows that the Progressive Era witnessed a synthesis of politics and economics whereby "ultimately businessmen defined the limits of political intervention, and specified its major form and thrust" (p. 280).

7. R. Miliband, *The State in Capitalist Society*, U.K.: Weidenfeld and Nicholson, 1969, p. 9.

8. See D. Horowitz, ed., *Corporations and the Cold War*, New York: Monthly Review Press, 1969.

9. C.W. Mills, *The Power Elite*, New York: Oxford University Press, 1956.

10. R. Miliband, p. 9.

11. R. Miliband, pp 66-67.

12. R. Miliband, pp 254, 262.

13. Sections IV and V of this article are condensed summaries of documentation found in Chapters Two and Three of the author's M.A. Thesis: *The Political Economy of American Postwar Higher Education: The Military-University Complex*, Edmonton: University of Alberta, 1971, pp. 21-90. The data presented here has not been updated to include events of the past six years, however, there is no reason to believe that significant qualitative changes have occurred in that period of time.

14. H. L. Nieburg, *In the Name of Science*, Chicago: Quadrangle Books, 1966, p. 252.

15. S. Lens, *The Military-Industrial Complex*, Philadelphia: Pilgrim Press, 1970, p. 15. For a detailed account of the State (military)-University network during World War II, see D. S. Greenberg, *The Politics of Pure Science*, New York, New American Library, 1967; H. L. Nieburg, *In the Name of Science*; R. L. Beals, *Politics of Social Science: An Inquiry into the Ethics and Responsibilities of Social Scientists*, Chicago: Aldine Publishing Co., 1969.

16. National Science Foundation, *Federal Support to Universities and Colleges, Fiscal Year 1967*, U.S. Government Printing Office, 1969, p. 36.

17. They are as follows: MIT, Michigan, Columbia, Harvard, Illinois, U of California (Berkeley), Stanford, U. of California (Los Angeles), Chicago, and Wisconsin.

18. A complete listing of Project Themis grants is available in C. Brightman, *Viet Report: Special Issue*, 1968; 3:4-5, pp. 2-48. Also see M. Klare, ed., *The University-Military-Police Complex: A Directory of Related Documents*, North American Congress on Latin America (NACLA), 1970.

19. R. Clarke, *We All Fall Down: The Prospect of Biological and Chemical Warfare*, London: Allen Lane, 1968, p. 45. Additional references on CBW research include: C. Brightman, ''The Weed Killers and the Universities at the Front'', in Viet Report, 1966, 2:4-5, pp. 9-14, 33-48; M. Klare, ed., *The University-Military-Police Network;* R. Lapp, *The Weapons Culture,* New York: W.W. Norton, 1968; S. Lens, *The Military-Industrial Complex*.

20. T. Asad, ed., *Anthropology and the Colonial Encounter*, Ithaca Press, 1973.

21. W. J. Crockett, quoted by M. Windmiller, ''The New American Mandarins'', in T. Roszak, ed., *The Dissenting Academy*, New York; Pantheon, 1968, p. 121.

22. J. Ridgeway, *The Closed Corporation: American Universities in Crisis*, New York: Ballantine Books, 1968, pp. 125-26.

23. Quoted in M. Windmiller, ''The New American Mandarins'', p. 121.

24. Quoted in M. Klare, ed., *The University-Military-Police Network*, pp. 10-11.

25. D. Horowitz, ''The Foundations: Charity Begins at Home'', *Ramparts Magazine*, 1969, 7:11, p. 46.

26. G. W. Domhoff, *Who Rules America?*, Englewood Cliffs: Prentice-Hall, 1967, p. 71.

27. D. Horowitz, ''The Foundations: Charity Begins at Home'', pp. 40-41.

28. D. Horowitz, "Billion Dollar Brains: How Wealth Puts Knowledge in its Pockets", *Ramparts Magazine*, 1969, 7:12, p. 39.

29. D. Horowitz, "Billion Dollar Brains", p. 37.

30. It should be pointed out that there is no official record of the exact number of foundations operating in American society; even the Internal Revenue Service does not have a comprehensive listing. The *Foundation Directory* (1967) has data on 6,803 foundations, those with assets exceeding $20,000, or annual grant expenditures of $10,000.

31. These foundations are, in order of size: Ford, Rockefeller, Duke Endowment, Kellogg (W. K.), Hartford (John A.), Lilly Endowment, Sloan (Alfred P.), Carnegie Corporation of New York, Pew Memorial Trust, Longwood, Moody, and the Rockerfeller Brothers Fund.

32. D. Horowitz, "Sinews of Empire", *Ramparts Magazine*, 1969, 8:5, p. 33.

33. T. C. Reeves, ed., *Foundations Under Fire,* Ithaca: Cornell University Press, 1970, p. 14.

34. U.S. Department of State Report, quoted in M. Klare, ed., *The University-Military-Police Network*, p. 45.

35. G. M. Beckmann, "The Role of Foundations in Non-Western Studies", in W. Weaver, ed., *U.S. Philanthropic Foundations,* New York: Harper and Row, 1967, p. 398.

36. Beckmann, pp. 396-403, gives an indication of the research priorities of these general purpose foundations: "$420,000 to Columbia University for research on the political evolution of modern China (1955), $277,000 to Harvard University for research on the economy of China in modern times (1955), $200,000 to the Massachusetts Institute of Technology for a study of economic development and social change in sub-Saharan Africa (1959), $200,000 to the University of Michigan for research on the political modernization of Japan (1961), $130,000 to the University of Florida for studies of the historical and contemporary forces shaping the territories and nations of the Caribbean(1961), $910,000 to the Social Science Research Council for research on the economy of Communist China (1961), $240,000 to the University of Chicago for research on education and socio-economic development of transitional societies (1962), and $250,000 to Northwestern University for research on intercultural relations."

37. D. Horowitz, "Sinews of Empire", p. 37.

38. D. Horowitz, "Sinews of Empire", p. 38.

39. D. Horowitz, "Sinews of Empire", p. 38.

40. North American Congress on Latin America (NACLA), *The Rockefeller Empire: Latin America*, 1969, Newsletter.

41. See M. Mandani, *The Myth of Population Control: Family, Caste and Class in an Indian Village*, New York: Monthly Review Press, 1972.

42. J. Carnoy, "What's Nu in Burma?", *Pacific Research and World Empire Telegram*, 1971, Volume II, No. 3, p. 4.

43. A. Guerrero, "Basic Problems of the Filipino People", *Pacific Research and World Empire Telegram*, 1970, 2:2, p. 18.

44. Paul Hoffman was in charge of Ford activities in the 1950s. D. Ransom, "The Berkeley Mafia and the Indonesian Massacre", *Ramparts Magazine*, 1970, 9:4, p. 40.

45. E. C. Lindemann, *Wealth and Culture: A Study of One Hundred Foundations and Community Trusts and their Operation During the Decade 1921-30*, Brace and Co., 1936; quoted in T. C. Reeves, ed., *Foundations Under Fire*, p. 80.

46. G. W. Domhoff, *Who Rules America?*, p. 65.

47. G. W. Domhoff, *Who Rules America?*, p. 73.

48. Space limitations preclude an investigation of any specific universities and the role they play in maintaining the American Empire. The original thesis looks at two case studies: Michigan State University (MSU) and Columbia University. The MSU example shows how a university literally went to war during the Vietnam era, while Columbia University reflects the extent to which members of the corporate ruling class can control the trusteeship positions of a major American university. Together these two examples symbolize the specificity and pervasiveness of university complicity in State monopoly capitalism. See original thesis, pp. 90-114.

49. P. Baran and P. Sweezy, *Monopoly Capital*, pp. 37-38.

50. T. R. McConnell, "Governments and the University — A Comparative Analysis," *Governments and the University*, Toronto: MacMillan of Canada Ltd., 1966, pp. 90-91.

51. N. Chomsky, *American Power and the New Mandarins*, New York: Pantheon Books, 1967, p. 41.

52. Quoted in G. W. Domhoff, *Who Rules America?*, p. 4.

53. D. Horowitz, "Sinews of Empire", p. 42.

Growth and Celebration
of the American Multiversity

RANDLE W. NELSEN

INTRODUCTION

Clark Kerr, former President of the sprawling multicampus University of California, wrote of education in 1960 that "it conduces toward a new equality which has nothing to do with ideology."[1] Yet, as Kerr clearly argued three years later in *The Uses of the University*,[2] education has to do with service and the development of a service ideology. This service oriented education, as well as his own participation in fostering and developing it, is celebrated in *Uses* where President Kerr coins the term "multiversity" in reference to universities similar to the very large (seven campuses then), rich, and distinguished institution he administered. Preliminary to his assessment of its current realities, Kerr asks and answers in rhetorical fashion:

What is the justification of the modern American multiversity? *History is one answer. Consistency with the surrounding society is another.* Beyond that, it has . . . no peers in all history among institutions of higher learning in *serving* so many of the segments of an advancing civilization. . . . *The multiversity has demonstrated how adaptive it can be to new opportunities for creativity; how responsive to money; how eagerly it can play a new and useful role*; how fast it can change while pretending that nothing has happened at all; how fast it can neglect some of its ancient virtues.[3] (my emphasis)

Some of these ancient virtues, American style, have been publicly stated by oil millionaire and former University of California Regent, Edwin W. Pauley, whose interest in higher education ought to be considered alongside his candid admission: "I dealt in everything I could make a profit in, in the good old American way."[4] During the mid-1960s Regent Pauley issued a defense of capitalist virtue with his condemnation of an experimental educational program known as the Tusman Plan. He charged that the professors planning the program were Marxists and "if not Marxists at least believe in the Marxist theory, or if not that, at least disbelieve in the Capitalist system." Summing up his resistance to the Tusman experiment Pauley concluded: "Before I go before the Legislature to ask for funds for the university I think I should at least have a letter from these men stating that they believe in the Capitalist system."[5]

Such a letter, then and now, would be redundant as is indicated in the summary history of the creation and expansion of America's universities

120

outlined in the paragraphs below. Not only does a vast majority of university regents and trustees continue to give silent support to the rationale behind Pauley's condemnation,[6] but such support also can be found among many faculty and administrators. In fact, President Kerr, using language more familiar to liberal educators than to successful industrialists like Pauley who continue to dominate the Kerrs and their educational institutions, presents a "balanced" view of higher learning in his multiversity which sounds strikingly similar to Pauley's capitalist thinking and philosophy. In Kerr's words:

The essence of balance is to match support with the intellectual creativity of subject fields; *with the need for skills of the highest level; with the kinds of expert service that society currently most requires....*

Knowledge is now central to society. It is wanted, even demanded, by more people and more institutions than ever before. *The university as producer, wholesaler, and retailer of knowledge cannot escape service. Knowledge, today, is for everybody's sake.*[7] (my emphasis)

One might add, in light of this statement by Kerr taken together with Pauley's comments and the perspective developed below, especially for the sake of the successful and powerfully dominant group of elite capitalists and the educators who serve them.

HISTORICAL GROWTH OF THE EDUCATIONAL-INDUSTRIAL PARTNERSHIP

The fact that it might be rather easy to mix, and at times confuse, the statements of educator Kerr and industrialist Pauley should not be viewed with surprise. Instead, this fact of today's corporate economy should be viewed as a logical outcome of the historical growth and development of the multiversity. To quote Kerr concerning the educational-industrial partnership upon which rests the multiversity's present-day pre-eminence:

The university and segments of industry are becoming more alike. As the university becomes tied into the world of work, the professor — at least in the natural and some of the social sciences — takes on the characteristics of an entrepreneur. . . . The two worlds are merging physically and psychologically.[8]

This merger and the resulting growth in higher education was greatly stimulated by increased Federal appropriations to land grant universities and the G.I. Bill following World War II. However, it is important to point out that this government spending and the attendant university growth did *not* result in as radical a transformation as some observers, including Kerr, like to think.[9] This transformation from a classical curriculum reserved for an aristocratic elite to a vocational (or technical) curriculum made increasingly more available to the masses had its beginnings about a century earlier. Thus, the G.I. Bill and other government funding which made university education possible for a greater number of individuals from a variety of socio-economic backgrounds, needs to be placed within a historical perspective emphasizing the much earlier beginnings of the change from a classical to a vocational-technical curriculum.

This perspective, in summary form, shows how the growth of higher education in the mid-1800s was dominated by a wealthy few (a socio-economic elite) capable of defining their pursuit of personal interests as being compatible with the best interests of the general public. Selectively bestowing their riches upon particular institutions of higher learning a small number of wealthy capitalists decided which few schools among the many (between 1780 and the beginning of the Civil War nearly 1,000 colleges were started[10]) were to survive. The price of survival for the "naturally selected" colleges was the continued development of a practical curriculum, a curriculum reflecting the discovery by these wealthy few that they might profitably apply a useful science to the technical problems they encountered in operating their manufacturing and industrial concerns. Thus, successful capitalists like Charles Goodyear and later the Armours, the Dukes, and George Eastman, hired professors to make their knowledge useful in suggesting the possible uses of rubber, and in finding scientific solutions to the problems of producing various consumer goods from hot dogs to cigarettes and cameras. While the professors acted as consultants, college administrators sought financial aid for their schools from wealthy manufacturers and industrialists. Two of the most successful fund-raisers among nineteenth-century college presidents, Harvard's Edward Everett and Brown's Francis Wayland, were outspoken advocates of the view that classical curricula should be made pragmatic — that is, profitably modern. They were eventually joined by Dartmouth's Nathan Lord and Michigan's Henry Tappan, staunch supporters of the classical tradition, whose views gradually changed to match their first-hand instruction in the economic reality of the growing educational-industrial partnership.[11]

This partnership developed rapidly during the late 1800s and early 1900s as the elite fashioned and refashioned higher learning corporations into training grounds for the scientist-technicians needed to operate its industries. It was given political sanction and impetus with the Federal Government's passage of the Morrill Federal Land-Grant Act in 1862, the related Hatch Act of 1887, the second Morrill Act of 1890 together with amendments in 1905 and 1907 which were further supplemented by the Smith-Lever Act of 1914 and the Smith-Hughes Act of 1917. In the initial legislation, sponsored by Vermont Congressman Justin Smith Morrill, the government in Washington agreed to give land to those states constructing agricultural and mechanical colleges. The result was a tremendous growth in the number of state-supported schools, a growth that not only increasingly secularized a curriculum moving away from a religious perspective in both management and content, but that also increased the dependency of higher learning institutions on the prosperity of business and industry.[12]

THE PARTNERSHIP TODAY: GOVERNMENT
SPONSORSHIP OF MULTIVERSITY RESEARCH

The relation between this increased dependency of higher education on the prosperity of business and industry, especially those corporations with government-sponsored contracts, and the development of an increasingly pragmatic curriculum is nowhere better illustrated than in the growth of the multiversities during the past thirty years. Leaving growth statistics aside,[13] and relying once again on a passage from *Uses*, Kerr accurately summarizes the growth of the multiversity when he confesses that he has often thought of the modern university as "a series of individual faculty entrepreneurs held together by a common grievance over parking."[14]

Professorial concern over parking attests, among other things, to the present predominant position of what might be termed a consultant/grantsman role model as a guide for professorial practice. Moving back and forth from university to government to business obligations, today's most successful and well-travelled professors spend a minimal amount of time at their schools, preferring instead the big-business, big-government "halls of power". They understand the importance of a reserved parking spot as they practise a social science that helps repair, and thereby sustain, the corporate socio-economic arrangements which have proven profitable to a wealthy elite. The overwhelming majority of Americans remains dependent upon and dominated by this elite as members of the academic establishment manipulate their educational "contacts" in attempts to serve, and thereby gain access to, the elite stratum. In a phrase, most professors try to become as proficient as possible in playing "the university game".

Success in playing this game not only contributes to, but also depends upon, the future growth of a science triangle involving big business-government-education. According to James Ridgeway, who has supplied documentation of how big business and the Department of Defense dominate American higher education, the money flows out of industry and/or government to the university where someone "hatches a utilitarian idea" which can be sold to a company that either makes a product or designs a test. "The object of the university game, then, is to control any two legs of the triangle, for by doing so, the university professor can establish the beginnings of power."[15]

During the past thirty years of multiversity growth the beginnings of professorial and university power have often been established through government grants. While in recent years contracts have replaced grants as the predominant mode of funding, recent research underscores the fact that the Federal Government remains a most willing consumer of social science research. As Keith Baker of the Department of Health, Education, and Welfare (HEW) writing about this new contract grantmanship has statistically shown, the government in Washington has been steadily increasing its support for social science research during the 1970s. Baker indicates that increased government research spending has moved away from so-called "basic" towards "applied" research.[16]

This applied emphasis should not startle anyone who is the least bit familiar with the historical development of social science in the United States. For just as the multiversity curriculum has changed over the years to become more vocationally (technically) specialized, more marketably pragmatic, in like manner the university research which gets funded has been made increasingly applicable to the changing needs of a corporate capitalism fashioned by relatively few manufacturers and industrialists who dominate higher education as regent and trustee benefactors. Documentation for this assertion comes from examining a cycle of servility, kept in motion by sociological research retailing overseas and at home an "official view of the social scene", which can be, and has been, historically traced.[17] This servility runs from the founding fathers of American sociology who developed sociologies providing ideological support for America's chaotic transition from laissez-faire to corporate capitalism;[18] to the time-and-motion students of the second generation who used sociological knowledge to serve the interests of their powerful capitalist employers by attempting to "humanize" management so as to pacify laborers both at the factory and in the increasingly problem-plagued cities where the workers lived;[19] to the statisticians of the third generation whose feverish attempts to make their sociology scientific and then demonstrate its practical utility to big business and government foreshadowed the ill-considered judgments of the present-day fourth and fifth generations regarding alternative possibilities for applying their newly-created and recognized expertise.[20] The latter two generations continue to research "social problems" which increasingly are being defined by the funding agency.

Over the past two decades sociologists have been busily and profitably engaged in applying their science to a wide variety of problems both foreign and domestic. Sociologists at Michigan State University received financial support from the Central Intelligence Agency for their assistance in planning the Vietnam War during the late 1950s;[21] scholars from American University in Washington D.C. and other institutions of higher learning throughout the land were offered handsome retainers in exchange for furthering the government's counter-insurgency operations in Chile with their Project Camelot participation in 1964-65;[22] sociologists worked together in a complicated corporate arrangement linking Columbia University's Bureau of Applied Social Research with professors at Johns Hopkins University and the Massachusetts Institute of Technology (MIT) so that they could administer over $700,000 in 1967 defense contracts awarded them for turning their research interest in political propaganda into active involvement in the Vietnam War;[23] subsequently, sociologists from Columbia, Harvard, and MIT found it a profitable venture to try transferring the lessons learned in attempting to educate (read pacify) the Vietnamese to Blacks in Roxbury, a Boston slum.[24] At about this same time, Regent Pauley's and President Kerr's Washington lobbyists were beginning to obtain sizeable funding to support the work of University of California social scientists for their participation in a Camelot subcontract, the Berkeley-run Himalayan Border Countries Project, an eleven university consortium known as the Institute for Defense Analysis, and a variety of other military/paramilitary projects. Monies from these projects supplemented the strong financial backing which Cal's physical scientists had long received for work at Berkeley's Radiation Laboratory used to design and build hydrogen bombs at the Laboratory's branch plants in Livermore and Los Alamos.[25]

The point is this. Whether it be Michigan's State University, Johns Hopkins of Maryland, New York's Columbia, Massachusetts' Harvard and MIT, or the many campuses of the University of California, the multiversity has fulfilled its research and teaching promise by serving. The question is, by serving whom? Not "society", for this is far too general a term and begs the question rather than answers it.

More specifically, the multiversity has served by maintaining and strengthening the socio-economic arrangements of a corporate capitalism upon which its continued survival in its present form depends. Investing government funds to create profitable research "spin-offs" in the "private sector",[26] multiversity employees have woven intricate corporate arrangements which vividly emphasize the fact that the scholarly activity of the most financially successful and well-known universities is big business. To borrow a phrase from steel market monopolist, Andrew Carnegie, used in 1902 to describe the prototype twentieth-century research foundation (the Carnegie Institute) he established to encourage the consolidation of government-business-university research efforts in a corporate form, the multiversity exists today as "an active force working by proper modes for useful ends."[27] This utility has turned Kerr's 1963 assessment of the role of higher education into accurate prophecy, for the last thirteen years of growth have demonstrated that the multiversity as a service institution has few, if any, peers.

DEVELOPMENT OF A SOCIOLOGY OF HIGHER EDUCATION: THE MULTIVERSITY CELEBRATED

Part and parcel of this service has been the analysis of American higher education's growth developed by that country's most established and eminent sociologists. Ample illustration of this service orientation is to be found in the celebrations of the multiversity constructed by three of their number — David Riesman, Christopher Jencks, and Burton R. Clark. Together they have developed a sociology of higher education that attempts to deny the historical relation of dependency which ties the growth of American colleges and universities to the maintenance of the prevailing socio-economic system. However, as is indicated by the following summary of the way in which their work fosters multiversity professionalism, this attempt to prove higher education autonomous only serves to affirm the subservient relation of education to the larger corporate economy.[28]

To summarize, Riesman argues that the intellectual veto power of professional educators gives them control in shaping a higher education that is autonomous — so autonomous, that the university, under the direction of the increasingly powerful professors, is fast becoming the dominant institution of the American social system. According to Riesman, professional fitness for service in this leadership position comes about as a result of training in one of the academic disciplines, those veto groups he labels "the racecourses of the mind". Tracking on one of these racecourses, in the view of both Riesman and *Academic Revolution* co-author Jencks, schools future educators to objectively separate their professional from their personal lives. Thus, the newly socialized professors come to learn that not only are the universities within which they run the racecourses autonomous, but as professional scientists, they too can act autonomously (that is, professionally). Stated another way, they learn to make few genuine attempts at gaining respect for their expertise from those outside of, and lower in the status hierarchy than, "the profession"; instead, they learn to professionally ignore the wishes and needs of "clients" in order to gain the approval of colleagues.[29]

Such ignorance is not usually, as Riesman and Jencks seem to suggest, synonymous with "the advancement of the human condition" — that is, if this phrase is to be made relevant to the great majority of people. Rather, it helps to make the education-as-autonomous thesis and a narrow scientific professionalism mutually reinforcing. Such reinforcement, in turn, helps the elite maintain current socio-economic arrangements by making sure that everyone, professional and non-professional alike, knows and remains in their place. In short, the human condition furthered by the colleague-orientation of the Riesman-Jencks view of academic professionalism protects Yale and its graduates against an influx of too many clients-turned-colleagues from "the wrong side of the tracks"; or to remain within the Riesman metaphor, his view of the racecourses he has been so instrumental in designing does not allow for much 'off-track betting'.

Similarly, the Jencks examination of *Inequality* suggests the futility of betting on those whose breeding is questionable — those without the benefits of being born into families where adults have been schooled in one or more of the academic racecourses. For Jencks, however, a bet on the Yale admission chances of the physician's son from New York City would be almost as risky as one on the Bridgeport boy from the other side of the tracks; for in his opinion, decisions as to who is permitted to run the racecourses (academic disciplines), like the benefits that might possibly obtain from successfully completing the race, have become personalized accidents.

These accidents and their relation to extreme differences in individual incomes become, in the Jencks view, sociologically unrelatable; as personal fortuities and adversities, they come to resemble the distinctiveness that he sees separating the factory from both the autonomous school and the independent nuclear family. As with the school and the family, individual accidents help eliminate dissatisfaction that results from the important inequalities *within* groups, as opposed to the less significant differences *between* groups. Therefore, Jencks argues, enlightened public policy would not attempt to monitor or control these accidents; instead, the Jencks analysis permits them to be molded to, and to serve, differences between groups as class distinctions of capitalism in its corporate form.

Clark too is concerned with, and develops an argument that fosters, this service orientation of higher education. For Clark, education is becoming "active"; the passive and traditional service function that has made schools "society's main vehicle of cultural indoctrination" is now being supplemented by education which is innovative — an "active force". Thus, Clark's colleges and universities, because they play an increasingly large part in creating and *Educating The Expert Society* they serve, are becoming increasingly autonomous.

This autonomy is necessary if higher education is to remain an "active agent". According to Clark, both professors and students are becoming much more important as interest groups, and like Riesman and Jencks, he sees development of the academic disciplines as being vital to the restructuring of society. Moreover, Clark argues that the research orientation of professional educators, when combined with the tolerant attitudes they teach their students, is not only able to create "new culture" but is also capable of sustaining the culture it creates. Clark contends, then, that pluralism, the supposedly increased differentiation caused by the proliferation of academic disciplines, can provide both creative and maintenance functions — but only if professional educators are allowed to develop their academic specialities with a minimum of outside interference. Briefly stated, the same pluralism that strengthens professionalism in order to solve problems within the educational institution, also can solve the problems of the larger socio-economic order, as professional (that is, objective) educational leaders "steer change in desired directions".[30]

Thus, in the writings of Riesman, Jencks, and Clark, the same theme, with variations, continually reappears: the expertise of professional scientist-educators makes them capable of an objective, an unbiased, and value-neutral, understanding of the socio-economic system. The implication is that since they stand apart from this system they are creating and serving, professional social scientists should be able, if given sufficient autonomy, to apply their supposedly non-partisan expertise to social problems — solving them in ways that will benefit the great majority of non-experts. By promoting this professional ideology, professionals with specialized expertise are able to create an ever-widening gulf between these non-experts and themselves. The result for scientist-educators is that objectivity and autonomy become ever more closely tied together; the problem-solving properties of an "unbiased" science are used by professional educators who, working in colleges and multiversities that supposedly stand apart from the value-relevance and bias of the present socio-economic order, plan the new society. This planning, as is argued in this review of the education-as-autonomous thesis and in the section which follows, places primary emphasis upon social control as opposed to social change. In Clark Kerr's view this control constitutes a kind of balance in which:

We should expect the most money and the brightest students and the greatest prestige to follow the most exciting new ideas. By and large they have done so, and this is one way of defining the nature of balance. (Economics was exciting in the 1930s: sociology was more exciting in the 1950s.)[31]

With sociological analyses that are as favorable to the continued domination by a wealthy corporate elite as are those of Riesman, Jencks, and Clark, it is small wonder that sociology continues to be "exciting" and well-funded in the 1960s and 1970s.

FACULTY-STUDENT PROFESSIONALISM AND BUREAUCRACY: THE MULTIVERSITY SETTING

Familiar professorial complaints, especially in vogue during the turbulent 1960s, have involved distaste, even hate, for administrators; a growing number of professors claimed that they wanted to join activist students in fighting the university administration. However, a 1967-68 study conducted by Edward Gross suggests that this was nothing more than liberal rhetoric. Thus, when Gross asked administrators and faculty members in U.S. non-denominational universities to rank organizational goals, he found that in both groups most of the goals placed at the bottom (three of the last four) referred to students.[32] In short, if professors, as a group, do not dislike students, few are interested in paying much attention to them. The domination of multiversity students, then, by consultant/grantsman educators occurs in the form of purposeful evasion and/or indifferent neglect, as professors use the multiversity bureaucracy to foster and enhance a professional image which students are encouraged to respect and emulate.

Not only can students be dominated, but as educators become more skilled in their manipulation of the professional norm of objectivity and the educational thesis (read myth) of autonomy, they can also define and solve professional problems. A refined professionalism is thought by many educators to offer the solution to vexing problems created as a result of professional scientists being employed within the bureaucratic setting of the multiversity — problems such as the supposed dichotomies between client versus colleague orientations and teaching versus research obligations. However, it is most important to understand that success in lessening whatever tension results from these conflicting tendencies is incorporated as an artifact of maintaining the present socio-economic system; in other words, success in this regard rests upon professorial ability to develop increasingly closer ties between the daily operation of schools and the other major institutions of the prevailing order.

Thus, as Project Camelot grantees accepted "the propriety of the Army to define and delimit all questions . . . it became clear that the social scientist savant was not so much functioning as an applied social scientist as he was supplying information to a powerful client."[33] And ten years later, Baker of the Health, Education, and Welfare Department explains that "the people who ultimately do the work have no involvement in many of the basic decisions of the research process." He also encourages multiversity-based researchers to accept the fact that "the project manager [government] is boss" and to scramble for a larger portion of the expanding applied research budget.[34]

Paradoxically, then, as consultant/grantsman professors attempt to sustain their professional ideology by combining the scientific norm of objectivity and the educational thesis of autonomy, they are fast becoming technicians who are neither objective nor autonomous.

As technically-competent and partisan "hired help" serving monied interests, they are becoming less able to delineate and maintain anything remotely resembling a value-neutral position. Rather, they make themselves and the educational organizations they represent more dependent upon preserving, fundamentally unchanged, the institutional arrangements of the current socio-economic system. In a phrase, professorial emphasis is on social control rather than social change.

This emphasis on social control has been a lesson well-communicated to students. Like their instructors, today's multiversity students seem satisfied to merely ignore and/or circumvent the unpleasant and destructive exigencies of specialized discipline professionalism and hierarchical academic structures. Furthermore, and of crucial importance, not only has classroom instruction effectively socialized current students to adjust to bureaucratic life in the multiversity without the protests of their 1960s predecessors,[35] but it also seems to have helped create passive acceptance of an American socio-economic system built upon a permanent "defense" economy.

Thus, while their professors continue playing "the university game" by submitting research bids in competition for an enlarged share of America's growing defense budget,[36] reporter Tom Buckley informs the readers of *Harper's* that many of today's most intelligent multiversity students have taken to playing war games for entertainment. Most of these war gamers are, by Buckley's description, "under thirty" and "dedicated pacifists" with "long, lank hair, beards" who infused the first national war-game convention at Johns Hopkins University with a tone that was "entirely anti-military".[37] Still, one wonders whether their game of "Clean Carnage" encourages the use of any non-entertainment time devoted to combating the rising public support for increased military spending?[38] Or, whether the work of Simulations Publications, number one retailer of war games, on a $25,000 Pentagon contract to develop a training game for platoon officers and non-coms holds any political significance for these reputedly intelligent, young players?[39] Or, to summarize other inquiries and doubts, will participation in this form of entertainment simply help reproduce the current socio-economic reality?

In this reality most professors continue educating in a manner which leaves the multiversity, as an inspirational setting for significant social change, increasingly hollow and tomb-like. Should we not also expect, then, that most of their well-socialized students will leave unasked the major questions their war-game entertainment raises concerning the interrelation between defense spending, the growth of multiversity education, and the multi-national, monopoly structure of a maturing corporate capitalism? The sad fact is that most of today's multiversity professors and their students no longer have any interest in asking a question raised by Robert S. Lynd some thirty-nine years ago: "Knowledge for What"?[40] The answers to such a question might constitute the beginnings of an anti-corporate, if not anti-capitalist, sociology.

CONCLUSION

The historical growth and predominant research orientation of today's American multiversity, as well as the professional sociology created and taught there, offer evidence that service to the dictates of corporate capital is lucrative business. *The Uses of the University*, as Kerr points out, are many and varied. However, they justify the modern multiversity not because of their useful variety but rather, because they in turn justify, and help to legitimate, the socio-economic arrangements of the prevailing corporate capitalism.

To return to, and reinterpret, Kerr's justification of the modern university, the historical growth of American higher education leaves no doubt as to the multiversity's "consistency with the surrounding society". Also, Kerr's emphasis upon the way in which the multiversity has adapted to "new opportunities for creativity" can be historically documented. However, what Kerr — and Riesman, Jencks, and Clark as well — fail to emphasize, and what is critically important, is the role of corporate capital and capitalists in defining these creative opportunities to which the multiversity has responded in translating its eagerness to play "a new and useful role" into money. In the process, the multiversity has, as Kerr notes, changed rapidly, while multiversity participants have been most successful at "pretending that nothing has happened at all."

The point is, as has been argued throughout this paper, there is really no need to pretend. Multiversity changes have been made in accordance with the changing needs of the socio-economic system which dominates its continued growth and development; and, until multiversity participants realize the extent of this domination, and with this realization, their lack of autonomy, the multiversity will continue to be an institution which, in Kerr's words, "cannot escape service". Therefore, why pretend? In fact, while the multiversity has changed, nothing at all has happened — that is, nothing with respect to fundamental social change. In the self-congratulatory grip of an increasingly profitable educational-industrial-governmental partnership which has concentrated wealth and power in the hands of a dominating corporate elite, most multiversity professors and their students continue in contented service. They continue to create, teach, and learn the ideology of scientific multiversity celebrations. In so doing, they render themselves incapable of practice which might fundamentally question and alter prevailing socio-economic arrangements by asking which groups of people representing what beliefs, values, and economic interests they are serving.

NOTES

1. Quotation is taken from Barbara Jacobson and John M. Kendrick, "Education and Mobility: From Achievement to Ascription", *American Sociological Review*, August 1973, p. 442. The original source is Clark Kerr et al., *Industrialism and Industrial Man*, Cambridge: Harvard University Press, 1960.

2. This book is based on the 1963 Godkin Lectures, delivered by Kerr at Harvard University on April 23rd, 24th, and 25th.

3. Clark Kerr, *The Uses of the University*, New York: Harper and Row, 1964, pp. 44 and 45.

4. Quotation is taken from Bettina Aptheker, *Big Business and the American University*, New York: New Outlook Publishers, 1966, p. 6.

5. *Ibid.*, p. 20.

6. This is simply to say that quotations from sermons against Marxist theory and in praise of capitalism are much less important than those from the stock exchange in determining the loyalties of most regents with regard to the maintenance of prevailing socio-economic arrangements. For an informative bibliography and data that provide the basis for a composite picture of the socio-economic backgrounds and educational attitudes of the trustees who regularly sit on the governing boards of American colleges and universities, see Rodney T. Hartnett, "Trustee Power in America", *Power and Authority: Transformation of Campus Governance*, eds. Harold L. Hodgkinson and L. Richard Meeth, San Franscisco: Jossey-Bass Inc., 1971, pp. 25-38.

7. Kerr, *Uses*, p. 114.

8. *Ibid.*, pp. 90 and 91.

9. In addition to *Uses*, see, for example, Frederick Rudolph, *The American College and University*, Toronto: Random House of Canada, 1962; Christopher Jencks and David Riesman, *The Academic Revolution*, Garden City: Doubleday, 1968.

10. See Merle Curti and Roderick Nash, *Philanthropy in the Shaping of American Higher Education*, New Brunswick: Rutgers University Press, 1965, p. 43.

11. For a more detailed treatment of the historical growth of this partnership, see Randle W. Nelsen, *Growth of the Modern University and the Development of a Sociology of Higher Education in the United States*, Ph.D. Dissertation, Hamilton, Ontario: McMaster University, 1975, pp. 41-54. For a similar analysis, see David N. Smith, *Who Rules the Universities?*, New York: Monthly Review Press, 1974.

12. Nelsen, pp. 79-81, for more detailed information concerning the provisions of the Morrill Act and related legislation. The part this legislation played in secularizing an increasingly practical curriculum has been well-summarized by Frederick Rudolph who writes: "In the end, what sold agricultural education to the American Farmer and overcame the hostility of the Grange was evidence that scientific agriculture paid in larger crops, higher income, and a better chance to enjoy higher living standards — in other words, an opportunity to make frequent use of the Montgomery Ward or Sears Roebuck catalogue." (*The American College and University*, p. 261) By 1961 there were 69 American colleges whose primary source of financial support came from benefits received under the Morrill Act and related legislation. While this Act has not been significantly altered since passage of the Smith-Hughes legislation in 1917, it should be noted that the Vocational Education Act of 1963, and later amendments in 1968, have increased the amount of vocational training funds and made funding requirements more flexible in an attempt to better serve "disadvantaged" groups by broadening the scope of vocationalism.

13. For data on endowments to higher education and financial support for research and development in the United States, see Smith, *Who Rules?*, Chapter 7 entitled "Capitalism and the Universities", especially pp. 161-169. It is common knowledge that since 1950 governmental spending on research and development has grown at an extremely rapid rate (pp. 165-166). However, it is worth emphasizing, as is indicated in Smith's table on expenditures for American higher education from 1920-1963 (p. 164), how remarkably well "donations" from private

sources have kept pace with the tremendous increase in public expenditures. This fact indicates the inadvisability of placing too much emphasis upon a separation between "private" and "public". For the two merge as the result of the daily activities of a wealthy, dominant elite and as Smith points out, "the capitalist class would greatly prefer to let the state continue financing basic research rather than shoulder the burden itself." (pp. 168-169).

14. Kerr, *Uses*, p. 20. The fact that Kerr probably intended this to be a light-hearted and humorous definition of the modern multiversity does not alter its accuracy as a description of today's reality.

15. James Ridgeway, *The Closed Corporation: American Universities in Crisis*, New York: Ballantine Books, 1968, p. 11.

16. See Keith Baker, "A New Grantsmanship", *The American Sociologist*, November 1975, especially pp. 206-208.

17. See Nelsen, especially pp. 23-90, 139-151, and 267-281. The phrase in quotation marks is taken from Martin Nicolaus, "The Professional Organization of Sociology: A View from Below", *The Antioch Review*, Fall 1969, p. 382.

18. For excellent analyses of the work of this generation, see Dusky Lee Smith, "Sociology and the Rise of Corporate Capitalism", *Science and Society*, Fall 1965, pp. 401-418; *Some Socio-Economic Influences upon the Founding Fathers of Sociology in the United States*, Ph.D. Dissertation, Buffalo: The State University of New York, 1970.

19. This generation has been well-analyzed by Loren Baritz, *The Servants of Power: A History of the Use of Social Science in American Industry*, Middletown, Connecticut: Wesleyan University Press, 1960. Also, see Alex Carey, "The Hawthorne Studies: A Radical Criticism", *American Sociological Review*, June 1967, pp. 403-416. Many second generation sociologists found employment at the University of Chicago. For a description of the way in which the University of Chicago school developed a useful sociology built largely upon the work of founding father Albion W. Small, see Robert E.L. Faris, *Chicago Sociology 1920-1932*, Chicago: The University of Chicago Press, 1970.

20. See Herman Schwendinger and Julia Schwendinger, *The Sociologists of the Chair*, New York: Basic Books, 1974. For an earlier and much briefer overall view of the development of American sociology, see Roscoe C. Hinkle, Jr. and Gisela J. Hinkle, *The Development of Modern Sociology*, New York: Random House, 1954.

21. MSU was a willing "clearinghouse and broker" for close to $5¹/₂ million of government money over the seven year period from 1955 to 1962. Among the many activities financed were the hiring of CIA personnel by the university to help train Vietnam's police forces, the routine advisement by MSU project members of the South Vietnamese as to what military hardware they would need, and research that led to Project Director Wesley Fishel's complete change of mind, within the twelve month period just prior to the overthrow of the Diem government, as to the democratic character of that regime. See Irving Louis Horowitz, *Professing Sociology*, Chicago: Aldine Publishing Co., 1968, pp. 306-307; Warren Hinckle, Sol Stern and Robert Scheer, "MSU: The University on the Make", *Ramparts*, April 1966, pp. 11-22.

22. Project Camelot, ostensibly concerned with anti-Americanism in Chile, became

essentially a counter-insurgency project attempting to forecast revolution and insurgency in underdeveloped areas of the world. Project members, sponsored by the U.S. Army in what was originally to be a three to four year, $4-6 million contract let to SORO (Special Operations Research Office), were to find and try to eliminate the causes of revolution and insurgency so that the developed nations (e.g., the U.S.) could more easily continue their control of the less developed countries. Bad publicity forced discontinuation of the project after only one year and made advisable SORO's name change to CRESS (Center for Research in Social Systems). In 1968 CRESS had its head office in Washington, D.C., and turned over some $250,000 of a $3 million annual budget to American University in return for that institution's services in managing the affairs of its world-wide offices. For a discussion of the role of social scientists involved in Project Camelot — a role that makes transparent the relation between higher education and the prevailing socio-economic system — see Horowitz, *Professing,* pp. 288, 300-301. For more detail and other interpretations of this project, see *The Rise and Fall of Project Camelot,* ed. Irving Louis Horowitz, Cambridge: M.I.T. Press, 1967.

23. See Ridgeway, pp. 54-57.

24. *Ibid.*, pp. 68-72, 169-171.

25. *Ibid.*, pp. 10, 112-113, 129-132, 137-150.

26. The phrase ''private sector'' is placed in quotation marks because any remaining opposition from individuals and/or institutions that would permit one to make a distinction between private and public has long since been repressed and negated. For an excellent presentation of this point of view see Herbert Marcuse, *One-Dimensional Man,* Boston: Beacon Press, 1964.

27. See Howard S. Miller, *Dollars for Research: Science and Its Patrons in Nineteenth-Century America*, Seattle: University of Washington Press, 1970, p. 174.

28. For a more complete presentation of this argument as well as detailed references to the work of the three sociologists reviewed in summary form here, see my other contribution to the present volume, ''The Education-As-Autonomous Argument and Pluralism: The Sociologies of Burton R. Clark, David Riesman, and Christopher Jencks''.

29. This statement seems to be especially true for sociologists, see Roland J. Liebert and Alan E. Bayer, ''Goals in Teaching Undergraduates: Professional Reproduction and Client-Centeredness'', *The American Sociologist*, November 1975, pp. 201-202.

30. This author rejects Clark's analysis because his pluralistic bias does not permit him to recognize that the subservient position of an institution such as education means schools (multiversities included) do not change the institutional arrangements of the larger socio-economic order; rather, schools are in fact changed and maintained by that order. However, I agree with Clark's emphasis upon the necessity of minimal outside interference as a precondition for establishing at least some autonomy in higher education.

31. Kerr, *Uses*, p. 62.

32. See Edward Gross, ''Universities as Organizations: A Research Approach'',

American Sociological Review, August 1968, Vol. 33, especially p. 530.

33. See Horowitz, *Professing Sociology*, pp. 300-301.

34. Baker, pp. 212 and 214.

35. For case studies of "student activism" on two American campuses during the 1960s, see Irving Louis Horowitz and William H. Friedland, "Five Years of Confrontation at Cornell" and "Sit-In at Stanford" in *The Knowledge Factory: Student Power and Academic Politics in America,* Chicago: Aldine Publishing Co., 1970, pp. 220-335.

36. See Baker, pp. 206-207; also an editorial entitled, "Summer Madness", *The Nation*, May 29, 1976, pp. 642-643.

37. Tom Buckley, "Clean Carnage", *Harper's*, May 1976, p. 31.

38. Evidence of the growing public support for increased defense spending was collected in an April 1976 Gallup poll. See "Summer Madness", p. 643.

39. For further details concerning the work of Simulations Publications, see Buckley, pp. 34-35.

40. Robert S. Lynd, *Knowledge for What? The Place of Social Science in American Culture*, Princeton, New Jersey: Princeton University Press, 1939.

SECTION III

Job Recruitment in the Capitalist System

In North America in the 1950s and well into the 1960s, employers journeyed to university campuses to wait in line with extravagant and often unrefusable offers for graduates. Today, in the 1970s, recent graduates journey from the campus to wait hopefully outside the doors of prospective employers and employment agencies, while an increasing percentage lose hope and mark time in lengthening lines of the unemployed.

These developments have brought about a growing controversy over the role of education in recruiting and placing graduates in jobs. At the centre of this controversy have been debates concerning the responsibility of educators for providing job-related curricula, job-placement assistance, and job-creation programmes which some feel might encourage both the State and private industry to create meaningful alternatives to government-supported unemployment. The following papers provide a class-based analysis useful in beginning to understand the relation between education certified in schools and finding work in the capitalist economies of Canada and the United States.

Norene Pupo's paper is an examination of the role played by Canadian universities in training skilled labour. She argues that growth of Canadian higher education can be directly related to development and transition of the Canadian upper class structure. She traces some important links between big business, government, and universities by examining the development of the University of Waterloo. This history, with particular emphasis upon growth of Waterloo's Cooperative Engineering Programme, is used as a case study exemplifying transformation of Canadian universities to teach more scientific and practical subjects required by the postwar economy when need for skilled personnel was most acute. Perhaps more important than technical knowledge and skills taught to students, as Pupo notes, is the way in which universities have served needs of the dominant class by graduating men and women equipped with proper values, attitudes, and beliefs.

Fred Pincus picks up this thesis in his analysis of attempts by American community colleges to "democratize" education. He finds that community college participants operate within the context of four commonly accepted, but not publicly avowed, goals — training a paraprofessional labour force, screening, cooling-out, and custodial care. Achievement of these goals helps to "track" community colleges and their students into an educational system that is rather rigidly stratified. Community college educators come to accept

136

as legitimate the unequal distribution of wealth and power in American capitalist institutions, as well as their training role in helping to provide a skilled labour force to meet institutional needs. Pincus shows how acceptance and defense of conventional academic standards helps reinforce the view that correlations of social class and race with academic ability and achievement are simply an unfortunate, and also unchangeable, reality. The result is that community colleges do not help to democratize education but instead are important in maintaining educational inequality, helping to reinforce today's class and ethnic stratification system in the United States.

The Postwar University in Canada and the Need for Skilled Labour: The Waterloo Example

NORENE PUPO*

INTRODUCTION

In Canada, as in other capitalist countries, there has existed an intimate and reciprocal relation between institutions of higher learning, and men and institutions of wealth and power. Generally, the most prominent men who played major roles in the political and economic institutions acted as promoters and financiers of universities. Universities, in turn, have responded to needs of the dominant class by graduating men and women equipped with the proper values, attitudes, and beliefs as well as the type of knowledge or skills required by the economic order during its various stages of development. The growth of higher education has been related to the development and change of the Canadian upper class structure.

As the modes of production underwent significant transformation from independent commodity production to the later stages of competitive capitalism and monopoly capitalism, universities responded by changing curricula, admission policies, general outlook, and purposes. For example, during the early 1800s, universities were mainly responsible for training clerics and educating sons of the dominant class. Common educational ideas during the time, as espoused by prominent educators and administrators, such as John Strachan and John G. Simcoe, proposed that institutions of higher learning function as socialization agencies to preserve and maintain close ties with Britain. This ideology served the dominant class, the Family Compact, which depended on the British connection for its power, position, and wealth.

By the 1850s, changes were evident in the Canadian social structure as a result of the reform era. Pressure was brought to bear on universities to revise classical and often times religious curricula. Programmes were broadened to include more pragmatic, rational, and scientific subjects, and teaching methods took on new dimensions as instructors moved from book learning to demonstrative teaching techniques. Increasingly, members of the dominant class expressed great interest in higher learning. For example, close connections were maintained between William Gooderham, William McMaster, Sir

---

* I wish to thank Dusky Lee Smith and John Barkans for their comments and criticisms during the preparation of this paper.

Edmund Walker, John Hoskin, and the University of Toronto, and Peter Redpath, William Molson, William C. MacDonald, and McGill University. These men not only provided funds for the colleges but also sat on the major decision-making bodies of universities.

During the last decades of the nineteenth century and well into the twentieth century, the question of state supported higher education was debated. Arguments persisted over the form support was to take. Gradually as changes were made in legislation concerning universities to incorporate further financial and administrative support from the state, both businessmen and university officials worried that the university's autonomy was threatened. Universities, however, were never autonomous institutions but rather were shaped by social, political, economic, and historical forces operating on the Canadian political economy as a whole.

Although the relation between universities and the socio-economic order had been established during the nineteenth century, it was not until 1906 that the Canadian state fully legitimated this relation with passage of the University Act. Subject to debate for many years, this Act empowered the government to appoint for each university a separate Board of Governors which was to make decisions regarding financial matters. A second body, the university senate, whose members were to be internally recruited from professorial and administrative staff, was to direct policy decisions. However, rules made at this level were subject to the Board of Governors' approval. The ideological justification for the Act was that state supported universities should serve "society at large" and a government appointed body was entrusted to ensure this. In reality, the measure tightened capitalist hegemony in higher education. It has been found both in Canada and the U.S. that university Boards of Governors, composed largely of representatives of the dominant class, function to check that the political and economic ideology of the university's educators and administrators is favourable to the status quo.[1]

Starting from the historical premise that Canadian institutions of higher learning were closely related to the socio-economic order, this paper examines higher education in the post-World War II era. In particular, it focuses on the University of Waterloo. This university's massive growth and unique curricula and programming not only provides an interesting case study of a Canadian university's development but, more importantly, allows insights into social and economic forces at work within the university structure.

THE DEMAND FOR HIGHER EDUCATION AND THE POSTWAR ERA

Canadian universities were largely unprepared to teach the more scientific and practical subjects required by the postwar economy when the need for skilled personnel became acute. Although the Scientific and Industrial Research Council, the forerunner of the National Research Council, had been established as early as 1916 and was backed by the influential Canadian Manufacturers' Association, neither trained workers nor the essential laboratories and equipment were readily available in Canada by the end of World War II. Unlike American universities which were noted for their pragmatic approach to curricula,[2] Canadian universities had traditionally placed more emphasis upon preparing students with the proper values, attitudes, and beliefs for their roles within the social order rather than as training centres equipping students with easily marketable skills. By the post war period, however, changes in the Canadian economy and in the outlook of prominent Canadians had prompted a re-evaluation of the purposes of higher education.

Canadian higher education steadily expanded except during the depression and the war years when serious cutbacks were made. During World War II, all physically fit male students were subject to military training, an integral part of the university curriculum. Those engaged in research directly relevant to the war effort were allowed to continue on to graduate school. When the veterans of World War II were discharged, they were channelled into the universities, creating what was called the "veterans' bulge". Full-time enrolment jumped from 40,000 in 1944-5 to 64,000 in 1945-6 (by more than 50 per cent) and to 80,000 in 1946-7. Enrolment peaked at 83,000 in 1947-8 and gradually dropped to a postwar low of 63,000 in 1952-3.[3] What was more important than increasing enrolment figures, however, was the change in popular attitudes towards higher education as compared to prewar days. It has been pointed out that "it was not until World War II that universities found wide acceptance as essential institutions."[4] In fact, the entire higher educational system was broadened with the development of the institutions of technology and the community colleges during the 1950s.

The policy of directing war veterans into universities served to lessen the severe postwar unemployment problem. The government, in other words, extended its help to the economic order which was affected by the change in production requirements after demobilization. The Department of Veterans' Affairs granted $150 to universities per year per veteran.[5] The grant was to be discontinued upon the veterans' graduation, leaving the universities with the dilemma of "falling revenues and rising costs."[6] In the short time between the huge influx of soldiers and their graduation, in order to accommodate the great increase in enrolment, universities were faced with the problems of creating new courses and programmes or expanding old ones, hiring qualified teaching staff, and providing the extra laboratory equipment and building space required.

The following table shows the source of Canadian universities' finances based on data gathered from eight universities. Government sources (derived

TABLE I

In Thousands of Dollars

	1943-4	1944-5	1945-6	1946-7	1947-8	1948-9
Income from	1,562	1,827	1,684	1,635	1,697	1,749
endowments	15.9%	17.9%	11.5%	8.1%	7.9%	8.0%
Income from	3,378	3,444	5,539	8,028	8,537	9,932
student fees*	34.3%	33.8%	38.0%	40.0%	44.2%	48.0%
Grants from	3,978	4,289	4,487	6,262	5,573	6,082
prov. govt.†	40.5%	42.2%	30.8%	31.2%	25.8%	32.8%
From Dept. Vet-	4	4	1,865	3,222	2,822	2,137
erans' Affairs‡	0.0%	0.0%	12.8%	16.0%	13.1%	10.3%

* exclusive of board and lodgings
† other than grants from specific projects
‡ supplementary to students' fees, included above

Source: *Report of the Royal Commission on National Development in the Arts, Science and Letters*, p. 141.

from taxes collected disproportionately from non-upper class members) accounted for 40.5 per cent of all revenue in 1943-4 and 43.1 per cent in 1948-9. However, provincial grants declined by 7.7 per cent and it was only the federal government's veterans' grants which caused the increase in government grants to universities in the five year period. During the same period, the institutions' total expenditures for academic purposes (excluding construction expenses) rose by 110 per cent but because of increased numbers and crowded classroom conditions expenditures per student had dropped by 16 per cent.[7] Financial difficulties for some students were exacerbated by the sharp 50 per cent rise in the cost of living.[8] Generally students were responsible for a larger share of the costs of their education. In concise form, Table II below indicates changes in university funding which have occurred over the two postwar periods.

TABLE II

% of total

Year	Grants	Fees	Endowed	Other
1921	50%	18%	17%	15%
1946	42%	39%	10%	9%
1948	41%	41%	7%	7%

Source: *Financial Post*, May 26, 1951, p. 17.

The most striking observation from Table II is that income from student fees increased by 143 per cent while endowment receipts decreased by 128 per cent. While veterans' grants ideally may have provided opportunities for men of working class origin to attend university, the Massey Commission Report concluded that "money played a too important part in determining the composition of the student body." Further, the Commission found that as tuition fees rose, the number of students from rural areas decreased while more and more were drawn "from those communities which . . . [had] greater financial resources." Even in university cities where expenses were reduced because students were able to live at home, promising students were "barred by the lack of necessary means."[9]

While government officials and politicians declared their concern over the excessively exclusive nature of universities, educators seemed to be worried more about losing this exclusiveness. This worry was expressed in terms of the university's image and maintenance of "standards" and "quality". In a 1954 address, G.P. Gilmour, President of McMaster University, stated that "a new problem" had emerged because a greater number of students were entering universities "from homes which do not naturally and continually prepare their children for university, homes where books are scarce, where taste is not severely disciplined and where education is looked on chiefly as a means of upgrading in the economic sense."[10] Taking the British system as an example, Gilmour concluded that students from the middle and lower classes lacked the necessary "mental furniture" because of their more immediate "problems" — "financial anxiety, lack of privacy and the continuance of non-university companionship."[11]

Fear by Gilmour and others that universities were becoming more open was real and was probably based on the assumption that the economic prosperity of the period would allow more students from various backgrounds to attend. Between 1946 and 1971, both the Canadian gross national product and the total earned income increased rapidly, especially in the periods 1946 to 1951 and 1961 to 1971, resulting in a rise in the *per capita* gross national product by 346 per cent and in the *per capita* earned income by 501 per cent.[12] Possibly, then, the new economic prosperity of the post war era did enable some non-upper class people to attend university.

However, worry that high standards of universities would be lowered with the influx of working class people was needless. In 1951 President F. Cyril James of McGill University wrote: "A young Canadian from a family in modest circumstances has less chance of getting a university education than the youth of any other country with which I am familiar."[13] In fact, it was reported in 1956 that about 50 per cent of those desiring a university education were unable to go for financial reasons and in the same year only 15 per cent of Canadian university students received financial aid of any kind.[14]

In order to evaluate the growing demand for higher education in mid-twentieth century, it is important to understand the changing nature of the economy at the time. Briefly, during the 1950s, the Canadian economy moved from mainly primary industries into secondary and tertiary industries. Agricultural production declined, resource and extractive industries grew at a rapid rate, transportation and communication trades increased, and government activities in the community expanded. Further, the Gordon Commission Report expected that a great improvement in the relative cost position of secondary industry would take place once the Canadian market or "demand" was increased.[15] The most striking feature of the period concerned creation of what is called "the branch plant economy". The Report states that "from 1945 to 1955 total capital invested in Canada by United States residents increased from $4,990 million to $10,289 million" or by 106 per cent. American investments in Canada "grew substantially more during that decade than in the whole period from 1900 to 1945."[16] By 1955 U.S. investments in Canada equalled 77 per cent of all foreign capital invested.[17] The increase in the postwar period was mainly in the form of direct investment.

The changing nature of the economy placed great demands on universities. At the National Conference of Canadian Universities in 1956, a "crisis" situation in higher education was declared. The Conference was attended by university presidents including J.G. Hagey, Waterloo College; Sidney E. Smith, University of Toronto; C.T. Bissell, Carleton College; N.A.M. Mackenzie, University of British Columbia; federal government representatives — such as W.J. Bennett, president, Atomic Energy of Canada; K.W. Taylor, Deputy Minister of Finance; R.B. Bryce, Secretary to the Cabinet; provincial ministers of education; delegates from national organizations such as the National Research Council, the Canadian Chamber of Commerce, Canadian Manufacturers' Association, Industrial Foundation on Education; and industrial representatives of such firms as Imperial Oil and International Nickel Company of Canada.[18] Many of the Conference sessions were devoted to the need to improve Canada's higher educational system so that it would be comparable to the systems of the U.S. and the U.S.S.R.

Dominant North American ideology at the time reflected a simultaneous fear of, and respect for, Russia's "Sputnik" experiment. With a desire to compete in similar scientific endeavours, the Canadian dominant class set down as one of Canada's primary tasks the amelioration of the university system. This ideology was reflected in statements made by prominent educators. For example, P.R. Gendron of the University of Ottawa said that for Canada to maintain its role as a leading nation, its universities "must be enabled to contribute to the advancement of knowledge in the field of applied science as they do in the field of pure science."[19] Similarly, N.A.M. Mackenzie stated that Canada's basic national interest is toward scientific progress if the country is to keep pace with other nations. [20]

Cold war attitudes reflected the stereotyped version of mass society under "communism" and encouraged a strong competitive sentiment. North Americans desired to assert superiority over the U.S.S.R. and in order to do this, higher education was necessary. In explaining his ideas on scientific and technological training, one M.I.T. dean said that Russia is training "swarms" of technicians, "but [I'd] rather bet the security of the world on a substantial number . . . of enquiring minds . . . than on a horde of skilled and obedient technicians."[21] In the "monolithic" U.S.S.R. where there was supposedly "no clear way to the top", technologists were accorded high salaries, status, and other rewards as "carrots", resulting in sufficient numbers of applicants for technical training.[22] Since Canada was a "free country", the answer to the question of how to attract people into technical fields lay in the creation of a meritocracy.

TABLE III

	No. in Higher Education	Per 1,000 People
U.S.S.R.	4.3 million	19.6
U.S.	3.0 million	18.0
Canada	70,000	4.9

Source: *Financial Post*, May 18, 1957, p. 7.

As 1957 statistics clearly show, the proportion of Canada's population enrolled in university lagged far behind the corresponding figures for the U.S.S.R. and the U.S. Thus, in the spring of 1957, N.R. Crump, president of the Canadian Pacific Railway, headed a campaign to raise $4 million for Queen's University.[23] Shortly after this, in another area of the province, Waterloo College was opened on July 2, 1957 to its first group of 100 engineering students. Speaking rather candidly several years later, President Hagey recalled: "Russia obligingly sent up Sputnik. The rush was on in 1958 and 1959 to train engineers."[24]

Ideally, full scale expansion of universities seemed to be the solution. Practically, there were problems — the universities lacked finances and facilities. Not only had there been no *real* increase in revenues over the twenty year period from 1936 to 1956,[25] but salaries for faculty employed in universities lagged far behind what would normally be offered in industry. To rectify this situation, two sources of revenue were sought: the state and the corporate sector.[26]

As cited above, statistics show that government sources accounted for an increasingly larger proportion of universities' budgets while income from endowment and other gifts steadily declined.[27] As discussed in the Gordon Commission report, the increase in U.S. investment in Canada was accompanied by a new technology and ultimately the need for skilled personnel.[28] The expansion of the Canadian public sector, therefore, was directly beneficial to the American private sector in that much of the skilled manpower employed by American branch-plants was educated and trained at Canadian taxpayers' expense. Further, merit scholarships were often given out to top students by companies to encourage research and more importantly to guarantee the proper training of future employees. This type of award was given directly to the student as an incentive. The institution, backed by government finances, still had to absorb overhead costs of laboratory facilities, faculty and staff salaries, and building space.

In 1956 the Ontario government announced a ten year programme of capital assistance to provincial universities and technical institutes, the aim of which was "to boost the output of engineers and technicians."[29] Provincial Treasurer Dana Porter (later Chancellor of the University of Waterloo) was in charge of the plan which operated on the assumption that "about $25 million was needed for Ontario university expansion in the . . . five years ending in 1960 and another $60 million in the five years after that."[30]

Shortly after this plan was announced, the federal government, responding to the Canadian Association of University Teachers' submission to the Gordon Commission, decided that it would double *per capita* grants to universities from $.50 to $1. Total federal grants thus climbed from $8 to $16 million.[31] This amount was subsequently increased to $1.50 in 1958-9, to $2.00 in 1962-3, and to $5.00 in 1966-7.[32] In the 1966-7 year, the grant was abruptly discontinued, leaving the bulk of university financing to the provinces. The federal programme, it seems, was mainly instituted in order to help out during the critical expansion period.[33]

That the universities and the corporate sector were mutually dependent on one another and mutually reinforced each other was clear. At the 1957 Conference of the Industrial Foundation on Education it was urged that financial aid to schools and universities be immediately increased, a policy most welcomed by the financially dependent "ivory towers". Members of the corporate sector decided that efficient and increased production of highly trained people was key to the nation's ability to maintain a competitive position among the industrialized countries of the world.[34] Another and perhaps more immediately recognizable reason for corporate donation to education was the belief that Canada had to catch up technologically to major world powers. On this subject James S. Duncan, Chairman of the Ontario Hydro-Electric Commission, said: "In my opinion, we are in danger today of losing the Cold War unless we do something very drastic about it and education is very close to the core of the problem."[35] Members of the corporate sphere had a vested interest in maintaining institutions of higher learning. Until further government support could be generated, they would partially assume responsibility of financing universities rather than risk the possibility of losing a respectable position in world trade and the cold war.

As the Table below indicates, in the four year period between 1956 and 1960, business and industrial grants to universities rose by 405 per cent. Besides these grants given to the institutions, business and industrial enterprises offered scholarships and other awards to students. However, the government provided the major source of support for the student as well as for the institutions. Of $11.5 million donated in the form of scholarships and bursaries to Canadian students in 1960, $1.2 million or approximately 10 per cent came from business and industry while the remaining 90 per cent came from various levels of government.[36]

TABLE IV

Business and Industrial Grants to Canadian Universities, 1956-60

Grants*	1960	1959	1958	1957	1956
Capital		9,039	7,627	7,046	1,484
Operating	12,400	1,009	648	922	421
Research		1,669	1,306	1,320	469
Other	1,224	719	847	2,335	323
Total	13,624	12,436	10,428	11,623	2,697

* in thousands of dollars

Source: *Financial Post*, August 5, 1961, p. 24.

Besides manpower needs of advanced technology, and nationalistic desire to improve Canadian higher education, the dominant class had a more fundamental reason to support the university. That is, universities were major socialization agencies and ideology producing mechanisms, promoting a strong identification with those values, attitudes, and beliefs necessary for maintenance of the capitalist system. As W.M. Compton, the president of the American Council for Financial Aid to Education said, "liberal education . . . provides the economic and political climate most favourable to business. If we lose the spirit of liberal education, we shall gradually lose the spirit of free enterprise." "Like advertising", education maintains the capitalist system by "making people dissatisfied with what they have."[37] Creation of new and often "false" needs within people ensures smooth running of corporate machinery from production to consumption.

David N. Smith suggests that the corporate order has built a system of higher education "corresponding not to the logic of industrial production *per se* but to the logic of capital accumulation underlying industrial production in capitalist society."[38] Such controls are reinforced in institutions of higher learning by the boards of governors with their relationships to the economic order and to the dominant class; as well as by the institutions' readiness to teach subject matter which deals both directly and indirectly with profit-making, industrial techniques, business practices and ideas of hierarchy, obedience, subordination, and competition. In order to understand such relationships, it is now time to turn to a specific case example of a modern university.

THE DEVELOPMENT OF THE UNIVERSITY OF WATERLOO

In 1955, J.G. Hagey, a former advertising and public relations man with B.F. Goodrich, recommended that a Faculty of Applied Science be established in affiliation with Waterloo College. Waterloo College was a small liberal arts college established in 1914 as an outgrowth of Waterloo Lutheran Seminary. Pressures of post war expansion, the Cold War and Russia's launching of Sputnik, and need for technical expertise had led Hagey and Ira G. Needles, president of B.F. Goodrich Canada, to agree that "it was in the best interests of the Twin Cities area that opportunities be provided for higher education beyond the general arts degree."[39] To discuss possibilities of developing an applied science programme in Kitchener-Waterloo, Needles and Hagey organized a meeting, mainly for businessmen, where it was decided that those in attendance would support the plan and would serve as members of the Board of Governors of the Associate Faculties of Waterloo College.

These governors were, for the most part, actively engaged in a broad range of industrial and commercial activities. Of twenty-two persons on the committee, eighteen were described in the university's official history as businessmen. Of the remaining four, two were publishers[40] and two were doctors. One was also Mayor of Waterloo. Seventeen were listed in *Who's Who in Canada, 1958-60* and/or *The Financial Post Directory of Directors, 1955*. A total of 33 directorships and executive offices were held by these seventeen. Some of the corporations in which governors held offices included: The Dare Company, Dominion Mortgage and Investments Association, Dominion Rubber Company, Superior Box Company, Doon Twines, Economical Mutual Fire Insurance Company, Waterloo Manfacturing Company, Dominion Electrohome Industries, Waterloo Trust and Savings Company, L. McBrine Company, Campbell Containers, Biltmore Hats, Central Ontario Television, Canadian Office and School Furniture, and Equitable Life Insurance Company of Canada.

Particularly outstanding was the governors' affiliation with financial institutions: seven governors held seven directorships in insurance companies; five were affiliated with Waterloo Trust and Savings Company; and two positions were held in two other financial organizations, Waterloo Bond Company and Dominion Mortgage and Investments Association. Also, the seventeen governors together held approximately thirty-five positions in manfacturing firms. It is clear that these men were prominent within local ''higher circles''. Because of the class specificity of ideology, it is certain that when they were called upon to make decisions concerning the priorities of the developing university, curriculum possibilities, or the administration of the institution, they did so in the best interests of their class positions within the economic order.

The rapid rate of corporate expansion in the 1950s meant that most employers were actively searching for trained personnel. At the time, *Financial Post* reported that there were approximately two or three times more jobs than graduates. At the University of Toronto, for example, nearly 200 companies sent recruiters to the campus and another 330 tried hiring by mail. Over 4,200 jobs were offered but only 1,500 graduates were available.[41] The highest ratios of jobs to graduates were reported in mechanical and electrical engineering, metallurgy, mathematics, physics, geophysics, chemistry, and technical, civil service and administrative jobs. Placement offices became shopping centres for employees and employers alike. The problem as one placement officer saw it was one of ''fitting an annual crop of some 11,000 graduates to many more than 11,000 jobs.''[42] One officer at McMaster University saw the need to create more of a liaison between the economic order and the campus as the solution to this problem.[43]

If, indeed, universities were to service the corporate sector by facilitating its task of finding proper employees, the Waterloo College plan was certainly ideal. Under this plan, President Hagey proposed that the Associate Faculties adopt a cooperative programme in engineering. According to the original plan, students were to spend alternate periods of thirteen weeks on and off campus. The scheme was later changed to four month periods. While on campus, students were to cover theoretical material which would equip them for the subsequent off campus period that they would spend in local industries. The Hagey plan, devised to overcome the shortage of engineers and trained technical personnel, was financially sound because it permitted maximum use of college investment capital by remaining in operation for 48 instead of the regular 30 weeks per year. Furthermore, by providing education for two classes annually it would release fresh ''crops'' of graduates at a relatively faster pace than other universities.

By October 1956, the Ontario government had acknowledged the ''Waterloo Plan'' with a $25,000 grant for initial research and development of the programme.[44] By May 1957, a course outline for the first three years had been prepared, faculty appointments had been made and a budget of

$125,000 had been approved for equipment. More importantly, 150 students had indicated their acceptance of the programme by applying and sending in cash deposits.[45] In addition, the provincial government granted a further $625,000, Joseph E. Seagrams and Sons contributed $250,000 for a football stadium and gymnasium, while the City of Waterloo promised $100,000 for the football field and surrounding lights.[46]

During the planning stages of Waterloo College, many contacts were made with representatives of the economic order and appropriate professional bodies. For example, opinions and advice on the workings of the cooperative programme were sought from such bodies as the Canadian Manufacturers' Association, the Canadian Engineering Institute, and the National Conference on Canadian Universities.[47] The governors sponsored a luncheon in Toronto where they met with thirty-five industrialists, and letters were written to 100 major Canadian corporations in order to receive reactions to cooperative education.[48]

Waterloo organizers were pleased with the results of their work. J.G. Hagey declared: "The response from industry has been so great that we will have to allocate to some companies fewer students than they ask for."[49] After its initial stages, industry did not lose interest in the programme. At a meeting the following year, Hagey was able to boast: "No difficulty has been found in placing Waterloo students and the fact that over 300 have found suitable industrial employment well in advance of current work assignment periods is a striking indication of industry's acceptance of the cooperative plan and . . . of the acceptance of the students themselves."[50]

The University of Waterloo was officially born on March 5, 1959 when the private bill creating it was given royal assent in the Ontario legislature. At that time, there were 173 companies, spread from eastern Manitoba to western Quebec, employing cooperative students.[51] According to *Industrial Canada*, "the list of participating firms [reads] like an industrial 'Who's Who in Canada'."[52] Moreover, it was reported in the *Monetary Times* in 1958 that "there . . . [were] few, if any, of the household-name companies in Canada, which . . . [were] not cooperating with the College and they included primary producers, manufacturers and service enterprises."[53] Once the Waterloo Plan was under way, headlines in the *Kitchener-Waterloo Record* read: "Twin City Industry Surges Ahead: Millions Poured into Expansion."[54] Since the university was developed in order to "serve the Kitchener-Waterloo area", it is probable that local concerns were taken into account when decisions were made with respect to the university's need to serve the corporate sphere.

Not only did the governors, to a certain extent, provide the link between the economic and educational orders, but in the case of the University of Waterloo, there also existed a "go-between" organization. The Industrial

Advisory Council was organized in 1958 to "keep abreast of industry's reaction to the college courses."[55] This Council was extremely important because it was a formal, institutionalized channel through which industry's viewpoint was aired.

In view of the findings of the Industrial Foundation on Education and the Gordon Commission, it is not surprising that industrialists in Kitchener-Waterloo and hinterland areas were convinced of the need for the university. In explaining Canada's deficiency in advanced technology, the Industrial Foundation on Education noted that "in the year end[ing] June 30, 1957, 23 per cent of our exports . . . consisted of products in which modern technology was predominant. At the same time, 48 per cent of our imports . . . consisted of products in the same category."[56] Also, comparative statistics showed that the U.S. employed 4.2 engineers for every 1,000 persons while Canada employed only 2.8.[57] Of the engineers employed in Canada, a great number were immigrants. For example, in 1956, 1,700 engineers were brought into the country; this number was equivalent to the engineering graduates from all Canadian universities in that year.[58] Waterloo College promised to meet all needs outlined in the report.

The Gordon Commission pointed out that an increasingly large number of skilled workers would be needed for the Canadian economy to maintain a steady and positive rate of growth. According to the Commissioners, it would be more and more mandatory that workers at all levels have a higher general level of ability with respect to technical skills.[59] As early as 1952, large U.S. subsidiaries in Canada were following the U.S. trend in demanding a university degree for job vacancies.[60] Furthermore, it was proposed that the government help by fostering in-plant training programmes so that as employees' skills became obsolete, they would be retrained. Given the shortage of engineers and other technically trained personnel, the advantages of going to university were clear. This was especially true at Waterloo where those who could not keep up with more advanced studies were given technical diplomas instead of being failed or forced out of the system altogether. The question for graduates, however, was not one of whether or not there were adequate job openings. It was a question of whether they could prevent the loss of responsibility and control within their positions during the following decades of phenomenal corporate expansion and technological advancement.

THE WATERLOO COOPERATIVE STUDENT AND THE WHITE COLLAR WORKER

The path between the campus and the plant should be open and unhindered.
—Samuel Bronfman[61]

For many years one of the guiding principles of business education had been that "contact with industry is the best possible lab and textbook."[62] University business departments wanted "to be regarded as the businessman's friend in need — a source of readily available information and advice."[63] This same principle became the guideline for Waterloo's cooperative engineering programme. The programme established one more formal link between the university and the socio-economic order. Through the participating students, the industrial sphere was able to keep abreast of all the new "products" of the "knowledge factory". Thus, when the University of Sherbrooke patterned its cooperative engineering programme after Waterloo, some companies decided to pair students from the two institutions to work in alternate terms in order that ideas from both schools would be brought into the company.

The idea that employers were able to "look over" future employees was particularly appealing both to university officials and employers. In 1956 it was reported that corporate officials were interested in hiring second and third year students for summer jobs in order to introduce them to the company. According to the *Financial Post*, this gave "the corporation a chance to look over the prospective employee and also a chance to sell him on coming back to the firm after graduation."[64] Similarly, one of the selling points of the Waterloo Plan was that students would acquire a "business outlook" and would therefore not be "green" employees.[65]

In order to simplify the task of fitting a student into the normal company pattern, most firms took two students per year on opposite schedules. This meant that the student position would be filled year round, creating no problem or loss for the corporation. It left the employer with a good choice in hiring at the end of the terms. Most students returned to the firm where they served throughout their university careers. Only 30 per cent of students shifted to new employers.[66] Most shifting students, however, had also decided to change their field of specialization. Overall, it was found that 61 per cent of companies and 50 per cent of students had their first choice in hiring for jobs.[67] Out of an average graduating class, 80 per cent of students entered industrial employment while 20 per cent went to graduate school or into teaching. Of those who entered industry, roughly 50 per cent returned to their last employer under the cooperative programme, 43 per cent were hired by another participating company and five per cent sought employment elsewhere.[68] Thus, corporation officials were able to hire well trained and educated workers while reducing costs of hiring, interviewing, and recruiting.

Attitudes toward the students were generally very favourable. For example, a Bell Canada supervisor described Waterloo graduates as job oriented, "more mature", "ready to produce", and less costly to hire.[69] Similarly, a Union Carbide of Canada executive said that the plan permitted the company not only "to assess undergraduates", but to select and develop those in whom they were interested "to the point where these [students] . . .

[could] undertake assignments of greatest responsibility'' compared to similar graduates of a non-cooperative university.[70] Another employer remarked that his company did not ''have to waste time on familiarization'' if it hired Waterloo graduates.[71]

Furthermore, it has been argued that education under the capitalist system prepares students for life as employees;[72] that is, education teaches them to accept the fundamental principles, workings, and values of capitalism. Ideas of division of labour and hierarchy, acceptance of the dominant class, and belief in competition, obedience, and respect for authority are, for example, part of the ''hidden curriculum''. In the case of cooperative education, the functions of education — the teaching of submissiveness, etc. — are shared directly with members of the corporate order. The transition, then, from one set of oppressors — educators and schools — to another — employers and corporate bureaucracies — is made smoother for the student who is gradually imbued with an employee mentality.

Hence, employers support higher education (and education in general) because of its function not only in training workers but also in *socializing* them. In answer to the question of why he supports higher learning, Philip Reed, Chairman of General Electric Company said that the most important function of higher education is not in creating technical specialists but rather, in ''maintaining the *social, economic and political climate* of . . . democracy. Without such a climate, business could not survive and certainly not prosper and continue to make progress.''[73]

Engineers increasingly socialized as ''employees'' in bureaucracies became part of the shift to a ''new middle class''. Whereas the ''old middle class'' referred to a society of small entrepreneurs and implied a degree of property, freedom, and security,[74] the ''new middle class'' according to C.W. Mills is composed of white collar groups, including professionals, clerical workers, technicians, administrators, civil servants, managers, and engineers.[75] The myth of the middle class, perhaps derived from the meaning of the term ''middle'', is that it occupies the levels of the social hierarchy between ''labour'' and ''capital''. This myth is based on social indicators such as status and prestige. However, Mills argues, in its relation to property, the middle class is ''*not* 'in between Capital and Labour' '' but is ''exactly in the same . . . class position as . . . wage workers.'' The middle class has ''no direct financial tie to the means of production, [or] prime claim upon proceeds from property.'' Like factory workers, members of the middle class work for those who own the means of their livelihood.[76] Rather than analyzing white collar workers as a separate social class, it is more appropriate to describe their position as a sector within the working class.

The expansion of the white collar sector in postwar Canada can be related largely to growth of the economy and of American corporate involvement in Canada. During the 1950s, the number of unskilled workers was decreasing while the number of skilled and semi-skilled workers increased. By the end of the 1950s, Porter wrote, 40 per cent of workers were in white collar and 10 per cent were in personal service occupations; although blue collars still comprised about one-third of the work force, they were generally more skilled. "During the decade the labour force grew by about one-quarter, but professional occupations grew by three-quarters and other white collar occupations grew by one-third."[77] In relation to working conditions, the white collar employee has no more control over the work process than does the blue collar worker. As Mills noted, "most of the old professionals have long been free practitioners; most of the new ones have from their beginnings been salaried employees."[78] This point has been amply demonstrated by Leo Johnson who found in Canada "an overall decline in the proportion of professionals in independent practice" between 1941 and 1971.[79]

White collar workers and professionals have thus become less independent and their work has become more routinized. Historically white collar jobs have become more similar to blue collar jobs with respect to gradual loss of worker's control over his or her work process, rigid and hierarchical division of labour and job tasks, loss of responsibility, authority, and freedom, and the more distinct possibility of one's job being terminated for disobedience and other employee infractions.[80]

The major factors separating white collar from blue collar workers are type of education and emphasis upon the ideology of professionalism and expertise. It was, according to prominent educators, the task of the university to prepare the "new middle class" to maintain "progress". As universities sustained myths and promises of upward social mobility, eventual job satisfaction, privileges, responsibility, and respectability for graduates, all those not barred from matriculating because of financial difficulties were increasingly compelled to earn a degree.

WATERLOO'S OTHER PROGRAMMES

Because the development of the University of Waterloo was closely related to Canada's search for technically trained personnel, the image of the university is most often associated with its engineering and science faculties. In fact, by 1963 the question of whether Waterloo would become "a Canadian M.I.T." arose.[81] Although Canadian universities in general have many direct and formal ties to the socio-economic order through their boards of governors, a relatively high proportion of Waterloo's officials, administrators, and teaching staff were at some time involved in industrial pursuits. For example, the first chairman of the Industrial Advisory Council had been an executive of Sun Oil Company; a Waterloo vice-president and chemistry professor, previous to his university appointments, had been associated with three large corporations; one physicist had formerly been with the Defence Research Board Electronics Lab and another was from Orenda Engines Limited; a chairman of the chemistry department had worked at E.I. DuPont Company and his successor had spent several years at Welland Chemical Works. This industrial partnership accounts somewhat for the pragmatic nature of the university's curriculum and reinforces a general business orientation.

In 1959 the Department of Science split from engineering to form a separate faculty. At this time the faculty offered four courses — honours chemistry, honours chemistry and physics, honours math and physics, or three year general science. By 1962 the faculty offered both a graduate programme and a cooperative course in applied science and in 1966 a cooperative course in chemistry was added. The nature of the teaching was very practical. Hence the chairman of the chemistry department declared: "The staff in the university is as much concerned with *practising* their subjects as with *teaching* them."[82]

In a similar manner, the Faculty of Arts is very much oriented toward a practical curriculum. The "nucleus" of the faculty is the math department which had in its first year of operation twelve out of the twenty-four arts faculty members.[83] In 1964 a cooperative programme was introduced in honours math with computer science and actuarial options and in 1966 the math department split from Arts to form its own faculty. The cooperative course in math, wrote the *Financial Post*, "answers requests by representatives of the Canadian insurance industry for a cooperative system to assist students to enter the actuarial profession."[84] Response from the financial sector was phenomenal. When the programme was announced, twenty-eight companies immediately agreed to take cooperative students.[85] Three years later headlines in the *Financial Post* read: "Big Insurers Still Call K-W Home".[86] It was reported that the heaviest concentration of Canada's insurance business was located in the Kitchener-Waterloo area. Thus, it is quite possible that pressure from financial circles, through the Board of Governors, was brought to bear on the university to institute a programme for the financial sector similar to the ones in engineering and physics which catered to the industrial sector.

Other programmes in arts included Russian and German, English, sociology, political science, Romance languages, history, psychology, economics, philosophy, classics, and geography. Again, the programmes were oriented toward more practical forms of curricula. Sociology, for example, is noted for its strong orientation toward quantitative studies as it was assessed by the recent Report of the Advisory Committee on Academic Planning.[87] Similarly, the department of geography and urban planning is noted for its pragmatic approach to urban studies and geography problems.

By 1960 adult education classes had been organized in the surrounding communities of Galt, Guelph, Hanover, and Stratford. These classes were sponsored by either the local Chambers of Commerce or sales and advertising clubs. There was a total of 46 classes, 58 instructors, and 1,212 students during the first year of operation. However, it seems that the "spirit" of higher education had not yet caught on. The Annual Report of the Adult Education Department noted that few top management officials were aware of opportunities for education for their employees. Nevertheless, the Report added that "where Top Management gives encouragement and recognition for courses taken, there is a much greater response from employees."[88] Perhaps the chance for workers to upgrade skills was not seen as an essential need in 1960. Most adult education courses at the time were non-degree courses. Four years later, in 1964, the Annual Report showed a more positive attitude. In projecting to 1970, the authors of the report expected less demand for non-degree courses and increased demand for degree programmes. This projection, moreover, included concrete plans to develop more programmes in marketing and management studies, taught by persons with "acceptable industrial or business backgrounds."[89] This attitude reflected the national push for expansion in higher education and for training and retraining programmes in the 1960s.

Although a complete analysis cannot be undertaken here, it is important to study not only the programmes like science, engineering, and mathematics which are directly useful for the corporate order, but also to realize that university curricula are generally supportive of the socio-economic system. There may be no fundamental ideological differences between courses in engineering and science and those in the social sciences and humanities. Structurally, the university's primary function is to train and socialize workers to fit into various slots in the social structure. The significant difference between the disciplines concerning ideology, then, is one of preparing students for different roles within the socio-economic order.

THE CURRENT SITUATION: STUDENTS, EDUCATION, AND JOBS

As previously stated, during the 1960s universities engaged in a massive expansion movement, largely financed by government.[90] The universities were mainly inadequate for the large numbers of people attending. Expectation of upward social mobility coupled with employers' demands for educated workers rapidly accelerated growth of higher learning in Canada. Between 1959 and 1965, nine new degree granting charters were authorized — Waterloo, Waterloo Lutheran, York and Royal Military College in 1959, Laurentian in 1960, Lakehead in 1962, Trent in 1963, and Brock and Guelph in 1964. Enrolment increased steadily. Between 1956-7 and 1968-9, full-time undergraduate enrolment increased by 217 per cent in Canada and by 212 per cent in Ontario. In the same period full-time graduate enrolment increased by 619 per cent in Canada and 509 per cent in Ontario. Ontario's lower percentage is accounted for by the fact that graduate facilities and universities there developed ahead of those in the rest of Canada.

Between 1960-1 and 1967-8 total enrolment increases were: for Canada, 120 per cent, for Ontario, 146 per cent, and for the University of Waterloo, 729 per cent. Although increases across Canada were substantial during the entire decade, the establishment of new universities and colleges slowed down toward 1970. Enrolment, however, continued to grow at a faster rate. Hence, between 1958-9 and 1963-4, Ontario's total full-time enrolment grew by 59 per cent while Waterloo's enrolment expanded by 130 per cent. In the years from 1965-6 to 1969-70, full-time enrolment in Ontario grew by 87 per cent and for the same period, Waterloo's increase was 134 per cent.[91]

Between 1960-1 and 1969-70, operating expenditures of all post-secondary institutions in Canada increased by 480 per cent. This represents an average annual increase for the nine year period of 53 per cent.[92] For a number of reasons, including the fact that it was a strategy to combat increasing unemployment, the federal and provincial governments poured enormous amounts of money into higher education during the late 1950s and early 1960s. Table V shows sources of income of Canadian universities from 1958 to 1967. From the table it can be calculated that government grants rose from 57 per cent of total income in 1958 to 66 per cent in 1967, while endowment and investment income decreased from four to just under two per cent.

Not only were universities receiving an increased percentage of budgets from government but also a substantial portion of scholarships, bursaries, and other awards. In 1960, 69 per cent of scholarships and bursaries available to Canadian students were supplied by the federal and provincial governments,[93] with the greatest percentage coming from the latter. At the University of Waterloo, a slightly higher percentage of awards, 73 per cent, was donated by government.[94] Further, government sources accounted for 57 per cent of all science scholarships and 75 per cent of all those in engineering at Waterloo in 1960. By 1964 Waterloo students received 79 per cent of all awards from the government.

Increased state financing in higher education did not serve to prevent business and industrial involvement. This was especially true for newer universities where capital expenditures were very high. Also, new universities wanted to create respectable images in order to attract students. All institutions embarked on fund raising campaigns. Universities, along with government, worked to satisfy the needs of the dominant class so that they would be ensured of at least a minimal amount of gifts and endowments.

Owing to the success of the cooperative programme in meeting the needs of the industrial order, in 1959 over $1.35 million was contributed by business and industry to Waterloo. Of this figure, over 50 per cent came from the Kitchener-Waterloo area.[95] The Waterloo fund raisers were, in fact, members of either the "inner core" or "fringe area" of the Canadian dominant class. They included: W.M. Rankin,[96] general chairman of the campaign, vice-president and general manager, Waterloo area, Bell Telephone Company of Canada; J.D. Barrington, president and director, McIntyre Porcupine Mines; J.P.R. Wadsworth, vice-president and general manager, Canadian Imperial Bank of Commerce; A.A. Cumming, president, Union Carbide of Canada; E. Brown, deputy general manager, eastern division, Toronto-Dominion Bank; and W.H. Reid, president, Spitzer, Mills and Bates. The university, then, was dependent on members of the dominant class not only for their contributions *per se* but also for their ability to perpetuate the established relation between higher education and the socio-economic order.

TABLE V

Current Income
In Thousands of Dollars

School Yr. Ended	Endowments & Investments	Govt. Grants	Student Fees	Misc.	Total
1958	4,375	60,293	30,867	10,304	106,166
1959	4,668	74,294	33,546	11,373	123,881
1960	5,082	87,863	40,789	14,132	148,659
1961	5,332	115,524	45,991	14,396	181,243
1962	7,834	121,461	56,249	25,062	210,606
1963	8,191	142,606	62,397	27,107	240,301
1964	10,308	168,626	75,573	28,785	283,292
1965	7,986	200,412	89,738	44,632	242,768
1966	9,030	256,915	110,624	49,780	426,349
1967	9,506	384,521	129,523	57,604	581,584

Source: *Canada Year Book*, 1969, p. 359.

Although universities continued to seek favours, approval, contributions, and acceptance from the corporate order, growing responsibility for organization and funding of these institutions lay with government. With university expansion came increased government coordination and bureaucratization. Between 1960 and 1965, the Department of University Affairs, Committee of Presidents, Council on Ontario Universities, Ontario Confederation of University Faculty, and Ontario Federation of Students were set up to coordinate the government's educational affairs. Such emphasis on expansion and centralized control required enormous amounts of capital. At the expense of the working class through the taxation system, the state increasingly took control and paid for the training and socializing of technical, scientific, professional, and other so-called post-industrial workers.

Expansion of universities in the 1960s was accompanied by phenomenal growth of the Colleges of Applied Arts and Technology (C.A.A.T.) which "produced in their first two years, some 20 'instant colleges' looking after about 50,000 full and part-time students."[97] Due to the plethora of institutions of higher learning, employers could expect to hire more highly educated workers. As universities and colleges increasingly became mass societal institutions, "the meaning of education had shifted from status and political spheres to economic and occupational areas."[98] Education has contributed to the rise of white collar work by providing training in skills required by the occupational structure.[99] Employers' demands for more qualified workers (and consequently the workers' fears of replacement by better educated employees) became the norm during the 1960s and is reflected by the tremendous growth of part-time enrolment and extension departments. For instance, it was found that the number of part-time students taking undergraduate credit courses had risen from 11,904 in 1962-3 to 20,317 in 1965-6 and that part-time graduate enrolment had increased over the same period from 1,828 to 2,065.[100]

The so-called knowledge explosion has had, according to James O'Connor, "far-reaching effects on production relations." State sponsored schools have rapidly replaced family, office, and factory as the main socialization agencies of young workers. Rapid growth of technology has, in turn, been facilitated by the availability of large numbers of technical-scientific workers. Advanced technology has "spurred the substitution of [people] by machines" and has served to "expand total production and accelerate the growth of the relative surplus population." Consequently, more "social expense programmes", including education, are needed in order to "turn the surplus population into capital" and also "to legitimate the system in an epoch when education is increasingly required to get and keep well-paying jobs."[101]

This process described by O'Connor has been analyzed in a different way by proponents of the post-industrial thesis. Canadian sociologists, John Porter and Bernard Blishen, relying on the works of Daniel Bell and John Kenneth Galbraith, have accepted the argument that power in society has passed from individuals to organizations and that a "technostructure" of educated and technically trained manpower has become the "new men of power". Galbraith argues that "it is not to individuals but to organizations that power in the business enterprise and power in the society has passed."[102] In his model of post-industrial society, a growing body of educators and research scientists, "directly nurtured by the industrial system" is of central importance. This group's role, which he compares to that of the banking and financial community in earlier stages of industrial development, functions conveniently to connect those within the "technostructure" to those outside, and therefore acts as an integrating agent for various levels of society.[103] Similarly, in Daniel Bell's post-industrial society, the university is the locus of power. Whereas inheritance and entrepreneurial ability were modes of access when power was based on property, he argues, "education is ... becoming the chief determinant of the stratification system of the society" and therefore "the post-industrial society necessarily becomes a meritocracy."[104]

In their analysis of future needs of the higher educational system in Ontario, Porter and Blishen have suggested that "the education processes of the future should be such that they provide for continuity and the acquisition of higher qualifications."[105] Further, these institutions must cater to the needs of "many dimensional man" and must not "be confined to the production of scientists and technologists."[106] Rather post-secondary education should be developed as a complement to "the world of work as it becomes changed by the creation of new occupations and specializations."[107]

Post-industrial theorists rationalize the need for educating more people for longer periods of time. As technology and automation (or as O'Connor suggests, "capital equipment" or "dead labour")[108] have increased and the need for "human capital" has declined, higher education has grown. Ideologically, this process has served the dominant class by perpetuating the belief that the "new middle class ... will inevitably ... assume political power" because modern society has become more and more dependent upon its skills.[109] The problem, as Mills points out, is that "technical and managerial indispensability is thus confused with the facts of power struggle and overrides all other sources of power.[110]

The rationalization that education is needed even for routinized, bureaucratic labour and that people must keep abreast of the occupational world by training and retraining, serves to mystify the fact that technological advances have created a surplus of labour power. Furthermore, it is this rationalization that provides an ideological smokescreen for the notion that "knowledge is power" and keeps large numbers in school and off unemployment rolls. Increasingly, higher education serves to create an oversupply of white collar employees.

In order to slow down expansion of universities, the provincial government imposed a five year freeze on university building plans in 1969. The university system had become an expensive and unnecessarily massive programme to alleviate the problems of automation, the replacement of human capital with capital intensive equipment, and consequently, the burden of unemployment. The system of higher education had become a panacea for the inconsistencies of growing monopoly capitalism.

By 1969 the job market for graduates had tightened considerably, prompting the *Financial Post* to write that "employers now have the upper hand in hiring." It was further stated that "the two largest employers of university graduates, the federal government and I.B.M. both reported 30-50 per cent hiring decreases from . . . the [previous] year."[111] Other firms such as Imperial Oil, Bell Canada, Stelco, and Ford of Canada were reported to be hiring about as many graduates as in 1968. Meanwhile, enrolment figures continued to rise; Waterloo received a record number of applications for 1969-70[112] and summer student enrolment in 1969 was higher than ever.[113]

Because of the steadily expanding university population, operating costs of all universities rose substantially. Under the Fiscal Arrangement Act, Ottawa had agreed to pay 50 per cent of operating costs or to transfer $15 *per capita* to each province for the universities. In 1970 it was announced the federal government would not renew this programme when it expired in 1972.[114] Waterloo's response was to keep enrolment increases to a minimum. However, the number of applications continued to increase in 1973 and 1974. This was due in part to high unemployment rates.[115]

In his analysis, O'Connor argued that more efficient production and distribution of education was the only solution to the fiscal crisis in schools. This included replacement of "traditional liberal arts programmes" with "career education" or, in other words, pragmatically oriented courses, increased tuition fees, elimination of duplicate services or facilities, a more centralized administration with stricter financial control, and the re-emergence of repressive measures in education with programmes designed to re-emphasize merit and disciplinary systems.[116] The Ontario government's recent decisions in response to the dilemma in higher education in the 1970s were indeed similar to those steps O'Connor believed would most likely be taken in the U.S.

In 1972 the Wright Commission Report on post-secondary education in Ontario was issued. It explained that after World War II, "modernization" combined with "higher technology, a world of administrative complexity and electric communication required new knowledge, as well as a better trained labour force and better informed citizenry."[117] Thus, the report states: "The logic of viewing prolonged schooling as a prudent personal investment in a future job or career, with a rapidly growing and industrializing economy, provided youth, parents, and an increasing number of adults with plausible practical reasons for wanting more formal education."[118]

Some major recommendations of the Wright Commission were that:

extensive guidance programmes which were to be separated from the educational institutions and placed in community centres be set up; the number of courses serving as more practical job training programmes be multiplied; more people attend C.A.A.T.s, thereby leaving the universities mainly for research; there be more programmes related to retraining of workers at various points in their careers; centralization and coordination among institutions of higher learning increase. Echoing the Wright Commission, John J. Deutsch, then president and vice chancellor of Queen's University, said in an address to the Empire Club that universities should be for those seeking "scholarly excellence" and "high professional competence". Instead of widespread university education Deutsch suggested that there should be a "variety of colleges and institutes" for "technical training and vocational skills", and that suitable opportunities and facilities be established for those wishing to "combine work and study" and "for continuing education throughout life."[119] Thus, during the financial crisis in higher education, universities are further pushed toward the fulfillment of labour market needs. In Canada this has meant a continuing shift toward preparation of employees for work in branch-plant companies and multinational corporations.

For students, the funding squeeze has meant crowded classroom conditions, increased tuition, high student-teaching assistant ratios, and less choice in course selection. Government cutbacks in higher education are, according to H. Adelman, indicative of a change in the relation between the university and the state. He has found that "direct government financial support to the universities not only failed . . . to keep pace with the increased cost of living" during the early 1970s, but had "declined absolutely on a unit basis."[120] For example, in Ontario the Basic Income Unit (B.I.U.)[121] increased by two per cent during the 1972-3 fiscal year while the cost of living rose by 3.5 per cent. In 1972 in order to make up for reduction in government support to universities by $100 per B.I.U., undergraduate tuition fees were raised by that amount.[122]

Loss of government support is indirectly passed on to students. Along with the $100 tuition increase in 1972, the provincial government raised the Ontario Student Awards Programme loan ceiling from $600 to $800, effectively reducing the grant portion by $200; dropped the bursary of $500 to those at the Colleges of Education; imposed a $250 tuition fee on nursing students. Overall, the government reduced its contribution to all forms of student aid from $51 million to $34.8 million and its provision for grant assistance from $44 million to $31.7 million. In 1970 the graduate fellowship programme was cut from $6 million to $5 million; in 1971 it was further cut to $3.5 million and in 1972 to $3 million.[123] While the Ontario Graduate Fellowship programme was cut back, at the same time, graduate students were forced to pay income tax, unemployment insurance, and their own medical coverage. Thus, net income of graduate students was reduced while their costs of living increased.

With this economic situation, the push for "marketable skills" was more apparent. At Waterloo, for example, there were plans to set quotas for arts students in 1970-1,[124] and by 1973 Waterloo officials were able to announce that enrolment in professional and practical oriented courses had increased while enrolment in arts had declined. At nearby University of Guelph applications for arts programmes were down by seven per cent.[125] It has been noted that "the University of Waterloo has taken on the job of converting graduate chemists into chemical engineers."[126] A cooperative Ph.D. programme was started in September 1976 as a joint project between the universities of Waterloo and Guelph "in order to land Ph.D.'s jobs in fields other than teaching."[127]

A university diploma primarily serves to fit students into particular occupational categories. The financial squeeze felt by institutions of higher learning reflects the process of the cheapening of degrees as marketable commodities. The argument that higher education is now available to greater numbers throughout the class structure and that working class people are no longer excluded from degree granting institutions has *some* support. However, an examination of job placement for university graduates may prove that they are "in the same boat" as others regarding dependence, lack of autonomy, and the routinization of their labour.

CONCLUSION

Historically there has been an intimate and reciprocal relation between universities and the Canadian dominant class. Passage of the University Act in 1906 legitimated and strengthened this relation which had, in effect, existed from the founding of the universities. The dominant class has relied on universities to train and socialize its researchers and manpower while universities have sought support of this class for funding expensive research programmes and for approval of curriculum, finance policy, and other solutions to key problems. Through positions on boards of governors, members of the dominant class acted as "gatekeepers" for the socio-economic order they represented.

Cold war ideology and pressures for scientific and technological progress led to massive university expansion in the post-war period. While channelling veterans into universities served to lessen the severe unemployment problem, more importantly, it perpetuated the ideology that universities were open to all who showed promise and that opportunities for individual advancement were abundant in Canada. Nevertheless, it was clear that there was (and there still is) uneven access to universities although the largest share of their funds is derived from government sources through taxation. Govern-

ments' increased funding of universities has not been met with a corresponding decrease in corporate involvement with, interest in, or benefit from higher
education. Rather, within the university, the state and the private sector
mutually and explicitly reinforce their coordinated interests. "Socializing"
the costs of maintaining schools, universities, and other aspects of the
superstructure is directly beneficial to the corporate order. Overhead,
"risks" of production, and costs of research and training are diverted to the
public sector while benefits and financial gains are accumulated within the
private sector. It is increasingly the case that the state has paid for expensive
training and retraining programmes. This is especially true in fields where
industry has become capital intensive, and where employers demand that
workers be skilled in a very specialized area. The present analysis of the
Waterloo cooperative programme in engineering and mathematics underscores this point. Expanding demand for "marketable skills" has in fact
turned the university into a job training centre and sophisticated employment
office.

Thus, changes in the economy and in requirements for job skills have led
to changes in higher education. The trend toward training and retraining
programmes has been felt not only in manual jobs, but has more recently
become popular among white collar groups. Employers have become accustomed to the type of skilled manpower provided by universities and colleges
in Canada and are wary of hiring less educated personnel. Whereas in the past
white collar and professional workers were hired for ability in making decisions
and judgements, capacity for responsibility, and perhaps their ability to deal
with a degree of autonomy on the job, this is not the case in "post-industrial"
Canadian society. Instead, demands by growing government and corporate
organizations for an increasing number of coordinators, managers, and
bureaucrats are being answered by Canadian institutions of higher learning
producing graduates well-trained in how to adjust to a new kind of work
situation. The new white collar labourers are skilled in working as harmonious members of the "management team" rather than in making decisions; in
appreciating the necessity of obeying orders rather than in seeking greater
autonomy; in learning how to live with boredom on jobs becoming ever more
routinized rather than in demanding and creating more stimulating work
environments. In sum, it is this kind of skilled labour force that is being
produced by the postwar Canadian university in the late 1970s.

NOTES

1. Reference is made to the fact that members of the dominant class sit on university boards in Wallace Clement, *The Canadian Corporate Elite*, Toronto: McClelland & Stewart Ltd., 1975; John Porter, *The Vertical Mosaic*, Toronto: University of Toronto Press, 1965; and Ferdinand Lundberg, *The Rich and The Super-Rich*, New York: Bantam Books, Inc., 1969. See also, John Barkans and Norene Pupo, ''The Boards of Governors and the Power Elite: A Case Study of Eight Canadian Universities'', *Sociological Focus*, Summer 1974, Vol. 7, No. 3.

2. It is argued that American higher education has historically been characterized by an extremely pragmatic curriculum and approach. See, for example, Randle W. Nelsen, *Growth of the Modern University and the Development of a Sociology of Higher Education in the U.S.*, Ph.D. Dissertation, Hamilton, Ontario: McMaster, 1975.

3. Edward Sheffield, ''The Post War Surge in Post Secondary Education: 1945-69'', *Canadian Education: A History*, eds. J.D. Wilson, R. Stamp, L.P. Audet, Scarborough: Prentice-Hall, 1970, p. 417.

4. *Ibid.*, p. 416. Sheffield was director of the educational division of the Dominion Bureau of Statistics.

5. Vincent Massey, Chairman, *Report of the Royal Commission on National Development in the Arts, Letters and Sciences*, Ottawa: King's Printer, 1951, p. 142.

6. *Ibid.*, p. 141.

7. Calculations are based on the data in *Ibid.*, p. 142.

8. *Ibid.*, p. 142.

9. *Ibid.*, p. 143.

10. G. P. Gilmour, *The University and Its Neighbours*, Toronto: W. J. Gage & Co., 1954, p. 54.

11. *Ibid.*, p. 56.

12. Leo Johnson, ''Poverty in Wealth'', Toronto: New Hogtown Press, 1974, p. 2.

13. F. Cyril James cited in *Financial Post*,* May 26, 1951, p. 17. *hereafter referred to as *FP*

14. *FP*, November 17, 1956, p. 15.

15. W.L. Gordon, Chairman, *Final Report of the Royal Commission on Canada's Economic Prospects*, Ottawa: Queen's Printer, 1957, p. 362.

16. *Ibid.*, pp. 40-1.

17. *Ibid.*, p. 41.

18. C. T. Bissell, ed., *Canada's Crisis in Higher Education: Proceedings of a Conference held by the National Conference of Canadian Universities*, Toronto: University of Toronto Press, 1957, pp. 270-72.

19. G.P. Gendron, "The Physical and Natural Sciences" in *Ibid.*, p. 1.

20. N. A. M. Mackenzie, "Government Support of Canadian Universities" in *Ibid.*, p. 189.

21. D. J. E. Burchard, cited in *FP*, November 17, 1956, p. 14.

22. D. J. E. Burchard, "The Role of the Humanities and Social Sciences in the Training of Scientists and Technologists" in Bissell, p. 52.

23. *FP*, May 18, 1951, p. 7. Crump is described as "one of the top Canadian executives who recognize that Canadian business and Canadian scholarship — in the broadest sense of the term — have to move forward together."

24. Hagey, cited in *FP*, June 5, 1965, p. 59.

25. *FP*, November 17, 1956, p. 15.

26. According to Rick Deaton, the growth of the state's expenditures, financial activities, and coordination among various levels corresponds directly to increasing economic needs of the private sector. In a financial arrangement designed to facilitate growth and stability of the corporate sector, the state has "absorb[ed] the costs of social overhead and made public . . . the costs of maintaining the infrastructure." Historically the Canadian state has served the corporate sphere through a variety of programmes. Corporations' most costly needs, research and development, the training, retraining and maintenance of the labour force, or generally the "private risks of production" have been met at public expense through various government grants, loans, subsidies and other allowances. Universities have shared in this corporate welfare scheme by training researchers and manpower for industry. See "The Fiscal Crisis of the State", *The Political Economy of the State*, ed. D. I. Rousssopoulos, Montreal: Black Rose Books, 1973, pp. 19-20.

27. Between 1955 and 1975 total annual government contributions to provincially assisted universities in Ontario have grown from $16 million to $650 million. *The Hamilton Spectator*, March 17, 1976, p. 7.

28. Gordon Commission Report, p. 41. Also, see chapter 20.

29. *FP*, October 13, 1956, p. 1.

30. *Ibid.*, p. 1.

31. *FP*, December 7, 1957, p. 3.

32. D.A.A. Stager, "Federal Government Grants to Canadian Universities, 1951-66", *Canadian Historical Review*, Vol. 54, p. 296.

33. Among educational circles, with increased government support of higher education, the question of "academic freedom" was often discussed. Heavily state supported programmes were seen as "socialistic" and fears were expressed that such measures would only be a prerequisite for Canada's following in Russia's footsteps. Academics who apparently believed in "knowledge for knowledge's sake" rejected notions of state-sponsored research. Notwithstanding critics, however, there was consensus that because Canada was a "democratic" country, government donations should be made without imposed conditions. Concern about external control of universities excluded the corporate sector. In fact,

educators often felt that the bond between corporations and universities should be strengthened. Because the more sophisticated level of technology in industry required highly trained personnel, various campaigns were led to increase the flow of private money into universities.

34. Industrial Foundation on Education, *The Case for Corporate Giving to Higher Education,* Toronto, 1957, Introduction, p. 1. The introduction to the conference report reads: "if Canada is even to maintain her position among the industrial nations of the world, the country will have to increase substantially the rate at which it can produce highly trained people. It was also agreed that if the universities, and indeed the entire educational system of the country, were to meet this challenge, financial aid to education would have to be increased."

35. Duncan in *Ibid.*, Part 1, p. 4. He also said that: "Science and engineering have made such remarkable progress in recent decades that the nation which holds the lead in these fields, holds the initiative in world affairs."

36. *FP*, August 5, 1961, p. 24.

37. Uses and purposes of education and the relation between business and education in general are clearly described by Compton who has further stated that "industry does not thrive in smog; and what happens to American education will eventually happen to America. Business is depending more and more on college educated men and women. We need only to look at the statistics. Education has added just as much to America's capacity to buy and consume as it has to its capacity to produce and sell. . . . If higher education were to wither, production, markets, and consumption would wither too." Cited by Somers in Bissell, pp. 201-2. Canadian educators, government officials, and businessmen at the 1957 Conference of Canadian Universities were urged to heed Compton's suggestions. Incidentally, Compton had experience in the corporate world as vice-president of American Forest Products Industries, director of Cameron Machine Company and founder of the Timber Engineering Company.

38. D.N. Smith, *Who Rules the Universities? An Essay in Class Analysis*, New York: Monthly Review Press, 1974, p. 63.

39. James Scott, *Of Mud and Dreams: University of Waterloo, 1957-1967*, Toronto: The Ryerson Press, 1967, pp. 25-6.

40. The publishers were John E. Motz of the *Kitchener-Waterloo Record* and Hugh C. Templin of the *Fergus News Record*. Scott's description of Motz as a publisher seems to underrate his activities in the economic order. Besides his position as president of the local newspaper, he held directorships in Central Ontario Television, Broadcast News, and Waterloo Mutual Insurance Company as well as in local philanthropic organizations.

41. *FP,* March 31, 1956, p. 19.

42. *FP*, June 13, 1953, p. 1.

43. He said, "we want to keep business right on coming to campus to hire graduates. But we want to find ways to make their visits more effective." *Ibid.*, p. 1.

44. According to Hagey, part of the grant was to be used to create a liaison between Waterloo and Ontario industries which employed engineers and technicians. Also, plans were made to hold discussions with engineering institutes and

associations in order to develop a curriculum in accordance with professional requirements. *FP*, October 27, 1956, p. 11.

45. Scott, *Of Mud and Dreams*, p. 40.

46. *K-W Record*, January 24, 1957, p. 6.

47. Further, contacts were probably made through members of the Board of Governors. For example, Carl Pollock was president of the Canadian Manufacturers' Association; Gordon J. Chaplin was a member of the Canadian Chamber of Commerce and the Society of the Plastics Industry; and A.W. Hopton was past president of the Society of Automotive Engineers.

48. Scott, pp. 37-8.

49. Cited in *FP*, June 29, 1957, p. 13.

50. Cited in D.G. Dainton, "Coop Education at Work", *Monetary Times*, December 1958, p. 22.

51. *FP*, March 14, 1959, p. 41.

52. "Waterloo's Engineering Students Spend Six Months on the Campus, Six Months on the Job", *Industrial Canada*, November 1959, Vol. LX, p. 48.

53. Dainton, "Coop Education at Work", p. 20.

54. *K-W Record*, January 26, 1957, p. 15.

55. Dainton, p. 22.

56. Industrial Foundation on Education, *Case for Corporate Giving*, Part 1, p. 5.

57. *Ibid.*, p. 22.

58. *Ibid.*, p. 9.

59. Gordon Commission Report, p. 447.

60. *FP*, May 10, 1952, p. 3.

61. Cited in Scott, p. 43.

62. *FP*, April 11, 1953.

63. *Ibid.*, p. 7.

64. *FP*, March 31, 1956, p. 17.

65. *FP*, June 29, 1957, p. 13.

66. Constance Mungall, "Coop Education at Work — How Good Is It?", *Canadian Business*, Vol. XL, No. 10, p. 56.

67. *Ibid.*, p. 54

68. *Ibid.*, p. 54.

69. Cited in *Ibid.*, p. 56.

70. *FP*, October 27, 1962, p. 36.

71. *FP*, September 30, 1961, p. 3.

72. See, for example, Joel Spring, *Education and the Rise of the Corporate State*, Boston: Beacon Press, 1972.

73. *FP*, October 29, 1955, p. 7. (emphasis added) Interestingly, headlines of the article read: "Our Varsities Need Cash to *Shape* New Executives." (emphasis added)

74. C.W. Mills, *White Collar*, New York: Oxford University Press, 1971, p. 7.

75. C.W. Mills, "A Marx for the Managers", *Power, Politics and People: The Collected Essays of C.W. Mills*, ed. I. L. Horowitz, New York: Oxford, 1972, p. 55.

76. Mills, 1971, pp. 71-2. (emphasis added)

77. Porter, p. 151.

78. Mills, 1971, p. 113.

79. For example, he writes, "In 1951 there were 24,992 professionally trained engineers and 1,740 architects in the work force; of this number a total of 2,210 (8.3 per cent) were self-employed. In 1961, while their numbers had grown to 35,721 engineers and 2,940 architects, only 2,785 (7.2 per cent) were self-employed." Leo Johnson, "The Development of Class in Canada in the Twentieth Century", *Capitalism and the National Question in Canada*, ed., Gary Teeple, Toronto: University of Toronto Press, 1972, p. 167.

80. An excellent historical analysis of work and work relationships is Harry Braverman's *Labour and Monopoly Capital : The Degradation of Work in the Twentieth Century*, New York: Monthly Review Press, 1974.

81. Scott, p. 75.

82. Cited in *Ibid.*, p. 100.

83. *Ibid.*, p. 111.

84. *FP*, February 1, 1964, p. 4.

85. *Ibid.*, p. 4. For example, among companies interested in the cooperative mathematics programme were the following: Canadian Life Assurance Company, Confederation Life Association, Dominion Life Assurance Company, Empire Life Insurance Company, Imperial Life Insurance Company of Canada, International Business Machines, Manufacturers' Life Insurance Company, Mutual Life Assurance Company of Canada, National Life Assurance Company of Canada, Prudential Assurance Company Ltd. of England, and Sun Life Assurance Company of Canada.

86. *FP,* October 14, 1967, p. O-13.

87. Council of Ontario Universities, Advisory Committee on Academic Planning, *Perspectives and Plans for Graduate Studies: Number 7, Sociology,* April 1974, p. A-58.

88. University of Waterloo, *Adult Education Department Annual Report*, May 1960.

89. University of Waterloo, *Report to the Senate and Board of Governors From the Department of University Extension and Adult Education*, October 1964.

90. Although the largest percentage of universities' budgets came from government, this does not mean that private endowments and corporate scholarships and funds were no longer provided, nor does it imply that members of the dominant class were less interested in or involved with universities than in previous decades. Rather, the university should be analyzed as an institution in which explicit coordination between the state and the private sector occurs. During the 1960s, a period of relative economic prosperity and stability, the Canadian state assumed more responsibility for the expensive task of providing higher education for a broader range of people. At this time needs of the corporate order required more university based research and university trained personnel.

91. The following figures have been calculated from data in *Canada Year Books*, 1960, 1965, 1969, 1972; W.G. Fleming, editor, *Ontario's Educative Society*, Volume 1, Toronto: University of Toronto Press, 1971; and John Porter, Bernard Blishen, et al., *Towards 2000: The Future of Post Secondary Education in Ontario*, Toronto: McClelland & Stewart, 1971, p. 15.

92. Stephen G. Peitchinis, *Financing Post Secondary Education in Canada*, Calgary, 1971, p. 1.

93. Calculation is based on figures in *FP*, August 5, 1961, p. 24.

94. This figure, however, includes municipal donations. *U. of W. Report to the Senate of the Committee on Scholarships*, May 1960.

95. *FP*, June 30, 1962, p. 8.

96. Rankin was elected chairman of the board of governors in October, 1975.

97. Porter, Blishen et al., p. 74.

99. *Ibid.*, p. 266.

100. *From the Sixties to the Seventies: An Appraisal of Higher Education in Ontario*, Toronto, 1966, p. 12.

101. James O'Connor, *The Fiscal Crisis of the State*, New York: St. Martin's Press, 1973, pp. 114-5.

102. J.K. Galbraith, *The New Industrial State*, New York: Mentor Books, 1968, p. 72.

103. *Ibid.*, p. 291.

104. Daniel Bell, "The Measurement of Knowledge and Technology", *Indicators of Social Change: Concepts and Measurements*, eds. E.B. Sheldon and W. Moore, New York: Russell Sage Foundation, 1968, p. 160. He further wrote, "in the post industrial society the university necessarily achieves a new, central role. It is the place where theoretical knowledge is sought, tested and codified in a disinterested way, and thus it becomes the source of new knowledge and innovation. It has a new importance as the gatekeeper for the society." (p. 159)

105. Porter, Blishen et al., p. 8.

106. *Ibid.*, p. 6.

107. *Ibid.*, p. 8.

108. O'Connor, p. 115.

170 Reading, Writing, and Riches

109. Mills, 1971, p. 298.

110. *Ibid.*, p. 298.

111. *FP*, December 27, 1969, p. 4.

112. *K-W Record*, June 19, 1969.

113. *K-W Record*, July 3, 1969.

114. *FP*, June 27, 1970, p. 1.

115. *K-W Record*, March 21, 1973.

116. O'Connor, p. 116.

117. D.T. Wright, Chairman, *The Learning Society: Report of the Commission on Post-Secondary Education in Ontario,* Toronto: Ministry of Government Services, 1972, pp. 4-5.

118. *Ibid.*, p. 5.

119. "The Universities of Today and Tomorrow", *An Address Given by John J. Deutsch to the Empire Club*, Toronto, March 15, 1973, pp. 5-6. Deutsch himself was a member of the capitalist class. In 1973 he held directorships in, among others, the Canadian Imperial Bank of Commerce, Alcan Aluminum, International Nickel Company of Canada and FP Publications.

120. H. Adelman, *The Holiversity: A Perspective on the Wright Report,* Toronto: New Press, 1973, p. 9.

121. The B.I.U. is the government grant to the university for one general arts student.

122. Undergraduates' tuition fees have been raised again for 1977-78. Even more drastic steps have been taken with respect to foreign students since the government will no longer support these students, forcing them to pay full cost of education themselves.

123. Data was collected from various newspaper articles.

124. *K-W Record*, December 3, 1969.

125. *K-W Record*, March 21, 1973.

126. *University Affairs*, February 1976, p. 10.

127. *K-W Record*, November 10, 1975.

Tracking in Community Colleges*

FRED PINCUS[1]

The quest for a college education has remained an unfulfilled dream for the vast majority of youth from poor and working class families. The same has been true for most young people who are members of ethnic minority groups.[2] Poor, working class, and ethnic minority students are *less* likely to attend college and more likely to drop out of college than their white middle class counterparts. This has been true in private and public institutions of higher learning. (Jencks and Riesman, 1969; Crossland, 1971; Folger, et al., 1970)

Explanations for the lack of success of these students in higher education are wide-ranging. On traditional tests of academic ability (I.Q. and aptitude tests) and academic achievement (grades and standardized achievement tests) middle class and white students consistently score higher than poor, working class, and ethnic minority students. (Folger, 1970; Crossland, 1971) Many point to these differences in aptitude as the main cause of the class and ethnic inequalities that exist in higher education.

Although some argue that these ability differences are largely due to genetic differences in intelligence, most would agree that environmental factors are *a* major cause, if not *the* major cause of the inequalities. Some argue that the "culturally-deprived" environment in poor and ethnic communities retard the development of intellectual skills and create low educational aspirations in students from these communities. Others argue that biased tests of ability, an irrelevant curriculum, and racist attitudes of teachers are the real causes of existing inequalities. The basic point here is that most scholars point to an entire set of economic and cultural factors that are crucial in determining a student's score on tests of academic ability and achievement, and consequently, a student's success in college.

The public community college[3] has been given the major task of providing increased opportunity for those students who have been excluded from higher education. Edmond Gleazer, President of the American Association of Community and Junior Colleges (AACJC) states that:

a much larger proportion of our population than is now doing so can benefit by education beyond high school, and that the student can best show what he can do by

---

*This paper is reprinted in its original form from *The Insurgent Sociologist*, Spring 1974, 4:3.

being allowed to try. . . . This "chance to try" is provided by the community college. (Gleazer, 1968:51)

Almost all those who are proponents of the community college stress its role in "democratizing" higher education and in providing "equal opportunity" in higher education. (e.g., Clark, 1960a; Medsker, 1960; Newman, 1971; Cross, 1971; Monroe, 1972; Carnegie Commission, 1970; Yarrington, 1973)

This paper will analyze the attempts by community colleges to "democratize" higher education. Have they succeeded or failed in providing equal opportunity for all? Before proceeding, however, it is necessary to develop a criterion for success and failure; i.e., exactly what does "equal opportunity" mean?

One view of equality conceives of higher education as a contest in which everyone should be allowed to compete. Students from all backgrounds and with a wide range of academic skills should be allowed to enter college, but only those with the appropriate kinds of academic skills should be allowed to succeed. These skills will probably not be found among most low income and ethnic minority students due to their "disadvantaged" or "deprived" backgrounds, but at least these students should be given a chance to try. For those who make it, so much the better. Those who don't can probably benefit from their limited college experience.

An alternate notion of equality in higher education looks not only to the "chance to try", but also to the "chance to succeed". Since a large part of the class and ethnic differences in educational ability and achievement are due to environmental factors, equality in higher education cannot exist until these environmental factors have been either eliminated or neutralized. In terms of the larger society, this would mean the elimination of income inequality and racism. Within the schools, it might mean having unprejudiced teachers, a more relevant curriculum, more effective tests of ability, and the like. At the very least, effective remedial programs would be necessary to "undo" some of the "damage" that has been done to low income and ethnic minority students by poverty and inadequate schooling.

The crucial point in this second conception of equality is this: as long as conditions in the larger society and/or in the schools continue to be an important cause of the unequal educational achievement between students of different social classes and between students in different ethnic groups, one cannot talk of equality. Ideally, one can talk of equality only when there is no correlation between achievement and social class, and between achievement and ethnicity. (Milner, 1972; Karabel, 1972)

This paper demonstrates that community colleges hold the "chance to try" concept of equality, and are much less concerned about the "chance to succeed". This will become evident after examining the goals that the community colleges have set for themselves. In fact, the community colleges play an important role in maintaining educational inequality and, as a result, help to reinforce the system of class and ethnic stratification that exists in the United States.

HISTORY OF COMMUNITY COLLEGES

Community colleges began to develop during the first quarter of the twentieth century, frequently as private institutions that were two-year extensions of high schools or were simply substitutes for the first two years of college. By 1922, there were over 200 community colleges in the country and most of them were private. The number of two-year institutions jumped to more than 600 by 1940.

During the decades of the 40s and 50s, community college growth slowed considerably and by 1960 there were only 656 community colleges. However, presidential commissions in the Truman and Eisenhower administrations and the 1960 Commission on National Goals recommended that community colleges be expanded. These commissions emphasized the fact that many people could benefit from two more years of education and stressed the importance of "flexibility" in the community college curriculum. Rather than simply being academic institutions, the community colleges were encouraged to develop occupational programs to meet the needs of government and industry, and to provide for the needs of millions of students who "would not otherwise receive college educations." This was the beginning of what came to be known as the "comprehensive" community college. (Monroe, 1972; Medsker and Tillery, 1971)

After 1960, the community colleges grew rapidly. By 1971, there were over 1,100 community colleges, most of them public. Between 1958 and 1973, community college enrollment increased by more than five times, from 525,000 to 2,917,000. In contrast, the number of students in all institutions of higher learning increased only two-and-one-half times, from 3,420,000 to 9,662,000. Almost all of the community college students (95 per cent) are enrolled in public institutions. (USOE, 1970; Chronicle, 1974)

In the fall of 1973, 30 per cent of all college enrollment was in community colleges, and all indications are that this figure will continue to increase. Over half of *all freshmen in public institutions* of higher learning are currently enrolled in community colleges, and some predict that this figure will rise to 70 per cent in 1980. (Monroe, 1972; Chronicle, 1974; Carnegie Commission, 1971) In the future, most freshmen will be having their first college experience at a public comprehensive community college.

Goals of Community Colleges

There appears to be almost universal consensus among community college administrators and planners on the basic goals of these institutions. The function of community colleges in higher education can best be understood by talking about the *public goals*, those that are discussed in school catalogues and public relations materials, and the *non-public goals*, those that are not discussed in catalogues and public relations materials but that are discussed in books, articles, and reports written by educators and social scientists.

Public Goals

There are five public goals of the community colleges — (1) a comprehensive curriculum, (2) an open-door admissions policy, (3) convenient location, (4) an attempt to give students a second chance, and (5) a community orientation.

The first public goal, a *comprehensive curriculum*, refers to the broad range of programs that exist in community colleges, enabling students with different "interests and abilities" to select the program that is "best suited to their needs." The curriculum can be divided into two basic categories: (i) *Transfer* or *College-Parallel* — courses that are equivalent to the first two years at a four-year school and that will prepare students to transfer to a four-year school; (ii) *Terminal Occupational* — programs lasting two years or less which provide students with the skills necessary to enter some form of employment after graduating from the community college.

In addition to these two basic curricula, there are also *remedial* or *developmental* programs designed to help students develop academic skills in which they may be deficient; *adult or continuing education programs* that help students gain their high school equivalency certificates and/or upgrade their jobs; and *general education programs* that provide courses of general interest that don't necessarily lead to any degree. This type of curriculum, then, provides something for everyone who enters community college. Diversity is the key word.

The second public goal of the community college is the *open door* principle, whereby any person who is a high school graduate or who is an adult citizen (over eighteen) is welcome to attend a community college. Thus, while other institutions of higher learning are selective in their admissions policies and expensive in cost, the community colleges will take everyone.

The *convenient location* of community college is the third public goal. Campuses should be developed in all areas of the country, but particularly in large urban areas, so that community colleges will be within commuting distance of 95 per cent of the population. (Carnegie Commission, 1971)

The fourth public goal of the community college is to provide students with a *second chance* to succeed, sometimes referred to as the "salvage" function. Students who have not been successful in high school will get a second chance at a college education. This could be useful for good students who have not applied themselves in high school, and for the mediocre students who need some remedial work.

The fifth public goal is *community orientation*. The community college should offer a relevant curriculum to the members of the community in which it is located. In addition, it should serve the community by providing cultural events, expertise in solving local problems, and a meeting place for community organizations.

These, then, are the public goals of the community college that are designed to bring equal opportunity to all students in higher education. These goals are accepted by just about everyone who supports the community colleges. (Gleazer, 1968; Koos, 1970; Carnegie Commission, 1970; Medsker and Tillery, 1971; Cross, 1971; Monroe, 1972; AACJC, 1973)

Non-Public Goals

The public goals tell only part of the community college story, however. In addition there are four non-public goals — (1) training a paraprofessional labor force, (2) screening, (3) cooling-out, and (4) custodial care.

Although *paraprofessional training* is publicly offered to students through the occupational tracks in the community colleges, students are not told how this training is related to the stratified labor force that they will enter. Most observers of the American economy agree that the fastest growing sector of the labor force is the category of "professional and technical workers". (e.g., U.S. Department of Labor, 1970; Berg, 1971) Institutions of higher education, in general, have the responsibility for training the vast majority of these workers, but the community colleges have the specific task of training the "technical" or "paraprofessional" part of the labor force; i.e., those middle-level workers who "assist" the professionals and who need more than a high school education but less than a college education. (Monroe, 1972; Medsker and Tillery, 1971; Carnegie Commission, 1970; Harris, 1964)

A division of labor has developed within higher education to provide American institutions with a skilled professional and paraprofessional labor force. The four-year colleges and universities will continue to train people for jobs that require a bachelor's degree — from teachers and social workers to doctors and systems analysts. The community colleges, on the other hand, will train people for jobs requiring only two years of college, including teacher's aids, x-ray technicians and computer operators. In other words, community college graduates will enter lower paying jobs that have less prestige, less job satisfaction, and fewer chances for mobility. (New University Conference, 1971)

The second non-public goal, *screening*, refers to the community colleges' job of differentiating those students who will complete four years of college and eventually enter one of the professions, from those who will complete only two years of college. Almost half of all high school graduates attend college, and many do not have the traditionally-accepted academic skills that are necessary to successfully complete college. More and more, these "non-traditional" students are entering the community colleges. It is the job of the community college to encourage and permit bright, motivated students to enter the transfer programs, and to encourage other students to enter one of the terminal programs.

The community college may not be conscious of performing a switch-man's role of sorting out individuals like freight cars in a switchyard and placing them on alleged abilities as minority spokesmen claim. . . . This sorting job is not a pleasant one since many of the persons involved feel that they have been switched onto the wrong tracks. Now that the community college has an open-door policy, the universities are relieved of much of this distasteful task of selecting between the "fit" and the "unfit". (Monroe, 1972:37; See also Roueche, 1968; Gleazer, 1968; Jencks and Riesman, 1969; Koos, 1970; Carnegie Commission, 1970; Newman, 1971; Medsker and Tillery, 1971; Cross, 1971)

Cooling Out

The third non-public goal, *cooling-out* students with unrealistic aspirations, is closely related to the first and second. The term "cooling-out" was originally used by Goffman (1952) to refer to the process where a swindler gets his mark (i.e., the person who has been swindled) to accept his fate and not to complain to the authorities. Burton Clark (1960b), however, applies this concept to community colleges.

Although two-thirds of the community college freshmen want to eventually transfer to a four-year school, data show that only one-third actually do transfer. (Medsker, 1960; Gleazer, 1968) Clark refers to those students who want to transfer but do not transfer as "latent terminals" — regardless of their ambitions, they are "destined" to be terminal students. These students, according to Clark, have "unrealistically high aspirations that exceed their abilities." For example, a student might want to be a doctor but cannot pass the necessary biology and chemistry courses. It is these latent terminal students that are likely to drop out of school.

Clark's solution is to cool-out these students by convincing them that they cannot succeed in the transfer program, but that they could succeed in the "appropriate" occupational program. Rather than being a doctor, the student might consider being an X-ray technician or a pharmacist's aid. This cooling-out process, it is argued, is not only good for the individual student, but also provides the larger society with another skilled person to enter the labor force. The main instrument of this process is the counselling service at the community college and the bulk of his paper is a description of a step-by-step process by which counsellors can help students to "redefine" their educational goals.

In his article, Clark stresses the non-public nature of the cooling-out function of community colleges.

One dilemma of a cooling-out role is that it must be kept reasonably away from public scrutiny and not clearly perceived or understood by prospective clientele. Should it become obvious, the organization's ability to perform it would be impaired. . . . If high school seniors and their families were to define the junior college as a place which diverts college-bound students, a probable consequence would be a turning-away from the junior college and increased pressure for admission to the four-year colleges and universities that are otherwise protected to some degree. This would, of course, render superfluous the part now played by the junior college in the division of labor among colleges. (Clark, 1960b: 575)

Many writers actually use the term "cooling-out" in discussing the goals of the community colleges. (e.g., Simon, 1967; Roueche, 1968; Monroe, 1972) Most others talk about bringing people's aspirations in line with their abilities, but do not specifically mention the term "cooling-out". (e.g., Knoell and Medsker, 1964; Gleazer, 1968; Cook, et al., 1968; Koos, 1970; Carnegie Commission, 1970; Medsker and Tillery, 1971; Cross,1971) A recent article in *Chronicle of Higher Education* summed things up this way:

Community colleges may be worth the money if they do nothing more than this: One student came here never having liked to read or write and never having been very good at either. Yet, he wanted to be a lawyer. After some counselling he realized the odds against him were high, so he joined the Air Force. "Apparently" says a counsellor, "he's quite happy about it." (Van Dyne, 1972:3)

The fourth non-public goal might be referred to as *custodial care*. A certain number of community college students will lack the motivation and/or the ability to succeed in any of the community college programs.

It has been maintained that junior colleges provide programs for low-achieving students in order to keep these young people out of the labor market, off the streets and out of trouble. (Roueche, 1968:23)

Although not all writers discuss this goal per se, they do talk about the large number of students who never receive any type of degree. In any case, custodial care is not inconsistent with the other non-public goals of the community college.

These, then, are the goals as discussed by spokesmen and spokeswomen for the community colleges. Although the five public goals — comprehensive curriculum, open door policy, convenient location, second chance, and community orientation — stress the importance of providing more educational opportunities to more people, the four non-public goals — training paraprofessionals, screening, cooling-out, and custodial care — make it clear that not everyone will end up with the same education. The bright students will transfer to a four-year school and be eligible to enter one of the professions. The students of moderate ability will be able to complete a two-year occupational program and be eligible to enter one of the paraprofessional occupations. Students of low ability might well end up leaving the community college and will be able to enter only the lesser-skilled jobs. These non-public goals make the community colleges an integral part of an educational system that trains people to enter a stratified labor force that serves the interests of the large corporations that dominate American society.

THE EMPIRICAL STUDY OF TRACKING IN HIGHER EDUCATION
Academic Characteristics

Students at community colleges have lower grades and score lower on standard tests of academic ability than students at four-year institutions. Cross (1968) summarizes the evidence:

The mean score for students attending four-year colleges exceeds that of students in two-year colleges, and . . . two-year college students score higher as a group than high school graduates who do not go to college. The research demonstrating these facts is national in score, it is unanimous in findings, and it is based on a staggering array of traditional measures of academic aptitude and achievement.

The American Council on Education national survey of freshmen in the Fall of 1972 not only replicates these differences between two- and four-year students, but they also show that freshmen at public universities have higher grade point averages and higher class ranks in high school than state college freshmen. (ACE, 1972) Thus, the brightest freshmen attend universities, the next brightest attend state colleges, and the rest attend community colleges or no college at all.

Social Class

The social class background of a student is a crucial variable in determining the likelihood of that student's receiving a college education. The research in this area may be summarized as follows: "The higher a student's social class, the more likely it is that the student will have a high grade point average in high school and a high score on a standardized test of academic ability or achievement." When academic ability is statistically controlled, the higher a student's social class, the more likely it will be that a student will attend college; and once entering college, the more likely it will be that a student will complete college. (Astin, 1972; Folger, 1970; Jencks, 1972; Lauter and Howe, 1970; Rothstein, 1971)

Given the way higher education is stratified, students from higher social class backgrounds with their higher grades and achievement test scores are more likely to enter universities. Students from lower social class backgrounds with their lower grades and test scores, on the other hand, are more likely to begin their higher education at a community college. (Cross, 1968; Monroe, 1972; Karabel, 1972; Hanson and Weisbrod, 1969; Windham, 1969; Birnbaum and Goldman, 1971; Trimberger, 1973)

To examine more precisely the effects of class background on college attendance, Table I was constructed. The table displays the median family incomes of freshmen at different types of public institutions since 1966 (the earliest available data). Four conclusions may be drawn from the data.

TABLE I

Median Income of Families of College Freshmen at Different Types of Public Institutions, of Families of All College Freshmen, and of All U.S. Families with Heads 35-44 Years of Age, 1966-1972

Type of Family	1966	1967	1968	1969	1970	1971	1972
Freshmen at Public 2-Year Colleges	8,600	3,760	8,900	9,520	9,900	11,000	11,000
Freshmen at Public 4-Year Colleges	8,140	9,000	9,320	10,200	11,180	11,530	12,180
Freshmen at Public Universities	9,860	12,900	11,350	12,250	13,080	13,330	14,450
All College Freshmen	9,580	9,990	10,150	10,950	11,770	12,200	12,580
All U.S. Families with heads 35-44 years of age*	8,590	9,000	9,830	10,730	11,410	11,880	13,119

Source: American Council on Education (1967a, 1967b, 1968, 1969, 1970, 1971, 1972)
Current Population Reports (1967, 1969a, 1969b, 1970, 1971a, 1972, 1973a)
*This is an estimate of families with freshmen-aged children. See Footnote 4 for details.

---

(1) Public higher education is stratified by economic class. The median income of public university freshmen is highest, followed by state college and then by community college freshmen. In 1972, for example, the median incomes of freshmen families were $14,450 in universities, $12,180 in state colleges, and $11,000 at community colleges.

(2) The pattern of stratification has remained constant since 1967. Two-year college freshmen come from families with the lowest incomes and university freshmen come from families with the highest incomes.

(3) The extent of stratification and its stability can be seen by the fact that since 1967, freshmen in two- and four-year colleges have come from families whose incomes were *below* the incomes of the families of all college freshmen and even below the incomes of all families in the country (where the head of the family was old enough to have a freshman-aged child).[4] Public university freshmen, on the other hand, come from families with median incomes well *above* the family incomes of all freshmen and of all U.S. families.

(4) In 1972, for the first time, the median income of all college freshmen was *lower* than the median income of all families likely to have freshman-aged children. If this difference persists, it will indicate some progress in getting persons from lower income families to enter college. However, these lower income students will be more likely to enter the two-year colleges than either the state colleges or the universities. In fact, there is no discernible trend that indicates any relative changes in the incomes of four-year colleges and university freshmen.

While the stratification of public higher education is both clear and consistent in the data of Table I, these data must be seen as an *underestimate* of the true degree of inequality that exists in higher education.

To begin with, the data in Table I refer only to public higher education. The family incomes of private four-year college and university freshmen are even higher than their counterparts in public institutions. In 1972, private four-year college freshmen came from families with a median income of $15,500, while private university freshmen came from families with a median income of $17,850!

Finally, the data given thus far refers only to those who *enter* college and says nothing about who finally receives a B.A. Available data indicate that even after scores on standardized tests of ability and achievement are statistically controlled, the lower a student's social class, the less likely it is that the student will complete four years of college. (Astin, 1972) Thus, if data were available showing the social class backgrounds of students receiving B.A.s from different types of institutions, the stratification would be even more dramatically illustrated.[5]

Ethnic Composition

The two largest ethnic minority groups in America — Blacks and Spanish-Americans — are also tracked into the different institutions of public higher education. Table II provides the data which describe the pattern of ethnic stratification. Clearly, both Blacks and Spanish-Americans are under-represented among all college freshmen.[6]

The Spanish-American population, comprised mainly of persons from Mexican and Puerto Rican backgrounds, is almost non-existent in public universities (0.6 per cent). They are considerably under represented in four-year colleges (2.0 per cent) and slightly under represented in community colleges (4.2 per cent). This pattern of tracking closely corresponds to the social class tracking described in the previous section, with low-income people being under represented at the universities and over represented in the community colleges.

Blacks, too, are considerably under represented among public university freshmen (3.2 per cent). However, they are surprisely over represented among state college freshmen (15 per cent) and slightly under represented among community college freshmen (9.1 per cent). The distribution of Black freshmen in higher education follows a different pattern than generally exists among other low-income people.

TABLE II

Ethnic Composition of the U.S. Population 18-20 Years Old, of All Freshmen, and of Freshmen in Different Types of Public Institutions in 1972, by Per Cent

| | Ethnicity | | | | |
	White	Black	Spanish-American	Other	Total
U.S. Population, 18-20 Years Old [6]	81.2	12.3	4.9	1.6	100.0
All Freshmen	87.3	8.7	2.1	4.0	*
Freshmen at Public 2-Year Colleges	83.8	9.1	4.2	5.5	*
Freshmen at Public 4-Year Colleges	81.6	15.0	2.0	3.5	*
Freshmen at Public Universities	95.3	3.2	0.6	3.0	*

Source: American Council on Education (1972)
*The American Council on Education permits multiple responses on the ethnicity question so the total percentages add up to slightly more than 100 per cent.

The explanation of this apparently atypical pattern is to be found in the regional differences in college enrollment. In the South, where the majority of Blacks still live, there are relatively few community colleges. Consequently, only 6 per cent of all Black students in this area are in public community colleges, while 55 per cent are in public four-year colleges. In the far West, on the other hand, where extensive systems of community colleges exist, about 70 per cent of Black students attend these two-year institutions. (Medsker and Tillery, 1971) Recent studies of Black students who attend predominantly White institutions show that they are most likely to attend community colleges and least likely to attend public universities. (Bayer, 1973; Chronicle, 1973a; Knoell, 1970)

Comparisons of enrollment changes are presently available only for Black freshmen in the 1966-1972 time period, and the data are presented in Table III. It is difficult, however, to draw many solid conclusions from these data because they show erratic fluctuations by year and by type of institution.

Blacks were under represented among all college freshmen during this entire period, but their position was somewhat better in 1972 than it was in 1966. However, at least part of this improvement is due to the *decrease* in college attendance of Whites. In the Fall of 1972, the percentage of White high school graduates attending college dropped 4.7 per cent from the preceding fall, while the percentage of Black high school seniors attending college increased by only 0.5 per cent during this same period. (Chronicle, 1973b)

TABLE III

Percent of All Freshmen and Freshmen in Different Types of Public Institutions that Were Black, 1966-1972

Type of Freshman	1966	1967	1968	1969	1970	1971	1972
All Freshmen	5.0	4.3	5.8	6.0	9.1	6.3	8.7
Freshmen at Public 2-Year Institutions	5.0	3.4	4.7	4.1	16.9	5.0	9.1
Freshmen at Public 4-Year Institutions	10.1	8.8	9.8	6.8	9.2	10.3	15.0
Freshmen at Public Universities	1.5	1.8	3.3	3.4	2.9	3.6	3.2

Source: American Council on Education (1967a, 1967b, 1968, 1969, 1970, 1971, 1972).

Black representation among two-year college freshmen does appear to show a modest increase since 1966. At the four-year colleges, Black representation was constant until 1971. The meaning of the large increase in 1972 is not yet clear. As far as Black representation among university freshmen is concerned, the data are fairly clear. Blacks increased their percentage of university freshmen from under two per cent in 1966 and 1967 to slightly over three per cent in 1968. Since then, Black representation among university freshmen has remained constant.

Preliminary data for the Fall, 1973 enrollment shows that the percentage of Black and Spanish American freshmen had fallen to 7.8 per cent and 1.3 per cent respectively (Chronicle, 1974a). This might well be due to the skyrocketing inflation in 1973, but it might also be an indication that any progress that had been made in the past might be levelling off.

Transfer and Terminal Students

Approximately one-third of all community college students are enrolled in terminal programs, while the remaining two-thirds are in transfer programs. (Medsker and Tillery, 1971) Students in the transfer programs score higher on traditional tests of academic ability and achievement than students in the terminal programs. In addition, students in the more prestigious terminal programs, called "technical" programs, score higher in academic ability and achievement than students in the less prestigious terminal programs, sometimes called "vocational programs". (Medsker and Tillery, 1971; Brue et al., 1971; Karabel, 1972)

As might be expected, students in transfer and terminal programs also differ in their social class and ethnic backgrounds. A recent study of 63 community colleges shows that lower-income students are more likely than upper-income students to be in terminal programs, and less likely to be in transfer programs. For example, students from families with incomes of less than $6,000 accounted for 14 per cent of all transfer students, 14 per cent of the terminal-technical students, and 24 per cent of the terminal-vocational students. On the other hand, students from families with incomes of more than $10,000 accounted for 36 per cent of all transfer students, 28 per cent of terminal-technical students, and 21 per cent of terminal-vocational students. Similarly, Blacks are more likely than Whites to be in the terminal programs, and less likely to be in the transfer programs. (Cross, 1970; Coordinating Council, 1969; Brue, et al., 1971; and Jaffe and Adams, 1972)

The lowest track in the community college is the remedial or developmental programs, and most discussions of these programs refer to the "nontraditional" or "educationally disadvantaged" students who enroll in them. Although no empirical data are available to measure the social class background of the remedial students, one recent study of five remedial programs indicated an over-representation of Blacks and Mexican American students that were enrolled in the remedial courses. (Roueche and Kirk, 1972)

The data presented above clearly demonstrate the pattern of social class and ethnic tracking within public higher education, in general, and within community colleges, in particular. Despite all the talk to the contrary, community colleges do not seem to increase a student's chance of eventually getting a B.A. Folger, et al., (1970) found after controlling for social class and academic ability, students entering community colleges were *less* likely to receive the B.A. degree than those entering four-year schools. Karabel (1972) shows that the regions of the country with the *most* well-developed community college systems have the *lowest* proportion of the age cohort completing four years or more of college. Rather than being part of the solution to class and ethnic inequality, the community colleges have become part of the problem.

COMMUNITY COLLEGE POLICY

Although community college officials have been aware of the data that have been discussed in the preceding pages, they have chosen to follow a set of policies that will inevitably lead to *more* rather than less stratification in higher education. This is particularly evident in the areas of occupational and remedial education.

Occupational Education

Almost all community college supporters are concerned with the emphasis both students and faculty place on transfer programs as opposed to occupational education. For example, a recent report of the American Association of Community and Junior Colleges (1973:146) states:

Career education as a concept can be the vehicle through which community and junior colleges undertake a fundamental reformation of their curricula to make them more responsive to emerging needs and less dependent on their tradition of the lower division of the four-year institution.

This concern for increasing the percentage of students in terminal occupational programs stems from two basic factors — the nature of the American economy and the nature of the community college students. Most discussions of community colleges include a section on the increasing need for people in paraprofessional or middle-level occupations.

The same AACJA report encourages its member institutions to: "consider the development of occupational education programs linked to business, industry, labor, and government a high priority." (p. 145; also see Gleazer, 1968; Medsker and Tillery, 1971; Monroe, 1972; Blocker, 1973)

The leaders of industry and government clearly agree with this analysis since they are strongly encouraging the development of occupational education. For example, the Higher Education Act of 1972 authorized $850 million to be spent on these terminal programs. Many corporations and private foundations have given written and financial support to occupational education, including North American Rockwell, the Carnegie Commission on Higher Education and the Kellogg Foundation, who also helped to sponsor the 1972 Assembly of the AACJC. Finally, it is not unusual to have an advisory board made up of members from industry and government for each different occupational program in the community college. (Karabel, 1972)

The second reason for stressing these occupational programs has to do with the nature of community college students. As was mentioned earlier, it is commonly believed that many of these students have "unrealistically high aspirations" in wanting to transfer to a four-year school and that if they persist in this direction, they are "doomed to fail". Although these students can be "cooled-out" once they enroll in the transfer program, most community colleges would rather have them enroll in the appropriate occupational program in the first place. One way to interest entering students in the occupational programs is through effective counselling and there is almost universal agreement that counselling services must be improved.

Another way of "selling" occupational programs is through public relations campaigns to improve the image of these types of curricula. In a book published by the American Association of Community and Junior Colleges, Harris (1964) outlines an entire public relations campaign consisting of slide shows, news-spots, paraprofessional career days, and the like. He even suggests talking to high school counsellors about the establishment of a "third track" that will prepare students specifically for community colleges.

The community colleges are rather explicit in their goal of providing a paraprofessional labor force to meet the needs of government and industry. In fact, the support given to the community colleges by government and industry is largely responsible for their rapid growth since 1960.

But public education in the United States has always served these same political and economic interests (Bowles, 1973). In the 19th century, public schools were established to train immigrants to work in the factories of New England. In the 1920s when there was a need for a more differentiated labor force, public education responded by developing a tracking system based on a student's "ability level". Students who were defined as "bright", most of whom also happened to be White and upper-middle class, were in the upper tracks and went on to college. The "slow" students, most of whom were also immigrants and working class, had to be satisfied with vocational programs leading to semi-skilled work. The large group of "average" students, most of whom were working and lower-middle class, would be able to enter skilled blue collar and lower level white collar jobs. This tracking system, which acts to perpetuate the system of class-based stratification is still in effect today, although the growth of ethnic minority groups has added an additional factor to the stratification system. (Lauter and Howe, 1970)

The community colleges are simply the next step in a tracked educational system that provides a trained labor force in an increasingly differentiated economy. The community colleges are succeeding in providing the paraprofessional part of this labor force. This explains their lack of concern about achieving social class equality in education since this was never their goal in the first place.

However, the students who end up in the occupational programs are not always happy about it. "The resistance to occupational programs by many students who might profit from them has long disturbed community college leaders." (Medsker and Tillery, 1971:60) Edmund J. Gleazer, President of the AACJC (1968:71) acknowledges this desire for enrollment in the transfer programs in order to enter these "top level" jobs, and says,

In a nation which encourages aspiration and puts its faith in economic and social mobility, there is nothing wrong with this — if a person can indeed qualify for the presumably greater responsibilities at the top of the ladder and if society can use him. Realistically, however, one must face the fact of an almost infinite variety of human talent and a bewildering array of societal tasks. It is to be hoped that talents and tasks can be linked up.

What the students are not told is that their two-year terminal degree will probably be worth less money than a four-year degree. All evidence indicates that the more education a person has, the higher that person's income will be. Men with three to seven terms of college make 120 per cent the income of a high school graduate, but only 80 per cent the income of someone with eight or more terms of college. Some college is better than no college, but not as good as a four-year degree. (Karabel, 1972) Unfortunately, there are no studies comparing the salaries of those with two-year occupational degrees and those with four-year degrees. However, the slogan promoting para-professional training programs that say "earn a College Man's Salary without Attending Four Years of College" are not consistent with the available data.

Remedial Education

Since many of the students who come to the community colleges have academic deficiencies in one or more areas, remedial programs have been set up to help students overcome these deficiencies. These programs are particularly important if the lower income and ethnic minority students are to "catch up" to their White middle class counterparts since academic achievement is related both to social class and ethnicity. Although there is not much research on the effectiveness of these programs, the data that exist are not encouraging. After reviewing some of the literature, a recent study concluded:

Even with the dearth of research the evidence indicates that remedial courses and programs in two-year colleges, and in all of higher education for that matter, have largely been ineffective in remedying student deficiencies. (Roueche and Kirk, 1973:7)

The authors cite numerous studies in different areas of the country which reach the same pessimistic conclusions. Not only do many of these programs fail to provide students with the skills to succeed in the college parallel programs, they also don't provide students with the skills necessary to succeed in one of the occupational curricula.

Perhaps as a result of these failures, some writers are taking a "value-added" approach to remedial education. Even though these "high risk" students don't receive any degrees, the argument goes, they are better off than they were before. According to Monroe (1972) many of these value-added programs, sometimes referred to as "developmental programs", first:

had the same goal as remedial courses, that is, to prepare unready students for successful participation in standard college courses. Developmental programs which were conceived with these unrealistic goals were bound to fail . . . . Since 1965, most developmental programs have had more realistic goals, such as to prepare a student for a vocation and a better way of life than that which his parents enjoyed. (114: Also see Cross, 1971)

Thus, most attempts at remedial education have failed, and it appears that some developmental programs are becoming more "realistic" and are giving up altogether. This all leaves little hope for those low income and ethnic students who come out of poor schools in search of a social mobility through the community college. Without effective remedial programs, community college talk of "equality" is merely an illusion.

Roueche and Kirk (1973) argue that in spite of all this some effective programs do exist. The authors then present data on "model" remedial programs at five institutions showing that the grade-point averages were higher, and the drop-out-rates were lower for students enrolled in remedial programs compared with a control group of "high-risk" students not enrolled in remedial programs. By the end of the fourth semester, the grade-point average for the remedial students still enrolled at the college ranged from 1.99 to 2.37, depending on the particular institution.

Although the results of these programs are certainly better than most other programs, the progress that does exist is quite modest. From the above GPA figures, it seems safe to conclude that between one-third and one-half of those students still enrolled are doing *less* than C work. In addition, only 45 per cent of the students who began the remedial program were still enrolled in the institution by the end of the fourth semester. No information is given about the type of curriculum in which the students are enrolled (transfer or terminal), and no information is given about the number of students who received the two-year degree. Finally, one of these "successful" programs was faced with a "minority student boycott" at the time of the study, although the authors present no further details. If these five programs are among the *best* that the community colleges have to offer, they simply aren't good enough.

CONCLUSION

All of the data presented in this paper are available to community college administrators and planners; and , in fact, much of the data were collected by people sympathetic to the community college movement. Yet in spite of the overwhelming evidence pointing to the rigid stratification that exists in the community colleges and among all institutions of higher learning, the educational establishment continues to talk about the important role that the community colleges are playing in democratizing higher education.

As was mentioned earlier in this paper, there are at least two different notions of "equality" and "democracy" that have been used with regard to education. The criterion used by this author has looked to the *outcomes* of the educational process and has stressed class and ethnic differences in who goes to college, what type of colleges are attended, and what type of curriculum students are enrolled in. By this criterion, equality does not exist in higher education and the evidence does not indicate much progress in this regard.

By this time, it should be clear that community college educators have a different set of concerns that can be best understood as a set of six interrelated beliefs.

(1) *American capitalist institutions and the existing unequal distribution of wealth and power are legitimate.* Free enterprise, individualism, competition, and the quest for social mobility are all acceptable values upon which to base a society.

(2) *Community colleges must help to train a skilled labor force to meet the needs of government and industry.* Community colleges will train paraprofessionals, while four-year colleges and universities will train professionals.

(3) *Conventional professional academic standards are legitimate.* In order to get a B.A. degree, students must be able to achieve these standards of excellence. For those who can't, more flexible standards can be used in the occupational and remedial programs.

(4) *The correlations of social class and race with academic ability and achievement is an unfortunate reality.* Economically-impoverished and/or culturally different environments will prevent people from learning the skills and attitudes that will enable them to succeed in traditional academic programs, but the community colleges can't do much about that.

(5) *Community colleges should strive to be meritocratic.* Some members of low-income and ethnic minorities do have the ability to compete and to enter the professions. Holding them back because of a lack of money or "biased" measures of ability would mean a loss of talent to industry and government. Therefore, more efficient sorting mechanisms should be developed and more sophisticated tracking systems should be established.

(6) *Most working-class and ethnic minority students can do no better than complete a two-year occupational course.* There is nothing really wrong with this since there is a need for people in these jobs and since many of these students will be better off as paraprofessionals than with no college at all.

Given these beliefs, it is not difficult to understand why community college supporters are not more concerned in their failure to enable more working-class and ethnic minority students to get bachelors degrees. One community college administrator in New York City expressed his low level of expectations this way:

Even if only a minority of them make it through, it is that many more who have been saved from going down the drain . . . I know it sounds like the Salvation Army, but when they make it, we have saved souls. (Maeroff, 1973:24)

The rapid growth of the community colleges since 1960 has been caused by an increased need for skilled labor and by the demands of the poor, working-class, and ethnic minority students for a college education. Community college development has been strongly supported by the government, the large corporations, and the educational establishment. Consequently, the community colleges use standards that are defined by people at the top, have programs that benefit the people at the top, and reward students for having skills that are more accessible for people at the top.

Bowles (1973) argues that the division of labor and the American stratification system have given

rise to distinct class subcultures. The values, personality traits and expectations characteristic of each subculture are transmitted from generation to generation through class differences in family socialization and complementary differences in the type and amount of schooling ordinarily attained by children in various class positions. These class differences in schooling are maintained in large measure through the capacity of the upper class to control the basic principles of school finance, pupil evaluation, and educational objectives. (p. 56)

The social class and ethnic tracking in the community colleges and the failure of the remedial programs has more to do with who *controls* the community colleges than with who enters the "open doors".

Some community college liberals seem to throw their arms up in despair when they discuss the lack of success of working-class and ethnic minority students. This feeling of despair is increased by recent studies which argue that educational inequality will exist as long as economic inequality exists. (Jencks, 1972; Milner, 1972) As long as contemporary political, economic and educational institutions are accepted as legitimate, there isn't much hope for those who want to bring about educational and economic equality.

Since the community colleges and other educational institutions are closely tied to the class and ethnic division of labor in American society, the only way to significantly change the educational system is to change the class nature of society. Those that profit from the existing institutions cannot be expected to reform them so that others can share in the rewards.

NOTES

1. The author would like to thank the following persons for their comments during the various stages of the preparation of this paper: Chris Bose, Howard Ehrlich, Byron Matthews and Natalie Sokoloff.

2. In this paper, the term "ethnic" will refer to Blacks, Mexican Americans and Puerto Rico Americans. It will *not* include the so-called White-ethnic groups.

3. In this paper, the terms "Community College", "Junior College" and "Two-Year College" will be used interchangeably.

4. The category "all U.S. families with heads 35-44 years of age" is an estimate of families with children old enough to be college freshmen. This is based on the following data: (1) 90 per cent of college freshmen are 18-19 years of age; (2) the age of first marriage for men is about 23 years of age; (3) the first child usually comes within two years of marriage; (4) children will be 18-19 by the times their fathers are 43 and 44, respectively.

5. The only measure of social class that has been used thus far is median family income. However, the American Council on Education also has data on the median years of school completed by the student's parents. When one examines the median years of education completed by parents, the same pattern of stratification emerges — university freshmen have the most educated parents, and community college freshmen have the least educated parents.

6. Estimates of the 18-20 year-old population in 1972 were made as follows: First, the percentage of Whites, Blacks, Spanish-Americans and others were obtained from 1972 data (Current Population Reports, 1973a, 1972a). These percentages were just about identical to the corresponding figures in 1970 (U.S. Bureau of Census, 1973a, 1973b, 1973c). The only detailed data for 18-20 year-olds was available for the 1970 data. It was assumed that these 1970 percentages were close estimates of the 1972 percentages and were thus used in Table II.

REFERENCES

American Association of Community and Junior Colleges
　　1973　"1972 Assembly Report" in *Educational Opportunities for All: An Agenda for National Action*, R. Yarrington, Ed. Washington, D.C.: AACJC, 141-152.
American Council on Education
　　1972　The American Freshman: National Norms for Fall, 1972, *ACE Research Reports*, Vol. 7, No. 5.
　　1971　The American Freshman: National Norms for Fall, 1971, *ACE Research Reports*, Vol. 6, No. 6.
　　1970　National Norms for Entering College Freshman — Fall, 1970, *ACE Research Reports*, Vol. 5, No. 6.
　　1969　National Norms for Entering College Freshman — Fall, 1969, *ACE Research Reports*, Vol. 4, No. 7.
　　1968　National Norms for Entering College Freshman — Fall, 1968, *ACE Research Reports*, Vol. 3.
　　1967a National Norms for Entering College Freshman — Fall, 1967, *ACE Research Reports*, Vol. 2, No. 7.
　　1967b National Norms for Entering College Freshman — Fall, 1966, *ACE Research Reports*, Vol. 2, No. 1.

Astin, A.W.
 1972   College Dropouts: A National Profile, *ACE Research Reports*, Vol. 7, No.
        1.
Bayer, A.E.
 1973   "The New Student in Black Colleges", *School Review*, 81, May, 415-426.
Berg, I.
 1971   *Education and Jobs: The Great Training Robbery*, Boston: Beacon Press.
Berg, E., and D. Axtell
 1971   *Programs for Disadvantaged Students in California Community Colleges*,
        Oakland: Peralta Junior College District.
Birnbaum, R. and J. Goldman
 1971   *The Graduates: A Follow-up Study of New York City High School
        Graduates of 1970*, CUNY: Centre for Social Research and Office for Re-
        search in Higher Education.
Blocker, C.E.
 1973   "A National Agenda for Community-Junior Colleges" in *Equal Opportu-
        nity for All: An Agenda of National Action*, R. Yarrington, Ed., Washington:
        AACJC, 125-140.
Bowles, S.
 1973   "Unequal Education and the Reproduction of the Social Division of
        Labor", in M. Carnoy, Ed. *Schooling in a Corporate Society*, New York:
        David McCay, Co., 36-64.
Brue, E.J., H.B. Engen, E.J. Maxey
 1971   "How do community college transfer and occupational students differ?",
        American College Testing Program Report No. 41.
Carnegie Commission on Higher Education
 1971   *New Students and New Places: Policies for the Future Growth and De-
        velopment of Higher Education*, New York: McGraw Hill.
 1970   *The Open Door Colleges: Policies for Community Colleges*, New York:
        McGraw Hill.
Chronicle of Higher Education
 1974   "Opening Fall Enrolment", 1972 and 1973, January 14.
 1974a "This Year's College Freshman", February 11.
 1973a "Minority Group Students Found Under-Represented in California", June,
        26.
 1973b "College-Going Gap Narrows Between Blacks, Whites", April, 9.
 1972   "9.2 Million in College, Up 2 Percent", December 18.
Clark, B.R.
 1960a *The Open Door College: A Case Study*, New York: McGraw Hill.
 1960b "The Cooling Out Function in Higher Education", *American Journal of
        Sociology* 65:569-576.
Cook, J.B., Hoss, M.A. and Vargas, R.
 1968   *The Search for Independence: Orientation for the Junior College Student*,
        Belmont, Calif: Brooks Cole Publishing Co.
Coordinating Council for Higher Education
 1968   *The Undergraduate Student and His Higher Education: Policies of Califor-
        nia Colleges and Universities in the Next Decade*, Sacramento, Calif.
Cross, K.P.
 1971   *Beyond the Open Door*, San Francisco: Jossey Bass.
 1970   "The Role of the Junior College in Providing Post-secondary Education for

All'', in *Trends in Post-secondary Education*, Washington, D.C.: U.S. Government Printing Office.
1968   *The Junior College Student: A Research Description*, Princeton: Educational Testing Service.
Crossland, F.E.
1971   *Minority Access to College*, New York: Shocken Books.
Current Population Reports
1973a *Money Income in 1972 of Families and Persons in the United States*, U.S. Department of Commerce, Series P-60, No. 87.
1973b *The Social and Economic Status of Negroes in the United States*, 1970 U.S. Department of Commerce, Series P-23.
1972a *Money Income in 1971 of Families and Persons in the United States*, U.S. Department of Commerce, Series P-60, No. 83.
1972b *Selected Characteristics of Persons and Families of Mexican, Puerto Rican and Other Spanish Origin: March 1972*, U.S. Department of Commerce, Series P-20, No. 238.
1971a *Income in 1970 of Families and Persons in the United States*, U.S. Department of Commerce, Series P-60, No. 80.
1970   *Income in 1969 of Families and Persons in the United States*, U.S. Department of Commerce, Series P-60, No. 75.
1969a *Income in 1968 of Families and Persons in the United States*, U.S. Department of Commerce, Series P-60, No. 66.
1969b *Income in 1967 of Families in the United States*, U.S. Department of Commerce, Series P-60, No. 59.
1967   *Income in 1966 of Families and Persons in the United States*, U.S. Department of Commerce, Series P-60, No. 53.
Folger, J.K., H.S. Astin, A.J. Bayer
1970   *Human Resources and Higher Education*, New York: Russell Sage Foundation.
Gleazer, E.J.
1968   *This is the Community College*, Boston: Houghton Mifflin Co.
Goffman, E.
1959   ''Cooling the Mark Out: Some Aspects of Adaptation to Failure'', *Psychiatry 15* (Nov.): 451-463.
Hansen, W.L. and B.A. Weisbrod
1969   ''The Distribution of Costs and Direct Benefits of Public Higher Education: The Case of California'', *Journal of Human Resources* 4:176-191.
Harris, E.C.
1964   *Technical Education in the Junior Colleges: New Programs for New Jobs*, Washington, D.C.: American Association of Junior Colleges.
Herrnstein, R.
1971   ''IQ'', *Atlantic Monthly* (Sept.).
Jaffee, A.J. and W. Adams
1972   ''Two Models of Open Enrollment'', in *Universal Higher Education*, L. Wilson, Ed. Washington, D.C.: American Council on Education.
Jencks, C.
1972   *Inequality: A Reassessment of the Effect of Family and Schooling in America*, New York: Basic Books.
Jencks, C. and Riesman, D.
1969   *The Academic Revolution*, Garden City, N.Y.: Doubleday.

Jensen, A.R.
   1969 "How Much Can We Boost I.Q. and Scholastic Achievement?", *Harvard Educational Review* 39 (Winter): 1-123.
Karabel, J.
   1972 "Community Colleges and Social Stratification", *Harvard Educational Review* 4 (Nov.): 521-562.
Knoell, D.M. and L.L. Medsker
   1964 *Articulation Between Two-Year and Four-Year Colleges,* Berkeley: Centre for the Study of Higher Education.
Koos, L.V.
   1970 *The Community College Student*, Gainsville: University of Florida Press.
Lauter, P. and F. Howe
   1970 *Conspiracy of the Young*, New York: World.
Maeroff, G.I.
   1973 "A kind of higher education", *New York Times Magazine,* May 27, 12-24.
Matson, J.E.
   1973 "Student Constituencies: Real and Potential", in *Educational Opportunity for All: An Agenda for National Action*, R. Yarrington, Ed., Washington, D.C., AACJC, 9-22.
Medsker, L.L.
   1960 *The Junior College: Progress and Prospect*, New York: McGraw Hill.
Medsker, L.L. and D. Tillery
   1971 *Breaking the Access Barriers: A Profile of Two-Year Colleges*, New York: McGraw Hill.
Milner, M.
   1972 *The Illusion of Equality,* San Francisco: Jossey-Bass.
Monroe, C.R.
   1972 *Profile of the Community College*, San Francisco: Jossey-Bass Inc.
Moore, W.
   1970 *Against the Odds*, San Francisco: Jossey-Bass.
New University Conference
   1971 *Open Up the Schools*, Chicago NUC.
Newman, F. et al.
   1971 *Report on Higher Education*, Washington, D.C.: U.S. Office of Education.
Rothstein, R.
   1971 "Down the Up Staircase: Tracking in Schools", *This Magazine is About Schools,* Vol. 5, No. 3.
Roueche, J.E.
   1968 *Salvage, Redirection, or Custody: Remedial Education in the Community Junior College*, Washington, D.C.: American Association of Junior Colleges.
Roueche, J.E. and R.W. Kirk
   1973 *Catching Up: Remedial Education*, San Francisco: Jossey-Bass.
Simon, K.E. and W.V. Grant
   1970 *Digest of Educational Statistics*, Washington, D.C.: U.S. Office of Education.
Simon, L.S.
   1967 "The Cooling Out Function of the Junior College", *Personnel and Guidance Journal* (June): 793-798.

U.S. Bureau of the Census
1973a Census of the Population: 1970; General Population Characteristics, Final Report PC(1)-1B U.S. Summary.
1973b Census of the Population: 1970; Subject Reports PC(2)-1E Persons of Spanish Surname.
1973c Census of the Population: 1970; Final Report PC(2)-1E Puerto Ricans in the United States.
U.S. Office of Education
1966 *Opening Fall Enrollment in Higher Education*, Washington, D.C., U.S.O.E.
1970 *Opening Fall Enrollment in Higher Education*, Washington, D.C., U.S.O.E.
Van Dyne, L.A.
1972 "The Big City Community College: Hope for the Academically Deficient", *Chronicle of Higher Education* 6 (May 30):5.
Windham, D.M.
1969 *State Financed Higher Education and the Distribution of Income in Florida*, Ph.D. Dissertation, Florida State University.
Yarrington, R., Ed.
1973 *Educational Opportunity for All: An Agenda for National Action*, Washington, D.C.: AACJC.

SECTION IV

Branch-Plant Marginality and the Capitalist System

A most noticeable feature of Canadian Left scholarship in the 1960s and 1970s has been the realization that American domination of Canada is a major feature in holding Canadians back from a complete mental and economic liberation.

Publication of George Grant's *Lament For A Nation: The Defeat of Canadian Nationalism* seemed like an epitaph in 1965. Since then, in response to Grant, much research by progressive scholars has documented the objective subordination of Canada to the U.S., in order to promote a national resuscitation. No longer is the U.S. seen as the source of all good influences — as it was to a large extent by Left and Liberal scholars of the 1930s. In his 1970 preface, Grant commented: "The Years of the Vietnam war have been an exposition (a veritable Expo) of the American empire."

The origin of American domination in Canada is, of course, based on American control of international capitalism. Capitalism has developed in a very uneven way so that just as over-class has dominated under-class, certain territories become production centres while other areas are sources of raw materials. The ideologies and idea systems of the advanced capitalist centres tend to be exported, along with finished goods, to the lesser and underdeveloped areas of the world.

The two papers which follow show two faces of the question about domination. In the peripheral areas of the capitalist world, students imbibe a passive, retreatist, and quiescent character structure. Since real economic opportunities and social mobility lie elsewhere, it is no surprise that the population in such peripheral areas lack what some scholars have called "an achievement motivation". But the solution is not another round of "blaming the victim", but an understanding that the process results from a marginality produced by branch-plant status. All of this is demonstrated by Edgar Z. Friedenberg. Marginality produced by the uneven development of capitalism has so effected the psyche of Maritime children that they cannot even take out crayons without permission. Such children will, no doubt, serve as quiescent employees, thankful for the crumbs left from the system.

Arthur K. Davis' article shows that imperial domination of ideas often results in an inability of peripheral areas to produce necessary self-awareness. Theoretical models developed in the advanced capitalist centres are particu-

195

larly inappropriate when perceived as explanations for behaviour in the peripheries. The production of ideas which correspond to the realities of the periphery is what is needed. According to Davis, this means that Canadian scholarship must cease to rely on American Weber-Parsons ''consensus'' models, and must develop class and economic related ''conflict'' models.

The Davis article was first presented as an address at the CSAA (Canadian Sociology and Anthropology Association) meetings in 1970. We anticipate that some readers, noting more recent work building upon several themes stressed by Davis, may criticize this article as being out-of-date. However, we choose to publish his address in its entirety (previously it has been available in abstract form only) because we consider it of vital importance as an emphatic reminder to make us aware that: (1) there has been, in earlier writings, a few educators speaking against American domination as they saw it in the static and ahistorical weaknesses of American import social analyses applied to the Canadian situation; (2) there are, as a result, historical antecedents of this different way of viewing and acting in the world which have helped produce present-day proposals for fundamentally restructuring the Canadian socio-economic system; (3) there is, therefore, an historical base upon which to continue building our struggle to significantly alter the status quo, the prevailing structure of a developing capitalism, and the kind of schooling created in capitalist North America.

Education for Passivity in a Branch-Plant Society

EDGAR Z. FRIEDENBERG

A year or so ago, one of the better students in my sociology class was discussing what she was learning concurrently in her practice teaching course. She reported an incident that had occurred a few days previously in her first-grade class — an incident that had shocked her. She had what she thought was a good and easy rapport with the class. Far from presenting "behaviour problems", these children were uniformly quiet and docile; enough so that their young teacher had been trying, within the narrow limits of the school situation, to get them to relax and feel a little freer in the classroom, on the rare occasions when the master-teacher left her in charge. Like many teachers before her, she thought that art might be a helpful way of loosening the children up; it was included in the first-grade curriculum and was presumably an acceptable classroom activity. So she passed out sheets of drawing paper, and suggested to the children that they might draw whatever they liked.

Nothing happened for a few moments. Then some of the shyer children began to cry. My student looked on bewildered and aghast; until one of the more outspoken children spoke out to explain: "You haven't given us permission to take out our crayons!"

This story shocked and angered me, too; but I responded to it as primarily negative — that is, as a striking example of the school's early success in repressing its pupils' capacity for spontaneity and eradicating any sense of autonomy they might have begun to develop. This interpretation is surely correct enough; but in making it I had tended to obscure from myself the positive significance of this educational process, which was only just beginning and would ultimately have very powerful cumulative effects.

By "positive significance" I do not, of course, mean to imply that this example suggests that anything beneficial was happening to these children in school: on the contrary. I mean only that my attention had fixed on the episode as evidence that the school was, from the outset, impeding its pupils' development and preventing them from becoming what they might have been. I had therefore neglected to consider it as evidence of the early effectiveness of formal education in making them what they would become.

Basically, I suppose, these are simply two ways of saying the same thing, since every human identity forms itself by foreclosing certain possibilities while developing others. But that is not quite what I mean; because the example my student-teacher cited does not, of itself, suggest that schooling had contributed *anything* to the growth of the pupils in her class — only that it had stultified them. My point is, rather, that even attributes that are wholly negative existentially are positive at least in the sense that they are, finally, what is there, immanent. Napoleon might, I suppose, have expressed his growing, if ill-judged, contempt for the character of his British adversaries by referring to their deficiencies; he might have called them timid, unimaginative, lacking in spiritual and intellectual interests, uncreative, banal. What he actually said, however, was that the British were a nation of small shopkeepers. That took it all in. But it also implied, though Napoleon didn't intend it to, that these were the people who would give the world Selfridge's and Harrod's though not, ultimately, Neiman-Marcus.

If there is such a thing as national identity — and those who enthusiastically support its claims arouse far less skepticism than those who, like the anthropologist Geoffrey Gorer twenty years ago, used the concept of "national character" in similar ways — then, surely, the schools are a major factor in its formation. We can never know exactly *how* major, because, as Henry M. Levin observes:

the educational system corresponds to the social, economic, and political institutions of our society and the only way we can obtain significant changes in educational functions and relations is to forge changes in the overall social, economic, and political relationships that characterize the policy. As a major corollary of this view I maintain that no educational reforms will succeed if they violate the major tenets of our social, economic, and political system . . . .[1]

If this is true, as I believe it is, there can neither be a way of isolating the effects of the school from those of other social institutions, nor a valid experimental procedure by which one might determine whether a totally different kind of school, established in the same society, might give widely different educational results — or rather, if it were done, the results would have very little meaning since the school wouldn't feel like a real school to its students and would not be a viable alternative in its society. But despite the difficulty of rigorous empirical verification, the idea that schooling plays a very important part in making us what we become is highly plausible. This must be one of very few propositions on which all Quebecers, like most Canadians, agree.

When I reflected, later, on what those first-graders who were too inhibited to take their box of crayons out of their desks without permission had already become, their plight seemed part of a larger and quite serious problem — not only *their* problem but the society's and indeed the nation's. It recalled to me an observation Mordecai Richler has made in lectures, and also in the following passage from an article in *Harper's* magazine:

Our problem, unique in the Western world, perhaps, was not an indigenous buc-caneering capitalist class, indifferent to those they exploited, yet intrepid and imag-inative nation-builders. Our problem was the Scots; the most inept and timorous capitalists in the West. Not builders, but vendors, or, at best, circumspect investors in insurance and trust companies.

If the pre-World War I American boy, at the age of sixteen, was dreaming of how to conquer and market the rest of the globe, his Canadian equivalent, at the same age, was already seeking a position with an unrivaled pension scheme.

And so, Canadian branch plants proliferate, there's an imbalance, corrections are called for.[2]

Richler's observation is, I should think, to be taken more as an illuminat-ing fable than a piece of solid historical detail; and it is, in any case, *historical*; the educations involved would have been those of entrepreneurs, or non-entrepreneurs, who went to primary school generations ago. Nevertheless, I was struck by the fact that a society that had evolved under the influence, primarily, of persons such as he describes, anxious to preserve their authority against the onslaughts of more confident and aggressive subordinates, could hardly do more to intimidate the potential competition earlier or more effectively than had been done to the first-graders in my student's class.

The role in history that Richler attributes to the Scots I would attribute to natural selection. So far as I can recall, Canada is unique in being the only nation to have been created as a confederation of colonies which had rejected, a century earlier, the chance to participate in a revolution which, whatever one may think of its outcome so far, had already turned out — even before Confederation — to be one of the most promising business ventures of all time. Canada came into existence through the repeated assertion of loyalty to existing political authority. This is not the way nations are usually born; and it seems safe to infer that it could only have happened to people who were, for whatever reason, more than normally prone to respect their betters, and demand a corresponding respect from their own subordinates — not like Germans, as an assertion of might and mission, but, because, on the whole, they generally trusted those in authority and preferred to depend, literally, on their good offices. Not always, to be sure; but William Lyon Mackenzie didn't really have much success; nor did he truly become a folk-hero. Francophones, as the implications of the Durham Report unfolded, have become considerably more skeptical. Still, even they have no marching-song called "Le Corps de Louis Riel" to assert that *son âme marchera toujours*; and there is no stirring tune called "The Battle Hymn of the Dominion" to which they might sing it if they had it.

So, whether or not Richler is right about why Canada developed a branch-plant mentality, he seems to me certainly right about what such a mentality is like. Moreover, as the United States replaced Britain as the location of the head office, leaving Canadians to feel more and more that they were indeed subject to a *siège social*, resentment has appreciably grown. Some of this is no doubt rationally attributable to the sheer magnitude and efficiency of American domination which does certainly constitute a threat to Canadian self-realization in every possible sense of the term. But some of the rise in anti-American feeling in Canada in recent years is also comparable to the resentment good little boys feel when their bad big brother gets by with things they are made to stand in the corner for, and is rewarded for his enterprise in bullying and breaking the rules by being allowed to take his kid brothers' things and use them up or break them; because, after all, the household economy has come to be dependent on the success of big brother's undertakings. The ensuing temper-tantrum leaves the weaker party feeling more passive and impotent than ever. Few legends and even fewer historical accounts have good boys as heroes; you can't stand tall with your finger in the dike.

The pervasive acceptance of authority in Canadian society is by definition conservative; it is the very heart of conservatism in Canada. A pervasive acceptance of authority is also characteristic of schools; at least, school officials assume it to be their due and can usually count on strong public support whenever the kids appear to be getting out of control; the legitimacy of that control is seldom effectively questioned. This, of course, is true of schools generally and not just in Canada; immigrants to Canada from countries other than the United States usually find the schools much freer than the schools at home. And American schools are no citadels of liberty, either, as is attested by the recent U.S. Supreme Court decision holding that beating children in school was not a violation of their civil rights even if there had been no sort of prior hearing at which they could defend themselves against whatever charges of misconduct had led to their punishment; and even if medically significant injury resulted, as it had in the cases brought before the Court. This did not quite mean that school children have no legal recourse whatever against battery by American school officials; but it does mean that the school officials can justify their actions totally by establishing that they were merely doing their duty as they saw it and malice could not be proved against them, whatever the consequences of the beating might be. No one else in the United States including, as the Court acknowledged in its judgment, convicted felons, enjoys so little protection from assault by authorities.

When Americans — or Canadians — express alarm about "mounting violence in the schools", beating children is never what they are talking about. Nevertheless, the American decision indicates a greater degree of support for children's rights than has so far been demonstrated in Canada. No such case has ever been brought before the Supreme Court of Canada, and it is hard to imagine that one might be, or that the Court would agree to hear it if it was, since no constitutional provision against "cruel and unusual punishment" exists here; while the British North America Act does define education as a Provincial rather than a Federal responsibility, and the Canadian Bill of Rights, limited as it is, specifically excludes any Provincial process from its provisions. The American Supreme Court decision was not only a split five-four decision, it was a decision in which four of the five concurring justices, including the Chief Justice, were markedly illiberal Nixon appointees. The two major professional education organizations in the United States both filed briefs in the case — but on opposite sides: the National Education Association supporting the plaintiffs and opposing the legality of the beatings as disciplinary measures, while the American Federation of Teachers, whose membership is composed almost entirely of classroom teachers who regard themselves as on what they often call, with dubious originality, "the firing line", supported the defendant school systems. The decision, when rendered, was roundly denounced editorially in *The New York Times* which abandoned its usually staid metaphor to suggest that the five miscreant Justices might be well served by a paddling themselves.

Whether American schoolchildren enjoy, on balance, more freedom than Canadian schoolchildren would be hard to say. American schools tend to be more informal but that also opens the way to more informal abuse of authority: the plaintiffs in the beating cases were seeking greater formality, not less. In the past few years, the American courts have established some formal rights for public school students that Canadians do not enjoy, but they are largely confined to issues like the right to distribute school newspapers published without prior censorship by the administration and without threat of confiscation; symbolic speech (the right to wear buttons or armbands expressing political views); and, paradoxically, the right to attend school, which sharply limits the power of the school administration to suspend or expel students and provides formal procedural safeguards when this is attempted. None of this is worth much except to middle-class students, with the sophistication and resources to go to court, or to poorer students militant enough to enlist the support of a civil-rights organization; so school routines in fact respond very slowly to judicial challenge even when this is successful.

But my point is not that American schools are freer but that American society itself is less like a school and feels less like a school than Canadian society. There is, notoriously, no Freedom of Information Act here in Canada; but, rather, an Official Secrets Act. Citizens are expected to raise their hands respectfully before they ask questions, and not to get smartassed about it, or the authorities may get very nasty. Judges in Canada still seem to inspire a kind of awe: contempt of court is regarded as a serious crime. It can get you into serious trouble in the United States, too; but the offense carries little stigma. Americans are more likely to regard contempt of court as either a natural state of mind or, occasionally, as when a judge sends a journalist to jail for refusing to reveal his/her sources, a civic duty.

Canada is not a more conservative country than the United States; in terms of the acceptable spectrum of political ideology and attitudes toward social welfare, it tends to be further to the left, as these things are conventionally seen. But its conservatism is of a different kind. It was in the writings of Northrop Frye, that *doyen* of Canadian literary critics, that I first encountered the word "costive". I had to look it up, and was delighted to discover that it just means "tight-assed", or, perhaps, "tight-arsed". The Canadian language really has need of this formal usage, because there are just too many occasions when this concept needs to be applied, without disrespect and sometimes not even pejoratively. Canadian conservatism is fundamentally costive; one cannot imagine William Buckley Jr., or Evelyn Waugh as Canadian — their approach to reality has been too fluid, though often venomous. This is not, of course, to imply that conservatism in this sense is peculiar to the Progressive Conservative Party or even especially characteristic of it. I am talking about a mentality that transcends party lines, but is well-illustrated by the events of a day last spring, when a document of a Parliamentary Commission enquiring into the Canadian Penitentiary Service and alleging gross brutality and incompetence against certain officials in Millhaven Penitentiary was leaked to the press. Not only did the leakage occasion more outrage than the reported and flagrant facts; the entire episode was utterly eclipsed by the apparently more shocking fact that the Prime Minister had snapped at one of his Parliamentary critics, "For Christ's sake, shut up!" Mr. Trudeau, though in some ways deeply conservative, is not costive; but, then, he is a francophone *manqué*.

Those who are disposed to doubt that costiveness is a central characterological problem in Canadian society may find themselves convinced by the brilliant and explicitly mythic fiction of Robertson Davies. The pivotal incident in his *World of Wonders*,[3] the culminating novel in his trilogy, is the retrospective account by the work's central figure, the magician and sorcerer Magnus Eisengrim, of the homosexual rape to which he was subjected as a ten-year-old boy in the pious village of Deptford, Ontario. So explicit an account of such an act is elsewhere to be found only in hard-core pornography. Yet, there is surely nothing pornographic in Davies' writing; there is nothing that could even be called gratuitous in the account, which leaves the reader curiously unmoved, though well aware that Eisengrim has told a classically diabolical story, of evil all compact. For Davies, like Mephistopheles, is sardonic; and Jungian rather than Freudian. This painful and humiliating experience does not traumatize little Paul Dempster forever — Davies is not even concerned about that aspect of the matter. What it *does* do —

literally, since he is then abducted by his assailant who takes him into a sleazy freak show in which he performs conjuring tricks — is get his arse out of Deptford and set him on the road to his apotheosis as the great Magnus Eisengrim. True, he becomes "a sufferer from a tiresome little complaint called *proctalgia fugax* . . . a cramping pain in the anus." But that is a common enough complaint in these troubled times, and it does not cramp Eisengrim's style as growing up in Deptford would have.

Costiveness precisely characterizes the approach to economic development Mordecai Richler describes, which is certainly inimical to either self-actualization or regional economic expansion. Its correlative in the schools is an excessive emphasis on decorum and control. Control is the traditional preoccupation of schoolteachers, especially in traditional schools. Preoccupation and occupation as well; whatever we may teach in our "social foundations" courses about student growth and the teacher's responsibility to nurture the potential of each child — especially those deemed disadvantaged — beginning teachers are rated on their ability to keep pupils quiet and orderly in class, and they know it; if they don't know it, they are soon enough informed.

Is this devotion to constraint especially intense in Canada? By world standards, certainly not; by North American standards, probably. In any case, international differences may be less significant than regional ones. I have lived in Nova Scotia and taught in the department of education at Dalhousie University for seven years now. Nova Scotia schools are reputed to be unprogressive, to say the least; and certainly, those of my colleagues at Dalhousie who have come here from other parts of Canada since I arrived, report with disturbing consistency incidents in which their own children have been punished for moving around or assuming that they might choose their seat in the classroom or talking out of turn in ways that were acceptable enough in the schools they had previously attended in Edmonton or Toronto. The most remarkable incident to come to my attention, which involved no student misconduct but did betray a certain lack of imagination on the part of the teacher, was a writing assignment given to a bright and sophisticated eight-year old who is the son of a close friend of mine, and who brought his graded homework home to show to his mother with wicked delight. It consisted of a sheet of ruled tablet paper on which each pupil was required to write on each line a simple declarative sentence prescribed by his/her teacher. The sentence which covered the page was "we play with our balls."

A plurality of Nova Scotia teachers are still "trained" at the Nova Scotia College at Truro, which is only now becoming a degree-granting institution as well. It has not hitherto shared very fully in the university tradition of commitment to critical inquiry. Relations between Dalhousie and Truro have been civil enough, despite rather considerable differences in our approach to the education of prospective teachers. But a major reason for this appears to be the prevalence among the Truro faculty and administration of a deep feeling of superiority to us based on their belief — undoubtedly correct — that most of the school systems in the province are delighted with their "product" and the way it accommodates itself to established expectations and demands. Our students, by and large, would like to make this accommodation, too — the problem comes up in a grievance session nearly every year at which many of them complain that we don't teach them how. This is, after all, what they came to university to learn, at great expense. Truro would have been cheaper.

These impressions are not very systematic; but one ought not to allow the prestige of the scientific method to blind one to what is plainly visible without resorting to it. My reason for attaching importance to them is that I think they are closely related to the Atlantic provinces' notoriously and persistently bad economic condition. Our labour force is widely regarded as relatively unproductive; it often behaves, as we say, like schoolchildren trying to see how much work it can evade, resists innovation as a threat, drinks a lot and walks off the job when one of its members is disciplined for doing it. These, of course, are faults of weakness rather than of militance; the attitudes of people who have never been permitted to consider seriously that they have a right to a strong voice in determining the pattern of their lives. When they do become militant, their tone is likely to be defiant and shrill, like that of angry children who have never been treated with any respect and who know that, whether they are right or wrong, they are likely to get spanked for being uppity. The head of the AFL-CIO may be an old Meany, but he has more confidence than that.

At the root of this difficulty, I suspect, is the residue of the entrenched British attitude toward social class, since labour conflict often takes a similar tone in Britain itself and in Australia. And certainly our managerial elite (there is no power-elite in Nova Scotia; we get our power, foolish virgins that we are, by burning foreign oil we cannot afford) rather consistently demonstrates precisely corresponding limitations. It behaves like a caricature of Richler's caricature and its distinguishing characteristic is a defensive passivity. For how many years has the proposal that the tides in the Bay of Fundy, the highest in the world, be utilized as an inexhaustible and non-polluting source of power been proposed? Nothing has been done about it, though tidal power has been a reality in France for years. The economy runs on taxes and Federal grants which are dissipated in subsidizing a series of fiascos; a heavy-water plant that doesn't work; an antiquated and unprofitable steel mill whose management flies into a snit, closes it down, and lays off the workers when the Federal Ministry of Mines and Resources complains that conditions are unsafe; more than six million dollars expended in the purchase and fitting-up of a German ship for tropical cruises which would cruise the coasts of Nova Scotia and Newfoundland during the summer tourist season, registered in the Bahamas with a largely Thai crew, though the unemployment rate in Nova Scotia is now running at about 15 per cent! The money invested in this undertaking is, incidentally, the sole investment (save for a small loan to an existing company) made by a tax-supported corporation established three years ago to promote economic growth in Nova Scotia, and involves about a third of its capital.

To call this managerial incompetence would be to miss the point. This kind of economic activity serves its actual, though not its ostensible, function very well. It channels money into the province or out of the pockets of its taxpayers in quantities adequate to sustain very lavishly the members of a closed society and provide them with the kinds of status and role to which they are accustomed. A thorough investigation would, I suspect, disclose very little that could be called corruption here; this is simply the way things are done; or rather, in which nothing gets done. Nova Scotia's managers do not act like Lockheed executives or Mafiosi; they act like Campus Leaders, whose roles carry snazzy perquisites but no real responsibility. The perquisites come from subsidies, not from economic productivity; and the roles, naturally, mostly go to members of the graduating class. This isolation of the upper bourgeoisie in the Atlantic provinces from economic reality is what gives their projects their characteristic loopiness: cruise ships to nowhere, gremlins and Bricklins, whatever happens to Come-by-chance. It is all as irresponsible as a suburban high school play, with as few roles open to the culturally deprived, and very expensive stage effects.

The economy of Nova Scotia is an extreme case, of course, a colony of a colony. But that is precisely why backward schools are suited to its demands. I am not suggesting that the schools are the source of the deficiency; to do so would be to contradict the proposition of Henry Levin's which I have already stated that I accept. The schools simply align themselves with the field of social forces that prevails, occasionally exerting some influence arising from their own purposes, like sailboats tacking into an unfavourable wind. One would, therefore, expect to find different approaches to schooling in regions, and among social classes, whose children anticipated a different set of demands and opportunities in later life. This is one of the most thoroughly investigated issues in the sociology of education; and some of the most sophisticated analysis has been made by Canadian scholars and deals specifically with schooling in Canadian society. I should like to consider three recent publications that seem to me especially relevant to the moulding of a branch-plant economy. All, as it happens, are by women, and I will introduce them in order of conceptual complexity. The first of these is a book by Carolyn Gossage, *A Question of Privilege: Canada's Independent Schools*.[4] The term "independent school" is much more limiting than private school; it applies only to the fifty schools in Canada whose heads are members of the Canadian

Headmasters' Association or the Canadian Association of Principals of Independent Schools for Girls — a criterion similar to that by which Britain's "Public Schools" are identified. These schools, though increasingly poverty-stricken, are still widely suspected of being citadels of privilege and the training-ground of Canada's ruling oligarchs.

Gossage's book casts a curiously revealing light on this proposition. The schools are certainly WASP's nests, and none is francophone though twelve, including the second oldest school in what is now Canada but wasn't when it was founded, are in Quebec, and some, — Upper Canada College in Toronto notably — have indeed been attended by a significant proportion of the Canadian establishment.

But as training-grounds for a power-elite, they sound, as Gossage describes them, strangely debilitating. More than half of their students are young women, girls mostly, in small underfunded, finishing-school-type places that are still training young women to be ladies qualified only for the most genteel employment. Truro is a lot more liberating.

The boys' and predominantly boys' schools, too, though, seem dreadfully repressive in ways surely inappropriate to the education of leaders. What I find most disturbing in Gossage's account is the way school after school treasures the memory of a putdown of somebody's initiative that might otherwise have led to a little more openness to human experience. Some of these are very odd, though the oddness may, of course, reflect a quirk in Gossage's interests as well as in the school. But she couldn't, after all, have made these things up. Thus, at Bishop Strachan school, "Thirty years ago, 'order marks' were liberally dispensed by the school prefects to anyone unable to stifle whispers, sighs, and girlish giggles during chapel. The one escape was to faint, a malady that from time to time reached epidemic proportions." Thirty years ago is since World War II! Or the incident around 1909 at Ontario Ladies' College, housed in a Charles Adams-like castle with a secret chamber, "when a group of girls on an exploratory foray stumbled upon the hidden entrance and crept inside. They emerged, festooned with cobwebs, to be greeted by the principal, who then padlocked the door and eventually arranged for the chamber's removal." Or the high old time at Ridley College, in Ontario near the Welland Canal, where "Fishing was also a popular pastime — at least until the day a group of boys lugged back a six-foot, seventy-eight pound sturgeon that had been trapped in the canal. The headmaster ordered its instant burial and the ungodly stench emanating from its shallow grave served to discourage future anglers from hauling home anything that would not fit into a frying-pan."

Such, such are the annals of Canada's independent schools. The fact that these events are all ancient history lends them retrospective significance. What kind of social group makes a humorous legend of an incident in which some of its prospective leaders are humiliated for having caught a fish too big to be convenient? In a capitalist society, especially, this seems odd, dissonant. Paul Bunyan may have been saved by the Webster-Ashburton treaty of 1842, which assigned his neck of the woods to Minnesota rather than Ontario. Schools in the Soviet Union do, indeed, suppress individual pupil initiative as severely as they deem necessary: Urie Bronfenbrenner's classic study *Two Worlds of Childhood: U.S. and U.S.S.R.* includes a detailed and horrifying account of his observation of the trial and punishment, in school, of a group of boys, all members of the Young Pioneers organization and excellent swimmers, for the serious offense of going swimming "without supervision."[5] But they are being socialized to fit a different economy; and the repression is evidently not carried far enough to make Soviet trawler crews timid fishermen.

The next study I wish to discuss here is altogether different: a brief article with a sharp focus: Eleanor Smollett's "Schools and the Illusion of Choice: the Middle Class, and the 'Open' Classroom."[6] Smollett's article is "based on observations in three working-class and three middle-class schools, several days at a time, over three successive years. In each school, rotating pairs of observers recorded in detail the events of each day in each of a number of classrooms. The observers, including the author and her students, had subsequent discussions with principals and teachers in these schools."

Smollett thus has a solid data base for her conclusions. The most important of these is that schooling subverts the powers of middle-class children to make meaningful policy choices about matters important to their lives and those of other persons who might be affected, by continuously indoctrinating them with the illusion of choice. But the range of possible choice is delimited by the teacher (whose range of choice is similarly prescribed and truncated by the school administration). The children are generally required to select among alternatives previously stated by the authorities — as in learning to get good grades on multiple-choice tests. Smollett describes a dreadful little pre-Christmas scene — this time, too, in a drawing class. The teacher "explains the task. They will do, altogether, two Christmas pictures each, one today in crayon, one next week in paint. One picture will be on the religious side of Christmas ... the other on Santa Claus or something on the non-religious side ... 'Miss Simms,' asks Brenda, 'can I make both pictures of the manger?' 'No,' says Miss Simms, 'you have a choice — one for one picture, one for the other.' "

The choices presented to pupils, Smollett further observes, almost invariably concern means, techniques — the children are never taught to consider the purposes or consequences of choice. They don't get time to.

Control is both subtle and absolute. It is achieved, in part, by the timing of activities. . . . In Miss Simms' grade three class, for example, activities rarely have a duration longer than a few minutes. Teacher explains the mechanics of the activity and very often, the choices available. The children begin work. Before they can lose interest in the task (or develop any thoughts of their own on the subject matter, or begin to elaborate in any way on the defined alternatives the teacher has offered), the activity is over, and the children are listening to the teacher again so as not to miss her description of choices for the next activity. Often, the next one involves different kinds of materials or a different location, so that the children must re-orient themselves . . . . In this manner, by a teacher who speaks to them with a sweet and quiet voice, they are gently led through the day, believing they are 'choosing' one activity after another, being given explanations of how to carry out this or that choice, rarely being given a straightforward order or reprimand, kept in control with subtle precision, while being regularly told that they are 'doing very well.'

Smollett's article is placed in Part II of *The Politics of the Canadian Public School* — a section entitled "Canadian Schools and the American Corporate Order." And not without reason. Today, when it isn't the Christmas season, do you suppose Miss Simms gives lessons about the Arctic Pipeline, in the Unit on Friendly Peoples of the Northland?

It is not possible for me to summarize the last publication I want to discuss so easily. Gail Regan's "Steps to the Reformation: An Evaluation of the Feasibility of Deschooling"[7] is one of the most intellectually complex and abstract essays I have ever read on any subject related to education. It is also one of the most fundamentally rewarding. What is novel and significant in her approach is her fresh and challenging insight into certain of the relationships between schooling and social class that few other scholars have even noticed. She begins by commenting that, though deschooling and even major educational reform are now usually thought to be highly improbable — precisely for the reasons Carnoy and Levin give — nevertheless:

My opinion is that the common-sense estimate of the improbability of deschooling fails to take into account the negative consequences that result from success in present-day schools. That is, I believe that deschooling *is* in the interests of those who most 'benefit' from school now, and, as the press for deschooling will come from those who currently have the most vested interest in schooling, the likelihood of deschooling is higher than common-sense might predict. But because deschooling will develop out of essentially conservative vested interests, *not* from the ideological and political left, its immediate future will be different from what [Ivan] Illich advocates . . . . It is tempting to view Illich's work as a proposal that, if implemented, would be of benefit to the objectively disadvantaged, i.e., the poor. This approach, I believe, blocks a full understanding of the prospects of deschooling. I think that present-day schooling, while providing for social mobility (and hence treatment of poverty to some extent), engineers subjective disadvantages, such as psychosomatic and mental disorders. The press for deschooling will come from those who, while objectively benefiting from present-day schooling, are paying the heaviest personal costs. What this means for deschooling is that deschooling is feasible, but that the course of its development will be somewhat different from what Illich predicts.

At this point, a few *caveats* are perhaps in order, just to keep the record straight. There is rather widespread agreement among historians of education — and certainly among "revisionist" historians of education like Herbert Gintis and Samuel Bowles, Colin Greer, and again, Carnoy and Levin, to name only the most widely recognized — that the schools never have, in fact, contributed much to social mobility or been, on balance, an aid rather than a hindrance to the children of the poor. Conversely, Regan presents no evidence that the parents of middle and upper class children understand that — much less how — their children "are paying the heaviest personal costs." And even if they did, they might not object, accepting it as a necessary part of the socialization process, as they themselves experienced it in school.

But this criticism does not affect the validity of Regan's basic argument about what schools do to children, though it does tend to weaken her conclusion that deschooling may come easier than most people now suppose. It is the former question — how the schools affect the moral and intellectual development of their students — that concerns us here. And what Regan maintains, brutally oversimplified, is that the schools drive them quite literally out of their minds — a greater disadvantage, presumably, to those whose status and role would permit them relatively full exercise of their intellect and judgment if they still had command of these faculties. For those who are willing to struggle with her abstract language, moreover, she does succeed in making clear exactly why and how she thinks this happens.

Regan's precision defies paraphrase; but the gist of her argument is that even schools with primarily middle-class clientele emphasize and reward with a record of high achievement the kind of conventional cognitive development needed in "skilled, routinized occupations". This, of itself, would to some degree penalize those destined for leadership positions. But what happens to the bright, independent-minded, or potentially bright, independent-minded students is likely to be much worse than what happens to their records; they have to live with this system for more than a decade, despite the fact that they see through it, and it violates their perceptions of reality. Broadly speaking, they have two alternative means of accommodating to the situation, both of which have their disadvantages.

They can, if their independence develops fast, cope with the school by what Regan calls *abstracting*; that is, retaining and developing their independent sense of what the world is but learning simultaneously not to be that smart in school — not just to play dumb but to grow accustomed to responding automatically to school as a situation with its own idiosyncratic, if not idiotic, set of right answers and view of the world. Most students, certainly by the time they get into high school, doubtless learn to do this light-heartedly enough, and without apparent damage. The damage, however, may easily be worse than it appears. The risk is that people who get through school essentially by abstracting become so alienated that they either begin to caricature their own experiences and blow it with the school when it finally learns what they think of it; or, much more seriously, learn to approach most situations in their lives with the same determination to manipulate them from within, like Michael Maccoby's *Gamesmen.*

But they may also respond to the school's demands in the converse way, which Regan calls *reification*: i.e., by convincing themselves that, if they really understood the way the world is, they would see that the school must be right; and that it is what they thought they had learned through their own experiences of life that is erroneous. Some societies — the Chinese, apparently — are so successful in insisting on learning through reification that its people lose or never develop the power to examine a public proposition critically in the light of their own experience. Their bullshit detector is bred out of them as an organ of negative adaptive value — skepticism decreases their chances of survival. But comparable processes occur in Canadian society as well. Regan states her position on this bitterly but clearly — once you grasp the rather unusual meaning she attaches to the concept of maturity — in another article.[8]

The reifier becomes oriented to myth-making, rather than to truth-finding. Unfortunately, those who learn through reification in classrooms are likely, not only to develop mature levels of cognitive and personality functioning, but to do well in school. The combination of maturity and school success will help them to achieve in later public life. Thus, the people who become faceless and authoritarian normatively, synthetic and accommodating in terms of knowledge, i.e., the people who are, in my opinion, the most morally bankrupt, are likely to end up in leadership positions. I think that Canadian schools play a role in the maintenance of this phenomenon.

Both abstractors and reifiers clearly have much to "contribute" to a branch-plant society; reifiers, especially, are useful in helping to ensure that the definitions of reality that emanate from head office are never seriously questioned. One might almost infer, indeed, that everything I have argued in this article merely serves to confirm that Canada has the kind of schools it needs in order to fulfill its manifest destiny. So, I suspect, does every nation. Schools play their appointed role in making us what we are; but they cannot make us what, through the centuries, we have "chosen" not to be.

NOTES

1. Martin Carnoy and Henry M. Levin, *The Limits of Educational Reform*, New York: David McKay, 1976, pp. 23-24.

2. Mordecai Richler, ''Letter from Ottawa; the sorry state of Canadian nationalism'', *Harper's*, June 1975, p. 32.

3. Robertson Davies, *World of Wonders*, Toronto: Macmillan Canada Ltd., 1975.

4. Carolyn Gossage, *A Question of Privilege: Canada's Independent Schools*, Toronto: Peter Martin, 1977.

5. Urie Bronfenbrenner, *Two Worlds of Childhood: U.S. and U.S.S.R.*, New York: Russell Sage Foundation, 1970, pp. 65-68.

6. Eleanor Smollett, ''Schools and the Illusion of Choice: the Middle Class, and the 'Open' Classroom'', *The Politics of the Canadian Public School*, Toronto: James Lewis and Samuel, 1974, pp. 92-102.

7. Gail Regan, ''Steps to the Reformation: An Evaluation of the Feasibility of Deschooling'', *Interchange*, 1974, Vol. 5, No. 3, pp. 31-43.

8. Gail Regan, ''Socialization Outcomes and Processes in Canadian Schooling'', *Education, Change and Society*, eds. Richard A. Carlton, Louise A. Colley, and Neil J. MacKinnon, Toronto: Gage, 1977, p. 404.

The Failure of American Import Sociology in Anglophone Canada*

ARTHUR K. DAVIS

THE FAILURE OF STRUCTURAL-FUNCTIONALISM TO COMPREHEND CANADIAN SOCIETY HOLISTICALLY

Wrote the late C. Wright Mills:

> Classic social analysis is . . . the concern with historical social structures; its problems are of direct relevance to urgent public issues and insistent human troubles . . . .[1]

Beginning with neolithic times — the discovery of agriculture, town life, writing, metallurgy, commerce, social classes, the bureaucratic State, and so on — the mainstream of social analysis has dealt (among other things) with historical, holistic social communities. It has done so in such a way as to be more or less relevant both to the major public issues of the times and to the more widespread personal troubles of ordinary people. These troubles generally included such matters as livelihood, relations to authorities, kinship and spouse roles, relations to cosmic entities, neighbours, enemies, and so on. Ever since the early civilisations of Greece, India and China, the social thinkers and teachers of the world's societies have had something relevant to say about their times. Doubtless this has not always been the case. It is reasonable to assume the co-existence of a category of irrelevant intellectual productions alongside the relevant.

In which of these two categories falls most of the teaching and research by angolphone academic sociologists in Canada is not a difficult question to answer. By and large, anglophone social scientists in Canadian universities have presented an abstract, bland, fragmental and static picture of Canadian

---

*A condensed version of this paper was one of five position papers presented at a plenary session of the Canadian Association of Sociology and Anthropology at Winnipeg in June, 1970. The condensed version was published, along with the other position papers, in Jan Loubser, ed., *The Future of Sociology in Canada/L'Avenir de la Sociologie au Canada*, CSAA.

society. Further, they see the world through a middle-class or bourgeois lens: conflict is underestimated. Finally, few of them deal with Canadian society as a whole.

Looking over the back numbers of the *Canadian Review of Sociology and Anthrolopology* and the various "readers" on Canadian society indicates a primary focus on micro-empirical aspects of Canadian social organization, and a relative neglect of macro-trends — especially those concerning Canadian-American relations in an exploitative context. In fact, a good number of those papers are essentially timeless and placeless, in the sense that the main focus is on variables abstracted from time and place rather than upon the time and place from which they are "lifted." Not many have anything to say to ordinary people, even about limited specific and local problems. For the most part, anglophone academic sociologists appear to be talking to each other about esoteric topics, although most of them are paid — fairly well— by Canadian public funds. For the average person (who pays the shot), Ann Landers is usually more relevant.

That a roughly parallel critique of academic economics in Canada is made by M.H. Watkins[2] suggests that the points raised in this paper stem from a general condition of anglophone Canadian society and of Canadian academia. Like orthodox economics, orthodox sociology is biassed toward the dominant Anglo, capitalist Establishment.

There are at least two related reasons for the aridity of anglophone academic sociology in Canada.

(A) The first is the pre-occupation with structural-functionalism, a cultural import from the United States. Whatever qualifications and exceptions may be cited, the prevailing tone of structural-functional approaches to social analysis is one of equilibrium, timelessness, value integration, and the natural harmony of interests. Deviance and conflict tend to be defined as fringe, short-term sub-cultures that will (hopefully?) never amount to more than sub-cultures. Having been made before, most of these points scarcely need repetition here. The only one that deserves re-emphasis is this: in the typical structural-functional perspective, which is of course a middle-class perspective, sub-cultures usually appear as, and remain, merely *deviant* sub-cultures. Their potential progression into large-scale structural changes is seldom seriously contemplated.

The concept *deviance*, though less negatively "loaded" and perhaps more sophisticated than the old category *social disorganization* (in general use one and two generations ago), still implies a single dominant and more or less stable normative order. This assumed order is the North American middle-class or bourgeois pattern. Measured thereby, other patterns such as hippies, peaceniks, draft-evaders, ghetto gangs, et al. come to be defined as sub-cultures. (*Sub* is short for subordinate in case the reader needs reminding.) Hence they are labelled or caricatured as minor variations going no-where.

However, in a dialectical, conflict-oriented perspective these "deviations" become "oppositions". Any of them might turn out to be sources of key structural changes. To estimate their respective potentials, even remotely, would require an historical view in a dialectical tradition. A structural-functionalist analysis gets us nowhere. Indeed, it sets us back.

For instance, here are some books that show rather conclusively how little our middle-class anglophone sociologists understand of the basic elements involved in (1) the situation of the American ghetto Blacks vis-à-vis the White bourgeois order (L. Rainwater and L. Yancey, 1967, R. Abrahams, 1970)[3]; (2) the refusal of Canadian Indians and francophone Quebecers to be assimilated into the dominant Anglo-Canadian pattern (Lévesque, 1968; Cardinal, 1969)[4]; (3) the meaning of poverty, which by the most conservative measure afflicts at least one-fourth to one-third of the Canadian people (Ian Adams, 1970).[5]

These cases are not mere "deviances". They are not simply "subcultures". In a few years, they could prove to be decisive in the changing mainstream of Canada tomorrow. In brief, structural-functionalism is culture-bound middle-class apologetics for a transitory, unstable capitalist vested interest.

(B) The second reason for the aridity of anglophone sociology and economics in Canada is the general identification of middle-class anglophone sociologists and economists with the Anglo-Canadian bourgeois Establishment, and/or with the latter's country-cousin status as a branch plant of the American capitalist empire. Even if the majority of our anglophone practitioners are indifferent to, or unaware of, Canada's hinterland subordination to the United States, still they can be said to support it by default. Many tacitly assume that Quebec separatism is wrong, that "federalism" is right, and that to make a big issue out of American economic and cultural imperialism in Canada is impolite, uneconomic and (most important) impolitic.

Surprisingly little attention is given to historical overviews or to the potentially massive conflicts building up both inside and outside Canadian society.

This is not to deny the value of limited specific insights and studies based on the strucutral-functional approach.[6] We have many such analyses in Canada. They are to be found in the collections of readings on Canadian society (Blishen, 1968; Mann, 1968; Laskin, 1964)[7], in the *Canadian Review of Sociology and Anthropology*, in Royal Commission and other governmental reports, in special monographs, and elsewhere.

Some of them are even published in American outlets. In the February, 1970, *American Sociological Review*, there appeared a study of the Saskatchewan Wheat Pool by John Craig and Edward Gross[8] — the latter is a famous name in American sociology. Only after reading one-fourth of the 13-page article does one realize that the topic is the Saskatchewan Wheat Pool, a large farmer-owned producer co-operative.

Six years of rural and urban research in Saskatchewan made the present writer reasonably familiar with the Saskatchewan scene. In the 1920s the Wheat Pool was an innovating and slightly revolutionary hinterland movement of western grain farmers fighting back against eastern metropolitan financial and industrial interests. By the middle 1950s the Pool had become part of the Saskatchewan Establishment. Something of the epic quality of that conflict-ridden historical cycle is recaptured in the work of both J. McCrorie (1964) and in J.F.C. Wright (1955a, 1955b).[9] However, it was difficult for me to recognize a real-life organization in the Craig-Gross analysis entitled, ''The Forum Theory of Organizational Democracy: Structural Guarantees as Time-Related Variables''. Though published in a prestige journal (according to the trade opinion in North America), this paper in my opinion conveys little about either the contemporary grass-roots activities of the Wheat Pool or the historical role of the Pool in Saskatchewan. Indeed, more feeling, insight, and essential perspectives on Sakastchewan is conveyed in Carlyle King's Saskatchewan literary anthology (1955).[10]

On occasion, to be sure, a structural-functional approach has attained a halfway holistic view of Canadian society: witness J. Porter, 1965.[11] This work contains much information and some useful historical data. But to find out what is really on-going in Canadian society today, one does not ordinarily resort to the writings of Porter or most other anglophone academic sociologists. One would be better advised to turn to philosopher George Grant (1965; 1969);[12] to economist Mel Watkins (1968);[13] to journalist Peter Newman (1963; 1968; 1975);[14] and to the documentaries of the Canadian Broadcasting Corporation (C.B.C.) and the National Film Board. For relevant reading on Canadian society, one should probably pass over at least half of the *Canadian Review of Sociology and Anthropology* in favour of *Canadian Dimension* and *Canadian Forum*. Lipset's well-known study (1950) seriously misinterpreted the Saskatchewan Co-operative Commonwealth Federation (CCF) movement as a transplanted offshoot of urban socialism,[15] when it was mainly an indigenous manifestation of western petty-bourgeois populism fighting back against eastern metropolitan capitalist domination. In the new up-dated edition of this book (Lipset, 1968), the record was set straight, not by Lipset or by some other sociologist, but by anthropologist John Bennett and political economist John Richards. Finally, the best study of poverty in Canada is by journalist Ian Adams (1970), or by novelist Gabrielle Roy (1947, 1958).[16]

In brief, then, concerning the contributions of anglophone middle-class sociologists to an understanding of Canadian society — with some exceptions — perhaps the less said, the better. If I were a C.B.C. official responsible for staffing documentary radio and television programs on what is going on in Canadian society, I would pass over most of the anglophone sociologists. I believe it would serve the Canadian public better to present the ideas of people like René Lévesque, Harold Cardinal, certain journalists, a handful of academics (mostly non-sociologists), and of the more sensitive and intelligent folk-singers like Buffy Sainte-Marie and stomping Tom Connors. They could do the job.

The reader has doubtless noted that I have concerned myself only with anglophone sociologists in Canada. This does not mean that our francophone colleagues have not been contaminated by over-concern with structural-functionalism. I believe that they have, but not nearly to the same extent as the anglophones. This is doubtless because they live close to the central conflict in contemporary Canadian society — the question of independence for Quebec. Hence they are more conscious of conflict and change than are most of the rest of us. Quebec is a nation, but anglophone Canada is a "banana republic", a colony of the American empire.

Another really sad fact is that the majority of anglophone sociologists do not know what their francophone counterparts are doing, because they do not speak or read French. If we anglophones want a dialogue with francophone intellectuals, we must learn their language and culture, read their writings, and attend their meetings, and talk to them in French. I believe that it should be a prime concern of the Canadian Sociology and Anthropology Association to re-establish communication with Quebec social scientists by pressuring anglophone members to take total-immersion courses in the French language. Indeed, it seems entirely likely, in my judgment, that even our western Canadian universities within a few years may give priority to appointing fluently bilingual professors to their faculties. The assumption of North American anglophones — "if someone wants to talk to us, let them learn English" — is simply a linguistic reflection and reinforcement of Anglo imperialism in Canada. Though not yet over, that era is rapidly passing. Few anglophone social scientists can see this.

THE NEED FOR A DIALECTICAL AND HISTORICAL PERSPECTIVE IN CANADIAN STUDIES

Roughly speaking, the dialectical premise is that major long-run changes in the institutional structure of a particular society stem from internal and external oppositions that develop immanently in that society and its milieu. These oppositions or confrontations of incompatible interests and values eventually work into a new institutional pattern which is not like either of the original opposing complexes, but which usually includes important elements of all. A good example is historian Crane Brinton's study of four major revolutions (1952).[17] The process of revolution obviously lends itself admirably to a dialectical analysis. For less "extreme" confrontations, the present writer prefers a modified version of the dialectic applicable to Canada, where political change has up to now been relatively moderate. The schema consists of a "metropolis vs hinterland" or "over-class vs under-class" frame of reference. It assumes a conflict of interests between metropolis and hinterland, between over-class and under-class, and an inherent tendency of hinterlands and under-classes to fight back — though these conflicts at different times may be overt or latent or counteracted by other factors, as conditions vary.

Metropolis refers to centres of economic and political control, usually in the larger cities. It may denote urban elites or regional or national or ethnic power structures. Its core is the boards of the great corporations, domestic and foreign. *Hinterland* means any comparatively underdeveloped or colonial area which exports for the most part raw or semi-processed extractive materials — including migrating people seeking better opportunities elsewhere. Hinterland also refers to urban under-classes as well as to rural proletariats and peasantries. Indeed, it seems convenient to use *metropolis* and *over-class* interchangeably, and likewise *hinterland* and *under-class*.

Finally, there are hierarchies of overlapping metropolis-hinterland relationships. Northern Manitoba may be viewed as a hinterland of Winnipeg — or perhaps, in certain respects, also as a hinterland of Ottawa. Manitoba itself may be seen as something of a hinterland of industrial and commercial central Canada: and Canada, of the United States' economic and political empire.

Needless to say, the metropolis — hinterland, over-class — under-class schema does not include all the relationships that may exist between or among these entities. Rather, it highlights the conflict, exploitative and dialectical aspects of such relationships. It is suggested here that the schema can be applied to Canadian and North American society with results that are insightful, dynamic, capable of taking account of unique local and historical conditions, and often relevant for tentative prediction. By contrast, structural-functional analyses are practically useless for prediction.

There is nothing really new in these remarks.[18] In fact, a good deal of work has been done along these lines by Canadian scholars, especially by such historians as Innis and Fowke. A number of sociologists have made consistent use of historical materials and perspectives — among them S.D. Clark, R. Ossenberg, S. Ryerson (1960, 1965)[19] H. Guindon — to name no others. But the contributions of such writers seem greatly outweighed, at least in volume, by work that leans toward the structural-functional, positivistic tradition. Consider, for example, the array of textbooks commonly used in anglophone introductory sociology courses in Canadian universities. The majority of them impress me as useless "mickey mouse" exercises imported (for a good price) from the United States, or produced by Canadian branch plants of American publishers. What they tell us about North American society is too often less important than what they leave out or cover up.

Even the bare handful of readers on "Canadian Society" leave much to be desired. For nearly a decade the Blishen reader (1968) has been a mainstay of anglophone Canadian university undergraduate sociology courses. First published in 1961, it has been used by thousands of students. It has probably widened the gap between Anglo and French Canada — willy-nilly — because it takes little account of conflict-oriented, dialectical views of Canadian society. Further, it has contributed — albeit unintentionally — to the obscuring of the one issue that can over-ride the Anglo-French issue: the stance of Canada vis-à-vis the American empire. In other words, the Blishen reader is — ideologically and doubtless innocently — a prime indirect supporter of the present middle-class Anglo-Canadian Establishment. The majority of the articles convey an Anglo, structural-functional bias. There are perfunctory bows toward French-Canadian patterns, Ukrainian patterns, Inuit patterns, and so on. Much the same could be said of the Laskin reader — except that it does a much better job on the Hutterites. And so likewise for the Mann reader.[20]

Here is the theme of two key papers, one by Naegele in Blishen (1961 and 1964 editions only) and the other by Lipset, in Mann (1968). In these two papers on Canadian society as a whole, a central idea is, "Canadians are not Americans, in terms of values, and they are not British, they are somewhere in between." Both writers rely mainly on the abstract, static, structural-functional Weber-Parsons concepts — an injustice to Weber, at least, because Weber had a keen sense of economic history.

Lipset's paper[21] in the Mann reader resorts to the well-known Parsonian pattern variables, and a more dismal exercise at explaining Canadian society I have never seen. It is not that Lipset is wrong; his approach is just irrelevant. What does it mean, for either American or Canadian society, when Lipset argues that the United States (and Canada only a little less so) is achievement-oriented rather than ascriptive with regard to status-assignment? That the United States pursues universalistic values over and above particularistic values? That it is self-oriented more than collectivity-oriented? Egalitarian rather than elitist?

Surely these jargonistic propositions do not capture the guts of American society or American history. Furthermore, they are not empirically true without serious qualifications: they fail to take into adequate account the obvious hierarchical, racist, elitist and special privilege aspects of American capitalist social structure.

How can we analyze the evolution of American and Canadian societies without central emphasis upon the differential development of modern capitalism in the two nations? Finally, if it is claimed that a neo-Marxian, dialectical frame of reference for sociological studies is bound up with ideological implications, then this claim is equally applicable to structural-functionalism, Parsonianism, et al.

What could be more ideological than Lipset's one-sided, special-pleading distortion of American social realities? If the reader has doubts about this charge, let him/her read Lipset, a recognized servant of the American Establishment, and then glance over the headlines of today's American newspapers. Lipset is listed as having received $95,000 from the U.S. Air Force to study the "Implication of Comparative National Development for Military Planning".[22]

It is regrettable that anglophone Canadian sociologists have not critically debated the relevance of the currently fashionable concepts of United States bourgeois sociology for analysis of Canadian society. Instead, there has prevailed a tendency simply to transplant those concepts. Occasionally, Canadian academics have displayed an almost supine attitude toward their American opposite numbers. Consider the following Foreword by Dr. Murray Ross for the W. Mann (1968) reader. Ross is not only a well known writer on community organization and higher education; he is also the president of York University, Toronto.

The popular view is that sociological analysis and study in Canada has lagged far behind similar work in the United States.... Unfortunately the popular view is correct... Canada has not yet produced original sociological theorists comparable to Talcott Parsons, Robert K. Merton, and C. Wright Mills.[23]

Two of these three eminent sociologists are structural-functionalists and generally irrelevant for un-American Canadians. But mainly, Ross is looking in the wrong place. The original theorists about Canadian society are not to be found in imported orthodox academic esoterica, but in such sources as Lumsden (1970), *Canadian Dimension*, *Monthly Review*, Harold Innis, Stanley Ryerson and Vern Fowke.

Not the least unhappy aspect of this deference to prevailing American intellectual concepts is the fact that it is unwitting. Yet it is not merely a function of ignorance. Rather, it is better described as stemming from class- and culture-bound blindspots. How ironic that professional social scientists should display this shortcoming in their own professional field!

But sociologists are not alone in being culture-bound. Consider the following Toronto *Globe and Mail* account of Prime Minister Trudeau's visit to President Nixon in Washington in March, 1969. The deferential attitude of the Prime Minister of Canada parallels that of the President of York University toward things American. The scene is Trudeau's reception at the White House in Washington.

Responding to the President's words about a commonality of background, Mr. Trudeau said this extended to 'a common outlook on the world. We have the same values and we tend to face the issues in a common way.' Because of that he was looking forward to the discussion . . . 'to listening to your views on world problems, on the information and the wisdom you will want to impart upon me in your talks.'

Some observers who have travelled extensively with Mr. Trudeau said that he had not sounded so humble, or looked so shy, since just before he decided to run for the Liberal Party leadership more than 13 months ago.[24]

Is it necessary to say here that we are not arguing for a unique "Canadian sociology"? There is no such thing as a "national sociology". But there are alternative ways of viewing society and history. And every society is geographically and historically unique in some essential respects. Structural-functionalism does not adequately explain, or convey a convincing image of, these unique aspects — least of all in a realistic context of flux and change. Structural-functionalism reflects and embodies the homogenizing universalism of *Pax Americana*.

Another way to size up our present condition in Canada is the *dialectical*. Not only is this appropriate for analyzing a semi-colonial society like Canada; it is equally indispensable for understanding imperial America.

Conversely, the structural-functional ideology obscures some key essentials of both Canada and the United States. Yet this is the prevailing school of sociology of North America. Its followers can fully understand neither Canadian society nor American society. The Canadian critic who complained that many American social scientists are not qualified to teach in Canada about Canadian institutions did not go far enough. Many Americans are not particularly competent to teach about the United States either.

Robin Mathews of Carleton University justifiably attacks the "Americanization of Canadian universities".[25] His solution is more Canadians — trained in Canada — on Canadian faculties. This is scarcely adequate. What difference would it make, so long as Canadian sociologists and economists continue to be trained in such obfuscating orthodoxies as structural-functionalism, symbolic interaction, and micro econometric economics? They will still remain junior lieutenants in the intellectual empire of the American imperial Establishment.

Conceptual orientation rather than nationality would be a more appropriate target for Mathews. No one wants or needs universities dominated by a particular viewpoint, any more than we want professional appointments to university faculties to rest heavily on non-professional criteria such as citizenship. Either outcome would make for parochialism — the very opposite of what a university ought to be. We should seek for variety of viewpoints and origins, and probably few people in the North American academic professions would disagree in principle. What I am contending is that, in practice, anglophone academic sociology in Canada has become top-heavy in its leanings toward structural-functionalism and similar approaches, and that in consequence a dangerous middle-class, continentalist, American-oriented parochialism has developed. Specifically neglected are the types of problems, conflicts and holistic perspectives best treated in historical, comparative and dialectical terms. Let us now sketch in tentative terms a dialectical view of Canadian and American societies in a metropolis vs. hinterland, over-class vs. under-class frame of reference.

CANADIAN SOCIETY AND HISTORY AS HINTERLAND VS METROPOLIS

Canadian society and history may be viewed as a series of hinterland or under-class reactions to foreign metropolitan imperialisms. First came the French, and soon afterward, the English. This European intrusion tied the native Indians to the capitalistic European fur trade. In the eighteenth and nineteenth centuries, the native Indians were reduced to a colonial status; the Inuit followed approximately a century later.

The conquest of French Canada by a British army in 1760 paved the way for the Anglo primacy in Canada that still prevails today. Despite the predominantly British orientation during the nineteenth century, relations vis-à-vis the new American republic became increasingly important. Confederation was basically a response to the mid-century American industrial and westward expansion. The "National Policy" that emerged by the 1870s included western settlement as a new investment frontier for eastern business, a transcontinental railroad, a protective tariff, shunting the Indians onto reservations, and so on.

There were some unintended consequences, however. From the beginning of western settlement, the under-class or hinterland colonials carried on chronic struggles to improve their status within the changing system of capitalist expansion and exploitation. The Métis and some Indians kicked up in 1885. From the early 1900s, western farmers entered one skirmish after another against the railroads, Winnipeg grain exchange, elevator corporations, and finally against the eastern-dominated political parties. Populist movements eventually came to power in the form of Social Credit and the CCF.

In effect, the broad course of events in Canada, as industrialization progressed, has followed the pattern anticipated by Marx in the *Manifesto* (1848) — but only up to the beginning of a socialist movement. Why socialism has so far been still-born will be discussed in the next section of this paper.

A similar metropolis-hinterland framework may be applied to Quebec. Quebec became another investment frontier for business interests that were predominantly Anglo, later American. In our own day, populist counter-attacks have appeared in the Caouette movement, speaking primarily for the northern Quebec colonials, and in the bourgeois "quiet revolution" more recently spearheaded by the drive for an independent Quebec. As "Canada" is colonized by the United States, Quebec is doubly colonized.

From a sociology-of-knowledge standpoint, structural-functionalism reflects and reinforces the interests of the Anglo Establishment — i.e. federalism in politics, capitalism in economic life. In my view, a conflict-oriented dialectic in the form of metropolis vs. hinterland is more realistic, and more revealing as an interpretation of Canadian society. It also implies a more openly political role for social sciences. Instead of tacitly supporting the institutional status quo, as most Anglophone social scientists do by default, a dialectical approach critically redefines the nature and transitory status of current institutional patterns in Canada. An excellent application of dialectical analysis of Canadian society by Drache appears in Lumsden (1970).[26]

Exploited colonials in the North American hinterlands have in the past battled to improve their status in the economic order, as shown for Canada by Fowke (1957)[27] and McCrorie (1965); and for the United States by historian William A. Williams (1969).[28] And the American empire has been able to carry the cost of concessions to its internal colonial under-classes by means of expanding its business interests into foreign colonial hinterlands.

But there are signs that the "Open Door" abroad is rapidly closing. A major crisis impends in American society, just when its monolithic rigidity and its lack of critically articulate and organized internal oppositions renders it incapable of adjusting to the new orders emerging in other parts of the world. It is doubtful, in my view, whether the United States will make it into the 21st century, alive and/or fit to live. This thought first occurred to me two decades ago.[29] It seems even more relevant today. If this is valid, then Canada is directly involved, for Canada has become in large part an informal annex of the American empire. This sell-out to "continentalism" took place without debate in the Canadian Parliament or in any other large Canadian public forum.

In this perspective of impending catastrophe south of the border, any large confontation in Canada may contribute to a Canadian-hinterland vs American-metropolis showdown. For this reason alone, the most promising recent development in Canadian society may well be the movement for Quebec independence. If, as seems inevitable, Quebec goes independent, it will almost certainly be forced to move toward state socialism. Genuine political independence requires economic independence. Anglo Canada may then be compelled to face up to its own self and to its alternative absorption into the homogenizing American empire.

The Anglo-Canadian Establishment has set its policy in favour of opting into the American empire as a junior partner, as George Grant and Mel Watkins have shown. Two-thirds of Canadian manufacturing is already under foreign control, according to the 1968 Watkins report. Certain large Canadian labour unions are controlled by American unions, which are very much an integral part of the American empire — also on a junior-partner basis. It seems too late for Canadian society to preserve its shrinking uniqueness and vanishing independence by normal negotiations. Quebec, however, may yet save Canada by going independent. And this sort of development in Canada may in turn, stimulate the United States to face up to its real problem — its own character and its own contradictory social structure.

Granted, this may be wishful thinking, yet just now it appears to be the most promising (i.e. the least costly) possibility. The alternative means might involve military defeat and conquest of the United States by rebellious hinterlands and rival metropolitan powers. But who would survive?

The francophone, Catholic character of Quebec may conceivably offer an adequate cultural and economic base for opting out of the American empire. The horrendous nature of that empire has been revealed in Vietnam, in the Black ghettos of American cities, and even on American university campuses. Let us turn to the nature of American society, into which the Anglo-Canadian Establishment is so blithely taking us. It is contended here that only a dialectical perspective can realistically illuminate the character of American society.

AMERICAN SOCIETY AND HISTORY AS METROPOLIS VS HINTERLAND

Two major confrontations mark the last century and a half of American history. The first was between southern agrarian capitalism and northern industrial capitalism linked with western farmers. Each had to expand in order to survive, and when expansion room ran out, civil war followed, 1861-65.

The second confrontation was the rising tide of agrarian and labour revolts that began to pile up against the burgeoning northern industrialism in the decades between the Civil War and First World War. Much as Marx had forecast, economic and political oppositions began to gather against triumphant business enterprise, and by 1900 a fledgling native socialist movement led by Eugene Debs was under way.

But after 1912, all socialist movements stagnated and declined. The agrarian colonials won concessions; militant labour for the most part became "business unionism" — safe for capitalism. Competition remained, of course, often nasty and bitter. Progressive reforms slowly materialized, especially in the 1930s. But these were basically conserving reforms — they conserved (saved) capitalism. After World War I, massive oppositions in America could hardly be said to exist. Everyone bought the prevailing American way of life — give or take a few modifications. Even the small civil rights movements marked by the National Association for the Advancement of Colored People and similar organizations accepted the bourgeois order. All they asked was — "Count us in".

What explains the collapse of the gathering, massive opposition to American capitalism? What explains the absence of any genuine "Left" on the American political scene after 1920? In theory, the absence of any important pre-capitalist order in America should have made for a classic example of the displacement of capitalism by socialism, as Marx predicted.

In a nutshell, what seems best to explain the absence of massive oppositions in the United States during the last half-century is the *over-success* of American capitalism. As historian Charles Beard (1927)[30] explained it, the triumph of business enterprise was due to fabulous resources, a protected domestic market, cheap immigrant labour, and a paternalistic national government that really looked after the business interests that controlled federal, state and local governments. Above all, two cheap world wars knocked off rival capitalist powers, and contributed immensely to American economic expansion abroad.

For what effectively smothered the gathering domestic crisis around the turn of the 20th century, after the interior frontier was "closed", was the launching of the economy on renewed expansion abroad. In other words, economic imperialism deferred the debacle of American capitalism. The only variations in this policy have been the "hard-sell" vs the "soft-sell". When Washington stressed "good neighbour" policies in Latin America, for example, that was "soft-sell". When American troops landed in some banana republic, that was "hard-sell". No major American party or interest has opposed American economic expansion abroad as the keystone of United States foreign policy. Splinter oppositions, of course, do not count. There are other factors, too, in the American success story: the Keynesian reforms, military and space budgets, farm subsidies, social-security concessions, etc. It all adds up to the most spectacular success story in human history — in the short run.

But in the long-run, disaster may be the consequence of this American over-success. If structural change depends on dialectical confrontations between massive oppositions in a society, then the USA must appear as a rigid monolith, incapable of adjusting to a changing world it cannot understand. Clearly, anti-colonial, national and communist revolutions in Europe, Asia and perhaps elsewhere, have slammed the door on American expansion in many such areas. The great watersheds of modern world history are the Russian, Chinese and Cuban revolutions. The massive oppositions to American society are now largely external, and a dialogue across national and racial lines seems unlikely because of the emotional blocks (both nationalist and racist) and the vested interests involved.

On a global basis, the existing tensions between the American metropolis and its foreign hinterlands must tend to increase, quite apart from whatever stresses or settlements may develop between the Communist empires and the United States. Hinterlands eventually are forced by their own internal conditions and aspirations to "fight back". If in the short run they — or their domestic "vendu" elites — gain a more favourable but still subordinate position within the metropolitan system, ultimately they cannot realize their aims for self-determination except by escaping entirely from capitalism, as China and Cuba have done.

Political economist André Frank has shown[31] (1967) that the capitalist metropolis actively creates underdevelopment in its satellites and in its internal colonized sectors. Underdevelopment, in other words, is immanent in the evolution of capitalism, and not an external or accidental separate system describable as "folk" or "traditional" or "pre-industrial" society. These terms may properly apply only to "undeveloped" societies, not to "underdeveloped" ones.

The latter are those which have been drawn into the world capitalist market and imperium, and then have been pushed aside into stagnation or confined to undiversified and even single-industry roles by new investment thrusts in other industries and other regions. In Canada, examples would be (in varying styles and degrees) the impoverished Indians, small farmers and an increasing proportion of middle-sized farm operators, large areas of the Maritimes and Newfoundland, francophone Quebec, and so on.[32]

The intensifying metropolis vs hinterland or over-class vs under-class syndrome, then, should make for mounting crisis in American society. There is still another factor pointing in the same direction. Why should the favored American six per cent of the world's population enjoy more than fifty per cent of the world's wealth and income? And this gap between rich and poor is widening, not only between advanced and "underdeveloped" nations, but within the advanced nations as well.[33] Can anyone doubt that the economic progress of Canada's native peoples is not keeping pace with the economic development of the advanced sectors of our national economy? S.D. Clark says much the same thing about the gap between French-Canadian farmers and labourers in Northern Quebec and Northern Ontario company towns, compared with Anglo managerial groups in the same northern communities.[34]

But the economic aspect by itself is only part of the relevant picture. Probably most Canadians want more economic goodies. But how shall they use them? What sort of community life do they want? Do they want to be addicts of suburban consumerism like the Americans? Do they wish to be accessories of the American napalming of Asian peasants? That appears to be the end-result of "continentalism" — the on-going drift into the increasingly reactionary American empire fostered since World War II by the big-business, Anglo-Canadian Establishment and its "vendu" francophone satellites who support Canadian "federalism".

Hopefully, not all Canadians want to be thus homogenized when they understand what is afoot. For if our analysis is even half valid, the American imperium is coasting toward disaster both at home and abroad. It has not been able to do anything significant about urban and rural poverty, the ghettoized Blacks, the disaffected students, the multiple hard-core problems centering in the cities. It is continually bogged down in military entanglements abroad and its economy appears headed for a serious recession. Assassination of leaders and shooting civilians have become standard political responses in the United States. Does any serious inquirer believe the official myths and cover-ups of the murders of the Kennedys, Martin Luther King, Malcolm X, etc.? Canada can expect to be dragged down in the American wake, if continentalism continues to prevail as Canadian national policy.

The opposite course would in some degree be anti-imperialist, anti-American, anti-capitalist, anti-continentalist, and anti-Anglo Establishment. What evidence is there that hinterland and under-class groups in Canada are leaning in any of these directions?

Outside of Quebec, the signs are scattered and weak. Let us cite statements by three different kinds of Canadians: Harold Cardinal, Alberta native Indian leader; René Lévesque, head of Le Parti Québécois; and George Grant, chair of the Department of Religion at McMaster University. Each is raising basic issues of non-economic cultural values — how we ought or ought not to live. In assessing the impact of these oppositions in a dialectical context, it is essential for us to remember that the non-economic aspects are at least as important as the economic factors. For instance, if the economic problems of our Canadian Indians could be met, the conflict of values would still remain. Many Indians simply do not buy Anglo middle-class norms and life style.

The new Indian policy promulgated by Prime Minister Pierre-Elliot Trudeau's government . . . in June of 1969 is a thinly disguised program of extermination through assimilation . . . a program which offers nothing better than cultural genocide . . . Indians have aspirations, hopes and dreams, but becoming white men is not one of them. [35]

There is no relief in our responsibility for creating or utilizing the potential that exists in our communities. There is very little place for non-Indians, simply because it is we who have to do the job. The Honorable Minister can never tell us the true meaning of Indianess. The Federal government with its billions of dollars can never buy us the true meaning of Indianess. And no White man, no non-Indian in any profession can tell us what Indianess means (Cardinal, speech to the Western Association of Sociology and Anthropology, Banff, Dec. 28, 1969).

We are Québécois. What this means first and foremost is that we are attached to this one corner of the earth where we can be completely ourselves, the only place where we have the unmistakable feeling that 'here we can be really at home.' Being ourselves is essentially a matter of keeping and developing a personality that has survived for three and a half centuries . . . . We are heirs to the group obstinacy which has kept alive that portion of French America we call Quebec . . . . This is how we differ from other men and especially from other North Americans. [36]

What our fate is today becomes most evident in the light of Vietnam. It is clear that in that country the American empire has been demolishing a people, rather than allowing them to live outside the American orbit . . . . The very substance of our lives is bound up with the western empire and its destiny, just at a time when that empire uses increasingly ferocious means to maintain its hegemony.[37]

Though none of these writers spells out his alternatives, the upshot of all three suggests sharp disagreements with some of the key policies of the orthodox Canadian Establishment. But it requires an historical, conflict-oriented frame of reference to assess these dissents.

In this grim evaluation of American developments, the one great question mark is the Black-power movement, and secondarily, perhaps, the student disaffection. Black power may yet save the United States, as Quebec may salvage Canada, and as Cuba may break the imperialist spell over Latin America. It is too early to say whether the Afro-Americans can come up with a mass-supported program of institutional reform along socialist lines. It is too early to estimate the significance of Quebec developments for Canada's future.

Meanwhile, the savage aspect of American society has been revealed in southeast Asia for all to see. The link between Main Street and Vietnam is direct and organic. Other such cases may arise any day in Latin America. Sooner or later, nuclear war seems likely, and that would be the end of all of us.

It is in the light of this urgent perspective that wider study and use of a dialectical, over-class vs under-class, metropolis vs hinterland, frame of reference for Canadian social science seems essential, both for advancing social theory and for informing national policy.

Only two truths seem clear. (1) The future of Canada will be vastly different from its present institutional forms — if indeed Canada with its self-destructive, high-technology, capitalist economy has any future at all. (2) Orthodox anglophone, structural-functional social science has totally failed to inform the people of Canada (who pay the shot for academia) — about the essential nature of the contemporary world, or about our options in that inexorably unfolding world.

NOTES

1. C. Wright Mills, *The Sociological Imagination,* New York: Oxford University Press, 1959, p. 21.

2. M.H. Watkins, "The dismal state of economics in Canada", *Close the 49th Parallel: The Americanization of Canada,* ed. Ian Lumsden, Toronto: University of Toronto, 1970, pp. 197-208.

3. See L. Rainwater and W. Yancey, *The Moynihan Report and the Politics of Controversy,* Cambridge: M.I.T. Press, 1967, and also R.O. Abrahams, *Positively Black,* Englewood Cliffs: Prentice Hall, 1970.

4. See René Lévesque, *An Option for Quebec,* Toronto: McClelland and Stewart, 1968, and also Harold Cardinal, *The Unjust Society,* Edmonton: Hurtig, 1969.

5. Ian Adams, *The Poverty Wall,* Toronto: McClelland and Stewart, 1970.

6. Symbolic interactionism merits some of the strictures here directed at structural-functionalism.

7. See B. Blishen, ed., *Canadian Society: Sociological Perspectives,* Toronto: Macmillan, 1968, also W.E. Mann, ed., *Canada: A Sociological Profile,* Toronto: Copp Clark, 1968, and also R. Laskin, *Social Problems: A Canadian Profile,* Toronto: McGraw Hill of Canada, 1964.

8. John Craig and Edward Gross, "The Forum Theory of Organizational Democracy: Structural Guarantees as Time-Related Variables", *American Sociological Review,* February 1970, 35:1, pp. 19-33.

9. See J.M. McCrorie, *In Union Is Strength,* Saskatoon, 1965, also J.F.C. Wright, *Saskatchewan: The History of a Province,* Toronto: McClelland and Stewart, 1955a, and *Prairie Progress: Consumer Co-operation in Saskatchewan,* Saskatoon: Modern Press, 1955b.

10. Carlyle King, ed., *Saskatchewan Harvest: A Literary Anthology,* Toronto: McClelland and Stewart, 1955. To go with the macro-historical and dialectical sociology for which I am arguing, we should foster an emphasis on realism in presentation of social data and social analysis. The leading questions should be of this sort: What was it really like (for example) in Saskatchewan in the 1950s, the 1960s, for the various occupational groups, classes, communities of various sizes and locations, age and sex groups, and for other categories of men and women? In answering this kind of query, the analyst, in my view, should deliberately include large subjective elements, descriptive materials, and emotional highlightings — including the analyst's own vantage point. In this way, we arrive at a micro-report that is somewhere between literature and conventional abstract sociology, as macro-dialectical historical lies between sociology and history. The common element is the confrontation theme. Examples would be certain works of W.F. Whyte and Oscar Lewis; R. Badgley and S. Wolfe, *Doctor's Strike: Medical Care and Conflict in Saskatchewan,* New York: Atherton Press, 1967; J.K. Howard, *Strange Empire: A Narrative of the Northwest,* New York: Morrow, 1952; William Hinton, *Fanshen: A Document of Revolution in a Chinese Village,* New York: Monthly Review Press, 1966; and numerous television, radio and film documentaries by the Canadian Broadcasting Corporation and the National Film Board.

11. John Porter, *The Vertical Mosaic: An Analysis of Social Class and Power in Canada,* Toronto: University of Toronto Press, 1965.

12. See George Grant, *Lament for a Nation,* Toronto: McClelland and Stewart,

1965, and *Technology and Empire,* Toronto: House of Anansi, 1969.

13. Melville Watkins, *Foreign Ownership and the Structure of Canadian Industry,* Ottawa: Privy Council Office, 1968.

14. Peter Newman, *Renegade in Power: The Diefenbaker Years,* Toronto: McClelland and Stewart, 1963, and *The Distemper of Our Times: Canadian Politics in Transition,* Toronto: McClelland and Stewart, 1968, and most recently, *The Canadian Establishment, Vol. I,* Toronto, McClelland and Stewart, 1975 (eds.).

15. S.M. Lipset, *Agrarian Socialism: The Co-operative Commonwealth in Saskatchewan,* Berkeley: University of California, 1950. See also the up-dated edition of the same book, Garden City: Doubleday Anchor Books, 1968.

16. Gabrielle Roy, *The Tin Flute,* Toronto: McClelland and Stewart, 1947 and 1958.

17. See Crane Brinton, *Anatomy of Revolution,* New York: Random House and Vintage Books, 1952.

18. They are amplified in the present writer's paper published in R.J. Ossenberg, ed., *Canadian Society: Pluralism, Change, and Conflict,* Scarborough: Prentice-Hall, 1971, pp. 6-32.

19. Stanley Ryerson, *The Founding of Canada: Beginnings to 1800,* Toronto: Progress Books, 1960, also *The Open Society: Paradox and Challenge,* New York: International, 1965.

20. However, note that Mann has heeded Davis' programmatic position since this paper was first delivered in 1970. In the third edition of Mann's reader (1976), Arthur K. Davis was invited to write the foreword. Also, papers by Davis' favourite authors, including Ian Adams, George Grant, Mel Watkins, etc. were published. Thus, since 1970 Davis has made an impact on the profession in Canada (eds.).

21. See S.M. Lipset, "Revolution and Counter Revolution: The United States and Canada", *Canada: A Sociological Profile,* ed. W.E. Mann, Toronto: Copp Clark, 1971, pp. 24-36.

22. See Ian Lumsden, "American imperialism and Canadian intellectuals" in Lumsden, ed., p. 335.

23. Murray G. Ross, "Forward", Mann, ed., 1st edition (1968), p. vii.

24. Lumsden, ed., frontispiece.

25. See Robin Mathews and James Steele, *The Struggle for Canadian Universities,* Toronto: New Press, 1969. Although Davis had certain reservations about Mathews, he has come to support a Canadianization hiring policy (eds.).

26. D. Drache, "The Canadian bourgeoisie and its national consciousness" in Lumsden, ed., pp. 3-26.

27. Vernon Fowke, *The National Policy and the Wheat Economy,* Toronto: University of Toronto Press, 1957.

28. See W.A. Williams, *The Roots of the Modern American Empire: A Study of the Growth and Shaping of Social Consciousness in a Market Place Society,* New York: Random House, 1969.

29. Arthur K. Davis, "Decline and Fall", *Monthly Review,* 1960, Vol. 12. pp. 334-344.

30. C. and M. Beard, *The Rise of American Civilization,* New York: Macmillan, 1927.

31. André G. Frank, *Capitalism and Underdevelopment in Latin America: Historical Studies of Chile and Brazil,* New York: Monthly Review Press, 1967.

32. Frank's work, based on a "metropolis-satellite" schema in a dialectical frame of reference, deserves to be better known among Canadian social scientists, because with little modification it is directly applicable to Canada — as a scanning of Harold Innis' work will easily demonstrate. For example, Canadian Indians and the reservation system today are to be understood primarily in terms of the relative decline of the fur trade (which originally reduced the Indians to the status of a rural, non-agricultural proletariat) and the shifting of capitalist development in the 19th century to new investment frontiers such as western agricultural settlement after confederation.

33. See W.A. Williams, *The Great Evasion: An Essay on the Contemporary Relevance of Karl Marx and on the Relevance of Admitting the Heretic into the Dialogue about America's Future,* Chicago: Quadrangle Books, 1964, chapter III.

34. S.D. Clark, "The Position of the French Speaking Population in the Northern Industrial Community", in Ossenberg, ed., pp. 62-85.

35. Cardinal, pp. 1, 3.

36. Lévesque, pp. 14-15.

37. Grant, *Technology and Empire,* pp. 63 and 65.

SECTION V

Native Marginality in the Capitalist System

The complex intricacies of capitalism as a system of production are often stressed by those who defend the essential worth of this system. This complexity, to which is commonly attached a connotation of "civilization", leads to the assumption that not only is a capitalist economic base superior and advanced, but also that our idea systems, ideologies, and values are far more advanced than those of more "primitive" peoples.

In the spread of capitalism as a way of life, there have been three basic attitudes to pre-capitalist tribal peoples: to kill them, to use them in some non-assimilative manner, or to assimilate them into capitalist society. The latter view came to be seen as the "humanitarian" policy which ought to be followed. The European humanitarian, so assured of the advantages of a capitalist-based society, could hardly believe that natives might resent the fragmentation of their own mode of production and way of life. Such humanitarians felt that no greater compliment could be paid to natives than to assure them that they too were sufficiently advanced to join a capital-based society. If natives did not agree, they were branded as backward reactionaries, and the suggestion was made that the ingrates must be *forced to be free* whether they liked it or not.

Seen in this perspective, it is clear that E.F. Wilson, the central figure of Nock's paper, was not an individual carried away with a somewhat romantic faith. The programme of social change which would lead the Indian away from traditional society, and towards acceptance of the capitalist world, was supported by governments and religious bodies all over North America. Schooling programmes like those used by Wilson were still in use in recent years. The Indians of this very moment are to a large extent products of an educational system different only in detail from that sponsored by Wilson. For example, the schools founded by Wilson in Sault Ste. Marie lasted until 1971. Until the final years, speaking the Ojibway language was forbidden. The native complaint against missionary-government schools was a major theme of Harold Cardinal's widely acclaimed book, *The Unjust Society* (1969).

Wilbert Ahern's paper demonstrates much of the same material in connection to the United States. This is consistent with our point that capitalism tends to produce the same general results across particular State

231

boundaries. American Indians too, had to put up with the ministrations of so-called friends, who wished to retrieve natives from the ranges or forests, and to put them into worker's garb.

What articles like those of Nock and Ahern reveal is that even "humanitarianism" must be understood within the limitations and requirements of specific economic modes of production. It is clear that many natives were satisfied with their traditional or semi-traditional mode of production; however, the humanitarianism of the western interlopers did not express itself by inculcation in natives of more refined hunting and trapping skills. Instead, their humanitarianism expressed itself in moulding the natives into acceptance of industrial-capitalism.

Sandra Steinhause's article is both a completion to this section and a preliminary for the next. Her description of an alternative to the missionary-government style of education meted out to Indians emphasizes the attractive features of an educational system which is adaptive and not directed or enforced. Currently, it is Indians in Atlantic Canada who are making use of this adaptive programme, but the skills they acquire should not become the exclusive property of racial and ethnic minorities. For Steinhause shows how the kind of reflection and action (praxis) encouraged by the Indian Band Staff Training Programme could be beneficial to any group of adults interested in learning how to develop alternatives to the oppressiveness of the status quo. While her paper is probably more descriptive than any other in this volume, there is enough analysis to suggest that such learning, rather than training people to survive by fitting into "the system", might instead constitute a kind of survival which contains the possibility of lessening dominant class control of the system.

The Social Effects of Missionary Education: A Victorian Case Study

DAVID A. NOCK

North American Indians have played several roles in the history of their interaction with Europeans. In areas which were thinly settled by Europeans, Indians served as labourers who toiled to trap furs for traders such as Astor. The Astors became multimillionaires; Indian trappers did not. In another role, Indians served as military allies to Europeans who found themselves in conflict with other European nations.

For example, in the War of 1812, Indians were allies of the British and Canadians in warding off American attack. But with the long peace established by 1815 in Europe and America, and with surplus multitudes pouring into Canada from 1815 until about 1920, the Indian began to lose his role as fur trapping labourer or military ally.

R.J. Surtees sums up succinctly: "The threat of hostilities with the United States had receded greatly by 1830 and the entire purpose of cultivating the Indians as 'prospective allies on the battlefield' was being questioned. It seemed that there were simply no more wars for them to fight."[1]

The fur trade, too, an enterprise which engaged the activity of both European and Indian, was noticeably on the decline after 1815. The fur trade and the military role had encouraged Indians to retain traditional or semi-traditional practises, and a semi-traditional lifestyle. Although the impact of the fur trade and the military role did have an effect on the Indian, and while this effect must not be underemphasized,[2] many Indians did tend to continue a semi-nomadic hunting, fishing, and gathering existence. Also, such change as did occur was frequently the result of non-directed or adaptive influence, rather than from directed or enforced culture change brought by Europeans.

But the impact of widespread European settlement, the introduction of agriculture and industry, meant that Indians were now seen as pests who got in the way of progress and profit. Surtees says, "As the settler moved into the wilderness he did not look upon the Indian as a potential ally, nor did he require Indian support. More often he considered the Indians as a retarding influence and a nuisance for they seldom used their land — often good arable land — for agriculture, but continued to live by hunting and fishing."[3]

233

Quickly a new policy was worked out in Central Canada around the year 1830 which involved reeducation of the Indians. Previously, as fur trapper or military ally, the Indian could be seen as a noble savage. The new policy, however, which Surtees calls the "paternal reserve policy which developed in the years 1828 to 1830", redefined the Indian "as a lost savage to be saved and civilized"[4] through education. Surtees describes this programme of directed or enforced culture change as follows: "Their final end, as the scheme developed, saw the Indian transformed from a migrant or semi-migrant savage to a settled, civilized, Christian, equipped with all the moral and mechanical skills necessary to compete in the European world of Upper Canada."[5] Enter the missionary!

Of course, missionaries had long been in contact with native peoples, trying to convert them to the soothing message of the Gospel. Now however, the missionary entered the scene as the bearer of an entire civilization and as the ambassador of a new economic mode of production. This new missionary function was supported and funded by the State, and incorporated into the educational system. In other words, the missionary became not just an apostle of Christ, but a government-supported civil servant who directed or enforced the ignoble savage into accepting Anglo-Canadian civilization, and the industrial-capitalist mode of production. The fate or role of the Indian henceforth was to become a Christian, British-oriented, proletarian who would work for other people either as a tradesman, unskilled worker, farmhand, or as a domestic servant.

* * *

Perhaps we can grasp the nature of this important process of directed social change if we look at the career of one representative missionary-educator[6] who was supported by the government. Let us look at the educational system implanted by E.F. Wilson in the Ojibway children of Northern Ontario.

E.F. Wilson was the offspring of a well-known Evangelical family. The Evangelicals composed the "enthusiastic" "born again" section of the Church of England. Wilson's grandfather had been Bishop of Calcutta, India, and his father was also a prominent Evangelical cleric in England. His father founded the Islington Annual Meetings for Evangelical clergy which are still held to this day.

Having first arrived in Canada in 1868 under auspices of the Church Missionary Society (C.M.S.), Wilson left that organization in 1872. Although the C.M.S. was concerned to "civilize" the Indians, it retained a primary focus on conversion.

E.F. Wilson had been led to the mission field more by a sense of Evangelical fervor than by any exact prior knowledge of the spiritual conditions of the Ojibway Indians of the Great Lakes. He found, much to his chagrin, that most Indians in the Lake Huron and Superior regions had already been converted to Christianity by Methodists, Roman Catholics, and occasionally by other Anglicans. There was a paucity of pagans around the Great Lakes!

In one missionary tour to Lake Superior, Wilson had to complain, " . . . I was a little disappointed that there was not a large number of pagan Indians among whom I might look forward to establish missions in the future."[7] Given that Wilson was an Evangelical, he also added that he "was disappointed to discover that they were all Roman Catholics."[8] The C.M.S. was dismayed at the mere handful of heathen who remained. They wrote to Wilson that they had "had no idea of the pre-occupation of the field by other Missionary Agencies to the extent which you say and statistics exhibit."[9]

After visiting the Sault Ste. Marie region, Wilson got the idea of establishing residential schools for Indians. Earlier, Wilson had been stationed at Sarnia. After he visited Sault Ste. Marie, Wilson felt the Indians near the Sault "were not nearly so far advanced in civilization as those of Sarnia . . . . there was something very attractive and fascinating about this first visit to the wilds of Algoma."[10] At this time "there first entered into my mind the idea of an institution for training the young."[11]

Having come to realize the small numbers of pagans in the Great Lakes region, Wilson increased his emphasis on education and industrial training of the Ojibway. Abandoned by the C.M.S., Wilson was able to collect funds on the basis of his Evangelical and upper middle class connections in England.

In September 1873, the first Shingwauk School was opened. Six days later the structure burned to the ground. With a fortitude sustained by his Evangelical faith in God's Word, he collected funds for a second school which opened officially in 1875, although some pupils had been admitted in 1874. Later on a separate school, the Wawanosh, was built for girls. In the later 1880s, Wilson also had a school built for Indian children at Elkhorn, Manitoba.

* * *

As indicated in Section I, a missionary-educator such as E.F. Wilson did not enter a situation which was void. By the 1870s, the government had been supporting education, Westernization, Christianization, and proletarianization of the Indians for some half-century. Reserve and residential schools were funded partly by missionaries or missionary societies, but also partly by the government. The government allowed a set sum per Indian child in attendance at school. It also contributed building allowances. Increasingly a standard curriculum from the Department of Education was imposed on the missionary schools.

For example, some missionary schools had been in the practise of having their pupils spend two-thirds of the day in classroom instruction. The Commissioner of Indian Affairs, Hayter Reed, objected: ''He thought that should not be done — 'unless it be intended to train children to earn their bread by brainwork rather than by manual labour, at least half of their day should be devoted to acquiring skill in the latter' ''.[12] Thus missionary schools came to adopt the half-day system — the Shingwauk included.

This directive from the Commissioner of Indian Affairs also shows the process of proletarianization which was intended to result. Proletarianization is the movement of a social group *en masse* into the lower orders of industrial society. When proletarianization occurs, it usually means that direction of industry is left in the hands of a dominant majority group which is able to benefit from the toil of a subordinate minority group. For example, E.F. Wilson received many testimonial letters from tradesmen who owned their own shops and businesses, complimenting the native boys on their steadiness and diligence.

It may be objected that the aim of missionaries and of government was not to proletarianize the natives at all. Ahern has made this point, that the ''humanitarian'' reformers ''did not intend that their educational programme would assure an inferior position for Indian children . . ..''[13] Wilson certainly did not think of his mission as intended to keep the natives in subjection. Quite the opposite. He stated: ''Our object in undertaking this voluntary work, is to raise the Indians from their present low degraded position, and to place them on an equal footing with their white neighbours.''[14] A number of Shingwauk graduates were successful enough to obtain middle class status as clergymen, teachers, clerks, or as civil servants. But the number was small, and the effect if not the intent of the schools was to produce a breed of sub-proletarians who were fully at home neither on the reserve or in urban industrial society. Harold Cardinal, modern Indian leader, speaks of a present which echoes the past: ''He [the Indian pupil] was turned toward a life that was foreign to him and one that he could not be part of. But he was a stranger to his people on his return. The child went to school an Indian. The young man emerged as nothing.''[15]

* * *

At this point, let us look in closer depth at the educational system used at the Shingwauk. It should be remembered, however, that the system used here was quite similar to, and representative of, that utilized in other schools.

Sociology as a discipline recognizes clearly that we are all end-products of a lengthy process of cultural indoctrination called socialization. Socialization begins when as a baby, our parents begin to shape our behaviour by a system of carrot and stick. Socialization continues, this time with government supervision and approval, when we go to school. Our methods of work, our concept of time, our habits and games, our ethics and mores, the holidays we observe, the music we like, all these are a product of our socialization.

Wilson realized that the school must socialize into Indian children many things which were normally left to the parent. *The Canadian Indian*, a journal he edited, editorialized:

The Indian child must be taught many things which came to the white child without the schoolmaster's aid. From the days of its birth, the child of civilized parents is constantly in contact with civilized modes of life, of action, thought, speech, dress; and is surrounded by a thousand beneficient influences . . . . He [the Indian child] must be led out from the conditions of his birth, in his early years, into the environments of civilized domestic life; and he must be thus led by his teachers.[16]

At least Wilson and his fellow missionaries did believe the Indian capable of resocialization into Anglo-Canadian capitalist society. Many people came to an unfavourable judgment of the capabilities of Indian or non-white peoples. Wilson *assumed* that the general Anglo-Canadian populace was willing to accept assimilation, or as he put it, "amalgamation" of the native peoples. These attitudes of Wilson — and of many missionaries — are expressed in the following letter:

I believe that there is through Canada a *kindly feeling* towards the Indian race, that it is only their dirty habits, their undisciplined behaviour, and their speaking another language, that prevents their intermingling with the white people. I believe also that there is in the Indian a perfect capability of adapting himself to the customs of the white people . . . but he wants the advantages given him while young, and he requires to be drilled into the use of those advantages.[17]

Not everyone in the white settler communities or in Britain agreed that the natives were so capable. For example, one British observer opined: "We cannot expect African cannibals to rise at one bound from the worship of lizards to an intelligent comprehension of the Athanasian creed."[18] A biased attitude that Indians were unimprovable is not infrequently seen in letters sent to Wilson. For example, he had to reply to a Mr. McMorine, "I am not surprised that people at the Landing [St. Joseph's Island] should speak hard of the Indians — I am used to that — but I believe that with patience and persistent effort much may be made of them,"[19]

H.A.C. Cairns has commented on such missionary enthusiasm as exemplified by Wilson:

The comparative missionary optimism as to the eventual success of his task was perhaps less a reflection of a generous assessment of [Native] capacities than a requirement of the faith — a belief in the special efficacy of the gospel as an instrument of social and religious change among even the least advanced members of the human family.[20]

At any rate, Wilson cannot be faulted for lacking in "persistent effort" to resocialize the Shingwauk and Wawanosh children into dominant Anglo-Canadian industrial-capitalist society.

* * *

In this combined missionary-government programme of cultural replacement, it was crucial that the children gain fluency in English, and if possible, lose fluency in Ojibway. In her study of the Blackfeet, Kozak says about the government's policy:

Increased demands for fluency in English were intended to spell the death of the Indian language. The native tongue was forbidden in all schools "because if the ideas and sentiments of white people are to be acquired it must be done by such contact as required a thorough understanding of their language."[21]

If the Indians were to be "amalgamated" into Canadian society, a good knowledge of English would be essential while native tongues would lose their importance. Since graduates of the schools were intended to integrate into the general industrial-capitalist work force, potential employers could not be expected to appreciate workers who failed to understand the language of command. *The Fourth Annual Report* of the Shingwauk said:

We make a great point of insisting on the boys talking English as, for their advancement in civilization, this is, of all things, the most necessary. Twice a week we have English class. The more advanced boys sit with their slates and write out definitions of English words; the rest of the boys form line in two classes and are taught *vive voce*, besides being put through certain manual exercises such as shutting the door, putting a slate on the bench, pulling down the blind, etc.; the object being to teach them to understand, and obey promptly, directions given in English.[22]

Some scope for speaking Ojibway was allowed in religious exercises and at tea time between six and seven p.m. But at other times, to speak Ojibway constituted infringement of the rules. Wilson sponsored a contest to encourage the speaking of English between the boys. Each Saturday buttons were distributed with new boys getting a greater number of buttons. If a boy was caught speaking "Indian", his companion was supposed to demand a button from the culprit. At the end of the week, an accounting was made with the boys who had returned the most buttons receiving a prize of nuts. Wilson considered this scheme "a goodhumoured way to keep a check on one another about talking Indian".[23] This plan or variants of it are quite common in situations where a dominant language is imposed on speakers of a minority language.

Later on during Wilson's stay at Sault Ste. Marie, he became stricter — the stick as well as the carrot was brought into use. "We bring this [proficiency in English] about principally by great strictness — sometimes punishing heavily any old pupil who presumes to break the rules."[24] This combination of positive and negative pressures resulted in Wilson boasting to the government: "Not a word of Indian is heard from our Indian boys after six months in the institution. All their talk among themselves while at play, is in English."[25] Any boy guilty of speaking "Indian", had at the very least, to face Wilson during the punishment period at seven p.m.:

One perhaps has broken a window, another was late getting up in the morning, another has broken the rules by talking Indian . . . each boy is admonished or punished as may seem best.[26]

The programme of cultural replacement which Wilson had planned for his pupils, extended down to the most elementary components of culture. Besides speaking English, the children were encouraged to learn European and British customs at all levels of significance. Once again Wilson was encouraged in this direction by government policy. As Kozak has pointed out:

The educative process revealed the department's intention of burying all that was Indian, including traditional games, dances, and native crafts. The government approved as principals reported that the children were being taught to forget their Indian games as well as habits and customs.[27]

The only Indian game that was tolerated at the Shingwauk was lacrosse, and this was at least one area in which the European had been influenced by the Indian.

With this exception the games played were European games, the boys engaging in cricket, baseball, soccer, and marbles. In the available accounts of the children at play, they are praised most when playing with and looking like white children. The basis of evaluation never has grounding in the culture in which the Indian children were originally socialized.

Examples of these standard comparisons to white children include an 1877 tour across Canada taken by Wilson and two of the Indian boys with the purpose of raising funds. Wilson wrote that he found it a "great pleasure and satisfaction to me, to see those two boys chatting freely and playing ball and cricket with their white companions . . . ."[28]

In a column intended for white Sunday school children, the writer "Barbara Birchbark" (probably a pseudonym for Wilson or his wife), was asked, "George W___ wants to know if the boys ever play games like white boys do, and what games they like best. Well, last summer base ball was all the rage." Barbara commented that in their new baseball suits the Indian boys "really looked exceedingly nice, 'quite like English boys' as some one remarked."[29] Other games included a swing, climbing pole, horizontal bars, and a covered skittle alley.

With similar motives, the boys were taught the music forms of Europe and Anglo-Canada. They were taught nothing of their own traditional Ojibway musical culture, but instead learned British patriotic, religious, popular, and folk songs. Wilson regarded the teaching of music as very important and always required that a prospective schoolmaster be able to sing or play the harmonium.

A brass band organized in the 1880s, was very popular. Both the band and the various sporting teams were aimed at encouraging interaction between the children and white residents of Sault Ste. Marie. The baseball team played against white teams from the community, and the band played for events in the village. "The band boys are going to play twice a week at Sault Ste. Marie, in the rink."[30] Among Indian residential schools, brass bands were quite popular, perhaps because of the discipline needed by the boys, and because white auditors would be impressed by the military precision of the boys.

Once again, the highest praise for the Indian children resulted from comparisons to white children of similar age. A visitor to Shingwauk wrote the following report of the choir organized by Wilson:

At four o'clock Mr. Wilson, his family, Mr. Wotton the organist, and about forty Indian boys were assembled for choir practise. It was indeed an interesting sight to see those children, many of them, no doubt gathered from homes where paganism, ignorance, and filth combined to make life wretched; and now there they stand, well dressed, clean, and wholesome looking, and unitedly lifting up their voices in the House of the Lord, in songs of praise to the Great Jehovah. The boys all seem to have some musical talent. As we listened to the practise, we could almost imagine we heard the strains of some surpliced choir in England.[31]

As might be expected, British and Canadian civil and religious holidays were celebrated at the Shingwauk. These included Christmas, Easter, Dominion Day, Guy Fawkes, New Year's, and Victoria Day. Emphasis was placed on teaching the children a proper respect for the Queen. It is evident that the custom of Santa Claus was unknown to Ojibway children. As Barbara Birchbark reported, "Many of them were new boys and had not the faintest idea what was going to happen."[32] The celebrations at Christmas included festooning with evergreens, a tree, distribution of candles, candies, and gifts, stockings, special games, exchange of cards and gifts, and Christmas dinner.

* * *

So far we have discussed socialization of the Indian children into the cultural and religious practises which were part of the Anglo-Canadian heritage. In dialectical or Marxist terminology, these cultural components are part of the "superstructure". The "base" or "substructure" is composed of the economic factors in society such as the type of mode of production, the class structure, class relations, and the work ethic peculiar to a specific mode of production. In Marxist analysis, one can trace the origin of the elements from the superstructure to the base. To do so is often a rather complicated and circuitous procedure since fields such as law, religion, ethics, morality, *do* have considerable autonomy to develop their own subsystems. Nevertheless, it can be claimed that some link, often a rather clear one,[33] binds the elements of base and superstructure. More acutely, retaining the notion of base and superstructure means that one can analyze a society as having some "coherence" or as composing a "totality". In other words, the evolution and composition of a society is not a random or chance event, nor is it produced by such a plethora of "little causes" that one cannot make any sense. A society can be explained by understanding specific processes, and key to this understanding is gained primarily from knowing the economic or substructural factors. Now let us turn to those elements which were to shape and resocialize the attitudes of the Indians into the thought patterns of Anglo-Canadian industrial-capitalist society.

Most importantly, Wilson and other missionaries were preparing their pupils to change participation in modes of production. Marx and Engels believed that societies had evolved through a series of stages (each called a mode of production). Each stage was characterized by a difference in class relations. The earliest stage was the "tribal". It was relatively egalitarian and lacked any clear means by which one class could exploit another class. This was true since many of these societies were so close to subsistence that little economic surplus was accumulated. Ancient or slave society followed, and in such societies, the ruling class appropriated the economic surplus produced by slave labour.

Feudal society followed and economic surpluses were garnered by the ruling class in the exploitation of serf labour. By the time of E.F. Wilson, the societal stage was one of capitalism. Capitalism is a system comprised of capitalists who own the means of production such as factories, land, etc., and workers who do not own any means of production and who therefore must sell their labour to others.

The Indians of Northern Ontario still lived a lifestyle that was essentially "tribal" — based as it was on hunting, fishing, and gathering. Governments and missionaries, however, thought little of such a mode of production. They underemphasized the skill needed to survive under such a mode of production. Thus, whites often portrayed Indians as being a people without "culture", or "civilization", or "technology". They also rejected hunting and fishing for being wasteful in that large tracts of land could only support a small number of people.

If the missionaries were to bring the Indians into industrial-capitalist society, the natives had to acquire a new set of economic values and norms. Wilson was preparing his pupils for entry into the general Canadian workforce. Therefore they had to learn those values and attitudes that would be of immediate importance on the job. From a Marxist perspective, missionaries and government agents expected Indians to "jump" from the first mode of production to the fourth mode of production. Given this "gap" which the natives were expected to "leap", perhaps one can understand better the difficulties on both sides.

* * *

Traits which might be thought to have been fostered because of their agreement with moral or Christian considerations, were actually taught because of their positive impact in "getting on" in the world of work. Missionaries such as Wilson, however, would probably have seen no discrepancy. John Maggrah, a model Shingwauk pupil, explained that honesty was literally the best policy to succeed in the world of work: "Hundreds of men and boys have got into high offices for their honesty. When a man looks out for a boy to work for him, he does not choose a strong and active boy, but an honest boy."[34]

Another value emphasized for its contributions to worldly success was politeness. "Politeness," said John, "often gives people a good situation." John also recounted the following style which emphasizes the material advantages of good manners:

Once a man wanted to choose out a boy among a crowd of boys to work for him. He got them to come into his office one by one. Some came in without shutting the door, and did not seem to care how they spoke. The last boy came; before opening the door he cleaned his feet, knocked the door, shut it quietly, and took off his hat. The man at once noticed how the boy acted, and for this reason he choosed [sic] him. The boy was polite.[35]

Wilson made sure his pupils learned such values as punctuality and cleanliness, so important to an employer. One boy wrote, "And anything we want to do we ought to do it at once and not to be late, and we ought not to be late in the roll call, and we must not get late in school."[36] Another boy emphasized the virtues of tidiness: "Now, when children are sent to school, they are taught to keep themselves tidy, and be like gentlemen and ladies after they leave school."[37]

The children at Wilson's schools had come from an environment in which their activity was largely unstructured. What structure there was, existed largely because the difference in seasons led to reliance on different food resources. But the general Anglo-Canadian society whose culture and economy the children were being trained to accept, was quite structured and formalized, and this structure and formalization was on a day to day basis. White people living in the industrial-capitalist mode of production live by the clock and a steady regular routine. The daily pattern at the Shingwauk was also a routine, one that encouraged the pupils to realize that time was not their own — that they had to react to clocks and bells, and to accomplish specific tasks within specific times.

The boys were awakened at six a.m. by a large bell set off by the captain; as soon as all were washed and dressed, the monitor in each dormitory called for silence for prayer, then "the stair gates are unlocked".[38] The roll call was taken by the teacher in the classroom; breakfast was eaten at seven a.m., the boys proceeding at the sound of another bell, "in an orderly manner" to their places.

After the meal the boys were dismissed "in the same orderly manner". Half of the school went to work and the other half to class, with some doing chores. At eight a.m. prayers were said except by those who had parted for work. After prayers was bed-making. "The boys file up in order to their dormitories, take their places at the head of his (sic) bed, and at word from the monitor, rapidly and neatly make their beds."

After this a half-hour play period for the morning scholars followed. At nine a.m. another bell rang out for the beginning of class, which ended at noon. At a few minutes past twelve, dinner was eaten. Then there was play for the morning workers until two, and the morning scholars till one. The two halves of the school traded places for the afternoon. Preparation under a monitor went on for half an hour until the arrival of the master at 2:30 p.m. Tea was at six, and evening prayers at seven. After prayers came singing or school preparation, with justice being dispatched by E.F. Wilson, "None are allowed to report each others' misconduct, only their own."[39] The boys went to bed gradually from 7:15 p.m. to 9:15 p.m., depending on the degree of seniority involved. Although the daily schedule held some differentiation of tasks and play, still there was a large amount of marching, bells and prayer.

Much of this emphasis on routine was to correct what was considered the Indian incapacity for regularity of conduct. If they were to amalgamate with whites, the Ojibway would have to be able to work the long tedious hours typical of the nineteenth-century working classes — 60 hours a week. Wilson admitted that even he was doubtful about this at first. But having seen the results himself, he was able to give a positive assertion: "Our apprentice boys work ten hours a day, six days a week, and very rarely ask for a holiday. Having once become accustomed to regular work, they like it, and will stick to it as well as any white man."[40]

Perhaps a final aspect that should be mentioned was the emphasis placed on competition. A four-tiered classification of the pupils was employed: victor, aspirant, below mark, and lag. "The result of the six examinations alluded to is that out of 85 boys — 10 were always victors, 28 victor or aspirant, 29 generally below mark or lags."[41]

The prize night was an important event at the school, with eminent whites and Indians attending. The children were encouraged to work towards individual distinction and there was a strong competitive element: "The pupils are thus obliged to keep constantly and steadily at work through the whole year in order to gain prizes."[42]

Wilson, as was a rather common attitude of the time, saw Anglo-Saxons as particularly blessed with a desire for accumulation and competition. At one time he thought of filling up the school with white orphans. Besides thus providing charity to the boys and aiding the Indian children in their English, the idea was advanced "with the view of imbuing the Indian boys with a little more of that spirit and perseverence which generally characterizes the Anglo-Saxon race and enables them to make their way in the world."[43]

These attitudes of competition and rivalry are seen in a letter written by David Waubegegis, one of the Shingwauk's prize graduates, about his efforts to beat white rivals at Trinity College School:

I am trying hard to get a prize. I hope the boys at Shingwauk are studying hard too. The boys here are studying till 10 o'clock at night. I think I will be head in Latin, for I am always ahead in our form, and the boys are so stupid they can't tell between nouns and adjectives. I am the only one that declined them right this morning.[44]

While boys were being taught trades, farming, and in a few cases the white collar occupations, girls were trained in domestic duties, either for future employment as domestics or as wives for Shingwauk graduates. The girls rose at 6:30 a.m. "as they do all the work of the Home, to prepare them for making good servants."[45] The essential qualities to be a good servant, as the following citation clearly shows, were docility, quietness, and obedience:

Several Wawanosh girls are now out in service. The mistress of one writes: "We find N. very satisfactory. She is kind and obliging, and if not hurried, does very well. She is also very honest. She seldom goes out except with one of the children or to Church with ourselves."[46]

The other future of the girls was to marry the educated male pupils. This proper mating was considered to be very important. "The officials hoped to see the educated marrying each other. A marriage comprised of a 'civilized' husband and an 'uncivilized' wife was seen as a disaster."[47] This aim is voiced by Mrs. Fauquier (wife of the Bishop of Algoma) as is also the idea that married couples were intended to serve as "the fifth column" for civilization:

Our hopes are also that, by and by, some of these Wawanosh girls and Shingwauk boys may be united in marriage, and by their good conduct, and tidily kept cottages, prove living recommendations to the benighted ones among whom their lot may be cast.[48]

As there was an imbalance between the number of boys and girls enrolled, there was a problem in the lack of females as prospective mates. From 1874 through 1879, the enrollment was 65 per cent male, from 1880-1885, it was 58 per cent male, and from 1886-1889, up again to 68 per cent male. In addition, the location of the Wawanosh School, some three miles distant from the Shingwauk, proved a barrier. It was a ticklish problem how much access to provide the boys and girls so that matrimony rather than scandal ensued. However, the boys and girls came together at least on Sundays, and there were a number of respectable unions.

* * *

Despite the optimism of missionaries and some governments, the process of directed culture change and resocialization did not work. Witness the complaints of Indian spokespersons like Harold Cardinal. This is evident from an analysis of the Indian Homes *Register* which Wilson kept from the time of his arrival to his departure. The *Register* gives the entry and exit dates of all pupils. The length of Wilson's curriculum was five years. The children generally entered the school at age 11 or 12. Even this period of five years would have been insufficient for the process of resocialization Wilson planned. But in fact, the *Register* reveals that the average stay of the Indian children was less than 2.5 years.

From 1874 to 1879, there was a total of 149 pupils. The average stay was 2.43 years. From 1880 to 1885 there was a total of 142 pupils. The average stay in this period was 2.37 years. From 1886 to 1889 with a total of 92 pupils, the average stay was only 1.8 years. This was partly because during the latter period, Wilson started to introduce Indian children from the Prairies.

Another way to look at the data is to break down Wilson's five year programme into shorter periods. Of the 397 pupils in attendance between 1874 and 1889, 43 per cent stayed only one year or less. Another 22 per cent stayed from 1.25 years to 2.5 years. Thus, if we combine these categories, 65 per cent of the pupils spent 2.5 years or less at the school.

Let us suppose that if an Indian child stayed at the schools for 3.75 years or more, this might be accounted a success in retention. In fact, only 21 per cent of the Indian pupils stayed for 3.75 years or more.

So it seems that participation in the schools was too little and too late for successful resocialization. More often than not, attendance at the Shingwauk was an "episode" in the Indian child's biography, rather than a major influence. By the time the children got to the schools, they were usually in early adolescence — far after cultural habits are ingrained during childhood.

Another indication of dissatisfaction was the recurrence of runaways. There were 39 reported cases of runaways in the period of 1874 to 1889; 14 per cent of the total enrollment of boys ran away. Only two per cent of the girls were runaways. This would seem to reflect sexual socialization practises. The runaways were avidly pursued by Wilson. He believed they should be forced to return and to remain their term at the school since (i) in many cases parents had signed a "contract" for their children to remain for a set period (ii) the runaway was usually wearing institutional clothing which rightfully belonged to the schools. Thus, Chapter XXIX of Wilson's book, *Missionary Work Among the Ojebway*, is devoted to rather dismal accounts of expeditions setting out after escaped boys:

A lamp was lighted and we told the boys who were lying on the floor and scarcely awake yet, to get up and come along, and then our sailor boys each took charge of one prisoner, and we marched them down to the boat.[49]

Wilson's disgruntlement with the Indians, both parents and children who rejected the freely given gift of missionary education, is seen in the following passage:

I think the Indians for their real advancement require to be held with a somewhat firmer hand, and that if they will not see what is good for them that they should be made to do so . . . . I am inclined to think that if the Department would procure the necessary legislation and pass a law for compulsory education of Indian children in the same way as a law has been passed prohibiting the sale of liquor to them, that the effect would be most beneficial.[50]

When these suggestions were not acted on, Wilson devised plans of his own. One such idea was to implement a school year in which the long summer holiday was removed. This prevented adults from getting used to having their children at home again for a period of two months. Wilson's opinion of the older generation was never high since he could not understand why they did not see things as he did. Obviously Indians did not have the societal stage model of "progress" that Victorians held (including an otherwise atypical Victorian, Karl Marx). Wilson was not noticeably endowed with the virtue of empathy. "The old people do not sufficiently realize the advantages of education themselves, and so seem to care little whether their children are in their place at class or roving about the bush with a bow and arrow."[51]

If Wilson had considered that to parents, the education their children were receiving was irrelevant and foreign from their own experience, the lack of enthusiasm might have been better understood by him. If the Shingwauk had been teaching improved methods of hunting or other aspects of Ojibway culture, the older generation of parents who did not agree with their chiefs in the need for Anglo-Canadian ways would have been more enthusiastic.

Besides cultural traditionalism and conservatism, there was one other main problem that Wilson faced with Indian parents. In English civilization, it is highly desirable to send one's children far away for education to a boarding school, the private so-called "public schools". However, with the Ojibway and other Indians, the matter was quite otherwise. The Ojibway educational system was based on imitation of the adults by children. Thus it was rooted in Ojibway culture that children had to be close to their parents:

While pre-adolescent girls follow their mother's activities, boys of this age take an increasing interest in those of their fathers . . . . By the age of fifteen a boy is out on the trapping line, helping his father, and running with the toboggan as a fledgling trapper.[52]

Again and again Wilson found that the Ojibway did not like sending their children hundreds of miles distant. Wrote the Indian Agent at Parry Sound:

. . . I explained the matter to the differing bands in Council showing them the advantages it held out for their children — but the answer was that although they wished for education for their children, they want not to send them so far from their parents.[53]

When Wilson visited the Prairies in 1885 and sought to bring back some Indian children, the Cree chief O'Keness "seemed to approve of the Indian children being educated, but did not think they would send their children so far."[54]

As a result Wilson was often forced to accept children who were a burden to their parents, either because of physical or behavioural defects:

It is also unfortunate circumstance for us if we can only take into our institution just such children and of such an age as the parents may offer us, and are obliged to pass over young intelligent looking children whom we feel sure would benefit far more by receiving a course of instruction.[55]

It was not that such missionaries as E.F. Wilson failed to understand the vast cultural chasms which lay between the Indian and European cultures. But most missionaries did not take the existence of this chasm as any reason to proceed cautiously in a programme of cultural replacement. Rather, they saw such differences as further proof that Indian aspects must be changed immediately and totally. Victorian missionaries believed in the need for drastic operations to ensure the patient revived from his debilitated condition.

Not all was gloom of course, and Wilson was able to record some successes. He was able to write of Joseph Esquimau in his *Register*:

Teacher. 5 years. Employed as a catechist and school-teacher at Neepigon. Married Oshkahpudkeda's daughter (the chief in that area) — had two children — wife died. Still at Neepigon '90. Returned to Little Current, fall 1891. Made great progress. Learned Algebra, Euclid, Latin, Greek.[56]

Or of John Wigwaus: "Bootmaker, 5 years. Living on Sugar Island 1887. Married with 1 child. Steady. C. of E. Doing very well '92."[57]

However, as indicated in the data cited earlier successes were outweighed by failures. A recent author on the schools, D. Geddes, has said, "Generally speaking, the children failed in attempts to use the trades skills learned at the Shingwauk Home. . . ."[58]

Some circumstances beyond Wilson's control also contributed to the failure of his plans. Prejudice against Indians was wider than he would admit. Wilson believed that if only the Indian would accept white culture, there would be no bias. Instead, Anglo-Canadians sometimes doubted the ability of the Indians, and were less than enthusiastic to have them resident in towns and cities. Nor did the widespread Depression of the 1870s to 1890s help, as this discouraged any process of "amalgamation".

In addition, increasing mechanization tended to render the trades learned at residential schools redundant:

In most cases jobs were scarce. The occupations that they were preparing for had few openings. For example, in the case of shoemaking, factory made boots were cheaper and quicker to obtain than those students made by hand. . . . Emphasis was placed upon more students becoming proficient in agricultural pursuits and the learning of trades was correspondingly de-emphasized.[59]

The result of this process of directed culture change, then, was not so much the shift from one culture and mode of production to another as hoped for by missionaries such as Wilson. Instead, the result was more like a process of marginalization with the Indian not quite fitting in his aboriginal culture and mode of production, nor quite into industrial-capitalist society. Other authors have cited the advantages of marginality. In the case of the North American Indian, the advantages of marginality would seem to have been rather thin.

NOTES

1. R.J. Surtees, "The Development of an Indian Reserve Policy in Canada", *Historical Essays on Upper Canada*, ed. J.K. Johnson, Toronto: McClelland and Stewart, 1975, pp. 264-65. This paper originally appeared in *Ontario History*, 1969.

2. For a good argument about considering the rate of change among native peoples as significant, see Charles A. Bishop and Arthur K. Ray, "Ethnohistoric Research in the Central Subarctic: Some Conceptual and Methodological Problems", *The Western Canadian Journal of Anthropology*, 1976, 6:1, pp. 116-144.

3. Surtees, p. 263.

4. *Ibid.*, p. 262.

5. *Ibid.*, p. 267.

6. For further information on Wilson's earlier career, see David Nock, "E.F. Wilson: Early Years as Missionary in Huron and Algoma", *Journal of the Canadian Church Historical Society*, 1973, 15:4, pp. 78-96. For information on Wilson's "radical" phase, see David Nock, "The Canadian Indian Research and Aid Society: A Victorian Voluntary Association", *The Western Canadian Journal of Anthropology*, 1976, 6:2, pp. 31-62.

7. E.F. Wilson, *Missionary Work Among the Ojebway*, London: S.P.C.K., 1886, p. 68.

8. *Ibid.*, p. 63.

9. Public Archives of Canada, Reel A-76, C.C. Fenn to Wilson, December 31, 1869.

10. Wilson, *Missionary Work*, p. 50.

11. *Ibid.*, p. 48.

12. Jacqueline Kennedy, *Qu'Appelle Industrial School: White 'Rites' for the Indians of the Old Northwest*, M.A. thesis, Ottawa: Carleton University, 1970, p. 91.

13. Wilbert H. Ahern, "Assimilationist Racism: The Case of The 'Friends of the Indian' ", reprinted in this volume, pp. 251-261.

14. *Correspondence*, Wilson to the Superintendent of Indian Affairs, August 2, 1877.

15. Harold Cardinal, *The Unjust Society: The Tragedy of Canada's Indians*, Edmonton: Hurtig, 1969, p. 87.

16. "Indian Training", *The Canadian Indian*, September, 1890, p. 29.

17. *Correspondence*, Wilson to the Superintendent of Indian Affairs, 2 August, 1877.

18. H.A.C. Cairns, *Prelude to Imperialism: British Reactions to Central African Society, 1840-1890*, London: Routledge and Kegan Paul, 1965, p. 211.

19. *Correspondence*, Wilson to McMorine, March 19, 1878.

20. Cairns, p. 214.

21. Kathryn Kozak, *Education and the Blackfeet: 1870-1900*, M.A. thesis, Edmonton: University of Alberta, 1971, p. 75.

22. *Fourth Annual Report of the Shingwauk and Wawanosh Homes*, Sault Ste. Marie, 1877, p. 20.

23. *Ibid*.

24. Dominion of Canada, *Sessional Paper, No. 3, 1884*, Ottawa, 1885, p. 24.

25. *Ibid*.

26. "A Day at the Shingwauk", *Our Forest Children*, 1888, 2:10, p. 16.

27. Kozak, p. 75.

28. "Third Annual Report", *Algoma Missionary News and Singwauk Journal*, 1877, 1:5, p. 35.

29. "Letter to the Sunday Schools", *Our Forest Children*, 1890, 4:4, p. 209.

30. *Ibid*., p. 210.

31. "Visit to the Shingwauk Chapel", *Algoma Missionary News*, 1886, 9:2, p. 21.

32. "Letter to the Sunday Schools", *Our Forest Children*, 1890, 3:12, p. 143.

33. For a good example of a work which uses the methodology of base-superstructure analysis, see C.B. Macpherson, *Democracy in Alberta: Social Credit and the Party System*, Toronto: University of Toronto Press, 1953. Macpherson shows how the political attitudes of Alberta farmers can be traced to the consequences and implications of their situation in the economic system of production.

34. Dominion of Canada, *Sessional Paper No. 16, 1888*, Ottawa, 1889, p. 23.

35. *Ibid*.

36. "On Tidiness and Punctuality", *Our Forest Children*, 1889, 3:4, p. 30.

37. *Ibid*.

38. "A Day at the Shingwauk", *Our Forest Children*, 1888, 2:10, pp. 15-16.

39. *Ibid.*

40. *Fourth Annual Report of the Shingwauk and Wawanosh Homes*, p. 23.

41. "Our Indian Homes", *Algoma Missionary News and Shingwauk Journal*, 1883, 6:5, p. 27.

42. Dominion of Canada, *Sessional Paper No. 15, 1887*, Ottawa, 1888, p. 26.

43. *Correspondence*, Wilson to H. Reed (Commissioner of Indian Affairs), June 30, 1886.

44. Dominion of Canada, *Sessional Paper No. 8, 1886*, Ottawa, 1887, p. 18.

45. "The Wawanosh Home", *Algoma Missionary News and Shingwauk Journal*, 1882, 5:1, p. 2.

46. *Our Forest Children*, 1890, 3:13, p. 163.

47. Kozak, p. 72.

48. "The Wawanosh Home", *Algoma Missionary News and Shingwauk Journal*, 1881, 4:4, p. 18.

49. Wilson, *Missionary Work*, p. 169.

50. P.A.C., RG 10, Vol. 2023, Wilson to the Superintendent of Indian Affairs, August 2, 1877.

51. Wilson, *Missionary Work*, p. 90.

52. R.W. Dunning, *Social and Economic Change Among the Northern Ojibwa*, Toronto: University of Toronto Press, 1959, pp. 99-100.

53. P.A.C., RG 10, Vol. 2023, Indian Agent at Parry Sound to E.A. Meredith, Deputy of the Minister of the Interior.

54. "The Rev. E.F. Wilson's Trip to the North-West", *Algoma Missionary News*, 1886, 9:2, p. 23.

55. Wilson to the Superintendent of Indian Affairs, August 2, 1877.

56. E.F. Wilson, *Our Indian Homes Register,* Sault Ste. Marie, 1894. Unpublished ledger.

57. *Ibid.*

58. Donald Geddes, "Indian Schools in Sault Ste. Marie", Sault Ste. Marie, n.d.-c. 1965. Unpublished essay delivered to the Sault Historical Society.

59. Kozak, p. 78.

Assimilationist Racism: The Case of the 'Friends of the Indian'*

WILBERT H. AHERN†

The subordination of racial minorities by reform movements claiming principles antithetical to racism constitutes an important theme in the history of racism in the United States. Too often, studies of race relations have assumed a direct relationship between race prejudice and racism. As our recent past has awakened historians to the pervasiveness of racism in the United States, we have emphasized the pervasiveness of racial bigotry in our history. Unquestionably, race prejudice at various levels of sophistication has played an important role in determining the distribution of resources in America. This paper should not be seen as a denial of the existence of deep hostility on the part of many European Americans toward Native Americans. But, as we have documented the existence of prejudice and oppression, we have also uncovered some paradoxes that require explanation. In the contrast between their stated goals and the results of their action, the Indian policy reformers active in the last two decades of the nineteenth-century present such a paradox and suggest an important pattern in the development of racism.[1]

Responding to a new crisis in White-Indian contacts born of the post-Civil War expansion of Euroamericans, a reform movement emerged to "save" the original inhabitants of the continent. Its membership, largely White, anglosaxon and protestant, came from urban, middle-class professional and business backgrounds. The periodicals through which they spoke and the record of their other activities as well as their socio-economic profile revealed their affinity to liberal reform of the period. Organized in such regional and national groups as the Indian Rights Association, the Women's National Indian Association, the Boston Indian Citizenship Commission, the Massachusetts Indian Association and the Connecticut Indian Association, these self-styled Indian reformers came together at Lake Mohonk, New York, each fall beginning in 1883. There, at Albert K. Smiley's tranquil resort, they

* This paper is reprinted in its original form from *The Journal of Ethnic Studies*, 1976, 4:2.

† I wish to express my appreciation for a Newberry Library Resident Research Fellowship and a University of Minnesota Graduate School Grant-in-Aid, which made this study possible.

discussed and adopted platforms addressed to the character and destiny of Native Americans.[2]

Sincere in their concern for the future of Indian peoples and adamantly opposed to a view of inherent racial differences between White and Red Americans, the "friends of the Indian" mounted a crusade to transform federal Indian policy. During the last two decades of the nineteenth-century, they were remarkably successful in implementing their plans. In retrospect, those reforms were disastrous for Native Americans. The allotment of land in severalty [to individuals] became a means of divesting the various tribes of about two-thirds of their land in the next fifty years. Educational programs failed to meet their goal of assimilating Native Americans, nor did they offer skills with which these peoples could resist assaults on their autonomy.[3]

Flaws in the reformers' vision made an important contribution to the devastating consequences of this shift in policy. Certainly other forces were involved in stripping Native Americans of their land and resources — the pressures of settlement, the demand of a booming industrialization for raw materials, the desire of the politician for more ways to grant and receive favours; but of interest here is the way in which their proclaimed "friends" contributed to the oppression of the Indians and the implications of this for the dynamics of racism.

The emphasis on schooling reveals most completely the paradox in the role of these assimilationist reformers. Perhaps because of its more concrete and dramatic nature, the Dawes Act of 1887 has appeared to be the culmination of the Indian policy reform movement, but to the "friends of the Indian" education was to go hand in hand with land in severalty.[4] Some differences over the nature of the schooling program — the role of the churches, proper location, use of the vernacular in instruction — characterized the discussions at Lake Mohonk or in the columns of periodicals. Further delineation of these differences is necessary for a complete understanding of this reform movement, but this paper explores the implications of a consensus that overrode these disagreements; an agreement on the central role of education in achieving the ends of the reform movement.

In his influential proposal of 1881 for land in severalty, Secretary of Interior Carl Schurz portrayed the school as the crucial assimilating tool. Alloted land would not be safe unless the Indian owner knew how to work and protect it. For this, education was necessary.[5] In the following years, the Indian defense groups lobbied for federal appropriations as well as church funds to expand educational facilities and staff. When the Dawes Act became law, they could point to an impressive increase in these appropriations.[6]

Yet now they turned even greater attention to schooling. Rather than believing that their job was done, they pushed for a comprehensive educational program. To Lyman Abbott's warning, "Put an ignorant and imbruted savage on land of his own, and he remains a pauper, if he does not become a vagrant and a thief,'' the Lake Mohonk Conference of 1888 responded in its platform. "Neither the land in severalty, nor law administered by competent courts will suffice for the protection of the Indian. More fundamental than either is his education.... It is the duty of the Federal Government to undertake at once the entire task of furnishing primary and secular education for all Indian children of school age on the reservations.''[7]

In 1889, Thomas J. Morgan, the new Commissioner of Indian Affairs whose experience in education and home missions gave him a deep affinity with those who gathered at Mohonk, presented a comprehensive plan for Indian education. Beginning with the reservation day school and culminating in the non-reservation high school, this system would do for all Indian youth what the public schools were "so successfully doing for all the other races in this country, — assimilate them.'' The "friends of the Indian'' saw their goals embodied in federal policy. They entered the last decade of the nineteenth century committed to assisting Commissioner Morgan and confident that they had blazed the trail to a prosperous future for the original inhabitants of the continent. They would, in Captain Richard Henry Pratt's revealing words, "kill the Indian and save the man.''[8]

This phrase captured the ambiguity of the reformers' program; it coupled ethnocentrism with egalitarianism. Their arguments for education stressed the inherent equality and the claim to equal opportunity for Native Americans. At a time when most Americans attributed inherent inferiority to non-Whites, the "friends of the Indian'' took the opposite position. In presenting his schooling program, Commissioner Morgan articulated its premise. "There is in the Indian the same diversity of endowment and the same high order of talent that the other races possess.'' Captain Richard Henry Pratt's statement, "[the Indian] is born a blank like all the rest of us,'' illustrated the fundamental environmentalism of their thought. Neither race nor culture were factors which irrevocably set one group of people off from another. Both reflected differences in the environment and thus could be altered by environmental changes. The experience of the Indian schools reaffirmed this article of faith. The record of Indian students at Hampton Institute and Carlisle conclusively demonstrated that they had the same ability as Whites.[9]

Their faith in the school revealed their belief in the plasticity of all men. They did not intend that their educational program would assure an inferior position for Indian children, despite some appearances to the contrary. The initial emphasis on separate Indian schools and the orientation toward industrial education smack of separate and unequal treatment. A closer look at the early programs refutes this too easy analogy with education for Black Americans. Separate institutions were temporary necessities reflecting particular problems of language, culture, location and relationship to the federal government. Because its model for the education of the freedmen predicted a separate and subordinate position for them, the approach of Hampton Institute to Indian education is suggestive. While they did see its mission in preparing Indian youth to return as missionaries of progress to their villages, the Hampton staff happily foresaw the intermingling of the White and Red races. The Indian schools should disappear in a generation.[10] Nor was the industrial approach geared to an inferior position in American society. The pestalozzian model as modified by Hampton and Carlisle, with its emphasis on building character through the gospel of work, should be applied to all youth. Higher education and professional schools were appropriate only for a talented few, be they White or Red. The founders of these two schools, General Samuel C. Armstrong and Captain Pratt, pointed with pride to their alumni who went on to professional schools.[11]

The attitude toward interracial marriage provided further evidence of the irrelevance of race to these reformers. Speaking with varying degrees of enthusiasm, most suggested that it represented the ultimate solution to the question. "The Indian problem is likely to disappear in the next century for want of a distinguishable Indian race" was a common sentiment in their "vanishing policy".[12]

This dream of racial fusion illustrated the other side of the reform thrust. Native Americans must abandon their ways and disappear into White society. Philip C. Garrett, a Philadelphia lawyer active in the Indian Rights Association and later Pennsylvania's Commissioner of Public Charities, expressed the one-sided nature of this exchange in unconsciously brutal imagery. "[I]t is the lion and the lamb lying down together, the lamb having been devoured by the lion. What happy result can there be to the lamb, but in absorption, digestion, assimilation in the substance of the lion. After this process he will be useful — as part of the lion."[13]

While insisting that the Indian could change, that he could clothe himself in White culture as easily as in White dress, the "friends of the Indian" maintained that he *must* change. Why? Because Native Americans could not and should not survive as they were. As Philip Garrett argued, they had been devoured by a lion — an expanding, aggressive society whose government, even in its best intentioned moments was unable to halt the depredation of tribal peoples.

The reformers fought such travesties as the removal of the Ute from Colorado, the attempts to redefine the Sioux territory in the Dakotas without their consent, the eviction of the Mission Indians in California, and many more, but they saw it to be a hopeless struggle as long as these peoples remained distinct and with land titles subject to the whims of Congress. In publicizing his program of education and land allotment, Carl Schurz discussed the assault on the Utes by the citizens of Colorado. It demonstrated the irresistible drive of White settlement and the necessity of his program.[14]

Not only was the reservation system ineffective in its protection, it was wrong. The annuities and rations system encouraged pauperism and undermined the character of Native Americans. It restricted movement and thus opportunity. Reformers would free their Red brothers from this "race-perpetuating system." Not all agreed with the immediatism of Lyman Abbott or his implications that legal obligations could be unilaterally discarded, but they accepted the general sentiment which he expressed at the 1885 Lake Mohonk Conference. "I hold that the reservation barriers should be cast down and the land given to the Indians in severalty; that every Indian should be protected in his right to his home, and in his right to free intercourse and free trade, whether the rest of the tribe wish him so protected or not; that these are his individual, personal rights, which no tribe has the right to take from him and no nation the right to sanction the robbery of."[15]

Central to an understanding of the impact of these "friends of the Indian" is the fact that they endorsed the expansion of Euroamerican civilization as natural and progressive. Reverend Abbott's statement illustrated their particular form of manifest destiny. It had its roots in laissez-faire liberalism as well as in social gospel Christianity. The key to progress was individual competition — the interaction of individuals on the basis of self-interest — not cooperation. Equal protection under the law, the sanctity of private property, the family and Christianity operated to distinguish this competition from warfare. This combination of institutions and ideals accounted for the magnificent achievements of the United States. Nothing must stand in its way.

These reformers seemed to face a dilemma. They endorsed both the expansion of American civilization and the claim of Native Americans to justice and equal rights. To most Americans these positions were contradictory, but a faith in assimilation resolved them. To "become an intelligent citizen of the United States" was the " 'manifest destiny' for any man or body of men on our domain."[16]

The school was the fundamental instrument. Through it they would "civilize" the Indian. "Education . . . is the Indian's only salvation," Thomas J. Morgan declared. "With it they will become honorable, useful, happy citizens of a great republic, sharing on equal terms in all its blessings. Without it they are doomed to either destruction or to hopeless degradation."[17] The tribal experience was too communal. It obstructed individual ambition and progress even in its most advanced forms. Senator Henry L. Dawes criticized one of the Civilized Tribes of the Indian Territory with classic ethnocentrism. "There was not a pauper in that Nation, and the Nation did not owe a dollar. It built its own capitol . . . and it built its schools and its hospitals. Yet the defect of the system was apparent . . . . There is no selfishness, which is at the bottom of civilization.''[18] The schools would teach self-relaince, which was to work and to keep. From this came the special emphasis on industrial education and the ''outing system'' in which individual students were placed with an employer, usually a farmer, during the summer. Such an education would allow Indians to disappear as a group and progress as individuals.

To themselves and to many observers, the ''friends of the Indian'' appeared to stand for that which was best in the values and traditions of the United States. Their classical liberal and Christian ideology led them to attack those in the society who would unabashedly exterminate or expropriate the material resources of the Native Americans. Yet this summary of their program and the place of education in it suggests certain flaws in their vision.

Significantly, these flaws were not tied to racialistic theories. In their crusade, they were consciously in a racial reform tradition that went back to the antislavery struggle. Parallels between the oppression of slavery and that meted out by aggressive settlers and/or a misguided governmental policy pervaded their speeches and articles.[19]

Nor was their concern for education invalid. The history of duplicity in treaty negotiations alone made a compelling case for literacy. An education which would provide literacy and enough knowledge of White Americans to improve their effectiveness at negotiation was attractive to many Native American leaders. Such reasoning led Spotted Tail of the Brulé Sioux to send thirty-four children East with a surprised Captain Pratt to attend Carlisle. So were Thomas Wildcat Alford and John King sent to Hampton Institute by the council of the Absentee Shawnee.[20]

Part of the problem, then, was not education, *per se*, but who should control it. The program initiated in the last two decades of the nineteenth-century placed that control squarely in the hands of the dominant society. When the reformers spoke for compulsory education under such rationales as ''A barbarian father has no right to keep his child in barbarism,'' they revealed that they as much as the exterminators denied self-determination to the Native Americans. The goals of such men as Spotted Tail or the leaders of the Absentee Shawnee foundered on the reformers' narrow vision of civilization and civilized values.[21]

The ill-effects of this colonial system of education continue to be felt and documented. The denial of worth of the child's past and family obstructed learning and contributed to self-alienation. To be successful in the eyes of the school reformers, the student had to wholly adopt White American modes of life. Despite these obstacles, some Indian students experienced success in school and went about creating new patterns of accommodation between their culture and that of White America. For many, the result was a Pan-Indianism that revealed a greater interest in their tribes' rights and traditions than their "friends" anticipated or desired. The latter ignored or opposed efforts of Indians to develop self-reliance with the necessary ties to their own cultures.[22]

While in no way wishing to de-emphasize the damage done directly by the schools, I would suggest that the broader implications of this emphasis on education were even more damaging. By placing so much faith in the school as the means of progress, the reformers weakened their own resistance to efforts to divest Indians of their resources and life chances. At best, their attention turned to methods of education and away from the physical needs and property rights of the tribal peoples. But their message actually supported assaults on Indian resources. Their opposition to annuities and rations contributed to starvation and desperate poverty. Captain Richard Henry Pratt revealed the dangerous implication of the idea that the Indians must learn to fend for themselves in White society. "I would blow the reservation to pieces," he said in typical brashness. "I would not give the Indian an acre of land. When he strikes bottom, he will get up." Other "friends of the Indian", observing that no one proposed giving land to Indians, repudiated the Captain's position.[23] Yet Pratt had captured the thrust of their reform. They agreed with the provision in the Allotment Act that much of the reservation land was surplus and should be sold off. The educated Indian would not need all that land. "A wild Indian requires a thousand acres to roam over, while an intelligent man will find a comfortable support for his family on a very small tract."[24] Despite continued criticism of fraud and corruption, their eagerness to see allotments assigned harmonized with the land hunger of less altruistic White Americans. The settlement of White farmers on reservations' "surplus" land furthered the assimilationists' goal of immersing Red people in White America.[25]

Basically, the Indian policy reformers comforted America. Their confidence in the school allowed them and the nation to avoid either admitting that they were involved in blatant conquest or confronting the complex task of recognizing the legitimate demands of Native Americans. Moreover, their argument that education would prepare the individual "to sink or swim" on his own merits in American society provided a dangerous rationale for a decline in the condition of Indian peoples. Education offered that opportunity for no one in America, especially not for peoples who had no desire to enter that society. Yet the implication of the reform ideology was that failure would be the responsibility of the individual.

By the end of the first decade of the twentieth century, to be sure, the extent of land frauds from Minnesota to Oklahoma and the spread of disease which seemed to be the main fruit of Indian boarding schools led to some criticism of the assimilationist approach. For most, however, the problems reflected too much optimism about Native Americans. Very few felt that the fault lay in the denial of self-determination to these peoples. Rather, these events strengthened a belief in racial differences.[26]

The paradoxes in this reform effort now came full circle. From a belief in the irrelevance of race and a policy of cultural imperialism, the reform effort contributed to a belief in the unchanging nature of race differences. Ironically, those that held such beliefs argued for a more protective policy. True, the loss of land and resources reduced the pressure of non-Indian aggression, but now race theory became a rationale for guarding the esoteric aborigines in their simplicity. Indeed, the Supreme Court, in a ruling protecting Pueblo land claims, operated from the premise articulated by Justice Van Devanter that the Pueblo ''are essentially a simple, uninformed, and inferior people.''[27] Lest we get carried away with the image that race theory helped its targets, we should note that this new approach was equally obstructive to Native American efforts to adjust to a new reality and became a rationale for reducing expenditures on behalf of them.

The episode of the ''friends of the Indian'' takes on greater significance for the history of racism when one observes its connections with the treatment of Black Americans. To the extent that the unforeseen results of this reform movement strengthened race theory, it operated against them as well. A race theory that denied equality and demanded segregation shaped the nadir of the Negro. He could not find even the saving grace of a protective isolation in the new climate.

That the Indian reform movement should indirectly contribute to Black oppression is not surprising when we recognize that liberal reformers had applied the same basic assumptions to their approach to the future of the freedmen. Many of the men and women who were active in the ''defense'' of Indians and others with similar ideals and social characteristics worked on behalf of the freedmen as well. Not only during the reconstruction period but after, they denounced the belief in racial inferiority and the denial of equal rights to the freedmen. Yet in their program to achieve equal rights, they opposed any federal action beyond the reconstruction Amendments to the Constitution. Those negative guarantees together with education would allow the ex-slaves to achieve their rank in society each according to his merits. Here too they applied the fallacious ''sink or swim'' theory, the corollary of what W.E.B. DuBois called the American Assumption, to the inevitable detriment of the freedmen.[28]

This connection between the reform of Indian policy and the approach to the future of the freedmen in America suggests some broader implications of this study. In the late nineteenth-century, the social assumptions of humanitarian reformers — their laissez-faire values and most importantly their confidence in the inevitability and universality of the American way of life — shaped a policy that hurt those that it was to help. A recent assessment of the work of Hampton Institute could be applied to the race reform movement as a whole; it ''was a device through which the white man's desertion of the Negro and his annihilation of the Indian was made more tolerable.''[29] Thus the ''friends of the Indian'' were racist in effect if not in intent. This analysis questions the presence of an American dilemma, a struggle between desires of justice versus exploitation of minority peoples. Liberal reformers subordinated the right to self-determination of the minority to the ''greatest good of the greatest number'' and the promise of assimilation. That such criticism can still be made reveals both a thread of continuity in and the limits to liberalism in its confrontation with racism.

NOTES

1. This paper discusses one component of the environment in which Native American peoples have operated in the post-Columbian era. I endorse the need for histories of Native Americans which reflect their perspectives, which give more emphasis to the tribal unit and offer a corrective to the emphasis on European action in shaping their destinies. At the same time, the dynamics of racism, that is, the manner in which Europeans interacted with Native Americans, is a part of the history of both groups and in need of more careful analysis.

2. For analyses of this movement which emphasize the pre-1890 period see Loring Benson Priest, *Uncle Sam's Stepchildren: The Reformation of United States Indian Policy, 1865-1887* (New Brunswick, 1942); Henry E. Fritz, *The Movement for Indian Assimilation, 1860-1890* (Philadelphia, 1963); Robert W. Mardock, *The Reformers and the American Indian* (Columbia, 1971). Francis Paul Prucha, ed., *Americanizing the American Indians: Writings by the ''Friends of the Indian'' 1880-1900* (Cambridge, 1973), provides a balanced and insightful collection of the opinions of these reformers. For the socio-economic profile of these reformers, I am indebted to Helen Bannan's unpublished ms., ''Who Were the American Indian Policy Reformers?''

3. William A. Brophy and Sophie D. Aberle, comps., *The Indian: America's Unfinished Business* (Norman, 1966), pp. 20; Brewton Berry, *The Education of American Indians: A Survey of the Literature* (Washington, D.C., 1969), pp. 15-30.

4. Mardock, *The Reformers*, p. 214, most explicitly sees the Dawes Act as the culmination of the movement, but the arguments of Fritz, *Indian Assimilation*, and Priest, *Uncle Sam's Stepchildren* suggest the same.

5. Carl Schurz, ''Present Aspects of the Indian Problem,'' *North American Review*, 133 (July, 1881), 12-18.

6. *Proceedings of the Sixth Annual Meeting of the Lake Mohonk Conference of the Friends of the Indian* (1888) (Boston: The Lake Mohonk Conference, 1888), 7-8. Later, these *Proceedings* are cited as *LMC, year*.

7. *Ibid.*, pp. 11, 94.

8. *LMC, 1889*, pp. 19, 16-34, 108; *LMC, 1891*, pp. 112-113; *LMC, 1892*, p. 121.

9. *LMC, 1889*, p. 21; Richard H. Pratt, "The Advantages of Mingling Indians and Whites" [1892], repr. in Prucha, ed. *Americanizing*, p. 268. For observations on Indian students, see *Report of the Board of Indian Commissioners* (1880), repr. in Prucha, ed., *Americanizing*, p. 195; *Lend A Hand*, II (Feb. 1887), pp. 103-104; Hiram Price, "The Government and the Indians,"*Forum*, X (Feb. 1891), pp. 708-15.

10. Prucha, ed., *Americanizing*, pp. 9, 41, 210, 223, 266; Larry E. Burgess, "The Lake Mohonk Conferences on the Indian, 1883-1916, "Ph. D. Diss., Claremont, 1972, ch. 6; Francis G. Peabody, *Education for Life: The Story of Hampton Institute* (N.Y., 1919), pp. 198-200; M.F.A[rmstrong], *Hampton Institute, 1865-1885: Its Work for Two Races* (Hampton, 1885), pp. 15, 19, 23.

11. Peabody, *Education*, pp. 244-245; Everett A. Gilcreast, "Richard Henry Pratt and American Indian Policy, 1877-1906: A Study of the Assimilation Movement," Ph.D. dissertation, Yale University, 1967, pp. 311-313, while accurate on Pratt, exaggerates his uniqueness.

12. M.F.A[rmstrong], *Hampton*, p. 23; Prucha, ed., *Americanizing*, pp. 60-62; Gilcreast, "Pratt," p. 102. Brian W. Dippie, " 'This Bold But Wasting Race': Stereotypes and American Indian Policy," *Montana*, XXIII (Jan. 1972), pp. 3-13.

13. Prucha, ed., *Americanizing*, p. 62.

14. Carl Schurz, "Present Aspects of the Indian Problem," *North American Review*, 133 (July 1881), pp. 20-21.

15. Prucha, ed., *Americanizing,* pp. 35-36.

16. Merrill E. Gates quoted in Prucha, ed., *Americanizing,* p. 46.

17. *Ibid.*, p. 224.

18. *LMC, 1885*, p. 43.

19. Mardock, *The Reformers,* ch. 1; Prucha, ed., *Americanizing,* pp. 36, 46, 247, 262-63, 269.

20. Richard Henry Pratt, *Battlefield and Classroom: Four Decades with the American Indian, 1867-1904*. Ed. with an introd. by Robert M. Utley (New Haven, 1964), pp. 222-24; George E. Hyde, *Spotted Tail's Folk: A History of the Brule Sioux* (Norman, 1961), pp. 278-79; Thomas Wildcat Alford, *Civilization* (Norman, 1936), p. 90, ch. 11, 12.

21. *LMC, 1888*, p. 14; Prucha, ed., *Americanizing,* p. 243; Hyde, *Spotted Tail's Folk*, pp. 290-93; Alford, *Civilization,* ch. 16.

22. Berry, *Education of the American Indian,* summarizes the literature. For an exhaustive documentation, consult the six volumes of *Hearings before the Special Subcommittee on Indian Education of the Committee on Labor and Public Welfare,* U.S. Senate, 90 Cong., 1 & 2 sess. (Wash., D.C., 1969). Hazel W. Hertzberg, *The Search for an American Indian Identity: Modern Pan-Indian Movements* (Syracuse, 1971), ch. 2, 10, p. 22.

23. *LMC, 1891,* pp. 65ff, 67.

24. Thomas J. Morgan quoted in Prucha, ed., *Americanizing,* p. 249.

25. Prucha, ed., *Americanizing,* pp. 25, 101, 251, 343.

26. Burgess, "Lake Mohonk Conferences," ch. 9, pp. 299ff, 318-319.

27. *U.S.* v. *Sandoval* 231 US 39 (1913) Ms. Helen Bannan brought this decision to my attention. Indicating the change of tone on race at the Lake Mohonk Conferences is G. Stanley Hall's address, *LMC, 1911,* pp. 225-32.

28. The Mohonk Conferences on the Negro Question held in June 1890 and 1891 illustrate the overlap of concern, *Mohonk Conferences on the Negro Question* (N.Y., 1969 [1890, 1891]). Wilbert H. Ahern, "Laissez Faire vs. Equal Rights: Liberal Republicans and the Negro, 1861-1877," Ph.D. dissertation, Northwestern Univ., 1968, and Ralph Edlin Luker, "The Social Gospel and the Failure of Racial Reform, 1885-1898," Ph.D. dissertation, U. of North Carolina, 1973, offer corrections to the view that reformers lost interest in the freedmen.

29. Robert Francis Engs, "The Development of Black Culture and Community in the Emancipation Era: Hampton Roads, 1861-1870," Ph. D. diss., Yale, 1972, p. 229.

An Adult Education Programme: Indian Band Staff Training*

SANDRA STEINHAUSE

Indians and education? Isn't that a contradiction? They're lazy, aren't they? They don't want to learn. What do they really want?

I had the opportunity this year to assist in a programme for Indian peoples. I watched men and women grow and bloom. I learned what certain groups of Indians *really do want*. I saw learning taking place.

The following is a descriptive report of the Indian Band Staff Training Sessions, 1976-77, undertaken at St. Francis Xavier University, Antigonish, Nova Scotia. These training sessions are offered through the university's non-degree programme of Continuing Education. This paper is not intended as a blueprint for other similar training programmes. It is an explanation of how certain educational principles, concepts and techniques are practiced. It is a report of an educational programme that, in the words of the students, "really works".

SOME RELEVANT HISTORICAL PERSPECTIVES

The theoretical and historical base for the Indian Band Staff Training Programme owes much to the pioneer work of William Godwin. Godwin wrote in the late eighteenth century; he clarified the link between methods of teaching and the type of character molded. He believed that it was the method of discipline and the techniques of teaching that undermined reason and eroded human freedom. Traditional teachers use *extrinsic motivation,* presenting material to the student "despotically, by allurements or menaces". He defined extrinsic motivation as that which is connected to a thing by accident or at the pleasure of some other individual; grades and other threats of punishment are examples of extrinsic motivators. Godwin argued that the type of education encouraged by these motivators prepares an individual for a government of despotic laws.[1]

The Scandinavian influence on adult education is fully recognized, as it is to Denmark originally that the world owes the idea of residential adult education. The People's High School, conceived by N.S.F. Grundtvig, the

* The author wishes to thank Randle Nelsen for his criticisms and comments during the preparation of this paper.

Danish teacher, educational reformer, and "Father of Adult Education", was given its first practical expression at Rødding in 1844. "It was inspired by the need to awaken a peasant community to a new sense of responsible nationalism, and there is no doubt that the People's High Schools have played a leading part in raising this sturdy people to the high position in the world which they occupy today."[2] These institutions have spread throughout Denmark, Norway, and Sweden and have inspired similar developments in Germany. They have become an essential part of the educational system of the three countries, generously supported by governments while preserving freedom of teaching.

The programme also derives some of its concepts from Max Stirner, a German schoolteacher during the 1840s. He stressed the idea of "ownership of self", making a distinction between a "freeman" and an "educated man". The educated man used knowledge to shape character; it became a wheel in the head which allowed him to be possessed by the church, state, or humanity. The freeman used knowledge to facilitate choice. "For the freeman knowing something was the source of greater choice, while for the educated man knowing something was the *determiner* of choice." The major problem with modern society, Stirner believed, was that it was full of educated people instead of free people.

If one awakens in men the idea of freedom then the freemen will incessantly go on to free themselves; if on the contrary, one only educates them, then they will at all times accommodate themselves to circumstances in the most highly educated and elegant manner and degenerate to subservient cringing souls.[3]

Other historical figures that should be mentioned in connection with the format of the Indian Band Staff Training Programme are Francisco Ferrer, Leo Tolstoy and Paulo Freire. Ferrer clearly stated that it must be the aim of schools to show the children that there will be tyranny and slavery as long as one person depends upon another.[4] Similarly, Tolstoy wrote, "Education is the tendency of one man to make another just like himself. When teaching is forced upon the pupil, and when the instruction is exclusive, that is when only subjects are taught which the educator regards as necessary, then education is restraining".[5] He argued that people should have full freedom to avail themselves of teaching which answers their needs and to avoid teaching which they do not need and do not want. Likewise, for Paulo Freire, learning is meaningful only if it is tied to the life processes of the individual. Traditional education is oppressive when "the teacher teaches and the students are taught, the teacher thinks and the students are thought about, the teacher acts and the students have the illusion of acting through the action of the teacher and the teacher is the subject of the learning process, while the students are mere objects."[6]

Luke L. Batdorf, initiator and director of the Indian Band Staff Training

Programme at St. Francis Xavier does not believe that you can instruct about freedom. You cannot learn by listening to information spouting from the mouths of "learned ones". He gives the example of an ancient Chinese proverb, "Give a man a fish and he will eat for a day. Teach a man how to fish and he will eat for a lifetime." However, Batdorf does not stop there. "The strategy should not be to give a man a fish, nor *tell him how to fish,* but to build up confidence in his ability to solve problems in his own style of learning. This way a person has the ability not only to learn to fish but to master any set of skills. Thus, he is free to fish or to do anything else he might choose."[7] In this way, a person will become a "free person" rather than an "educated person".

The following rationale, concepts, principles and objectives are excerpts from Batdorf's Training Proposal.[8]

RATIONALE FOR THE BAND STAFF TRAINING PROGRAMME
The Problem

In communities where serious problems exist, many attempts to solve them are largely unsuccessful. Often these attempts are solutions imposed upon the community from outside.

Sometimes a more constructive approach is taken, such as placing money in the hands of local people to follow their own initiatives, or providing them with necessary technical and vocational skills. However, even these more constructive approaches can also be unsuccessful. Failure is most often due to three major factors:

(1) Powerless communities have learned to fail and to have a low opinion of themselves because of their experience of failure. They do not see themselves as a major resource for change.

(2) Necessary skills needed to achieve in a highly complex, technical, and fast-moving society have not been sufficiently developed in many local people. Consequently, they are unable to participate in, and take control of, their own development.

(3) Many people have not acquired the skills of organizing and marshalling their own resources well enough to obtain resources they do not as yet have, but which they need in order to develop.

The Human Resource

Too much attention in development has been placed on counting trees and rocks and on finding ways to locate sewers and roads in the appropriate places. Too little attention has been given to helping people to develop — to human development as the major resource in the community. Too much emphasis has been placed upon formal education for children and very little upon helping adults master control of their skills.

A decision was made by the Band Councils in the Maritime Area, in co-operation with the Union of Indian Brotherhood and the Department of Indian and Northern Affairs, to seriously participate in a Band Council Training Programme in order to develop their human resources. The Programme would be available to Chiefs, Band Counsellors, Social Counsellors, Band Managers, and School Committee Members.

SOME BASIC CONCEPTS UNDERLYING THE PROGRAMME

Adult Education Experiential Model

(1) The learners are all adults who bring with them years of experiences. The emphasis is always upon direct experience of the learner, rather than upon vicarious experience of the facilitator.

(2) All learning goals come from the needs of the learners. All learners use themselves as the model from which they draw the information needed to build their curriculum of learning.

(3) The theory/knowledge content elements of the programme are not stressed, but "learning by doing" and "evaluating the doing" are considered the important issues.

(4) Experience and/or discovery needs to be shared. The learners must be able to share their reactions and observations with others so that they can secure feedback and thereby, confirm the learning. Therefore, group learning is the format offered.

(5) Reflection upon experiences and the practice of required skills is guided by experienced resource persons.

Competency Model

(1) The main purpose is to increase competency. This implies learning which is based on behavioral change. The emphasis upon skill development is more relevant to the learner than acquisition of academic knowledge or creation of theory.

(2) The learners each have different experiences and different starting places. As a result, the programme is individualized from the beginning. There is no competition between learners as each person is considered an individual with the right to their own pace of learning.

Evaluation

(1) Evaluation must be measurable and visually apparent to the group and/or the learner and/or the community.

(2) Because behaviors are modified in the process of "learning by doing", the latter portion of the training is open-ended so as to provide freedom for the learners to concentrate on acquiring skills they know they need to have but were unaware they needed at the onset of the programme.

(3) Terminal learning objectives and the learning process are always subject to the learners' revisions and/or modifications.

SOME PRINCIPLES OF TRAINING

(1) *Individuals must accept responsibility for their own learning*. Skills are more effectively acquired and used if people are encouraged to accept responsibility for their own learning. Learners participate by specifying what they need to know and what they need to learn to do.

(2) *Individuals must be free to have the experience of discovery*. The process of learning will be "doing" or experiential through laboratory situations. Learners will have experience upon which to reflect and make discoveries.

(3) *Individuals must have the right to make mistakes*. In a programme of skill development it is not usually possible to be successful at the first or second attempt. Mistakes *should* occur. Performance can be improved by evaluating mistakes.

(4) *Content areas must be evolutionary*. The basic content of a programme can be specified in the beginning, but it must always remain open enough to add new content as new needs arise.

OBJECTIVES OF THE TRAINING PROGRAMME

The primary objectives of the Indian Band Staff Training Programme are:

— to provide for the Maritime Indians of Canada learning experiences designed to enhance their skill development.

— to make available resources which will facilitate learning experiences.

— to provide an opportunity for native persons to secure an organized programme of personal and social development.

— to promote, encourage and reinforce continuous learning by native persons to become masters of their own destiny.

A DESCRIPTION OF THE PROCESS

In order for readers to better understand the Indian Band Staff Training Programme, I will use School Committee Members as an example and follow their development. Two learning environments were used in the training programme.

The first learning environment

The training programme began November 15, 1976 with a five-day learning event. Fifteen trainees lived together in a University residence and attended sessions from 9:30 a.m. to 4:30 p.m. with an hour and a half for lunch. The atmosphere was informal; learners met in a training room setting with comfortable lounge chairs. There were no "formal" lectures. Frequently small groups formed to work on specific tasks.

A week before the session began, a letter was sent to all the Band Council Offices in the Maritimes reminding school committee members of the upcoming sessions. They had the option to arrive the night before or the early morning before the first session.

The first morning was spent mainly on introductions, providing information about the town and discussing principles of the programme. These principles are constantly reinforced throughout all sessions as most learners are not accustomed to the fact that they are responsible for their own learning and that there is no "supreme authority".

In the afternoon, it was explained that they were going to design their own curriculum. This was met by: "That's ridiculous, none of us ever finished school!" "Are you kidding?" "I can't even spell curriculum." These remarks were accompanied by a lot of nervous laughter and some stony silences. The facilitators assured school committee members that by the end of the week they would have a curriculum designed by themselves.

The first task suggested by the facilitator was for the group to compile a list of what a School Committee *actually does*. The committees from the different reserves do many similar but also many different jobs. It was common to hear, "That's a good idea, we should try that at home."

The last hour of each day is spent either discussing a controversial subject, in order to better communication skills, or reflecting upon and stating what each person had felt that day. This first day only a few people spoke during the discussion hour. A common theme among speakers had to do with how important they felt it was to learn what each School Committee was doing on different reserves.

The second task the group worked on was what they thought a School Committee *should be doing*. For example, they had listed that school committees were responsible for school lunches, but no one thought that lunches should be their responsibility. However, they did think that they should be making sure that Mic-Mac legends were told in classrooms. The facilitator helped to elicit comments as to the role of school committee members but final decisions were left to the group.

After the above was finished, the group was asked to list what they thought they *needed to learn* in order to eliminate those demands they felt were not their responsibility and to accomplish those tasks they believed were a legitimate part of their job description.

One woman said, "I need to learn to talk better to the band counsellors so that I won't end up doing those lunches." Another person said, "Well, we have all those meetings, we have to know about meetings." It was also mentioned that in order for a new item to be offered in the schools, a proposal must be sent to Indian Affairs. Therefore, they needed to learn how to write proposals. Someone else realized that they would have to find people in the community who knew the Mic-Mac legends.

By Wednesday afternoon the group had developed a good deal of consensus regarding what they needed to learn. The facilitator offered his opinion that the group now had done the necessary research to write their curriculum the next day. It was important that learners were aware of the processes evolving, as learning takes place when people can reflect on the process. During all sessions there was a lot of positive reinforcement given to participants as to the fact that tasks were difficult and the group was succeeding excellently.

Thursday, the group examined and discussed, in detail, all items they had listed as needed to learn. For example, the question was raised as to what actually went into a meeting. After analyzing what happens in a meeting, the group listed the following as part of their curriculum: communication skills, parliamentary procedure, how to arrive at consensus, how to give a talk, how to write a report, and how to organize a meeting. Below is the complete curriculum designed by the school committee, with the various items weighted in order of priority:

Communication Skills
Consensus Training
Research Skills
How to Write a Letter
How to Motivate the Community
Proposal Writing
How to Organize an Effective Meeting/Workshop/Seminar
How to Write a Report
Parliamentary Procedure
Problem Solving & Decision Making Skills
How to Use Community Resources in Curriculum
Negotiating Skills
Interviewing Skills
How to Understand Bureaucracy

That afternoon, there were a few more people participating during discussion period. There was a feeling of a job well done. One man said, "If we can write our own curriculum, like all those college people, then we can learn anything."

I wish to mention, in particular, the experience of one woman whom I shall call Nancy. She had not spoken since everyone introduced themselves on Monday. She sat with her head down and her hands covering her mouth. She came over to me at break time on Thursday and while looking at the floor, said that she was looking forward to learning how to speak in public.

Friday mornings were devoted to evaluation. The facilitator re-explained that everyone there was a learner and we learned from each other's feedback. We wanted to be better at our jobs. What should we do to be better facilitators? How should the programme be changed to be a better programme? The feedback for the first Friday was all positive. This was expected, as at the beginning people are shy when it comes to voicing negative reactions. However, as time progressed, the group became more confident and trusting. By the next session, in February, three people were able to give such comments as: "We were doing too much listening on Tuesday." "I think you have to tell Jim to keep quiet, he doesn't listen to us."

The second learning environment

A twelve week period of field practice constituted the second learning environment. During this period participants completed an Action Plan. They had selected three skills upon which they wished to concentrate while at home. The object was to practice what they had tried during training sessions. A skill is only learned when one has become both competent and comfortable with it.

School committee members decided that for this first field work, they wanted to practice helping others assess their needs and set objectives. They realized they had done this while writing their curriculum.

When the group returned in February, two members from one reserve excitedly recited their experiences relating to the setting of objectives. They had interested three other people in becoming working committee members and the newly formed group had written their job description, listed their school committee goals, and had these signed by the Chief and Counsellors. It should be pointed out that these accomplishments are of vital importance to all school committees at this time as the latest governmental education policy calls for Indian control of Indian Education.[9]

Another incident which occurred during a field work period, (Feb.-May), concerned the development of a different skill. The group had decided that they needed to learn how to write a proposal. This is a difficult task — including researching, budgeting, forecasting, etc. When the training sessions about proposal writing were over, the group decided that they each would like to write a proposal as part of their action plan at home. One school committee member wrote her practice proposal for a playground for her reserve. She was so enthused while she was doing this work that she sent it to Indian Affairs. The response was very optimistic and the reserve is almost positive they will have a playground by the summer of 1977. Because of her proposal, there will be work for six students and two maintenance people.

CONCLUDING COMMENTS

It was, for me, a beautiful experience to watch and participate in the growth of people. For example, one of the skills on the curriculum of the school committee was how to negotiate a conflict. This involves, at one point, participants acting as mediators for others who are role-playing a case study.

The first person who volunteered to be a mediator was Nancy. Her development during the intensive communication skills training had been exciting to observe. Her hands no longer covered her mouth and she would look people in the face when she talked. She said she was still very nervous but she was enjoying being able to voice her opinions at meetings. She and the group felt that her self-confidence had grown amazingly.

There were many sessions on all facets of communication skills as the group had decided that this was a definite priority. I noticed in June that the last hour discussion period had changed considerably from September. Everyone was participating and people were often asking others for their opinions. Two members of the group now serve on the Indian Education Committee for the province.

The school committee will meet again after the summer as they petitioned Indian Affairs, Union of Indian Brotherhood, and their band counsellors to have their programme continued.

There are questions that can be raised about the continuation of the Indian Band Staff Training Programme. Are we training Indians to be white? Are we once more imposing our values upon another culture in the name of "this is good for you"? Are we training people to fit into "the system"?

The Maritime Indians come into constant contact with whites and have for hundreds of years. They already live in "the system" but with few benefits; they are treated as second-class children. *Since they are in an industrialized and technological society, they want to learn how to live in that world. They want to be able to choose what to accept and what to reject.* They taught white women and men the skills of survival when the whites arrived in their world and now think they should have the opportunity to learn the new skills of survival.

In the words of Programme Director Batdorf, "If enough adults develop to the point where they have high self-esteem and have mastered human relations and basic technical skills, they will be able to organize their resources sufficiently well to manage their own development and maintain their own value and cultural future."

NOTES

1. William Godwin, *Enquiry Concerning Political Justice and Its Influence on Morals and Happiness,* Toronto: The University of Toronto Press, 1946, Vol.2, p.272.

2. Robert Peers, *Adult Education,* London: Butler and Tanner Ltd., 1959, p. 250.

3. Max Stirner, *The False Principle of Our Education,* trans. by Robert Beebe, Colorado Springs: Ralph Myles, 1967, p.23.

4. See Joel Spring, *A Primer of Libertarian Education,* Montreal: Black Rose Books, 1975, p.25.

5. *Ibid.,* p.28.

6. *Ibid.,* p.31.

7. Luke Batdorf, *A Training Programme for Human Resource Development for Native Peoples,* Antigonish, Nova Scotia: Continuing Education Programme, St. Francis Xavier University, p.1.

8. *Ibid.,* pp.7-10.

9. See letter of Minister of Indian Affairs and Northern Development to President of the National Indian Brotherhood, February 2, 1973.

10. Batdorf, p.26.

SECTION VI

Educational Change and the Capitalist System

The four articles in this last section, like the Steinhause article, are focused upon ways in which practice and theory are unified in particular educational programmes. They all raise the questions of how much change and what kind of change can be incorporated within the present socio-economic order.

Some analysts argue that no major change is possible under the present capitalist system; others argue that waiting around for "revolution" is a futile waste of energy best directed in developing programmes which can be incorporated in the system. The problem with the latter course is that incorporation by the capitalist state may lead to cooptation, and that piecemeal reforms may in fact dampen demands for more deepseated change.

There is no easy solution to such problems. The papers in this section do, however, seek to address the issue. For Jim Harding, survival-related education must be developed for adults as well as the young. He points out that real education is not just a matter of preparing the young for a slot in the system. There may be no system at all unless food production, nuclear energy, and healthcare are brought under popular control. Harding also points out that present classroom instruction actually "educates" most people to be unaware of the real dangers which a corporate capitalist bureaucratic education causes. It is one of the merits of this article that Harding avoids the one-sided institutional approach of some Marxists by concretely relating the effects of the larger oppressive system to the psychological development of individuals within a community context.

The articles by David Hanson and Malcolm Garber are meant to be read together as they provide opposing answers to the questions concerning social change raised above. Hanson has been a participant in a particular programme of educational reform funded by the State, implemented to increase upward mobility of poor black and white ("minority/disadvantaged") high schoolers. Showing how requirements for admission to "Upward Bound" keep students in a perpetual "Catch 22" position (for example, they must be certified as both educated and therefore, educable, before being allowed to participate further in school learning), he typecasts this particular programme as typical of band-aid solutions in an unchanged socio-economic environment. In brief, Hanson is convinced these solutions constitute inadequate educational reform that is doomed to failure without fundamental change in the prevailing socio-economic arrangements of today's capitalism.

Garber provides contrast to Hanson's argument as he uses education to illustrate and advocate institutional innovation which falls short of Hanson's "tipping society over". Garber's argument, unlike most others in this volume, assumes continued existence of the current capitalism in the forseeable future and urges innovative reform as opposed to more radical social change. Given this assumption, we anticipate that many readers might find this article out-of-step with the major themes uniting this collection. However, Garber's argument makes it clear he shares our view that social change should be initiated by the residents of local communities in order to serve their needs and eliminate the wasteful inefficiency of professionally-oriented, self-perpetuating service bureaucracies. The key feature in his description of a family-based, community-oriented education project in the North York district of Toronto, is joint-evaluation by both community participants and professional programme administrators. Thus, Garber, like Steinhause, Harding and others in this volume, is strongly in favour of community-based, less professionalized adaptive change. This kind of change, based upon community involvement with professionals *on a voluntary basis*, is opposed to the enforced or directed state-sponsored bureaucratic programmes of change which end in stultifying local communities.

The final article by Chris Bullock attacks a notion of "progressive education" which remains tied to the present socio-economic order. Bullock supports Paulo Freire's Latin American developed approach that the Marxist educator must work with the life experience of students and demonstrate how their own lives are affected by the capitalist system. In other words, students are no longer seen merely as piggy banks collecting the coins of wisdom from above. Instead, the educator brings a coherent and unifying perspective, and this is applied to the experience of the students themselves as they engage in a dialogue with the educator. It is out of this dialogue that the potential for fundamentally changing the larger political economy may eventually be realized.

Making Education Relevant to the Issues of Survival

JIM HARDING

In pre-industrial societies the education of the young was linked directly to the survival activities of the community. In these societies educational activities stressed one's place within the social and natural world and the skills required for individual and communal continuity. As we discover the fundamental deficiencies of the existing industrial society,[1] we are beginning to realize how colonial are the images we have learned about these past cultures. It is no accident that while we are discovering the negative impact of industrial capitalism upon indigenous cultures throughout the world, we are also discovering that we have much to learn from the direct way that educational activities in these cultures dealt with matters of survival.

It will take time for people raised in industrial systems to fully grasp the significance of this past direct link between education and survival. As urbanization and centralized technology have removed more of us from direct knowledge of the land, the seasons and survival, we have all become somewhat presumptuous about our continuity as individuals and as a species. This is why there is the need for greater concern about the detached nature of today's educational system, and its inappropriateness for raising consciousness and generating activities that bear directly upon the issues of survival and development that humanity now faces.

We have all been taught to view education as a *personal* means for mobility within the capitalist economy. Such an individualistic perspective, and concern for collective, long-term survival have definitely become incompatible under the present system of education. The recognition of this incompatibility has been impeded by the influence of the middle class ideology of upward mobility. Yet, in spite of all the claims by tax collectors, people are realizing that the existing educational system *has not* challenged the system of class and caste in Canada or other capitalist societies.

Such inequality of educational opportunity was one of the issues that sparked social activism in the 1960s. But no matter how accurate was the criticism that education helps maintain a hierarchical society, the 1960s did not focus on the failure of education to address the issues of survival. There are several of these issues that result from the detachment of today's education. Is education today helping us understand what the industrial system is doing to the social and natural environment upon which we and our children's children depend for survival? Is education preparing us for a false future and, at the same time, indoctrinating us about a non-existent past? There is an urgency to such questions, for the rulers of this society continue to channel massive social resources into an educational system which has become historically irrational.

THE NEED FOR HEALTH EDUCATION

Some educationalists, especially those disillusioned with the bureaucratization of education, are starting to grapple with these questions. Many of these people have left educational institutions to organize alternatives. Some have been purged from the educational system. Some are hanging on in public school bureaucracies and multiversities while others have been drawn to the community education system which has grown so quickly in Canada and the U.S. in the 1970s.

If this general re-evaluation of educational goals is to have collective relevance there must be a systematic understanding of the pressing issues of survival. In particular, we need to consider: (1) the fundamental alteration of the system of food production and distribution in recent years; (2) the fundamental change in how pain and illness is being managed; and, (3) the present push by government and industry to tie this society to nuclear energy.

We could concentrate on other issues which are pressing in their own way. The above three issues all directly bear upon our individual and collective health, which is, after all, how our or any mode of survival can be directly evaluated. They therefore have a special relevance in re-evaluating the role of education. Clearly, a human culture and species whose food system alters too drastically may have its survival threatened. And there is growing evidence that the centralized food technology which has developed under corporate capitalism is leading to such a drastic alteration.[2] Also, the escalation in the production and consumption of prescription and other drugs including alcohol to manage the emotional and physical symptoms associated with rising economic and cultural stresses, has profound implications for our collective survival.[3] Finally, nuclear energy has frightening implications for our biological survival and threatens to make political institutions in industrial societies more and more totalitarian.[4]

These three issues relate to the main structural shift which has occurred in the economy in recent decades. This shift involves the new mechanization of labour which has become known publicly as "the technological revolution". The development of the mass, standardized educational system was a prerequisite for this so-called technological revolution. The term "technological revolution" is itself misleading, and the mass system of education tied to the research and development of the centralized food, drug and energy industries is greatly responsible for perpetuating such a conception. The term leaves a false impression that advances in knowledge alone have been the reasons for new methods of processing food, drugging the body, and generating electricity. It obscures the impact of the economic, military and political context within which these technological changes have been planned and designed. It totally ignores the point that alternative technologies would have, and still could be, developed in a different context.[5]

To begin to understand the origins and consequences of these industries it will be necessary to *unlearn* this pervasive and overriding bias in the education system. Most people who go through this system are not even aware of these issues of survival. Eating over-produced, carcinogenic food with poor nutrition value; depending upon pharmacological inventions for managing our emotional reactions to social and economic strife; and accepting the inevitability of nuclear energy, are all taken to be part of the present "way of life". They *are not issues* in the minds of most people. They are facts of life. And present education prepares people to accept them as facts, as given realities, rather than as issues over which we could assert control.

It is because present education does not treat these survival issues *as issues* that the existing technologies of the food, drug and energy corporations can be called totalitarian. What makes this totalitarian technology qualitatively different from past human techniques is the ability of the rulers of this society to make a complete population dependent upon a system of "survival" which is, at the same time, undermining the environmental and human conditions which support human and other habitats.[6] Since the mass education system has played a major role in legitimizing this technology it is not surprising that it is incapable, as a system, of enlightening us about the dangers of such corporate totalitarianism. It is because of this inherent limitation that we have seen such a growth of theories within educational and academic circles which propose technological determinism as the reason for the threat to our collective health and survival.[7]

EDUCATING OURSELVES FOR HISTORICAL OPTIONS

We will not be able to understand the origins and consequences of these totalitarian industries by focusing on the artifacts of this system any more than we would ever have gained perspective on our biological evolution by focusing on the existing anatomy of the human body alone. Technological artifacts and historical conditions are as interdependent as are species and their ecology.

We therefore require an historical analysis of the conditions that have given rise to these technologies. Such a historical approach has to fully understand the existing political economy, especially the role of the state in mass education and medicine.[8] The tendency towards total, standardized technologies does not come from the techniques themselves but from the increasing *monopolization* in the food, drug and energy industries.[9] It would be more accurate to call the so-called technological revolution a managerial revolution. It is a complete distortion of the nature of scientific activity to claim that the reason why more and more people are consuming harmful "food" is because the knowledge existed to refine flour, sugar and add various synthetic colours and other additivies to the food products. In actuality, such food technology was developed to stabilize the food commodity and expand the food market.[10]

Because it is possible to kill everyone using military applications of physical, chemical and biological methods does not mean that this should or will be done. Nor does it mean that the related knowledge of the material world would be responsible for our obliteration. The neutron bomb has not been developed because there exists the knowledge to do so. It has been developed because the military-industrial complex wants a nuclear weapon which will kill people but not property. It is the centralization of the economic system into a corporate empire which underlies the technologies of food, drugs and energy. And it is possible to develop alternative technologies, appropriate to the local needs of a population rather than the organizational needs of a corporation, by dismantling the world-wide corporate empire.[11]

THREE WAYS TO UNDERSTAND EDUCATIONAL IRRATIONALITY

To ever develop educational activities which can deal with the above issues of survival we have to fully understand how the present, irrational educational system has developed and is maintained. There are three general ways we can approach this task — the ideological, the structural-functional, and the strategic.

These three modes of analysis are reflected in the following questions: (1) How have the assumptions of liberalism in education counteracted the ability of people to understand the development of the corporate system of production and consumption? (2) How is the structure and function of education integrated into the corporate economy? and, (3) How can the contradictions within the existing educational system be a spark for progressive developments in education and the larger society? It is significant that we know a good deal about the first and second questions but very little about the third. This shows that our present knowledge is primarily critical (what is wrong) rather than strategic (what to do). It also indicates that strictly ideological and structural critiques can remain academic, while strategical analysis[12] can become political in an active sense.

THE LIMITATIONS OF ACADEMIC CRITICISMS

The emphasis on value-free science which developed during the post WW II cold war and educational boom came under growing criticism when the social movements of the 1960s gained political momentum. This occurred primarily when anti-war and anti-poverty militancy began to challenge the liberal ideology in mass education and people began to understand that the corporate system grew out of colonialism and was creating a new imperialism.

Once the false, value-free notion of scientific objectivity was shaken it was possible to begin to do research on the actual relationship between the structure of education and the corporate economy. Initially this research concentrated on the interlocking directors of education and business. Because of this emphasis, such criticism tended to reinforce a conspiracy theory. This shows the limitations of research with a focus on the formal structure of decision-making. Certainly mass education and the concentration of economic power under the multi-nationals have developed as a single historical process. And there have been government and industrial game-plans to achieve this structural integration, and these can be seen as "conspiracies". These game-plans, however, have taken place within the context of the overall centralization of the state and economy. The state and corporations now form a system, what is now being called *state capitalism*, and education has played a major role in cementing this new system. The fact that this system has internal contradictions between government and industry does not make it less of a system. It just points out that static models of social structures are not the way to understand historical changes.

Most investigations of the relations between education and the economy have unfortunately had such a static bias. This is partly because this research has been done by people trained in a system of education which compartmentalizes levels of problems and ritualizes methods of analysis through professional organizations and semantics. The initial structural research on education has expectantly mirrored such compartmentalization of both thought and language, even when the problem being addressed is critical of the educational system which creates such compartmentalization. Marxist ideology[13] has often been adopted as a way to overcome this compartmentalized training. This has sometimes led to the redevelopment of an appropriate Marxian methodology for contemporary conditions. More often, unfortunately, it has led to vulgar and mechanistic organizations and formulations.

DEVELOPING A STRATEGIC PERSPECTIVE OF EDUCATION

Rather than conspiracy theories and ideological clichés there is a need for the concrete analysis of concrete conditions. Such an analysis will have to view education as much more than what goes on in institutional settings. *The development of education as a formal and separate activity was the necessary condition for the integration of learning and teaching into the corporate realm. The rejection of this view of education is a precondition of any reversal of this and the development of educational activities which directly confront the issues of survival.*

Once education is reseen to be a concern of the community, not a monopoly of the state and corporations, an expanded understanding of the present irrational system of education is possible. With this expansion it becomes possible to see the way the social relations of the family, the school, the workplace, the office and the factory presently form an ideological and structural system. It therefore becomes possible to understand the function and impact of education on people's everyday lives.

There are four general areas we need to examine to gain this expanded, strategic perspective: (1) We need to evaluate the way pre-school experiences in the nuclear family can lower human resistance to corporate education. (2) We need to assess how our years in school remove our attention away from issues of collective survival and development. (3) We need to outline the shortcomings of past attempts at educational reform, whether they were freeschools or progressive university departments. (4) And, lastly, we need to outline the lessons we can draw from these above points for present projects in community and development education.

OUR OBSESSION WITH VERBAL DEVELOPMENT

The present educational system is not directly concerned about the impact of pre-school experiences on the child's later activities in the school. The main concern of educational authorities is that by the time children enter school they have learned to understand verbal instructions from the teacher. The concern is with social organization, not human development, and, as we shall see, the two goals are not at all complementary under the present system.

The overriding assumption of the educational system is that *formal language is the medium of education*. This is a very powerful and convincing assumption, accepted by many otherwise critics of present education. The overwhelming bias of this society towards verbal skills blinds most educationalists to the impact of early emotional development on later uses of language and thought. This is not surprising since it is the education system which has mass produced this verbal dimension. The ideology of liberalism treats all change brought about in this society by the concentration of corporate power as ''progress''. This has kept educationalists from understanding the implications of the verbalization of society. The alternative to this ideological view is to look at how verbal education actually functions in this society. To do this we have to look at the transitory role of the school between the family and the workplace in the human lifecycle under capitalism.

The separation of education from physical survival, which came with industrialism, meant that the child was no longer being prepared for work by the extended family. This became the function of the first state school. In spite of all the clichés about education being for self-fulfillment and creativity, the school's fundamental role has always been to socialize the child for the workplace and the State (e.g. war). Often the cultural heritage of the child has had to be overcome by the school so that the person can be made to function more smoothly within the workforce. This is true whether it is immigrant children or children of indigenous ancestry who are being enculturated by the school system.[14]

An institution under capitalism does not survive if it cannot adjust its form to meet new marketplace functions. The authoritarian, hierarchical organization of the school directly prepares the child to work within a particular stratum in the hierarchical workplace. This relationship is blatant in vocational schools where lower class students have to punch a time-clock as they enter school.[15] But we should not underestimate the many more subtle ways that this early internalization of social relations can act as a lifelong social control. Critics of education have tended to look at the content of instruction without seeing that the social form of the school acts as a pervasive control on the child. The fact that so many critics of the school concentrate on the verbal dimension of school socialization, and totally miss the nonverbal controls (the structure of time, of seating, of classes, etc.), shows how successful the school has been in integrating people into the functional dimension stressed under capitalism.

The hierarchical organization of capitalist work is, then, the main structural reason why the present school system emphasizes verbal perception. People have to be taught to take and comprehend orders to make a mass system of production, distribution and consumption work. Without the school teaching people the three R's, the capitalist organization of work would be in chaos. To perform as an efficient worker there is the need to internalize the symbolism of instructions of the corporate world. The school system is where people obtain their first systematic experience working passively in a corporate organization. If school has its desired effect, corporations don't have to focus on the socialization of workers. If it works, mass education teaches people to "be their own boss".[16]

This paternalism is so deeply imbedded in the school system that deviation from it in any form — to assert a female, ethnic or a working class identity — is suspected of being a symptom of psychological illness. The "good student" is the person who complies with all the nonverbal and verbal instructions about how to act, and performs well within those constraints. The student who attempts to expand beyond the institutionalized bounds is said to have a "behaviour problem".[17] The growing use of drugs on school children labelled in this way shows how far authorities in this society are willing to go to preserve their impersonal institutions.[18]

The school's emphasis on verbal performance to the neglect of nonverbal feelings and thoughts actually undermines the ability of people to develop positive nonverbal resources. Instead of learning to communicate on many levels — which would make the child more of a social individual — negative nonverbal habits are learned. Self putdowns and competitive projections of these upon others — all the stereotyping of sex, race, class and age that pervade this society — presently dominate the nonverbal life of the child. With its emphasis on blood, gore, status and heroes, television, for the most part, just perpetuates this. It is in this sense that the school (and television) presently ensures that the interests of the corporate economy are served even by our unconscious processes.

Any strategy of change which is concerned with liberating this human potential will have to fully consider ways to counter and prevent this deep level of socialization. Most approaches to resensitizing our nonverbal perception have not been linked to a general critique of the institutional context within which the initial desensitization occurs, and many of them are actually techniques to try to reintegrate people into a "participatory" corporation.[19] The fact that many dogmatic critics of the corporate economy have uncritically accepted their socialized obliviousness to nonverbal perception only goes to further show how effective the educational system has been.

CORRECTING OUR THEORIES OF LANGUAGE

The incentives of the educational system for verbal performance, and cognitive processes that relate to these verbal skills,[20] keep our children from developing a healthy integration of feeling, thought and language. And the dominant theories of language development actually ignore the child's potential for this integration. Typically they don't even accurately describe the role of feeling in the development of thought and the implications of this for the way language is learned and used. Rather than being a theory of the real problems of language development, the dominant theories today are really ideological statements which support the existing oppression of children.[21]

The real problems of language development can be shown by the way that the different emotional treatment of boys and girls affects their respective language development. Boys receive far less touching, they are picked up less and later when crying, and held further from the body.[22] After receiving such treatment during their formative years it is not surprising that so many men end up emotionally constipated. It is not that men don't have feelings, which is a false stereotype some feminists have reinforced. *Rather, it is that boys and men are systematically trained, through physical deprivation, to keep feelings inside.* The greater dependency of men on alcohol to release feelings can certainly be traced to these early experiences and their reinforcement throughout school and work.[23] The tendency to talk abstractly about personal experience and to intellectualize feelings, which is not exclusive to but is certainly widespread among men, is the end result of the early separation of thought and language from feelings.

EARLIER ANTECEDENTS OF EMOTIONAL DEVELOPMENT

The impact of emotional development upon language development actually goes back much further. The growing use of medical technology during pregnancy and birth has a direct impact on the earliest emotions of the newborn child. In most modern hospitals babies are removed from their biological environment immediately after birth. Though we know that touch is a basic human need, and that extreme deprivation can lead to death, the routine efficiency of hospitals systematically deprives most children of this need right at birth.[24]

The common belief that the child does not have emotional needs at birth, and the predominance of hospital rules over human needs, both relate to the bias towards verbal, institutionalized rationality which has been generated throughout the whole society with the aid of mass education. Bureaucracies typically operate as if humans are not emotional beings. If your feelings are hurt by the impersonal standardization, it's a sign of your, not the system's, weakness.[25] Rules which are rational from an administrative stance are assumed to also be humane. But time is not taken to honestly check this out. Since the baby can't talk, or, to be more accurate, since the baby's crying is not understood to be the first attempt at communication, the baby's needs aren't taken to be real. The baby is treated as though discomfort can be managed rather than expressing real, evolving personal needs which need to be met in a personal way.

This rupture in the child's biological continuity with the mother is the first assault on the emotional integrity of the person in this society. *It is the first act to socialize an asocial individual*. As the children are ripped from their biological web, lined up and diapered as if in a factory, they are *forced* to learn to stand apart and to hold back energy from others. This self-destructive form of adaptation begins at the moment of birth under the present social organization. With each experience that further assaults their emotional and social integrity, children become closer to being the kind of human who can separate decisions from consequences, to think without feeling, and to act without intent. They become more and more like the kind of person needed to run the compartments of the corporate society.

There are many other ways that the early experiences of the fetus and child establish the pattern upon which the detached educational system builds. The low nutritional quality of mass processed food and some drugs which get prescribed during pregnancy have been shown to have a direct impact on the child's fetal development.[26] Many occupational and environmental health hazards have been shown to be detrimental to both male and female reproduction. Past and present nuclear testing has had a horrendous impact on the unborn, and the nuclear energy system now being planned by the pro-corporate state has tremendous implications for the future of human reproduction.

The fact that people are allowing these things to be done to the newly born and unborn shows how resigned, uncritical and well behaved most of us have learned to be by the time we leave school. The fact that they are happening on the present scale shows how child negligence has become institutionalized into the corporate society. The added fact that groups *who totally ignore* the systematic oppression of children and adults are sometimes accepted as the spokespeople for the rights of the unborn, shows how compartmentalized are our feelings about life and death.[27]

MISEDUCATION IN THE NUCLEAR FAMILY

Once we face up to the emotional treatment of our children we can begin to see how formal schooling is just one step of a process already well underway. Before school age arrives the nuclear family has maintained an emotional assault on newborn children's sensitivities,[28] preparing them to enter a formalistic, insensitive school system already greatly desensitized.

Educationalists of various persuasions have assumed that the child is not engaged in significant learning until he or she enters school. When preschool influences are acknowledged, the emphasis is placed on the type of parental guidance and not on the direct experience of the child. This again shows the concern with authority roles rather than the living, breathing, curious child. Such an approach totally ignores the pervasive impact of the *social field* created by the nuclear family upon the child's perception and feeling about him or herself in the world.

Even such a child-centred psychologist as Piaget initially upheld such a limited perspective. Such a view, typical of all those who rigidly accepted Freud's dichotomy between the pleasure seeking of the child and the reality testing of the adult, totally failed to evaluate the social dimension of the child's pre-verbal activity.[29]

The form of family (e.g. nuclear, extended, communal, etc.) establishes the social field within which pregnancy, birth and early emotional development occurs. In the present nuclear family, language and thought are systematically divorced or separated by the polarized sex roles and the related division of labour into housework and factory or office work. This internalization of an inherently polarized social situation happens in a different way for boys and girls, but there is a common fragmented reality. Rather than comparing, idealizing or denigrating male or female socialization it seems more helpful to pinpoint this common source of the oppression of all children.

In the nuclear family both sexes identify with both parents and each sex therefore faces a unique conflict making future transitions from home to school, school to work, and work to home. The girl may have had more continuity from childhood to adulthood when the traditional role of mother was stable because she was socialized from the beginning in the home. The emotional price for such traditional continuity, however, was high.[30] Now that women are going into the factory and office in large numbers they face new disorientation because they have lacked a female model for full "participation" and exploitation in the workplace.[31]

Though the boy has this model in his father, boys never experience the model directly since they are also at home. The male role in the nuclear family is therefore also inherently precarious. Also some men are now going through a *reverse socialization* and becoming interested in domestic life and caring for children. There is an element of self-interest in doing this since this involvement with children opens up an emotional dimension which has been constricted since early life. But this transition is stressful, nevertheless, since it typically has to be undertaken without positive models from the boy's past.[32]

The difficulty we all face making the transitions from home to work, or work to home, greatly result from the isolation of the nuclear home from the neighbourhood and community. The sex roles learned in the isolation of the nuclear family separate feelings and language from each other for both sexes. Because of this the child ends up unable to connect feelings and words, usually more in touch with one or the other. This shows how later introverted and extroverted characteristics can be linked to the child's early social field. In either case the person, whether boy or girl, will have difficulties connecting private experience and public behaviour.

Our emotional *integrity* comes from this *integration* of internal feelings and external relationships. We constantly confirm or disconfirm our experience to ourselves by communicating fully or miscommunicating with others. The isolation of the home from school and school from work constantly jeopardizes our ability to communicate fully and develop into complete, social individuals. This has such a fundamental effect on the later development of the child that it is worth discussing it from the postulated point of view of the child.[33]

THE PHENOMENOLOGY OF LANGUAGE DEVELOPMENT

From the beginning of one's life the child is trying to figure out the meaning of his or her bodily feelings. At the same time the child is struggling to figure out the meaning and intention of the words spoken in the home. The steady integration of the meaning of experienced feelings and behaviour associated with words is the healthy ideal which can not be fully realized without a perceptive human environment. If there is an authoritarian role system in the home, the child's struggle to bring feeling and language together, into a positive thought process, can easily be undermined.

If language is used to maintain and manipulate a family order rather than to facilitate an environment which supports human development, the child's thought can easily become separated into privatized feeling and conforming words. With time, aging and a continuation of this splitting, feelings can become so privatized that they are unconscious. With each added reinforcement of such a *schizoid* socialization, the chance of a person ever partaking in the kind of play or other activity which will evoke these privatized bodily feelings into conscious experience will decline.[34]

Someone whose emotional make-up has become fragmented from this schizoid socialization is unlikely to be sensitive to the needs of children to integrate their earliest feelings and language. This shows how the nuclear family perpetuates itself at a cultural level. In the extreme this self-perpetuation is shown by the tendency of children who are abused to also abuse their children.

CHANGING OUR THEORIES AS WE CHANGE OUR PRACTICE

Once we begin to understand how early socialization prepares people to adapt to the miseducation of school, and become detached from the issues of survival, then *the task of changing education also becomes a task of humanizing the social relations of the home*. As more people become aware of this need, and its relation to educational and social change, we are also recognizing the misconceptions in the existing theories of maturation, development and the family.[35]

Past ways of understanding the split between the privatized self and public roles have either attributed the emotional fragmentation of the child to "human nature" or have looked for changes in the *"self"* or the *"role"* as the way to overcome this problem. The Freudian approach, especially in its vulgar form,[36] tends to do the former and therefore ends up as an apology for the present organization of the home, school, office and factory. Sociologists and psychologists who use a functional mode of analysis also tend towards this apology by seeing personal salvation in social conformity. And vulgar Marxists, who think they are critical of the Freudians and functionalists, often end up with a similar obsession with (a new) social conformity because they also ignore *the experience of the child in the system*.[37] And the self psychologists who focus on the perceptual dimension of experience tend to ignore the social field and, as such, encourage people to withdraw rather than transform social relations as a means to meet their deeper, suppressed needs.

If we are to be able to trace the continuity between early emotional experiences and miseducation we will need a much more inclusive perspective than any of the above. Rather than looking at only the organism or the person, or the environment or social field, we need to learn to understand the organism as a living person developing within a particular social field, *as a system*.[38] This ecological view applies as much to social systems as to the natural systems on which they depend. The person, as an organism who has developed in a particular way in a particular social environment, carries into the future the potential of recreating that same social environment. As we develop we directly internalize the quality of the natural and social world in which we live. What happens to one generation because of its emotional fragmentation in the nuclear family is easily, almost "naturally", done to the next generation. This continuity is of course not static or predetermined solely by past socialization. It is also determined by the existing place of the home in the economy. Parents who have been emotionally constricted by earlier *sex and family roles* and have this damage maintained and increased by constricted *work roles* are not likely to alter the cycle.

The extensive influence of behaviourist psychology in education greatly explains the inability of educationalists to grasp the qualitative significance of this early experience. The growth of phenomenological approaches to education, to counteract the past emphasis on behaviour, has helped to balance this picture. But an ecological approach, which deals at both the level of experience and behaviour, and does not analyse the person separately from the social field in which he or she develops, will be needed to grasp the continuities and discontinuities from home to school to office and factory.

Such a perspective will be required so that progressive interventions can be taken at various points in the contemporary life cycle. The belief that education can only be changed by changing the school, or changing the economy, is contradicted by everything we have learned about human development. Preschool socialization in the nuclear family prepares people for their passive role in school. Emotional fragmentation and the learning of detached uses of language have already disconnected self-expression from the self-determination of the child so most are ready to take instructions from the teachers by grade one. After completing school people are prepared for compartmentalized tasks in the corporate economy, often without having to be instructed. Interventions to counteract this passivity, to prevent it from occurring and to build a society that can meet deeper human needs, including the need for freedom, obviously have to occur at *all* points in this system.

THE SHORTSIGHTEDNESS OF EDUCATIONAL EXPERIMENTS

Once the subtle but pervasive influences of early emotional and language development are acknowledged it becomes clearer why the various attempts at "free schools" did not have the instant success that many desired. The movement towards unstructured education in the 60s was based on the half-truth that the external, imposed structure is what keeps us from engaging in a relevant, meaningful education. What it did not admit was that the repressive structure is also internal, backed by years of habit formation.[39] Calling something "free" because it is unstructured is an example of the unembodied, detached use of language which has been learned through corporate schooling. It is not a reflective use of language that tries to understand how changing experience involves social changes.[40]

With this one-sided view of alternative education, it is not surprising that so many people who became disillusioned by the lack of instant success in the free schools turned to a political or religious ideology. Rather than reflecting on the shortcomings of the experiments and their assumptions, and trying to connect personal and political processes to create an inter-subjective and truly co-operative consciousness, many people have further abstracted their external focus into an ideological rhetoric. Rather than learning historical lessons from their personal history, always trying to relate feelings, thoughts and words so that authentic commitments could develop, many have turned to a god or a revolution with a big R for personal salvation. In the process they have abandoned the potential for collective action based on principled reflection and criticism.

Now, in the late 1970s, many people have become active in community and development education. We should not remake the mistake made in the 1960s and romanticize these attempts to bring education into the community. Nor should we dismiss these attempts because they often occur within community colleges which were set up to serve the needs that the corporate economy and state has for a para-professional stratum of workers.[41] Rather, we should recognize that the contradictions within the present economy and society are also within educational institutions. For one thing there is an inherent contradiction between basic community needs and the strategies of the multi-national corporations. Community-based education therefore has the potential of helping to catalyze an informed political community which can begin to resist these corporate forces. Facing up to the issues of survival, and facilitating education about the food, drug and energy issues so that learning becomes linked to collective survival and development can do this in a concrete way.

STARTING TO OVERCOME THE CONTRADICTIONS OF COMMUNITY EDUCATION

To do this, we will have to face up to the major contradictions within community education. First, we will have to work to overcome the tendency we have all learned in our schooling to polarize the form and content of learning.

Universities tend to become fixated on content and lack insight into the impact of the form of ideas and presentation, and of the social context, on the consequences of education. Many people in community colleges have reacted against this ivory tower mentality and attempted to personalize and humanize learning through training in life-skills, sensitivity and assertiveness, and other workshops. In the process, however, they have often abandoned the search for *methods which integrate this perception of form with the development of concrete knowledge about the social world*. Such an integration of changes in form and a renewed development of relevant, critical knowledge, which includes knowledge of alternatives to the present, is needed to fully overcome existing miseducation.

Second, we need to work to overcome the other tendency we have all learned in our past schooling, to polarize theory and practice. Universities typically separate theory from practice and tend to make ideas and theories into things. Such a reification helps create the elitist professionalization of this society. And it is a way to obscure vested interests of some professions (most people in law, medicine and engineering) and the corporations, and the potential conflicts between students being trained and their later corporate bosses.

Community colleges have tended to do the reverse of universities and to fetishize practice. Since state money has been invested in colleges to train a lower-paid stratum of para-professionals this is not surprising. But the potential of developing relevant critical theory[42] out of front-line practices nevertheless remains. There is much in the direct experience of students with working class backgrounds, and the economic conditions that they will face, that suggests they may surprise the educational planners.

Third, we need to overcome the self-defeating polarization between personal and political matters that we have all learned through our schooling. The university teaches people that knowledge is apolitical *at the same time as it trains people to work to carry out the political strategies of the corporations*. It separates knowledge from the needs of the community through its appeal to such so-called professional objectivity. As such, people come to believe that they are dependent upon the experts and cannot develop and translate knowledge directly to meet their needs. This myth has been so ingrained in us that many otherwise progressive people set themselves up as *counter experts* for the people and also perpetuate the view that knowledge can only be used to serve a political organization and not people in the community directly.[43]

Convincing people that they have to keep their personal problems to themselves, and use education only to deal with public issues, means that they *can't* link personal problems to public issues. It means that people will deny personal needs in favor of abstract ideology or become self-indulgent and politically disinterested. It means that any solidarity developed will be based on personal denial rather than common fulfillment.

These needs of individuals have to be addressed directly if education is not to remain the monopoly of corporations and groups that have set themselves up as counter-elites. The depoliticization of the population results from the privatization of consciousness, and traditional "political" activities primarily reinforce this depoliticization because personal and political concerns cannot be integrated through them. Education about the issues of survival can begin to address these personal and political needs but this cannot happen until self-interest is liberated from the confines of the individualism of the corporate economy. The problem is not self-interest itself, but the inability of people to connect and conceptualize their self-interest in a collective way.[44]

Collective consciousness cannot come from teaching revolutionary morality or abstract class consciousness. It can only grow out of principled educational activities which overcome the polarization of the personal and the political in everyday life. The choice of issues around which such activities can grow has to be consistent with the overall process. Teaching people ideologies is by definition in contradiction to such a process. Confronting the issues of survival, at all levels, in a renewed community education can at least start us in the right direction.

NOTES

1. The term "industrial society" is often used as a way to obscure important historical, structural and ideological differences between capitalist and socialist societies. Though this issue is complicated by the development of state capitalist societies, I want it to be clear that I am talking about education within industrial capitalism in this article.

2. The most dramatic example of this is the refining of sugar and the qualitative change this has brought to the diet of the whole population. There is amassing evidence that the increasing consumption of refined sugar and carbohydrates is directly linked to a host of contemporary diseases. See T.L. Cleave, *The Saccharine Disease*, Bristol: Keats, 1975; J. Yudkin, *Sweet and Dangerous*, New York: Bantam, 1973; and William Dufty, *Sugar Blues*, New York: Warner Books, 1975.

3. We are finally beginning to understand how industrial capitalism undermines the health of the population thereby creating yet another profitable market. For a discussion of the pharmaceutical industry see *Who Needs The Drug Companies?*, London: Haslemere, 1976.

4. There are a number of helpful sources on the dangers of nuclear energy. See Fred H. Knelman, *Nuclear Energy: The Unforgiving Technology*, Edmonton: Hurtig,

1976; Denis Hayes, *Nuclear Power: The Fifth Horseman*, Washington: World Watch Institute, 1976; *The Nuke Book*, Ottawa: Pollution Probe, 1977, and the bibliographies in these books and pamphlets. I still know of no source that has adequately integrated the critique of the environmental health implications of nuclear energy into an anti-imperialist perspective.

5. David Dickson, *Alternative Technology*, London: William Collins & Sons, 1974 and E. Schumacher, *Small Is Beautiful*, New York: Harper & Row, 1975.

6. Apparently George Orwell saw the loss of control over one's food as the critical beginning of totalitarianism. The struggle against corporate totalitarianism is a struggle to regain social control over the production of food.

7. The best known argument along this line is Jacques Ellul, *The Technological Society*, New York: A. Knopf, 1964. It would be a mistake to dismiss the problem of technological domination even though his method reflects the reified position of education and theory in industrial societies.

8. The dramatic growth in government expenditures in Canada, now 40 per cent of the GNP is mostly a result of mass education and medicine. In both cases these government activities act primarily as infrastructure for corporate activities although there are some signs of a growing contradiction between government and industry over matters of educational relevance, prevention of illness, etc. See V. Navarro, *Medicine Under Capitalism,* New York: Prodist, 1976; and I. Illich, *Limits to Medicine,* Toronto: McClelland & Stewart, 1976.

9. The monopolization in the food, drug and energy industry is now extensive. See references under notes 3, 4, and F. Moore Lappé and J. Collins, *Food First: Beyond The Myth of Scarcity*, Boston: Houghton Mifflin, 1977; D. Mitchell, *The Politics of Food*, Toronto: Lorimer, 1975.

10. The most dramatic example of this is the global push of multi-nationals to get infants off breast milk and onto bottle milk. By severing this biological link capitalism creates a profitable baby food industry and, at the same time increases demand for products of the pharmaceutical industry because of increased infections and malnutrition. See Lyn Dobrin, "Infant Formula Abuse", *Food Monitor,* P.O. Box 1975, Garden City, N.Y. 11539, September 1977. This and related issues have also been discussed in *New Internationalist,* 113 Atlantic Ave., Brooklyn, N.Y. 11201.

11. An historical perspective on the present social structure shows the continuity of feudal and capitalist social forms. The over-emphasis of a class analysis of capitalism often obscures the corporate tendencies of the system and the analogies with feudal forms of social control.

12. I am using the term "strategic" instead of "dialectical" since the latter is often used to proselytize a deterministic form of historical change. This is particularly true of Stalinist and neo-Stalinist forms of "Marxism".

13. It may seem like a paradox that Marxist ideas have become reified into an ideology which can mask class interests in much the same way as Marx defined ideology. As long as the conditions persist which create the need for illusions, revolutionary ideas also risk this fate. An anti-dogmatic approach to educational change will need to constantly develop ways to prevent this from occurring.

14. I had not realized the brutality of this function of the school until I left middle class circles and heard personal stories about the way the RCMP was used to take Doukhobor and Indian children from their parents to begin this forced assimilation into the corporate marketplace. Many people shocked by such stories about educational colonialism from other countries still have not recognized that the Canadian educational system was built by similar tactics as those used on children of indigenous, conquered people and immigrant workers throughout the world. See my article "Political Repression in Canadian History, Part 1", *Our Generation*, June 1969, Vol. 6, No. 4, pp. 103-112.

15. See my article "Two Winnipeg Schools", *Student Power and the Canadian Campus*, eds. Tim and Julyan Reid, Toronto: Peter Martin, 1969. Also see S. Bowles and H. Gintis, *Schooling In Capitalist America*, New York: Basic Books, 1976; and the good critique of the non-class view of school authoritarianism by Sherry Gorelick, "Undermining Hierarchy", *Monthly Review*, October 1977, Vol. 29, No. 5.

16. I do not want to be misinterpreted here as being anti-intellectual. There would be a totally different effect if learning to read and write was directly related to personal and social self-determination.

17. The oldest son of a friend had this put on his report card in the early grades. He had been used to being treated as an equal among adults and expected the same treatment from teachers when he started school. He had to learn how to survive across this double standard, before the authoritarian pressures he felt so confused him that indeed he would have had a "behaviour" and an "experience" problem.

18. There is growing awareness that what usually gets labelled as a clinical problem among children is actually a combined problem of nutrition and oppressive home and school environments. But, instead of changing these environments, the drugging of the children continues.

19. This criticism applies to most of the group therapy approaches linked with the human potential movement. This is partly because of a misapplication of the ideas and techniques, notably in Gestalt therapy, and because the actual approaches were conceived in an apolitical manner. Approaches with potential political relevance are bioenergetics, an outgrowth of the Reichian tradition in psychotherapy, and some aspects of assertiveness training.

20. There are clearly cognitive processes that complement nonverbal perception. These are typically stereotyped as being the privilege of the few who become artists, but such potential exists throughout the population. The public artist is only the tip of the iceberg of creativity — the one who has kept cognitive imagination alive in spite of the school system.

21. I am thinking of all behavioristic theories of language. (See the writings of Noam Chomsky for a helpful critique of the theory of language perpetuated by behaviorist psychology.) I also think Piaget's theory is being used in this way, especially when it turns into a mechanistic theory of the correct stages of cognitive development, something that can easily cover over ideological and structural forces acting on the child.

22. This study was mentioned by W. Farrell the author of *The Liberated Man* (New York: Random House, 1975) during a recent television interview.

23. It is generally known in the addiction field that men tend towards the drug alcohol whereas women tend towards the psychotropic (mood-modifying) prescription drugs. The former can be seen as an attempt to release pent-up feelings while the latter can be seen as an attempt to control such feelings as anger which result from frustration and isolation in the home.

24. See A. Montague, *Touching*, New York: Columbia University Press, 1971, and F. Leboyer, *Birth Without Violence*, New York: Alfred A. Knopf, 1975.

25. W. Ryan, *Blaming the Victim*, New York: Vintage, 1971.

26. Poor food during pregnancy has been shown to detrimentally affect later mental potential. Also, some drugs as common as antihistamines, which get prescribed to women before they know they are pregnant, have been linked to increased birth defects.

27. The controversy over birth control and abortion has not yet been generally conceived in a progressive way. Those who have favored abortion on demand tended to be uncritical of chemical and technological approaches to birth control which have proven to be harmful and dangerous. Those who opposed abortion have tended to be unconcerned about the oppression of women and children here and in the developing countries. Clearly this controversy has reflected the degree to which we have become alienated from our bodies and life around us by both commodity-consumer fetishisms and an authoritarian moralism. There is some sign that we are going beyond this with the growing use of the mucous (Billings) method of birth control. See P. Thyma, *The Double Check Method of Natural Family Planning*, Fall River, Mass.: Married Life Information, 1976.

28. In no way is this indictment of the nuclear family to be taken as a criticism of the struggle of parents, especially those who face severe economic problems, to maintain a family. It is rather an indictment of the present social organization of the family and society which systematically undermines the potential of child and parent alike.

29. The best discussion I have found of this is L.S. Vygotsky, *Thought and Language*, Boston: MIT Press, 1962.

30. The overproportionate prescribing of central nervous system drugs to young married women is an indication of the deep dissatisfaction with this situation. See J. Harding, N. Wolf and G. Chan, ''A Socio-Demographic Profile of People Being Prescribed Mood-Modifying Drugs In Saskatchewan'', Regina: Alcoholism Commission of Saskatchewan, November 1977.

31. As women have moved from the home into waged work their rate of smoking has greatly increased. This may result from use of this stimulant to maintain the momentum of secretarial and other pressured work that most working women now face. For a discussion of changing rates of smoking see, *The Health Consequences of Smoking*, Washington: U.S. Department of Health, Education and Welfare, 1975.

32. Because of this incongruence between the early and later experience of both sexes, relations between the sexes presently lack cohesion and reciprocity. The sexes are like ships passing in the night. The inability of both men and women to find a personal common language, which transcends stereotyping, is not a

problem of communication so much as the result of having very different experiences.

33. Social criticism based on sex role has its place but it can easily lead people to the false conclusion that what is needed is another form of programmed socialization.

34. Maurice Merleau-Ponty's writings on the phenomenology of the body add a necessary dose of reality to discussions of child development. Also useful is R.D. Laing's *Politics of the Family*, Toronto: CBC, 1969 and Arthur Janov's *The Primal Revolution*, New York: Simon and Schuster, 1974.

35. The best synthesis of these criticisms that I know is E. Zaretsky, *Capitalism, The Family and Personal Life*, Winnipeg: Canadian Dimension Pamphlet.

36. For a discussion of vulgarizations of the Freudian perspective see H. Marcuse, *Eros & Civilization*, New York: Vintage, 1962, pp. 217-51.

37. Sartre once commented that "Today's Marxists are concerned only with adults; reading them, one would believe that we are born at the age we earn our first wages. They have forgotten their own childhoods." See J.P. Sartre, *Search For A Method*, New York: Alfred A. Knopf, 1963.

38. A good starter on a systems orientation to human problems is G. Bateson, *Steps Towards an Ecology of Mind*, New York: Ballantine, 1975.

39. The fact that Freire has this "dialectical" view is what makes his theory of education so potent. People in the industrial societies are finally realizing that this dialectical view is as appropriate here as in the more colonized world. See Paulo Freire, *Pedagogy of the Oppressed*, New York: Herder, 1970.

40. I tried to tackle this problem when I was a resource person in a B.C. free school in the late 60s. See "Being In The World at Knowplace", *Free School Journal*, Vancouver: 1970, Vol. 1, No. 1. A.S. Neill discussed the same problem in his *Freedom Not License,* New York: Hart, 1966.

41. Though I agree with Fred Pincus' structural critique in his article "Tracking In Community Colleges", also in this anthology, I think he tends toward the kind of sociological criticism and reductionism which ignores the potential for altering the planned effect of community college programs.

42. Critical theory in the university has more often than not created a massive communication gap between the way criticisms are conceptualized and the common sense of the people who experience oppression and exploitation. While there clearly is a need for a new level of abstract thought to be able to criticize state capitalism, this is no justification of left wing theoretical elitism. A U.S. journal, *Telos*, more than any other, reflects this ungrounded critical theory.

43. Elsewhere I have tried to show how this counter-productive notion of political leadership directly arises out of the kind of education people get within the capitalist division of labor. See "Dogmatic Materialism", *the chevron*, Waterloo: Student newspaper, March 26, 1976.

44. Polarizing individual self-interest and social altruism has been the error of all Christian-influenced forms of socialism. This tendency to build collectivity upon personal denial can be seen in the Canadian New Democratic Party (NDP) and left wing vanguard parties alike.

Catch-22 in Band-Aid Land

DAVID HANSON

On May 17, 1954, Chief Justice Earl Warren delivered the majority opinion in the Brown v. Board of Education case: "We conclude that in the field of public education the doctrine of 'separate but equal' has no place. Separate educational facilities are inherently unequal."[1] For the silent 1950s this proved to be the thunderbolt that preceded the skirmishes over desegregation in the South. These events provided an interesting backdrop to the passionate 1960s. The New Frontier of Kennedy and the Great Society of Johnson brought forth legislation that was to be the tool for equalizing educational opportunities. Programs were begun and the Department of Health, Education and Welfare became a full partner in governmental activity. The question for the 1970s seems to center around what has been wrought.

The greatest attention in the 1960s was focused on adapting education to the needs of that group of people that is commonly labeled "minority/disadvantaged". Specifically, this meant paying more attention to the interests of Blacks, Chicanos, and native Americans. Along with government programs, a concomitant shift was advised in the area of curriculum content. This sort of change, commonly subsumed under the rubric of "awareness", sought to calm some rather restive minorities and convince them that the white majority did indeed recognize that Blacks, Chicanos, and Indians had a heritage and had contributed to the strength, wealth, and progress of the nation.

It has been assumed, and more often assumed by the middle class than any other class, that education is the key to advancement in American society. In a very limited sense, it is. Realistically though, this represents only wishful thinking. The upper class sees through this with an air of "comfortability" and the lower class disregards the notion in different ways. The working class, the middle income group that does not usually espouse traditional middle class values, identifies with this idea in a qualified manner (i.e., the son or daughter should finish their high school education and then move as quickly as possible into the working world). The upshot of this is that a substantial portion of the population could and can agree with the seemingly liberal plan of opening up opportunities for "minority/disadvantaged" students, recent complaints about reverse discrimination notwithstanding.

By 1965, the way was clear for the Higher Education Act. Section 417, Subpart 4 of that act deals with "Special Programs For Students From

Disadvantaged Backgrounds''. Authorization is granted to "carry out a program designed to identify qualified students from low-income families, to prepare them for a program of postsecondary education . . . ."[2] Reading further on, activities authorized to advance this purpose are such "programs, to be known as Upward Bound . . . which are designed to generate skills and motivation necessary for success in education beyond high school . . . and in which enrollees from low-income backgrounds and with inadequate secondary school preparation participate on a substantially full-time basis during all or part of the program."[3]

In terms of operation, Upward Bound deals with tenth, eleventh, and twelfth graders. During the academic year, tutoring in some form is offered to participants. The project that employs me provides one tutoring session each week that lasts for two hours. In the summer, Upward Bound students attend six weeks of school where they take secondary level core and elective courses. These courses are intended to provide remedial and skill-building help and at the same time afford the student credit toward his or her graduation. After the senior year in high school, six hours of college credit may be taken free of charge. Upon completion of the whole cycle, it is hoped that the young person will pursue some kind of postsecondary education. During all phases of the program a nominal stipend is paid to the student if he or she participates fully.

Upward Bound projects are quartered on university campuses. They receive money for operation from the federal government and certain considerations along with a helping of moral support from the institution of higher learning involved. Theoretically, the government can shut down any program that does not justify its existence through the grant proposal it submits. Similarly, the host college may dismiss an Upward Bound program from its premises if it is straining the accountant's imagination too much to keep it alive. As in the marketplace, projects compete with each other for target areas and funding. This situation tends to foster a rather tight-lipped demeanor in directors when they are gathered with one another for conferences of some sort. Few give away any trade secrets.

Catch-22s abound in operations like these. The best illustration of this fact is provided by the very guidelines that are intended to create a structure for recruitment and implementation. Three requirements must be met by the prospective Upward Bound student. First, he or she must be from a low-income background. The criteria for low-income status established for the 1977-78 program year indicate that a family of four must make less than $5,500 annually in order for one of its children to be accepted. Even the least perceptive person has to wonder how four people can possibly survive on less than $5,500 a year, much less be concerned with anything called postsecondary education. In the February 26, 1977 issue of *The New Republic*, Michael

Harrington, in his article "Hiding The Other America", points out that the mechanism for arriving at figures for "low-income" or "poverty level" is assuredly outdated and in need of some sane and humane adjustment. However, this does not change the ways of the world in 1977. One cannot negotiate his or her way into Upward Bound if the family income figure is even fifty dollars over the amount cited by the government. The second requirement a student must meet has to do with school transcripts. He or she should be struggling a bit in the grade department or not performing up to par. The third requirement involves "academic potential". Those who hope to be a part of Upward Bound should display evidence of this quality in some way, shape or form. The indices usually employed for evaluating this sometimes elusive attribute range from high school counselor's evaluations to scores made on achievement tests administered in the ninth grade year to a knowing glimmer in the eye of the one on trial.

The second and third preconditions present an interesting paradox. Ideally, an applicant should look smart but appear dumb in the school files. Likewise, the successful program would be that one which recruits the "A" or "B" students who earn grades of "C" or lower. But this ideal is not often realized. A good share of Upward Bound students end up being those kids who have simply not passed many classes and are short of credits. Typically, they are identified as "motivational" problems or "discipline" problems. Helping these young people graduate from high school is nice but this calls into question some of the basic assumptions of the whole equalizing process.

The program I work for has been in existence since 1965 on the campus of Pacific University in Forest Grove, Oregon. Pacific is a small college most noted for its School of Optometry. Upward Bound at Pacific draws its students largely from the more depressed areas of the city of Portland as well as from some of the rural communities that abut Forest Grove. Over the eleven full years of the program, a total of 413 young people have been served. Of that number, 155 enrolled in postsecondary education. This means that approximately 37 per cent at least registered at a university, college, or community college. No reliable evidence exists which shows how many of these students completed their educations. No information is available which tells how many former pupils enrolled in postsecondary education after some time elapsed. Other programs may claim a higher "success rate" but it is likely that this project is representative.

Of the graduates from the program following the summer session in 1976, four (4) are working, one (1) is unemployed, one (1) is in vocational training, four (4) are in college, and four (4) are in the category of "status unknown". Again, roughly the same percentage obtains.

Because little or no history on the program is extant or was ever documented, it is difficult to state things in quantifiable terms. However, in talking with former and present Upward Bound employees, some facts become clear. In general, students have tended to show markedly lower reading levels and a poorer mastery of mathematical concepts than what would be expected of someone at their grade level. Also, their orientation toward school has often been decidedly anti-intellectual. The response to this attitude was, and perhaps is, to create courses that promote a higher interest level than the fare of the traditional school normally does. Since there has been equal representation of blacks, whites, Chicanos, and Indians in comparison to their numbers in the target population, it is appropriate to assume that lower ability levels and a frustration with traditional methods cut across racial lines.

Recruiting done this year when the enrollment was down to a negligible figure has perhaps introduced a different breed of student to Upward Bound at Pacific University. The average grade point of those presently on the rolls is 2.19 (on a scale of 0.00 to 4.00). There are four persons with a 3.00 or better. Reading levels, as measured by the Nelson-Denny Reading Test, average out to a grade equivalent of 9.8. The score used for computing this is a combination of vocabulary skill and comprehension totals. Of the young people so far recruited, at least half express a firm interest in furthering their education upon completion of high school. Perhaps the 37 per cent "success rate" of the past will immeasurably improve when these folks graduate from the program. However, there are still slots to be filled and from applications presently being considered, it is evident that the students with better skills are currently a part of this group of applicants.

The ups and downs of any enterprise, be it an educational project or a business, should not disguise reality. Just as the business will one year show a greater profit, so might the Upward Bound program. Both are amenable to certain gimmicks and string-pulling. The Upward Bound director with an instinct for survival and an eye toward the future will wisely try to draft the more creative students available to him or her and hope that sometime during their high school experience they will catch fire. Upward Bound takes credit for a job well-done. In the cases of those who don't pan out there would seem to be little problem. After all, the programs work with "high risk" students and failures are expected.

Probing deeper into this issue, serious questions must be posed concerning programs which seek to equalize opportunities. Anyone familiar with problems in teaching knows that inept performance at the high school level often indicates an established pattern of what could be termed poor development. Elements of basic skills are missing from the student's repertoire by the time he or she is sixteen or seventeen years old. Frustration is invariably the result of trying to learn. Simply attempting to catch up becomes an exercise in tedium. This problem of lag can be attacked and remedied to some extent by intensive one-to-one tutoring provided the proper attitudes and goals are present in the minds of both the teacher and the pupil. A program like Upward Bound can reduce the teacher/student ratio to 1:9 but this is probably not enough to make up for lost ground.

It is true that an equalizing program can provide a base at which to maintain contact with a disaffected young person but it cannot deliver the goods as it claims it will. The obvious analogy here is of Upward Bound as a type of federally funded ''sweathog'' class of the variety made popular by the television show, ''Welcome Back, Kotter''. But the problem that is being identified is only a manifestation of something much larger which cuts right to the core of American society and its economic arrangement. The essence of this is that plans of this sort, in the best progressive tradition, attempt to mainstream individuals so that they come to recognize the value of doing things the way everyone else does them. In this process, all the rough edges are blunted. By toeing the mark, the student affirms the value of hard work and perseverance. He or she comes to believe heartily in both of these values and the larger society understands more emphatically how things can be accomplished in only one way. That way represents the ethos of the majority. Little time is spent worrying about those who fail. They had their chance. Why didn't they make the most of it?

The successes, that minority of 37 per cent in this case, are held up as examples. They are this generation's Horatio Algers. They also serve as proof to many that social engineering works. But the fact is that most of these people would have ''made it'' whether an Upward Bound project existed or not. For everyone who benefits, many do not. The protective sieve of the capitalist society need not let too many through. Clearly, all this program does is make the whole competitive network slightly more accessible. It deals in dreams and represents illusion and fantasy rather than substance.

There can be no equal opportunity in education as long as people are forced to live in substandard housing, exist on food budgets that hardly allow for necessities, and worry about where their next few cents are coming from. Equal opportunity cannot be imposed on a few youngsters when they reach the age of fifteen or sixteen. That is not equal opportunity. It is a cruel joke. In short, and without becoming too hortatory, equal opportunity can be effected only by tipping a society, which thrives on bought and bitten flesh, over on its back. Only with a total change in structure will America ever get the largest possible number of its citizens to appreciate the responsibilities and benefits that accrue to them.

Edward Bellamy, in *Looking Backward*, states it all very plainly. Doctor Leete, while discussing the new society declares ''that the right of a man to maintenance at the nation's table depends on the fact that he is a man, and not on the amount of health and strength he may have, so long as he does his best.''[4]

NOTES

1. See William Manchester, *The Glory and the Dream*, Boston: Little, Brown and Company, 1974, p. 735.

2. *U.S. Code*, Title 20 (1964 edition, Supplement V), Washington: U.S. Government Printing Office, 1970, p. 1441.

3. *Ibid.*, p. 1441.

4. Edward Bellamy, *Looking Backward*, New York: New American Library, 1960, p. 98.

The Threat-Recoil Cycle in Relation to Early Childhood Education

MALCOLM GARBER

I would like to share some thoughts on institutional change with you. I wish to illustrate that our current stance on institutional change must be revised. If we continue to develop early childhood programs according to our current model for change, these programs will not succeed. If, on the other hand, we change our approach to institutional innovation, a better chance for success should result.

THE THREAT-RECOIL CYCLE

According to Rhodes, the community may be separated into three sectors: the public sector, the power sector and the exile sector. Rhodes states that, ''We might think of the the power sector as the protector, the public sector the protectorate, and the exile sector as the threat provokers.''[1]

The public sector is composed of the middle majority, the bulk of citizens who have been socialized to behave in ways which most of us have learned to value as good, proper and acceptable. We have learned to be honest, industrious, law-abiding, trustworthy individuals. You can count on us to act in predictable and acceptable ways. We were not always that way. As children we were playful, mischievous, unpredictable, in other words, ''unsocialized''. However, our families soon taught us right from wrong. As a four-year old, I can recall the silvery magnetism of a flashlight on the counter of the local Metropolitan store. Somehow, that flashlight landed in my coat and was stored in my dresser drawer. When the purloined bauble was discovered by my father and mother, overwhelming disaster followed. I learned — Thou Shalt Not Steal — through the discovery method. How could anyone with such thorough training, steal? Almost all of us have learned to behave according to standards set by society and transmitted first by families and church, later by schools.

We, of the middle majority, have learned to behave within the rules set by our culture. Somehow, we learned what was socially acceptable as well as what was socially unacceptable. We have been punished enough to avoid breaking the rules and rewarded sufficiently to follow them. And we have profited: we hold jobs, own property, and seek security. We have a piece of the rock. Because we have earned our franchise on social and economic status we are more cautious and circumspect about our own behaviour. Since we have something to lose we try to guard against losing it. We distrust the divergent — the hippie, the artist, the intellectual. The tragedy of Lennie Bruce's life story is that this poet-comedian exposed us to our own hypocrisies concerning language usage five years before we could tolerate looking at them. For that, he was punished. We find it intolerable for someone else to behave in ways which we ourselves have learned are unacceptable. We want protection from the divergent — the exile sector.

The exile sector is composed of individuals who for several reasons do not conform to middle majority norms. A large segment of this sector is lower class. Others who provoke threats are the alcoholic, the drug addict, the mental retardate, the delinquent, the psychotic, the underachiever, etc. Rhodes says, "Individuals existing in any of these states, and producing any of the behaviours associated with that state, are rejected from the mainstream of social life. As long as they exist in this state and until there is adequate retribution for their illicit behaviour they are relegated to a tabooed caste."[2]

It should be pointed out that any person or group of persons can shift from one sector to another depending on circumstances. For example, the ex-president of the United States, Richard Nixon, shifted from protector in the power sector to threat provoker in the exile sector following the Watergate disclosures.

The retardate and the delinquent are threat provokers who diverge from middle majority norms. The retardate learns more slowly, requiring more careful and repeated instruction. We have been taught to appreciate people who learn quickly. In our world, the fast worker reaps profits, while the slow worker suffers consequences. The retardate is relegated to a tabooed caste because he is perceived to be different from the rest of us. One who does not conform to our expectations does not find ready acceptance.

The delinquent also does not behave according to rules established by the middle majority. His deviance is even less tolerable since we have been so severely trained not to break rules. We find such deviance extremely disturbing. At the same time, illicit behavior which is punished, serves to diffuse some of the fears, anxieties and tensions we experience as we play out our proper middle majority roles. Thus, the current trend toward capital punishment may be understood as the public sector's need to displace its anxieties and reduce its frustrations. As the public sector meets with further frustrations it probably will clamour for more severe retribution. In seeking retribution and protection, we turn to the power sector for help.

The power sector is composed of two segments: "(1) the decision making or power segment (particularly decision makers in the judicial, legislative and executive branches of government), and (2) professionals and agencies allied with government in shaping and regulating human behaviour to fit the pattern of social requirements of the public sector. These are made up largely of systems affiliated with education, legal correction, social welfare, and medical mental health.''[3] Legislators, judges, lawyers, educators, psychologists, psychiatrists, social workers, etc., are all members of the power sector. They are the people from whom the public sector expects protection. Members of the power sector have to be ''free of taint'' as well as highly competent in detecting and diverting any appearance of threat. Before the public, members of the power sector must appear calm, controlled, never flustered or threatened, if they are to maintain their role as protectors. In the 1975 Davis-Nixon television debates prior to the 1975 Ontario elections, both appeared angry — to their mutual detriment.

''The power sector activates the socializing agencies and maneuvers them into a position between the alarmed public and the threatening sector.''[4] When the threat arises from criminal activity, the power sector often responds by building more prisons. When the threat arises from parental breakdown, the power sector responds with more staff, and more hospital service. When threat is generated by low academic performance, the response has been to mobilize agencies to provide more training. Recoiling from threat produces a treatment of symptoms approach. Yet, as the power sector becomes larger and more bureaucratic, the crime rate does not drop, the incidence of mental illness does not decrease, and the academic excellence of students does not improve.

A far more efficient model for generating change would be removing sources of social problems. Social programs that are designed to educate potential criminals in the social skills necessary to succeed in the middle majority culture are ultimately more valuable than maintaining an ever increasing prison system. Early identification and preventative treatment of the potentially mentally ill should prove more effective than our present treatment system. Similar early identification and treatment programs for very young children would be a far more efficient way of dealing with problems of children who require special education in the schools. A planned early childhood education program could attack problems early enough to substantially reduce them. A planned approach to the prevention of illicit behaviours is needed rather than more and bigger symptom treating agencies.

When the public sector sees the new buildings, the extra staff, the special programs, it is lulled into believing that something has been done and that the problem is being treated. But more agencies are not needed; planned preventative intervention is needed.

The public gradually becomes aware of a threat. The threat can be either direct or simulated. A direct threat is one which is precipitated by the occurrence of illicit behaviour such as murder, rape, theft, etc. A simulated threat is one which we do not see as immediately dangerous but which our leaders show us is dangerous. The public alarm over the population explosion is an example of a simulated threat. In the past, large families were highly valued, now with food shortages and overcrowding, family size is curtailed in the hope of enhancing the quality of life for future generations. The responsibility for alerting the public sector to simulated threats rests with the power sector. When the power sector has acted in response to simulated threats with good program development which can be evaluated, it is acting responsibly.

When the threat is direct, the reactions to it are influenced by the following: (1) the frequency of occurrence in a given period of time, (2) its location in the hierarchy of community taboos, (3) the intensity of the commission of the behaviour, (4) its degree of visibility in the open community, (5) its geographical location and distribution in the community, (6) the drama of its circumstances.[5]

Once the public sector becomes aware of a direct threat it calls upon the power sector. Although legislation is passed and agencies are mobilized on behalf of the public, seldom is this action evaluated.

In the United States, the public was made aware that their children lacked mathematical skills. The new math program, a recoil against the threat of growing mathematical incompetence, was instituted and implemented for over 20 years. A generation of children grew up with this unevaluated approach that is now proving to be ineffective. Programs must be evaluated carefully before they are put into widespread use.

Billions were spent on the war against poverty. The Headstart program was another attempt on the part of the power sector to reduce threat. Vast sums of money were funneled to local community action agencies which were supposed to set up early childhood education programs. While these programs were to be tailored to the needs of specific communities, specific program goals were not set and the programs became difficult to monitor. Local bureaucracies were formed which did little to implement their communities' early childhood education programs. Programs must have specific guidelines if they are to provide effective community services.

Community programs often turn into bureaucracies dedicated to self-maintenance instead of public service. This travesty occurs because the public sector is concerned with protection from threat rather than with the evaluation of program effectiveness. But as more programs prove ineffective, and agencies sponsoring these programs become more bureaucratized and expensive, a new threat looms. The entire economic system could collapse under the weight of such unevaluated, recalcitrant bureaucratic programs.

One important role of university educators should be to teach prospective professionals and legislators to develop programs with goals which can be evaluated. I see little reason for stressing the development of arithmetic skills in schools if government does not use these skills to determine whether their own programs add up.

It is true that early childhood education is important; however, various approaches should be tried and evaluated. Should day care be provided in large centres or small ones? Should it be private or public? What sort of educational programs should be added; a progressive open approach, a family-based approach, a cognitively oriented approach, a competency-based approach? Which groups of people would benefit from which special approaches in which communities? Who should be responsible for managing these approaches? Should we look for the social, emotional, educational, and physical development of our children in early childhood education? If so, who should pay? At what age should we begin our programs: the third trimester of pregnancies, at birth, three months of age or older? What rights and responsibilities do parents and children have in the direction of early childhood education? Many of these questions can be answered best through program development and evaluation. The time has come to initiate and carefully evaluate several programs. Those that prove satisfactory should be maintained, those that prove otherwise should be replaced.

Program evaluation should provide answers to two types of questions: (1) What effect is the overall program having? (2) Is the program operating the way it was intended to operate? In order to answer these questions, both the program goals and the necessary steps to reach these goals must be specified. Programs in which these evaluative types of questions are not asked should not be funded because such programs lead to the formation of a power sector that costs large sums of money for small and erratic services.

Children of the poor often suffer through school until, at the merciful age of 16, they can drop out. They often experience enough failure, despair, and hopelessness to become social and emotional cripples — fodder for courts, jails, and psychiatric hospitals. In the Everystudent survey, a study of all secondary students in Metropolitan Toronto Schools conducted by Wright,[6] 52 per cent of the children whose mothers received welfare payments were in special education programs. Less than two per cent of the children whose parents were professionals attended these same special education classes. Obviously, the school system needs to revise its procedures. Early childhood intervention, in the form of day care services, and educational programming may help to correct the gross inequities experienced by the marginal groups in our society. Surely we must respond to their needs.

A comprehensive early childhood education program could provide an early screening system for physical and emotional disabilities. Treatment of shortcomings as well as enrichment of special abilities could be undertaken. In addition, such programs could provide an extra work force of parents who otherwise would remain isolated at home.

A collaborative effort among various agencies within the power sector must be mounted on behalf of young children.

Leaving the task of educating these children to early childhood educators alone, no matter how competent they may be, is absurd because the child is embedded in a family, a social institution that is dependent upon many others for its effectiveness. No single professional group can tackle a problem with so many dimensions. A collaborative, well coordinated community-based effort is needed to provide the wide spectrum of services which are necessary for effective early childhood education.

The Ontario Institute for Studies in Education has funded a family-based project which aims at developing academic competence in four, five, and six-year old culturally divergent children in North York. The program is not a recoil against threat but rather a planned response emanating from prior educational research. This approach, directed by the present author, is in its third and final year of operation.

Two groups of children and their parents are taking part in this program. One group, the non-treatment group, receives regular junior kindergarten, kindergarten, and grade one instruction from trained and competent teachers. In another school the treatment group receives a similar type of educational experience with one additional factor: each week the parents are given a teaching task designed for home use. The tasks are enjoyable games that the parents play with their children and that lead to the development of such academic skills as reading, spelling and arithmetic.

The tasks originally were developed by a trained task writer at O.I.S.E., but, currently are being created by teachers and their assistants in the target school. These assistants are called Trained Outreach Paraprofessionals (T.O.P.) workers. They are parents from the target community who have children in the program and who are trained and paid to make home visits and assist teachers in the classroom. Their training consisted of three days preservice experience during which they learned (1) how to develop a task, (2) how to deliver the task, (3) how to evaluate the task, and (4) how to assist the classroom teacher. Regular, weekly, inservice training is undertaken and their working behavior evaluated. Preservice and inservice training also is provided for the teachers who, by the third year of the program, have taken over many of the program's administrative duties. Results are promising, but not spectacular. Certain academic gains may be attributed to the program. For example, children whose parents are actively involved in the program perform better in spelling and arithmetic than those in comparison classrooms. The parent advisory group, a group of parents and teachers who meet periodically to discuss the progress of the program reports that the children like the program and appreciate the effort.

However, much more could be done. Vocational training and placement for parents who are unemployed could be undertaken with this paraprofessional outreach model. Medical, legal and social services also could be provided. One key insight developed from this experience is that parents of culturally divergent and lower-class background can become remarkably proficient. With a career ladder and proper training, they can do a great deal to assist themselves and help others in their community. However, a collaborative interdisciplinary effort is required to foster such growth.

This approach was designed as a response to people's needs rather than in response to public threat. Probably, if it began when the children were three months instead of 48 months of age, it would be more responsive to the needs of people and even more effective.

This program is evaluated by those receiving the service as well as by those who administer it. This helps to insure that people in the program are getting what they want because they play a prominent role in program evaluation. Programs which benefit the exile sector and over which the control is shared, are needed. We do not need more self perpetuating wasteful bureaucracies. Programs developed as recoil against direct threat may never be effective.

In summary, the threat-recoil model for program development was described. It was suggested that programs developed as a recoil from public threat can produce wasteful bureaucracies. Though many questions remain about the course of early childhood education in Ontario, answers will be provided as new programs are implemented and evaluated. A family-based, early childhood intervention model was described which aimed at providing needed services rather than reducing public threat. We must provide more carefully evaluated programs which are responsive to the needs of those in the exile sector, if we wish to remain a protected public.

NOTES

1. William C. Rhodes, "Institutionalized Displacement and the Disturbing Child", *Educational Programming for Emotionally Disturbed Children: The Decade Ahead*, ed. Peter Knoblock, Syracuse: Division of Special Education and Rehabilitation, Syracuse University, 1964, p. 42.

2. *Ibid.*, p. 45.

3. *Ibid.*, p. 47.

4. *Ibid.*, p. 45.

5. *Ibid.*

6. E.N. Wright, *Student's Background and Its Relationship to Class and Programme in School*, Toronto: The Board of Education for the City of Toronto, Research Department, 1970 (#91).

The "Futility of Changeless Change": The Worth Report, Progressivism and Canadian Education

C.J. BULLOCK

The evident acceleration of production and consumption in the economic sphere, and hysteria and frenzy in life itself, does not preclude the possibility that a fixed society is simply spinning faster. If this is true, the application of planned obsolescence to thought itself has the same merit as its application to consumer goods; the new is not only shoddier than the old, it fuels an obsolete social system that staves off its replacement by manufacturing the illusion that it is perpetually new.

— Russell Jacoby[1]

Early in 1977, Alberta's Progressive Conservative government indicated that it was reassessing the shape of basic education in the province and might move to enforce an increased emphasis on 'basic' skills. *St. John's Edmonton Report,* Edmonton's version of *Time* magazine, greeted what they called the government's "brief and guarded statement"[2] with a blast of editorial good-will entitled: "Will the Schools Outlast Progressivism?"

The villain of this particular piece was the Alberta Teachers' Association (ATA) which, aided and abetted by the University of Alberta's Department of Education, under Dean Walter Worth, was engaged in perpetuating a " 'child-centred' . . . approach to education [that] had become a calamity".[3] Ranged against this evil crew were, in order, university faculties worried about student literacy, property owners' associations worried about vandalism, police associations worried about juvenile delinquency, employers' associations worried about workers' unwillingness to take on tough (read unpleasant and unrewarding) jobs, parents, students, individual teachers breaking ranks, not to mention the provincial government itself. In case the ATA didn't feel sufficiently cowed by this formidable, if still somewhat hypothetical, opposition, the *Edmonton Report* pointed out that the tide of history was running against them, that "Ontario and British Columbia had already reversed the progressivist tendency, were reinstituting a provincial curriculum and working out various forms of examinations to make sure it was being taught."[4]

Despite its bluster, however, the *Edmonton Report* did have a point. The dominance of Progressivism in educational theory *is* being challenged, and not only here in Alberta, or just in Canada, but also in Britain (where the Black Papers on Education mount an annual attack on comprehensive schools

307

and supposedly declining literacy) and in the United States (where *Newsweek* discusses "Why Johnny Can't Write" and a mounting barrage of studies question the achievements of 'egalitarian' education).[5]

My thesis in this study is that Progressivism, at least in its Albertan and Canadian form, *does* indeed need to be challenged. However, it needs to be challenged not from the standpoint of the present 'back to basics' movement, but rather from that of a critical assumption made by Brazilian educator Paulo Freire: "that man's ontological vocation . . . is to be a subject who acts upon and transforms his world, and in so doing moves towards ever new possibilities of fuller and richer life individually and collectively."[6] The task of dealing with current Albertan progressivist theory is made easier by the fact that much of this theory informs and is summed up in *A Choice of Futures,* the 1972 Report of the Alberta Provincial Government's Commission on Educational Planning, popularly known as the *Worth Report,* after the Commissioner, Walter Worth, (whose sudden move from the post of Deputy Minister of Advanced Education to that of the Dean of Education at the University of Alberta might seem to make him an apt bellwether for the approaching storm). Before analysing the report I briefly point to the tradition of criticism of so-called 'basic' education that Progressivism belongs to; after this analysis the traditional and progressive educational options are situated in their economic and historical Canadian context. Finally, a genuine alternative to these options is suggested.

General elementary education in Canada was a result of the surge of economic expansion around the turn of the century. In this era, the Canadian elementary school was "strongly teacher-centred, highly regimented . . . emphasizing factual learning . . . and 'good behaviour'. This all represented what progressivists were to refer to as traditionalism".[7] One classic critique of first-phase industrial revolution education comes in the description of the classroom at the opening of Dickens' *Hard Times* (1854). Dickens' memorable description of "little pitchers"[8] being filled to the brim with facts by the all-knowing teacher and visiting inspector (and struggling against the process) helped to initiate a continuing tradition of educational and social criticism. A contemporary spokesman for this tradition is Paulo Freire who attacks the "narrative" or "banking" concept of education which "leads the students to memorise mechanically the narrated content . . . [which] turns them into 'containers', into receptacles to be filled by the teacher."[9]

In *Hard Times,* Dickens makes the connection between school and work-place very clear; Utilitarian education springs from a view of the working class as "Hands"[10] who need nothing beyond the skills that will be required for their working lives. This connection is equally clear in early twentieth century Canadian education, particularly in the contrast between the regimentation of the elementary school and the tradition of scholarship and free enquiry in universities still, at that period, reserved for a governing elite. The social criticism embodied in Dickens' work is part, to a greater or lesser extent, of Progressive educational theory, which had its origins in the demand that elementary schools (and later high schools, colleges and universities) evolve an education more suited to the needs of their expanded clientele. I offer a brief overview of the evolution of this demand later in the study; here I want to consider that evolution through the lens provided by one monument of its advance, the Worth Report.

Let us start with the language of the Worth Report, since that is, after all, the aspect which we first encounter. A personal idiom, an engaged voice, are quite foreign to the Report, and its occasional approach to such a voice, usually at the beginning of a new section, seems woefully contrived, as in the reflection that "the educational skyline is already ablaze with neon offerings of patent remedy."[11] Such excursions into metaphor are, however, mercifully brief; the Report is far happier in the neutral observer stance of respectable social science, in which all references to agency recede. Thus "*it can be argued* that the realization of a second-phase industrial society is undesirable, if not self-destructive, since it is directed by values that *do not appear* workable"[12] (my italics) or "in this Province, as elsewhere in North America, we *appear to be* reaching the end of a period of preeminent staff power"[13] (my italics). The Report's language is curiously weightless, eminently forgettable. Take, for example, one of the futures forecasts with which this markedly future-oriented document begins, the forecast that "the value of individuality, combined with an emphasis on the welfare of mankind, holds the promise, however, of resolving the age-old conflict between the individual and society".[14] The claim is astonishing, to say the least, but the language in which it is presented is so inert, and so fuzzy in focus, that the claim has the impact of a weather, rather than a futures forecast.

The contradiction that a work arguing the Progressive case for the uniqueness of each learner, and for the necessity of learning by doing, should use language at once impersonal, inert and passive is explained by the fact that the one force whose real *activity* the document acknowledges is technology, the "major agent of social change",[15] which is dragging us into the future faster than we can comprehend the process. "Impermanence is permanently at the centre of Alberta life,"[16] we discover. Education's obsolescence requires "no blame . . . . Its causes lie in the fact of change, the pace of which has reached incredible proportions in recent years. The technology which has spun man about the moon has also set society spinning. Evidence of this surrounds us: the plight of the poor . . . the fluctuations of our economy . . . ."[17] In this version of time without agency or history, the past acquires the role of Original Sin. "The idea that a traditional general education will suffice in the future is 18th Century logic"[18] apparently. No doubt such an idea is inevitable, coming from people who are "colonised by the past".[19] But, never fear, technology will rescue us. If the "common theme" of their proposals is to "increas[e] the autonomy of the learner", the Commission concludes, then this means that "the teacher will be teamed with technology so that instruction can be tailored to the individual's needs and modal preference".[20] There is a strong family resemblance between this and the ATA's vision of the future:

The most noticeable change in curriculum by 1999 will be in packaging. Today students carry books. Tomorrow, they will carry kits of videotapes, film loops, voice tapes... and other as yet undreamed of products of technology.
... To force the teacher to work on higher levels of thinking... the task of imparting information will be relegated to kits and aides.[21]

One of the rare moments of moral passion in the Worth Report comes when it castigates teachers still determined to use technology as an *aid* to instruction.

No one could accuse the Report of failing to be responsive to the *fact* of technology; rather, what is missing from its formulations is any concept of the *control* of technology. Nowhere is this more apparent than in its glancing comments on the world of work.

As regards work, the recurrent emphasis in the Report is that of its opening section. The "major shift [that] will occur in the economic, social and spiritual functions and significance of work in the lives of many people" is conditioned by the fact that "the harnessing of technology for human purposes can be expected to render work for remuneration neither feasible nor possible for increasing numbers of citizens".[22] That is, work will lose its centrality, and simply become a "preferred activity",[23] one choice among many, for certain people. Later the Report retreats from this improbable vision a little, admitting that "participation in the world of work will remain an economic necessity for most..." [24] But what is most interesting is that this area is the one place that the Report allows a breath of contradiction into its social scientific heaven. Having extolled the virtues of learner-structured education, the Report goes on to assert "the need for more effective planning of schooling to meet occupational needs".[25] Then it notes that "a query is in order.... How can individual destiny control be extolled on the one hand and manipulation of that destiny be suggested on the other?"[26] Its answer is that individuals can choose whether to accept incentives or not, and that "this discussion is about the world of work and an individual's destiny will consist of much more than the world of work — especially in the future".[27]

What we find, then, is that "individual destiny control"[28] simply doesn't apply to the *structure* of work in modern Canadian society. In fact, quite the reverse: the structure of work in this society — particularly the intensified division of labour characteristic of advanced capitalism — is actually reproduced and advocated in the Report's proposals for education.

Take, for example, the treatment of institutional organisation. The Report inveighs against insidious distinctions between 'noble' and 'less noble' institutions, but the key word of its institutional program is 'differentiation'. At the two major Albertan universities discovery and criticism functions can be exercised; as we move through the rest of the field of further educational institutions, these functions are replaced by those of career and "integration" (personal development and socialisation). The same principle is even more explicit in the organisation of staffing, where the guideline is "differentiated staffing [which] means translating the division of labor and specialisation-by-function concepts, which have worked so well in business and industry, into terms appropriate for schooling".[29]

As a critique of these positions one could not do better than point to the discussion in *Schooling in Capitalist America,* Samuel Bowles and Herbert Gintis' recent work, of how progressivism has helped to meet the demands of advanced capitalism: how, that is, the increasing fragmentation of jobs and studies within institutions, and the stratification of institutions, has served to legitimise the job situation of increasingly skilled and specialised, but structurally powerless, sections of the labour force.[30] The gains of this process, even as regards efficiency, as Bowles and Gintis point out,[31] are dubious. The losses are admitted even by those administering the process; witness the Carnegie Commission on similar changes that they proposed in the United States: "We recognise that some of these options reduce the chances of a common culture among college graduates within which people communicate, but this has been happening anyway . . . .[32]

Now if we take the Progressive case that self-actualisation occurs through the activity of transforming one's environment at face value, we can see a crucial contradiction in the Worth Report's comments on work. For is not work, in its broadest sense, precisely the most decisive area of one's transformative activity? If we accept that it is, we can see the *real* loss involved in the strategies of the Worth Report. If the learner is powerless to control the structure of the most decisive realm of one's activity, which is also the realm in which one acts with others, with the collectivity, and if the organisation of both this and the educational realm militate against a "common culture", then what can be the *content* of the self-actualisation to which the Worth Report, and Progressivism generally, devotes itself?

As an example of the loss I'm speaking of, consider the case of the high school students enrolled in their first university English course. Their deficiencies there have become a recent *cause célèbre* for Canadian scholars such as Joseph Gold.[33] These deficiencies are described by the 'back to basics' movement simply as an inability to spell, construct grammatical sentences and so on. But what is the source of this inability, when it is present? The key to the answer is in the comment on contemporary poetry with which every university English teacher must surely be familiar: ''I like it because readers can interpret it in the way they want to.''

This, I submit, is the kind of attitude which springs from an advanced capitalist democracy, and is validated by Progressivist theory. When thought is ''free'' but can neither relate to the arena of collective action and transformation nor have influence upon a common culture, then it becomes non-instrumental ''opinion'', a personal characteristic, a private possession. The effects of this process are alarming, and the reason they show up most readily in English courses is that most of the writing in these courses is based upon the persuasive essay; the theory is that students will refine their language and linguistic strategies in the attempt to persuade the reader. But students who have been taught, however implicitly, the non-instrumentality of thought will only go through the motions; it is not that they would rather write about *Hawaii Five O* than *King Lear,* but rather that they can't see why they should persuade anyone about either.

What the discussion so far indicates is that the autonomy of the learner which is the most basic ''common theme'' of the Worth Report, and, I regret to say, of the ATA's document on education in 1999,[34] is the *privatisation* of meaning and knowledge referred to by York University's John O'Neill as the major means of social control in a liberal society.[35] How Canadian Progressivism came to fulfill that role, and why it is under attack at the present time are the questions to which I now must turn.

The starting point for an answer to these questions is to understand the ambiguity of the Progressive demand for an education appropriate to the public school system's expanding clientele. This demand could mean, and did mean for many Progressives, teaching which started from, and respected, the child's own experience of the world. However, an economic context of industrial expansion and declining individual production could instead make this demand mean teaching which equipped the child for a place in industrial society.

The contradiction between these demands is very apparent in the case of the introduction of manual training programs into the Canadian elementary school. The man most responsible, J.L. Hughes, School Inspector for Toronto from 1874 to 1913, was a leading disciple of one of the fathers of Progressive education, Friedrich Froebel, and his justification for the innovation was impeccably Progressive: humans are productive creatures who must learn by doing. However, the impetus the innovation gathered, and the trade union hostility towards it, undoubtedly sprang from its function of training future manual workers at the public expense.[36]

The contradiction in Progressivism is, then, as follows. Progressivism's emphasis on activity rather than passivity, and community rather than elite, led to the development of vocational training in North American schools, training which, given the structure of work under capitalism, inevitably led to stratification and 'tracking' within junior high and high school, and the narrowing rather than the expansion of areas for student creative activity. Instead of the Deweyan dream of the transformation of society by education, we see, rather, the transformation of education by society.

What Progressivism finally provided, despite the intentions of CCFers like Alberta's H. C. Newland, was a rationale for the provision of skilled labour. This was particularly evident in the sixties. Education, according to Hugh Stevenson, came to be seen "as a vital element of an expanding economy where success depended on the availability of a large highly skilled labour force".[37]

A long series of official documents inspired by Progressivism, a series beginning with Ontario's *Living and Learning* (The Hall-Dennis Report, 1960) and ending, rather belatedly, with the Worth Report (1972), saw the light of day.

What is interesting (and eventually infuriating!) is to see the way in which the demands of the capitalist economy in the sixties emerged in these documents as moral imperatives.[38] The rapid expansion of the economy created increasing job obsolescence;[39] the Worth Report insisted that the future is leaving us behind, and recommended continuous education as a major life-goal. Public money was poured into educational expansion on the premise — made explicit in Acts like the Technical and Vocational Training Agreement (1960) — that vocational training be the expanding sector; the demand was for a work-force with increased, but also increasingly differentiated, skills. The Worth Report responded with proposals for streamlining the differentiation of institutions and staffing.

Educational expansion meant that education itself became a promising market for corporate expansion. As Hugh Stevenson puts it:

In addition to television, a vast array of audio-visual hardware came into use in the schools during the sixties . . . [and] commercial interests . . . were equally industrious in producing software to be used in mechanised education. . . .

Quietly but surely technology and business assumed large controlling interests in education. Such combinations possessed the power to dominate an area of society traditionally reserved for public control, largely because educators were not equipped to judge accurately between technological advances with valid educational usefulness and others advocated by sales pressure from private enterprises' cherished profit motive.[40]

In this context, where specialisation worked against judgment and control, innovation and ideal became "subject to a futility of changeless change".[41] None of this, of course, bothers the Worth Commission; their answer is an embrace, the "teaming of the teacher with technology."

However, Alberta Progressivist dreams of millenia of endlessly improving ''packaging'' were to be brought low; between the inception of the Worth Commission in 1969 and its production of the Report in 1971/2 came the beginnings of the recession which is still with us, and growing unemployment in the skilled labour force which the sixties had created. Clearly the time had come for an education that asserted more direct social control, and created less expectations as to the qualities of work and life. And so Walter Worth returns to the University of Alberta's Department of Education; the call for a return to 'basic education' is heard throughout the land.

* * *

The burden of my argument so far is that Albertans and Canadians who wish to base their educational efforts on the kind of values for which Paulo Freire's work stands, must be critical of both options in the present education 'debate'. The argument thus raises the question as to the nature of a more authentic, yet still practical, option. Such an option requires elaboration and testing on various levels (institutional, economic, etc.); here I will confine myself to some of its structural and epistemological aspects.

The basic tenets of Freirian education are that teacher and learner must regard themselves as co-subjects, that their relation must be one of dialogue, and that ''true dialogue cannot exist unless it involves critical thinking . . . thinking which perceives reality as process and transformation, rather than as a static entity — thinking which does not separate itself from action, but constantly immerses itself in temporality without fear of the risks involved.[42]

The differences between these tenets and those of the ''back to basics'' option are crystallised in Freire's critique of 'narrative' and 'banking' education, and in his comments on what he calls ''naive thinking'': ''Critical thinking contrasts with naive thinking which sees 'historical time as a weight, a stratification of the acquisitions and experiences of the past', from which present should emerge normalised and 'well-behaved'.[43]

The vocabulary of Progressivism sounds closer to Freire, but my earlier critique should have made apparent the difference between the Freirian subject and the Worth Report's privatised individual, between the view of reality as process and the Worth Report's view of reality as uncontrollable change.

If we describe Freirian education as that in which teacher and student approach all aspects of reality as problems which demand their co-investigation, we have described something very close, in a great many respects, to what the Canadian teachers H.I. Day and Florence Maynes call the ''guided discovery'' method.[44] In this method ''problems are presented in ways that engage the dynamic of uncertainty'' in students, whose ''chosen solutions are challenged by suggesting other alternatives and implications''.[45]

From Day and Maynes' discussion several crucial advantages of the 'guided discovery' method become clear. Firstly, the work of certain psychologists interested in the effects of conflict upon the individual seems to show that *"whenever an individual is faced with an optimal level of uncertainty he responds with interest, attention and exploration"* [46] (authors' italics), and this conclusion is supported by the authors' own research. "Problem-posing"[47] education may, then, be able to justify itself on the most pragmatic criteria of efficiency.

Secondly, the 'guided discovery' method can be applied to both "the learning of simple factual material and the examination of complex concepts and theories"[48] and can be so applied, I would add, right across the spectrum of subjects and disciplines. As Day and Maynes put it:

Ottawa is the capital of Canada. There are seven days in the week. . . . Within every culture there are bodies of facts that must be learned if people are to communicate with each other. . . . We must have a common base of knowledge in order to build ideas and to communicate them to others in a comprehensible manner. . . .

[But] even the learning of the mundane fact that Ottawa is the Capital of Canada can be exciting if the teacher can approach it by showing the conflicting claims of Upper and Lower Canada. . . .

However education is more than the learning of mundane statements. It is learning to examine critically so-called facts and to interpret ideas.[49]

The example given recalls Freire's insistence that to learn that "the capital of Para is Belem must involve realising the true significance of 'capital' . . . that is, what Belem means for Para and what Para means for Brazil."[50] As to the second point: Day and Maynes take the practice of a science teacher in the laboratory as the main examplar of their method. However it is clear that, for example, the teacher of literature who discussed literary traditions, or the teacher of history[51] who discussed historical conclusions, not as facts, but rather as ensembles of facts, judgments, class preferences and the like, and thus as problems requiring the investigators to bring their own vision of things to bear, would be employing the methods of "problem-posing" education.

Thirdly, the absurdity of assuming that self-actualisation can proceed without real content, without struggle, and outside the community of one's fellows, is avoided. A true 'problem-posing' education demands that reality be confronted, that all available evidence and all available disciplines are brought to bear upon it, and that it is the class as a whole who perform the confrontation and consider the options for thought and action.

The 'guided discovery' method, 'problem-posing' education, can avoid the weaknesses of both Progressivism and so-called 'basic' education; it can both "avoid the rigidity of children coerced into accepting a teacher's dictum as correct, and . . . avoid some of the weaknesses of the non-directive approach''.[52] It demands on the part of the teacher a fundamental reorientation. The teacher must ''project himself [sic] as someone who also speculates, inquires, withholds judgement and becomes excited with uncertainty. He[sic] must not only act the role, but must truly be tolerant and investigate uncertainty, so that his [sic] students will respect him [sic] and emulate his [sic] example.''[53] This role of co-investigator is a mile away from that of the Progressive 'facilitator'; it demands a concern with content, judgement and the *disciplines* of enquiry and communication.

Day and Maynes provide a model of educational method which seems particularly appropriate for Canadian education. However, despite the correspondences between the two, there can be no doubt that their model lacks the explicitly critical dimension of Freire's. In particular, they fail to deal with the social and economic order, which endorses the practices they criticise, and which will be threatened by the practices they advocate (as also, I should add, would a bureaucratic state socialist regime). For there can be no doubt that neither Canadian capitalism's need for a skilled but powerless labour force (as in the sixties), nor its need for a lessening of expectation in the event of the over-production of such a force (as in the seventies), can be served by a critical and 'problem-posing' education.

Thus, it should be clear that the struggle for this form of education cannot simply remain a struggle within schools. This struggle must develop its own distinct epistemological and institutional objectives. The current provincial and federal strategies with regard to 'basic' and Progressive education make the present a decisive moment for those who reject both these options. We urgently need to consider how to organise ourselves in order to start a real, practical and ongoing, rather than a phony debate about the direction of educational development in Canada.

NOTES

1. Russell Jacoby, *Social Amnesia,* Boston: Beacon Press, 1975, p. xviii.

2. *St. John's Edmonton Report,* March 14, 1977, p. 19.

3. *Ibid.,* p. 20.

4. *Ibid.*

5. See Samuel Bowles and Herbert Gintis, *Schooling in Capitalist America,* New York: Basic Books, pp. 6-7.

6. Richard Shaull, ''Foreword'' to Paulo Freire, *Pedagogy of the Oppressed,* Harmondsworth: Penguin, 1972, p. 12.

7. F. Henry Johnson, *A Brief History of Canadian Education,* Toronto: McGraw-Hill, 1968, p. 133.

8. Charles Dickens, *Hard Times,* eds. George Ford and Sylvere Monod, New York: Morton, 1966, p. 3.

9. Freire, p. 44.

10. See Dickens, p. 49 in particular.

11. Commission on Educational Planning, *A Choice of Futures,* Edmonton: Queen's Printer, 1972, p. 152. Henceforth cited as *The Worth Report.*

12. *Ibid.,* p. 33.

13. *Ibid.,* p. 129.

14. *Ibid.,* p. 6.

15. *Ibid.,* p. 16.

16. *Ibid.,* p. 176.

17. *Ibid.,* p. 36.

18. *Ibid.,* p. 179.

19. *Ibid.,* p. 37.

20. *Ibid.,* p. 237.

21. Alberta Teacher's Association, "Teaching and learning 1999", in *The Best of Times/The Worst of Times,* ed. Hugh A. Stevenson and others, Toronto: Holt Rinehart, 1972, p. 567.

22. *The Worth Report,* p. 3.

23. *Ibid.*

24. *Ibid.,* p. 47.

25. *Ibid.,* p. 168.

26. *Ibid.*

27. *Ibid.*

28. *Ibid.*

29. *Ibid.,* p. 237.

30. Bowles and Gintis, pp. 204-8.

31. *Ibid.*

32. *Ibid.,* p. 208.

33. Joseph Gold, ed., *In the Name of Language,* Toronto: Macmillan, 1975.

34. See Note 21.

35. John O'Neill, *Sociology as a Skin Trade,* New York: Harper and Tow, 1972, p. xi.

36. This paragraph is based upon Robert M. Stamp's discussion of Hughes in

Wilson, Stamp and Audet, eds., *Canadian Education: A History,* Scarborough: Prentice Hall, 1970, p. 320.

37. Hugh Stevenson, "Crisis and Continuum: Public Education in the Sixties", *Ibid.,* p. 472.

38. For evidence that my comments do not simply apply to the Worth Report see George Martell's discussion of Hall-Dennis in George Martell, ed., *The Politics of the Canadian Public School,* Toronto: James Lewis and Samuel, 1974, pp. 14-19.

39. Hugh Stevenson, p. 493.

40. Hugh Stevenson, pp. 496-7.

41. John F. Ohles, "The Fertility of Change?", *The Educational Forum,* November 1964, vol. 29, no. 1, pp. 15-16.

42. Freire, pp. 64-65.

43. *Ibid.,* p. 65.

44. H.I. Day and Florence Maynes, "The Teacher and Curiosity: A Third Way", *Must Schools Fail,* eds. Niall Byrne and Jack Quarter, Toronto: McClelland and Stewart, 1972, pp. 69-82.

45. *Ibid.,* p. 76.

46. *Ibid.,* p. 72.

47. "Problem-posing" education is the way Freire describes his system throughout *Pedagogy of the Oppressed.*

48. Day and Maynes, p. 74.

49. *Ibid.,* pp. 74-75.

50. Freire, p. 45.

51. E.H. Carr's *What is History?,* Harmondsworth: Penguin, 1975, elaborates a very similar vision of historical method.

52. Day and Maynes, p. 76.

53. *Ibid.,* p. 80.

CONTRIBUTORS

Wilbert H. Ahern is Associate Professor of History at the University of Minnesota-Morris and Director of the West Central Minnesota Historical Research Center. His research concerns liberal reformers and racial minorities in post-Civil War America. He received his Ph.D. from Northwestern University in 1968.

John Barkans received his M.A. in Sociology from McMaster University where he is currently a doctoral candidate. His article with Pupo is a revision of their prize-winning undergraduate paper published in *Sociological Focus,* Vol. 7:3, 1974.

Graham Bleasdale received his M.A. from the University of Waterloo in 1976, and has taught sociology at the community college level in British Columbia. His experience in helping to establish a community day care centre in the Fraser Valley taught him much about both the different ways social services can be adequately provided and the way in which social values affect social relationships in a cooperative and egalitarian educational setting.

Chris Bullock received his Ph.D. in 1974 from the University of Leeds (U.K.). He is currently Associate Professor in the Department of English, University of Alberta, where he has taught since 1969, and is former Chairperson of the Marxist Literary Group Workshop on English Literature. He is involved in a major research project on Saul Bellow and has published an article entitled, "On the Marxist Criticism of the Contemporary Novel in the United States: A Re-evaluation of Saul Bellow" in *Praxis,* Vol. 1:2, 1976.

Arthur K. Davis was trained at Harvard and has spent the last twenty years in western Canada. He has been Research Director of the Centre for Community Studies at Saskatoon (1958-64), Professor of Sociology and Anthropology at Calgary, and since 1968, Professor of Sociology at Alberta. He is a former President of the Canadian Sociology and Anthropology Association, and a board member of the Social Science Federation of Canada.

Edgar Z. Friedenberg is the author of *The Vanishing Adolescent* and *The Disposal of Liberty and Other Industrial Wastes,* among other works. Since coming to Canada from the State University of New York at Buffalo — "a longer journey than it appears to be" — in 1970, he has been Professor of Education at Dalhousie University.

Malcolm Garber, a former high school teacher in Watts, California, and educational psychologist in Albuquerque, New Mexico, has become convinced of "the need to generate worthwhile educational programmes". After directing the Florida Planned Variation Head Start Program, he returned home to Toronto to work as an Associate Professor of Special Education at the Ontario Institute for Studies in Education. Recently, he has been directing a paraprofessional outreach project designed to help parents of mentally retarded children to more effectively teach them at home.

David Hanson lives in Portland, Oregon and currently works at Pacific University in Forest Grove, Oregon. Much of his non-work time is spent studying for an M.Ed. in Counseling at Lewis and Clark College in Portland. He has a novel set in the Pacific Northwest in progress.

Jim Harding completed his Ph.D. in the sociology of knowledge at Simon Fraser University in 1970. Prior to that, as a research assistant for the Centre for Community Studies, he did his M.A. on the education aspirations of native people in Northern Saskatchewan. He has taught at the Universities of Regina and Waterloo, Lakehead

University and Confederation College in Thunder Bay, and is presently Director of a research programme studying alcohol and drug disabilities in Sask. He has been active in anti-war, educational reform, environmental health, and development education organizations, and has published widely in the alternative press.

Ken Luckhardt finished an M.A. thesis in Anthropology at the University of Alberta (1971) from which the article in this volume has been drawn. His doctoral research focuses on hinterland capitalism and trade union history in Northwest British Columbia. He has been active in the Free Southern Africa Committee (FSAC) and in the compiling of *Canadian Complicity in Southern Africa: An Inventory of Corporate Connections,* Edmonton, 1977.

Randle W. Nelsen is the author of journal articles published in both Canada and the United States. He has taught in colleges and universities in both countries, and is presently employed at Lakehead University. Currently, he works with the Union of Injured Workers to change the Ontario Workmen's Compensation Act and some practices of the Workmen's Compensation Board. He is also involved in a study assessing the implications of traditional sex role stereotyping of Indian women by governmental agencies, and is a member of the Citizens Committee Studying Nuclear Waste.

David A. Nock completed an M.A. thesis for the Institute of Canadian Studies at Carleton University from which the article in this book has been drawn. After completing a Ph.D. in Sociology at the University of Alberta, he accepted a position at Lakehead University in 1976. His paper on the "History and Evolution of French Canadian Sociology" appeared in *The Insurgent Sociologist,* Vol. 4:4, 1974. In Edmonton he was affiliated with the alternative newspapers, *Poundmaker* and *Prairie Star.*

Fred L. Pincus is an Assistant Professor of Sociology at the University of Maryland, Baltimore County. He is presently doing research on vocationalism in community colleges and on higher education in the People's Republic of China, while he continues putting together an anthology on U.S. higher education. He is an associate editor of *The Insurgent Sociologist* and a member of the Advisory Committee for *Politics and Education.*

Norene Pupo received her M.A. in Sociology from McMaster University where she also, like Barkans, is currently a doctoral candidate. Her article concerning the postwar Canadian university and the need for skilled labour is drawn from her Master's thesis entitled, "Education, Ideology and Social Structure: An Examination of the Development of Higher Education in Nineteenth Century Ontario."

Sandra Steinhause is Director of the Regional Resource Centre for Energy Conservation in Thunder Bay, and Consumer Analyst and Broadcaster for the local C.B.C. station (CBQ) in Thunder Bay. She received her M.Sc. in Sociology from the Université de Montréal and did graduate work in Adult Education at St. Francis Xavier University, Antigonish, Nova Scotia.